WARRIORS TO MANAGERS

WARRIORS TO

MANAGERS,

THE FRENCH MILITARY

ESTABLISHMENT SINCE 1945

MICHEL L. MARTIN

The University of North Carolina Press Chapel Hill

© 1981 The University of North Carolina Press

All rights reserved

Manufactured in the United States of America

ISBN 0-8078-1421-0

Library of Congress Catalog Card Number 79-28114

Library of Congress Cataloging in Publication Data

Martin, Michel L.
  Warriors to managers.

  Bibliography: p.
  Includes index.
  1. France—Armed Forces—History   I. Title.
UA700.M36   306'.2   79-28114
ISBN 0-8078-1421-0

*To an officer of the Armée
d'Afrique and his wife:
my parents*

CONTENTS

Appendixes

FIGURES AND TABLES

Figures

Tables

ACRONYMS

ACF	Avion de combat futur
ALAT	Aviation légère de l'Armée de Terre
ANT	Arme nucléaire tactique
BTEMS	Brevet technique d'Enseignement militaire supérieur
CAFDA	Commandement air des Forces de défense aérienne
CEAA	Centre d'entraînement de l'Armée de l'Air
CEIPAA	Centre d'Etudes et d'Instruction psychologique de l'Armée de l'Air
CESM	Centre d'Etudes et de Sociologie militaire
COTAM	Commandement du Transport aérien militaire
DEUG	Diplôme d'Etudes universitaires générales
DIT	Défense intérieure du territoire
DOT	Défense opérationnelle du territoire
DPMAT	Direction des personnels militaires de l'Armée de Terre
DRME	Direction des Recherches et Moyens d'essais
EMEG	Ecoles militaires d'Enseignement général
EMIA	Ecole militaire interarmes
EMSST	Enseignement militaire supérieur scientifique et technique
ENA	Ecole nationale d'Administration
FAS	Force aérienne stratégique
FATAC	Force aérienne tactique
FOST	Force océanique stratégique
FNS	Force nucléaire stratégique
GMS	Groupe de Missiles stratégiques
ICBM	Intercontinental Ballistic Missile
IDS	Information et droits du soldat
IFOP	Institut français d'Opinion publique
INSEE	Institut national de la Statistique et des Etudes Economiques
IRBM	Intermediate-Range Ballistic Missile
MBFR	Mutual Balance Force Reduction
MIRV	Multiple Independently Targetable Re-entry Vehicle
MPR	Military Participation Ratio
NPT	Nonproliferation Treaty
ORSA	Officier de reserve en situation d'activité

RPR	Rassemblement pour la République
SAM	Surface-to-Air Missile
SIRPA	Service d'Information et de Relations publiques des Armées
SFIO	Section française de l'Internationale ouvrière
SLBM	Submarine-Launched Ballistic Missile
SOFRES	Société française d'Etudes par sondages
SSBM	Surface-to-Surface Ballistic Missile
TNW	Tactical Nuclear Weapon
UDR	Union des Démocrates pour la République
UNEF	Union nationale des étudiants de France
UNIFIL	United Nations Interim Force in Lebanon

FOREWORD

In the cross-national analysis of trends in civil-military relations in the Western nation-states, France has not figured prominently. Until recently, this has been in part because there has been relatively little adequate research on the French armed forces and society for the post–World War II period. This is unfortunate, because France is a crucial case. Obviously it has political and strategic importance; in addition, its patterns of armed forces and society do not conform, at first glance, to those of other nations in Western Europe.

Michel Martin's important and comprehensive *Warriors to Managers* is thus a most welcome contribution to the literature on comparative civil-military relations. It covers the period from the end of World War II until 1976. It draws on both political science and sociological perspectives in order to focus on the military and the internal sociopolitical role of the French armed forces. The reader will find a highly effective fusion of the grand tradition of French historical scholarship with a systematic detailed analysis grounded in organizational behavior.

Martin probes all the ingredients essential for assessing the effects of the French military establishment on domestic society and on military policy and practice. His trenchant study probes the institutional outcome of the changed military mission, and the resulting trends in personnel, arms, and budget. He carefully analyzes the internal organization of the three services and the vital issues of the "citizen-soldier" and the political problems of conscription. His original analysis of the sociology of the professional cadres—both officers and non-commissioned personnel—is especially important. He examines their social origins and their career motivations and lines, and their emerging professional perspectives and linkages with civilian society.

It is a commonplace in the study of the military, but a useful one, that armed forces, although they have characteristics that are widespread throughout the world, reflect the political arrangements and culture of their respective societies. The French armed forces represent this duality, and in this sense they are hardly unique when compared with those of the United States, the Federal Republic of Germany, or Great Britain. But there is a second duality as well. France operates as a modern advanced industrialized society with a most elaborate technological base; at the same time, French society maintains social, cultural, and political conventions that are traditional and long-standing. The French military conforms to this duality as well.

It is this duality, plus its military's extensive involvement in colonial missions since 1945, that has generated the impression that the French military do not conform to the trends in military organization and civil-military relations found in the other Western political democracies. It has been argued that the French do not conform to the "decline in the mass armed forces." No element in this argument appears to be more important than the continued reliance on and importance of conscription in France.

Martin's penetrating analysis highlights the special features of the French armed forces. He documents the high degree of self-recruitment into the officer corps, the maintenance of traditional forms of discipline, especially in the ground forces, and the concern with tradition and military honor. But he is original in trying to present a balance between those special features and the trends in the French military establishment that are common to the armed forces of the Western democracies. These common organizational trends are indeed powerful and point to increases in operational convergence with the forces under NATO command. Of course, convergence in an operational format is dictated by technological and administrative considerations, but it hardly implies similarity in political outlook and practice.

The trends in convergence are paradoxically strongly documented by Martin's detailed investigation of the transformation of conscription. In France, the continuation and "sanctity" of conscription are no longer taken for granted. Conscription is being debated politically, and the intensity of the debate is likely to continue. French youths are indifferent, if not actually hostile, to conscript military service. Of equal or even greater significance, French military leaders, under the influence of political realities and operational requirements, have gradually moved to a more constricted system of conscription and toward a stronger reliance on a volunteer "force-in-being," especially for the cutting-edge military formations. In essence, conscription remains, for the time being, as a contribution to traditional political arrangements, while the effective French military converges in format with that of the rest of Western Europe.

The Inter-University Seminar on Armed Forces and Society is pleased to include this valuable study in its publication series. French scholars are prone to claim that only a French person can understand the realities of French institutions, especially the military. We are therefore pleased that our first venture in the study of the French military satisfies this requirement. But research and scholarship have international aspirations. Michel Martin is a Frenchman who has immersed himself in the literature on the comparative analysis of military institutions. He has traveled and studied abroad extensively, and participated actively in the international community of international scholars concerned with the comparative study of civil-military relations. As this book clearly attests, the Inter-University Seminar has the best of both worlds, that is, the duality of French scholarship and the search for a meaningful internationalized perspective.

Morris Janowitz
The University of Chicago

PREFACE

After nearly ten years of total indifference following the settlement of the Algerian conflict and the related political instability, the French military establishment once again became a central focus of attention in France. True, such an interest mirrors the present givens of an *actualité mouvementée*. The malaise overcoming the career military personnel and the raucous restlessness of draftees and would-be draftees tended to be at the center of this renewed interest in military questions. But what is worth noting is that such a concern for military affairs was not simply a volatile craze, feeding on street events and orchestrated by the news media in search of sensational topics. It was also a testimony to an increased awareness of the importance of military affairs by a noticeable segment of the social community, and especially by members of the academic establishment.

In university circles, for example, this nascent preoccupation with military issues was evident in the growing number of courses offered dealing with military and defense questions, as well as in the development of new research institutes exclusively centered on military matters which are today recognized as integral parts of the university system (some of these are even qualified to grant degrees in the field of military history or defense issues at the doctoral level).

Today, one gets the impression that French social scientists seem ready, less reticent at least, to admit that the study of the military institution, like that of the educational system, the psychiatric asylum, or the criminal justice system, is of a nature to help provide a better understanding of the social system in which we live. More and more historians, political scientists, and sociologists, from all ideological backgrounds, realize that military institutions have occupied and still occupy too conspicuous a place in the functioning of modern industrial democracies, to say nothing of nonindustrialized societies, to be treated only by denial, as was the case when the currents of thought of the eighteenth and nineteenth centuries guided intellectual activities away from the military universe.

The nineteenth-century Comtean or Saint-Simonian pacifism-tainted myth of the coming demilitarization of modern societies, which, in one way or another, impregnated the belief system of generations of "liberal scholars" and nourished their indifference to military affairs, has faded away, permitting the military to become a field worthy of investigation. Interestingly, the same trend also affected radical social scientists who, because of a belief that the military was by definition antagonistic to the revolutionary aspirations of the working class, and, as a bourgeois item, could not figure on the eschatological horizon of the socialist consciousness, seemed to be inclined to consider military studies as an unholy intellectual pursuit, pretending to ignore that this topic was an important preoccupation of social thinkers like Karl Marx, Freidrich Engels, Jean Jaurès, or Karl Liebknecht. It is possible that, influenced by their fellow intellectuals and ideologues outside the university and by the changing posture of the French Left on national defense questions, leftist social scientists will soon engage in closer analysis of military institutions, thus giving a new impetus to military studies.

It can be said that a sort of consensus is now being formed by scholars regarding the fact that any understanding of social organizations must include the military institution and the role of force. However, this change in the intellectual attitudes of French social scientists varies according to academic discipline. If there were, for example, a special area of study called military studies, it would still be dominated by historians, because they have traditionally shown less hesitation in venturing into the field. In addition, what has been called the "renewal of military history in France" is further proof not only of the continued interest in the military but also of the desire to extend the field of historical investigation and to go beyond the punctilious factualism that has generally characterized the approaches to military events. Although political scientists have exhibited an increasing concern for military affairs during the last ten years, their concern is thematically limited to the questions of national defense, arms control, and the like. As for sociologists, their participation remains quite distant. The number of sociological studies of the military establishment is rather deceptive. The "classic" studies were written in the early 1960s by sociohistorians, not by sociologists. Recently a few case studies dealing with a particular aspect or specific sector of the military establishment have been undertaken by a number of sociologists or sociopsychologists—among them, it should be stressed, a number of military officers—but, on the whole, sociologists have done little to expand the field of military studies. As a social system, the contemporary French military remains virtually unexplored, and, except for a few sectional analyses, no comprehensive study of the modern military establishment in France exists.

It is the objective of the present work to attempt to fill this gap by sketching out a sociological portrait of the contemporary French military institution and of its evolution after 1945. Although intending to contribute to the accumulation of material, if not of knowledge, in the field of military sociology, this study has little theoretical ambition. It seeks, to borrow Karl Jasper's formula, to understand rather than to explain; it attempts to relate observations to a larger framework of analysis derived from recent intellectual formulations in the area of military sociology, in particular those derived from the theory that has come to be known as "the decline of the mass armed forces model."

In leafing through this study, the reader will rapidly realize that there is a certain lack of thematic continuity. The reader will also find that the number of topics addressed is limited; many issues were excluded. The reasons for such a limited scope of analysis are related to the paucity and disparity of information and statistical data available to the civilian researcher; documentary chastity is still one of the characteristics of the French military institution. Like other practitioners in the social sciences, I had to accommodate myself to what could be collected; in this I followed the advice of those experienced scholars who encouraged me to persist in my undertaking.

While attending a seminar in Cambridge, England, I met Professor Morris Janowitz. In a conversation he remarked that sociological studies of the contemporary French military were conspicuous by their scarcity and that perhaps someone should try to rectify that situation. By rescuing me from my doubts about being able to complete such a work, he arranged for me to come to The University of Chicago. Beyond all expectations this stay was an extremely rewarding intellectual experience. For that, and for his stimulus, it is a distinct pleasure for me to express my gratitude to Morris Janowitz. I would also like to record my appreciation to Professor Edward Shils, who also had a part in my Chicago sojourn, for his encouragement and confidence. His monumental knowledge made the time spent with him at the university and in various Chicago neighborhoods a delightful and enriching experience. I am sad to be able to offer only collective thanks to the many persons and friends for their suggestions and kindness, among them Ms. Ellen Stern, Professor Jesse Pitts, and many members of the Inter-University Seminar.

On the European shores of the Atlantic, I am much obliged to General Robert Vial and Colonel Jack Garcette, Director and Assistant Director of the former Centre d'Etudes et de Sociologie militaire. Colonel Garcette provided me with the most current information available and spent much of his valuable time *à éclairer ma lanterne* about the French military establishment. I am also indebted to Colonel de Suchet and Lieutenant Colonel Tixier from the air force staff, Monsieur le Médecin Chef Croq, Director of the psychosociology department of the Direction des Recherches et des Moyens d'essais, and members of the Service d'Information et de Relations publiques des Armées, for all the documents they kindly gave me. While finishing this study in France, new elements were brought to my attention thanks to various colleagues, in particular, Professors Jean-Pierre Marichy, Jean-Pierre Thomas, and Pierre Dabezies. Special thanks also are due to Professor Paul Ourliac of L'Institut and head of the Institute for Political Studies of Toulouse, who, besides his interest, granted me liberal research time; and last, but not least, to my colleague and friend Lucien Mandeville and Madame Mandeville, who, outside professional concerns, unfailingly offered me support and encouragement.

An undertaking such as the present one could not have been completed without financial assistance from outside sources and here I am very grateful to the Ford Foundation for the generous fellowship awarded to me and to Mr. William Bader and Ms. Marion Beber for their help in this regard. The Inter-University Seminar on Armed Forces and Society gave me an additional grant to complete this study and to engage assistance in the colossal task of preparing the manuscript for publication. The typing proficiency of Mrs. Jane Salinas and especially Ms. Jean Duncan Hall, who prepared many drafts, should be acknowledged, as well as Ms. Erika Hugo's much-needed editing skills, for, to paraphrase Conrad, I have been quarrying my English out of a black night, working like a coal miner in his pits.

I would like to add that although many people helped to make this book a better one, none of them should be blamed for its shortcomings, its omissions of fact or its interpretations; these are solely my responsibility.

M.L.M.
Chicago-Toulouse, November 1979–80

WARRIORS TO MANAGERS

INTRODUCTION ● THE FRENCH
CASE IN A THEORETICAL PERSPECTIVE

The latest theoretical efforts in the field of what is today known as military sociology sought, following major macrosociological undertakings concerning the military establishments of the nineteenth century, to understand and define with precision the nature, the causes, and the consequences of changes that affected Western military organizations during the second half of the twentieth century.

Modern Western military institutions, in effect, as highlighted by observation, seemed to be undergoing a mutation similar in importance to that undergone in the fifteenth century with the decay of feudal forms of military deployment, or in the nineteenth century with the rise of the mass armed force—a format derived from the revolutionary principle of the nation-in-arms and based upon universal conscription and national mobilization in time of crisis. The newest transformation, which came to be labeled with expressions such as "the decline of the mass army model," the "rise of quasi- or all-volunteer forces," the "emergence of force-in-being military" resulted in the nascence of a type of military organization that is, according to Morris Janowitz's words, "a smaller establishment recruited permanently on an all volunteer basis and organized predominantly on a force-in-being basis, with a de-emphasis of the older tradition of a cadre for mobilization."[1]

The causal factors generally associated with this recent mutation were numerous indeed, though they did not have the same weight within the process of change. A review of the theoretical analysis of the question, as well as the close inspection of specific case studies, reveals that sociocultural variables, such as the erosion of traditional forms of nationalism and patterns of citizenship and of commitment to the state's authority and the rejection of violence with subsequent declining legitimacy of military activities, must not be neglected. For example, it is certain that with the changing mentalities resulting from the emergence of advanced industrialized welfare social systems, all styles of life and behavior based upon asceticism and discipline, as they still exist in the military, became more intolerable to a rapidly growing segment of the younger generations. Moreover, the multiplicity of social roles through which the young individual today is able to manifest his quality as an adult and as a citizen, together with the extension of the concept of national security to various tasks such as social welfare and environmental protection, have inevitably limited the more decisive functions of military service. In so doing, these trends struck at the very source of the legitimacy of this institution, a legitimacy essentially resting on the monopoly it had on access to citizenship, entrance into adulthood, and socialization of the citizen to the dominant values of society.[2]

However, the key variables in the shifting pattern of military organization were essentially of a technological and strategic nature. One can assume that the decline of the mass armies born during the early nineteenth century's revolutionary struggles was to be attributed first to the introduction of sophisticated technology, especially the inception of nuclear weaponry in the military, and the reliance upon such technologies in the elaboration of defense strategy and second, to the alteration of the traditional distribution of dominant power centers in the international system together with the fading of the classic forms of imperial hegemony.

In effect, the military employment of atomic technology with its strategic corollary, deterrence, replaced the prenuclear concept of total war and led to the establishment of a fully alert and highly modernized armed force, in other words, to a type of posture inconsistent with the use of mobilization that, in any case, the redefinition of global military ends in essentially nonbelligerent terms (war being the failure of deterrence) no longer justified. This tendency was reinforced also by the obsolescence of the traditional means of creating and defending zones of imperial hegemony that necessitated the employment of large military contingents.

Though it can be said that from a macrosociological perspective, these factors had, in the long run, uniform effects upon the Western military organizations, the rate and the scope of the change tended to be dissimilar. In the case of the United Kingdom and of the United States, change was more thorough and more rapid than elsewhere in the Western world; the process of "all-volunteerization" of the armed forces was completed in the 1960s and early 1970s. In Austria, Belgium, Denmark, the Netherlands, and, to a lesser extent, West Germany, although the process was much slower, reliance on selective forms of conscription, the introduction of paramilitary styles of active service, and the formulation of contingency plans for the creation of quasi-volunteer military forces clearly emphasized the extent of the decline of the mass army model in the West.

Several factors can be credited for such discrepancies in the rate of military organizational change in Western societies. For example, in the United Kingdom, the lack of a strong citizen-mobilization tradition, postwar realism about the disintegration of the colonial empire, and rapid nuclearization of the British national defense and strategy facilitated the emergence of an all-volunteer armed force formally mandated in 1963. In the United States, though swift technological breakthroughs led to an early revolutionizing of the defense system, the Korean War and overseas military deployments, organized along classic imperial styles, preserved the need for the mass army posture; it was not until the end of the 1960s that significant organizational changes took place. In the rest of the West, mainly in continental Europe, factors that help to explain the relative slowness in the decline of the mass army model included the revolutionary tradition linking the mass mobilizing army with citizenship and democracy, and the NATO division of labor confining diverse European armed forces to the performance of conventional functions in the defense structure of the organization.

The postwar French military establishment belongs to this last category of cases, though it seems even to lag behind most of them. A preliminary examination reveals that until the early 1960s, the French military establishment unmistakably presented most of the features by which the classic mass armed force is defined. Even after 1965, though the institution theoretically tended to move away from the mass armed force archetype, it continued to retain some of the most blatant, obvious characteristics of the traditional model. Until the early 1960s, for example, the French military manpower level was among the highest in the world. As in any defense organization patterned on the mass mobilization model, the role of the reserves was crucial; the Military Participation Ratio was the highest of all NATO countries, with the exception of Greece. Until 1959, the French citizen's military duty lasted nearly thirty years, eighteen months of active service and twenty-six years of reserve duty. Conscription, until 1965, lasted one and a half years and the level of citizen participation in the active military service reached its maximum during that period. There was no dispensation from military service other than disqualification for medical reasons, and the level of exemption remained between 6 and 10 percent of the total eligible age-class.

After 1965, the picture changed. The armed forces strength fell to half of what it had been previously; the citizen mobilization level, both in active and reserve duty, decreased; the internal division of labor became more heterogeneous; the ratio of military to civilian personnel declined; and so on. Yet, one could see that key features derived from the mass armed forces model persisted: for instance, the existence of a still functioning universal and egalitarian conscription continued.

In short, the contemporary French military establishment became an organization in transition. It was a pluralistic (actually dualistic) institution with a mixture of characteristics derived from both traditional and modern forms of military organization. To understand the persistence of the mass army morphology into the 1960s and the dualistic or transitional structure that followed, two series of elements must be examined. This pattern of evolution was first the effect of a set of general causes, that is, of a system of causes that affected the institution in its entirety. The introduction of nuclear equipment into the military and the involvement of the armed forces in a defense policy patterned on nuclear deterrence were part of this. The second set of factors, most of which were rooted in the history and the social and political culture of the French polity or in the particularisms of the French military establishment, had little overall effect upon the military establishment as a whole, but tended to affect certain of its professional, organizational, and social components. Such factors either accentuated the impact of the general causes or opposed them, hence adding to the persistence of features that were expected to phase out. The maintenance of conscription, for example, resulted from specific factors working at crosscurrents to the general causes.

Such are the assumptions upon which the present analysis of the French military establishment is based. This book deals with the examination, from a sociological viewpoint, of the military institution between 1945 and 1976, with special emphasis on the contemporary period. Its purpose, above all, is to describe the evolution and the idiosyncratic nature of some of the major organizational, professional, and social components of the French military establishment and to assess their underlying logic. Such reflections, as suggested, will be made in the light of recent conceptual developments concerning the theory of the mass armed forces model and its mutation into the volunteer force pattern.

It should be stressed that thematically the following study is far from a comprehensive one. Though the choice of topics to be analyzed was guided by a concern for relevance (relevant with regard to the current intellectual preoccupations and practices of the discipline), many topics whose analysis might have been expected in such a study have not been entered into—for example, career patterns, personnel inflows-outflows, or lifestyle. The reasons for such a fragmentary approach are technical and are essentially due to the paucity of systematic (hard and soft) empirical material; this is felt all the more acutely in the present situation, where the focus is on both the diachronic and the synchronic (interservice) dimensions of the subject matter. Moreover, there is no doubt that discrepancies in the levels of the data—some refer to the macroscopic universe, others to the microscopic—and the lack of continuous statistical series, constituted a serious obstacle to the elaboration of valid and consistent inferences, and were thus conducive to taking some liberties with established research protocol. Unless one risked sheer paralysis, there was no choice but to cross back and forth over the frail bridge between the macro- and the micro-analytical level, as well as to rely upon the dominant idealized type characterizations by which we tried to trace and make apparent the tangibility of long-term change.

Although this study seeks mainly to understand, rather than to explain, we shall throughout our descriptions attempt to uncover the causes of the evolution, particularly when such evolution seems to be in contradiction to what might have been expected. Part One, starting with an examination of defense policies and the subsequent level of technological change for the military, defines the effects of these policies on the format of the military, with regard to the mass army/all-volunteer force continuum. Next, particular aspects of the military institution are studied in detail—at the organizational level in Part Two, at the professional level in Part Three, and at the social level in Part Four. Eventual deviations from the expected pattern of evolution are assessed with regard to these specific factors that, as we have said, tended to either reinforce or impede the effects of the system of general causes for change, and consequently, to affect the logical configuration of the paradigm established in Part One.

Notes

1. Morris Janowitz, "The Emergent Military," in *Public Opinion and the Military Establishment*, edited by Charles C. Moskos (Beverly Hills, Ca.: Sage Publications, 1971), p. 259.

2. The extramilitary dimension of conscription deserves detailed theoretical treatment in its own right. Most analyses describing (or denouncing) the socializing functions of this institution in terms of the degree of infringement upon personal freedom, as is the case with the prolific current literature on conscription in France, tend to ignore the historical role conscription played in developing and consolidating democratic political systems. In this regard, Mosca, *Elementi di scienza politica*; Engels, *Herrn Eugen Dührings Um-*

wälzung der Wissenschaft and *Der Deutsch-Französische Krieg*; Rousseau, *Considérations sur le gouvernement de Pologne*; and even Machiavelli, *L'Art de la guerre* are enlightening. Recently this theme has been the object of reflections by David C. Rapoport, "A Comparative Theory of Military and Political Types," in *Changing Patterns of Military Politics*, edited by Samuel P. Huntington (Glencoe, Ill.: The Free Press, 1962), pp. 71–100; Samuel E. Finer, "State and Nation-Building in Europe: The Role of the Military," in *The Formation of National States in Europe*, edited by Charles Tilly (Princeton: Princeton University Press, 1975), pp. 84–163; Morris Janowitz, "Military Institutions and Citizenship in Western Societies," *Armed Forces and Society* 2 (1976): 185–204; and Maury D. Feld, *The Structure of Violence: Armed Forces as Social Systems* (Beverly Hills, Ca.: Sage Publications, 1977).

PART ONE ● THE CHANGING ENVIRONMENT OF THE FRENCH MILITARY ESTABLISHMENT

INTRODUCTION

Fundamental changes in social institutions are always the result of the interplay between several, and often numerous, factors. It is the role, if not the very raison d'être, of the social sciences to offer a simpler and more comprehensible image of the real world by choosing from among the infinite variety and complexity of these factors those that account for the greatest part of the variance. In military institutions, long-term changes are the result of a large assortment of variables, but obviously only a few can be relevant. Among the few that can be designated as critical, the nature of the functions to be performed and the technological level associated with the performance of these functions are foremost. If the primary role of the military establishment is combat, the multitude of combat forms also has a wide range of distinct consequences for the institutional format of the military: guerrilla warfare, conventional warfare, and nuclear warfare obviously require very different, if not mutually exclusive, systems of military organization and levels of technology. Technological change itself has important repercussions for both the defense deployment and the format of the military: numerous studies have shown how technological change in military equipment has contributed to the transformation of the shape of the military institution over time. During the nineteenth century, for example, progress in armament techniques and the mass production of individual weapons had a crucial impact on the rise of military systems modeled on the mass army. With later innovations, in particular those born of the introduction of nuclear technology to the military and their subsequent effects upon world actors' defense strategies and upon the basic functions of armed forces, the mass army format, oriented toward combat functions, was drastically altered. The emergent model developing out of these transformations, and congruently with deterrence-oriented missions, took the form of what has been defined as the force-in-being format.

It is our assumption that the analysis of the roles performed by the military establishment after World War II, as well as the resulting level of technology at which the military had to operate to successfully achieve these roles, is a determinant in understanding the evolution and in assessing the nature of its format, particularly its position on the mass army/force-in-being continuum.

The following discussion examines the role and the missions performed by the French armed forces and the subsequent constraints imposed upon them during the three or so postwar decades. The best means of achieving this goal is the analysis of the change in the guiding principles of French foreign policy, at least of those aspects related to defense and security, and the examination of their technological implications for the military. A tangential discussion of national defense budgeting policy, defining the volume and the direction of resources within the military, will help to further pinpoint the areas in which the constraints of change actually occurred.

CHAPTER ONE ● *GRANDEUR* AND SECURITY

Foreign policy usually refers to a system of parameters relating to a nation's conception of world order. It is tied to the objectives and priorities the nation seeks to achieve as a member of the larger interacting social structure of the international "universe," and shaped by its perception of the changes, threats, and entangling processes produced by the dynamics of this universe. The following remarks are not aimed at presenting a comprehensive account of French international policy, nor at assessing this policy in regard to its external and internal sources, the goals it seeks to achieve, or its contribution to world security. The subject matter will simply define the guiding principles, the underlying philosophy, so to say, of French external policies in order to suggest the kind of environment in which the roles and tasks of the military establishment were specified and, as a consequence, the forces and the constraints to which this establishment was exposed.

For this purpose it can be said that the fundamental logic of French politics since World War II has been based on three intertwining concerns: the search for security (a continuous concern since 1870), the attainment of prosperity, and the restoration of national prestige. Though always sought concurrently, these goals could not always be achieved simultaneously, perhaps because the means utilized in the pursuit of one goal tended, in general, to be detrimental to the achievement of one or both of the others. *Grandeur*, for example, might have been realized by a strengthening of national independence, yet excessive independence could have been antagonistic to security and prosperity, particularly in a world in which a nation's economic and technological, not to mention military, survival was increasingly linked to national interdependence. Conversely, integration into larger supranational units in which power is a priori unequally distributed could frustrate any individual freedom of action and ultimately diminish national prestige. Therefore, though these priorities were collectively pursued, in the end one or another tended to be privileged, and one or another to be sacrificed. To a certain extent then, behind an appearance of byzantine complexity, sometimes even contradiction, the postwar dynamic of French foreign policy was animated by attempts to solve the dilemma created by the need to achieve these key demands. In this regard, it is possible to distinguish two separate periods roughly coinciding with the Fourth and the Fifth Republics.

The Foreign Policy of the Fourth Republic

In the course of the years following the liberation of French soil from German occupation, the new regime sought to revive the greatness and to reestablish the security of the country, according to the same principles which had been in force before 1939. This was particularly obvious in France's immediate attempt to reassert domination over her colonial territories, particularly those in Indochina; to devise an efficient control over Germany (in a fashion unmistakably reminiscent of that advocated by Ferdinand Foch or Georges Clemenceau in 1919, for example, de Gaulle's 1945 blueprints for dividing Germany into "deindustrialized" city-states); and to resume her special diplomatic ties with the old Russian ally. However, such views hardly fit with the new balance of the postwar world order, a new order in which the European powers, including France, had lost a great deal of influence to two non–Western European industrial nations. Within the two years following liberation, France had to recognize the impracticability of a return to the status quo ante bellum. Despite her attempt to emerge from the war as one of the four great victors, France reluctantly had to accept the immutable givens of the growing, antagonistic bipolarization of the international system and to admit her implicit membership in the Western bloc. The Moscow Conference of June–July 1947 dramatically severed the French dream of being a neutral arbiter, as the country became a nation threatened by the same "danger" as all other countries in the Western world. Indeed, the sheer dimension of the potential menace arising from new opponents beyond the Elbe added to the historical concern with the threat from beyond the Rhine and the necessity for economic recovery led France to take shelter, if not a participatory role, in a new military alliance, one in which she was only a minor power. With her security being ensured mainly by the American military umbrella, France's energies and resources could be invested in the recovery of prosperity. Partly to balance a diminished status in the Western world, but above all to promote her wealth, France, under the leadership of those Jean-Baptiste Duroselle has called the *néo-réalistes*,[1] undertook the reconciliation with Germany and the reconstruction of

Europe. European economic cooperation and the Marshall Plan put economic recovery within sight in a few years. *Grandeur*, however, remained an unfulfilled demand. Even before the war's end France experienced the bitter taste of second-class power status. Not only was she not invited to Yalta and Potsdam, but her military and civil leaders found themselves continuously confronted with the callousness of the big powers. That was the case in Alsace in 1945 and the Val d'Aoste Affair with the Americans and during the German partition proceedings with the Soviets. In the late 1940s, the country, though tagged as one of the postwar "Big Four," failed in its attempt to act as a referee power. Later, in the cold-war climate created by increasing bipolarization, security again became a critical issue and France realized that with her bewildered economy and next to no military means, she could not alone cater to this priority. Thus the French nation was led to abandon to a bigger and integrated alliance, one in which the United States was conspicuously visible, a part of her sovereignty in an area from which she had drawn most of her prestige and *grandeur*, an area in which she had been a leading power—national defense. And yet, particularly after the Soviet Union exploded its first hydrogen bomb in 1953 and exhibited its superiority in the technology of remote-control delivery systems in 1957, France's alliance-dependency, like that of every other country in Western Europe, increased. As a result of Soviet technological prowess, the American military protection grew, for evident reasons, less unconditional, and France found herself confronted ever more acutely with the predicament of dependency.

In a manner of speaking, all the bickering initiated by the French since 1953 about the nature of the military integration, about the behavior of her partners in the alliance, or about the role of the United States in favoring German rearmament, in meddling in Indochina, the Middle East, and North Africa, and in conspicuously reigning over the alliance was a result of France's increasing perception of her diminished prestige and of a sense of dispossession. The same can be said of French attempts to tighten European bonds and to strengthen a network of nonmilitary organizations. But, notwithstanding several declarations advocating withdrawal from the military alliance, the Fourth Republic, at least until 1957, never really intended to question NATO's existence and functions, nor its American support.[2] The feeling that the alliance, and particularly the United States' support thereof, was absolutely imperative was widespread. To some extent it could be said that the French decision to embark upon the construction of a nuclear force was not entirely guided by the desire to escape dependency, but was paradoxically a corollary of dependency, because it was conceived as an eventual trigger of the American atomic umbrella whose reliability was now being questioned.

However, though the tools for the preservation of national prestige, including military and economic independence, had to be abandoned for the sake of security, the resulting loss of prestige could be alleviated by other means and the enhancement of greatness could feed itself at another scource. The battered nation, humiliated by defeat and dependency, sought her lost preeminence in the task of nurturing imperial hegemony, exactly as she had done after the 1870 defeat.[3] Though the reasons for France's concern for the preservation of the integrity of her colonial possessions throughout the Fourth Republic are numerous and diverse, it can be argued that the search for ways to resuscitate her status as a big power, thus compensating for the predicament of dependency, was certainly an important one. One author rightly refers to this dialectic between *grandeur* and colonialism: "For time and again throughout the history of the Fourth Republic, beneath the invective of political division, one finds a shared anguish at the passing of national greatness, a shared humiliation at a century of defeats, a shared nationalistic determination that France must retain her independence in a hostile world—all brought to rest on the conviction that the colonies, and especially Algeria, would remain French."[4] But the postwar world was a difficult one in which to assert imperial pretensions. The fundamental objective contradictions that colonization bears in the germs of its own essence and that are ultimately detrimental to its existence had already given birth to the ideology of nationalism.[5] The participation of diverse members of the colonial empire in a combat aimed at the defense of democracy, racial and religious equality, civil liberties, and self-determination further nourished the indigenous peoples' conviction, at least that of their leaders, of the righteousness of their desire to be freed from alien domination.

Conscious of such changes, the British quickly admitted the unavoidability of the movement and prepared themselves to grant autonomy, and in the long run independence, to their colonial possessions. As for France, seeking to enhance her status, her dilemma consisted of preserving the integrity of the empire without completely antagonizing nascent nationalism. To simplify an exceptionally complex and contradiction-ridden view, it can be said that the Fourth Republic's colonial plan, though it rejected autonomy and independence outside the *bloc français*, admitted the equality of all members of the colonial community—to which France also belonged—without racial or religious distinctions, and the equality of each national aggregate within the community. From these syllogisms the implication could be drawn that equality of members would lead to access to a common citizenship, to a common system of right and duty, and that the equality of the national collectivity would lead to the emergence of equal status sovereignty. Yet autonomy and independence continued to be rejected. Because of the basic contradictions, such an organization was bound to fail. Common citizenship and diversified national sovereignty do not go together: the first is in the Jacobinic tradition of centralization and assimilation, the second in the federalist tradition of decentralization. And precisely because France had to keep the upper hand in such an organization in order to assert her special status, and because federation was not at all in the French political tradition, a tradition pervaded by unitarian and centralization-oriented proclivities and the inconceivability of a delegation of power, the federalist path was bent in such a way that the distribution of powers between the members remained uneven and the preponderance was left in the hands of France. As for the unitarian-centralization bias, it ultimately led, at least in the context of liberty and equality in which the Fourth Republic was willing to operate, to assimilation. Here again, France, unwilling to accept the consequences of such a policy, avoided implementing it for fear that "France would become the colony of her former colonies."[6] Basically the country was not ready for decolonization. Her inability to conceive of decolonization as an ineluctable element of the dialectic of social change was reflected in the search for reasons that would legitimate her attitude and actions. This view was not held by conservative ideologues alone. The Left, as well as numerous Resistance figures, concerned with the importance of the colonial heritage as a source of prestige, took up the defense of the empire. Pretexts such as the protection of Indochina from further encroachment by Japanese or Chinese imperialism served as ideologically consistent arguments for the sending of expeditionary forces. For example, the liberation movements and other struggles aimed at acquiring independence undertaken by colonized peoples tended to be interpreted as Machiavellian conspiracies organized by jealous powers seeking to undermine French prestige: Great Britain in the Middle East, the United States in Indochina and North Africa, and the conniving superpowers in the Suez fiasco took turns at playing the villain. Even when forced to admit the inevitability of the forthcoming disintegration of the empire into self-governing nations, France was not able to grant her possessions unfettered independence. In this complex institutional construction that was the French colonial community, juridical and affective discrepancies were numerous. In this vast conglomerate made up of the *départements d'outre-mer* (Algeria and the four old colonies), *territoires d'outre-mer* (black Africa and the Malagasy colonies), *états associés* (Indochina—Vietnam, Cambodia, and Laos), protectorates (Tunisia and Morocco), and *territoires associés* (United Nations mandates—Togo and Cameroon), all of these components did not have the same importance, the same quality. It was like a living body in which each organ has a different structure, function, and relation to the survival of the whole. Some colonies could be amputated, others could not. Some could not escape the orbit in which they were set; they were too much a part of the whole to be taken away. It was even denied that they were colonies—they were French (even if in practice they escaped the logic of integration). That was the case of Algeria, for which France stubbornly refused to accept the legitimacy of an indigenous nationalism: Algeria, it was claimed, was as French as Brittany or Alsace, and Algerian subversion was seen as a matter of domestic disorder. As Alfred Grosser pointed out: "About the most important problem, Algeria, there is a complete deadlock, there is a refusal to consider that this ultimate problem of domination overseas could be considered under the rubric 'decolonization.' In this regard, not only did the Fourth Republic refuse to consider this possibility, but it denied that the choice even existed. Algeria was not a part of the territories to which the idea of colonization would apply."[7]

Thus, throughout the twelve years of its existence, the Fourth Republic was oriented toward maintaining the integrity of the colonial community. To achieve this priority, despite increasingly unfavorable circumstances, France relied on many methods. The *donner et retenir* policy, to borrow Grosser's term, was a common diplomatic formula. Vietnam and, before the war, Syria and Lebanon, are cases in point. The voluntary granting of independence was used to introduce new patterns of relationships that constrained the new states to remain within French influence. For domination, only presence was viewed as an appropriate substitute. Military coercion was the ultimate weapon upon which the Fourth Republic relied to repress local nationalist uprisings in critical areas. Thus in Indochina as early as 1946, then in Algeria from 1955 on, the Fourth Republic was drawn into more than a decade of colonial warfare in which it mobilized a significant part of its military resources and energies.

To those within the Atlantic organization, of which France was a member, who criticized French involvement in colonial conflicts, either on moral grounds (an incompatibility between the ideals of the alliance and colonial repression) or on technical grounds (by fighting overseas nationalist rebellions France would weaken the united military strength of the alliance), the Fourth Republic responded that her wars against nationalist uprisings were fully legitimate in that they actually proceeded from the basic objective of the organization, namely, the containment of communism, the progenitor of these rebellious movements. It should be noted in passing that this argument, though an oversimplified view of the reality since there were, at least at their origins, no links between nationalism and communism, caught, particularly in the wake of the Korean War, the fancy of the leading actor of the alliance, "mistaking a colonial revolution aimed at independence for an element in the global Cold War . . . being drawn ever more disastrously into the area [Indochina]."[8]

Throughout the duration of the Fourth Republic, all sections of the political and military community seemed to have been convinced of the righteousness of this vision; thereby justifying French commitment to the maintenance of her national imperial hegemonic pretensions.[9] After 1954, the idea of fighting for the moral and territorial security of the Western world was added to the thesis of participating in the containment of Soviet influence. The security priority thus came to justify the prestige priority. The most conspicuous application of such an approach to international and colonial affairs was the famous military theory of revolutionary warfare contrived in the Indochinese rice swamps or POW camps and put into practice in the early days of the Algerian revolution. Conceiving the Algerian rebellion as the second stage of the Bolshevik encircling movement against Western civilization (the first one having been the communist victory in Indochina), the theory of revolutionary warfare was not only a military tactic to deal successfully with the Algerian rebellion, but also a means to justify, at both the domestic and the international levels, the legitimacy of French political and military response to colonial uprisings.[10] Interestingly enough, this conviction that the security of the nation was at stake on the Mediterranean and African fronts of the European continent was shared not only by the military and conservative politicians, but also by the Socialist Left for whom the Paris-Algiers-Brazzaville axis was central to French security.[11]

Thus *grandeur* together with security came to justify French readiness to maintain the integrity of the colonial empire and the country's involvement in two military conflicts that have had very important repercussions on the profile of the French military establishment.

The Foreign Policy of the Fifth Republic

The fall of the Fourth Republic signaled not only a change in leadership, but also a drastic reform of French external policy. Though the imprint of each new leader of the Gaullist succession had given to this policy a new physiognomy, there was, nonetheless, a definite similarity throughout the first seventeen years of the new republic. It is on the elements that contributed to such a continuity that we shall concentrate, as, more than the differences, this continuity helped shape the environment in which the French military establishment found itself immersed.

It should also be noted that the following summary actually addresses itself to the period running from 1962 to 1976 since, in effect, the policy following the fall of the Fourth Republic to 1961 was similar to that which had preceded it. And, though France had grown more and more distrustful of the Atlantic alliance at that time, the existence of the alliance was not yet questioned; French external policy, on the whole, was aligned with the alliance's position and its participants' conceptions: for example, the French government had a sympathetic attitude toward the United States during the Cuban Missile Crisis. One can also say that, though the government position toward the integrity of the colonial community, or what was left of it, was about to change drastically, the colonial policy that followed was in continuity with that of the Fourth Republic, as evidenced by the breadth of the military involvement in Algeria after 1958.

Therefore, it was really after 1961 that the originality of what was to be the Fifth Republic's international policy materialized; it was after 1961 that the pattern of accommodation among the three basic priorities took a radically new direction, particularly as concerned the prestige and the security of the nation. This change was due partly to the modification of the objective environment that included the world structure and the domestic context and partly to the personal and political philosophies of the new leaders concerning attainment of these priorities. By 1960, economic recovery had been achieved and prosperity was in view; new resources had become available. The threat against security had lightened as a result of the thawing of East-West tensions. On the "imperial front," however, where the battle for the prestige of the country was taking place, the situation deteriorated rapidly. Not only had the campaign launched to keep Algeria French produced no tangible result other than that of exposing France to the growing opprobrium of the rest of the world, but it had become an impediment to France's newly blossomed prosperity.

Crucial to the emerging leader of the new Republic was the fact that the preservation of colonial integrity, now symbolized by the Algerian War, had become detrimental to the very function it had been designed to fulfill—the prestige of the country. Neither the colonial hegemony ideal nor the actions undertaken in its pursuit could continue to be a source of prestige. And if prestige could be gained in this area, it would be in giving up such an ideal. This erosion of prestige occurred on two levels: not only did the conduct of colonial war, especially when conducted on such a scale as in Algeria after 1956, weaken the colonial power prestige, but it also significantly increased France's dependency on the Western alliance for the defense of her home front.

Though the exact amount of tactical planning and sheer improvisation in the Gaullist strategy remains a riddle, these facts obviously guided the colonial policy of the new regime.[12] At heart, de Gaulle was probably favorable to the colonial hegemony ideal—one recalls that between 1944 and 1955 he opposed any idea of colonial liberalization and ardently advocated the integrity of the empire.[13] But he came to recognize that Algeria could become France's Achilles' heel; Algeria could become the main obstacle to France's achieving greatness. He realized that the prestige of the French nation could actually be enhanced, particularly among the new Third World countries, by playing the game of self-determination. Nevertheless, de Gaulle always managed to act in such a way that the means used to resolve the problem constituted an acceptable and honorable solution in the eyes of the nation. For this reason he supported military engagement in Algeria until 1961; while preparing for the negotiations, he gave the impression of imposing his conditions on the National Liberation Front. Following the January 1961 referendum, negotiation became possible and acceptable.

As the curtain was drawn over colonial domination, it became clear that the country's *grandeur* had to be nourished from other sources. For himself, as well as for those who succeeded him in office, de Gaulle set up a model that was to be followed and that was to provide continuity, despite variations on the theme, over the ensuing years: national independence was the best way to restore and enhance the country's prestige. "It is by acting as the inflexible champion of the nation and the state that it will be possible for me to gain followers and even enthusiasts among the French, and to gain from foreigners respect and consideration," de Gaulle declared.[14] Thus the history of France's disengagement from the military network of the Atlantic alliance and her watchful posture against any further outside encroachment expressed the feeling that "it is intolerable for a great state to have its destiny subject to decisions and acts of another state, no matter how friendly it may be"[15] and symbolized the new path chosen to safeguard national prestige. The relationship with the Atlantic organization was so affected precisely because one of the key elements of the nation's independence was at stake—national defense. The Gaullists, whose views on that issue were fully endorsed by the political opposition and by public opinion, were deeply convinced that the only means by which the state could ensure national independence was national defense. "For the president of the Republic, each nation must keep complete control of its defense . . . for two reasons; first, because defense is the fundamental mission from which the state cannot be separated without mutilating itself or without risking the mutilation of the nation; then, because whatever the degree of consensus, of viewpoints, and interests between one or two countries, these interests can never be rigorously intermingled and it is the duty of each of them to give priority to the satisfaction of its own concerns."[16] Now, because of the nature of the integration and of the military division of labor between the Atlantic partners, France's exercise of the functions of national defense and her control over the exercise of the alliance's defense missions and over the definition of common interests were greatly limited. Independence, therefore, became two-sided. On the one hand, independence meant total exercise and control by the state over a number of functions, including national defense, perceived as relevant to its sovereignty; on the other hand, independence meant that the state could refuse to be drawn into the defense of alien interests, even those of its allies, without its consent. On the level of national defense, this last argument survived as one of the most salient and enduring characteristics of the Fifth Republic's external policy;[17] it spawned the concept of "sanctuarization,"—that is to say, the refusal to compromise the national defense for purposes other than the security of the nation—which was interpreted more or less strictly by each administration.

Independence was but one dimension of prestige enhancement; military might was the other. Not only did military strength enable the nation to insure her security without the inconvenience of entanglement, but it also permitted the nation to play a leading role in the world of nations. Armed force was thus seen as a powerful instrument of diplomacy.[18] In this General de Gaulle echoed a feeling that had already been expressed by a number of politicians and military leaders during the Fourth Republic, particularly by those advocating the construction of a French nuclear force. But for these harbingers the building of a strong military had more limited goals than for the Gaullists. As stated previously, during the Fourth Republic the construction of an atomic device was guided by concern for enforcing security, and, by proxy, it was thought that such a device would eventually secure American military assistance. In regard to greatness, military strength was seen as a means of upholding French status, but always within the Atlantic alliance. Under the Fifth Republic the objectives were surely less pur nimous. The development of a nuclear military force was now aimed at disentangling France from the burden of the network alliance, at guaranteeing the nation against any type of subjugation by a foreign power, and at glorifying French leadership over nonaligned nations.[19] Under the Fifth Republic, therefore, the same means, an independent national defense, was to serve in achieving both prestige and security priorities. Therein lies the difference between the Fourth and Fifth Republics; during the Fourth Republic the means by which security had to be attained were somewhat detrimental to the search for prestige since security implied a close dependency within an integrated organization in which France had only a minor role.

Thus, the Fifth Republic's history started with the disentanglement from the integrated organizations of the Atlantic alliance and continued with the avoidance of all encroachments on French national independence and with the enhancement of national defense credibility through the systematic development of an independent nuclear force.[20]

As pointed out, such was the rationale underlying the Fifth Republic's external policy. Variations on the theme occurred according to each government and the personalities of its leaders. Yet the continuity is quite clear.

Nineteen hundred sixty-one began a period of about seven years during which what has come to be considered the genuine Gaullist foreign policy developed. Yet the battle for independence, the fight against NATO, and particularly the struggle against American control of the alliance actually started before 1961. For example, a policy, later systematized by the Fouchet plan, that encouraged greater Franco-German cooperation and that was seen as the nucleus of a future third center of power capable of challenging the hegemony of the two existing blocs started in March 1959. Moreover, the famous memorandum of September 1958, requesting the formation of a tripartite decision-making direction for the alliance and the Western world, can be considered as a quid pro quo by which France initiated her action toward disentanglement. Further actions and various criticisms followed; these included attacks on the United States and further withdrawal measures. Critics of the United States' new flexible response strategy supplemented the attack with opposition to Nassau-style agreements, to the Multilateral Force Proposal, and to other test-ban treaties.[21] Then came the decision to withdraw the French fleet from the Allied command: the Mediterranean Fleet in 1959, the Atlantic Fleet in 1963. Next came the recall of all naval officers from the command organization, the refusal to engage French aerial defense equipment and cadres without the authorization of French command, the opposition to the reintegration under allied command of the forces repatriated from the Algerian front, and the refusal to participate in the 1965 NATO maneuvers. Finally, on 7 March 1966, in a message to President Johnson, France announced her intention to terminate all participation in NATO command structures. Though France did not withdraw from the alliance, she had no other obligations than to consult her allies; yet this consultation did not necessarily become a common policy.[22]

To a certain extent, it can be said that the growing visibility of the United States in European economic, monetary, and technical matters, together with the relative decline of the Soviet world pressure (due to its growing concern with domestic and economic problems), increased France's discontent with the United States and even led her to think that American imperialism had become a threat to global security; France's perception of external threats was affected.[23] Less biased against the East, France entertained the idea that the asymmetric development of power in favor of the United States made the latter a potential menace. Not only would further links with the United States not be a safe guarantee for allied partners because of American reliance on the flexible response paradigm, but it would also have unforeseen consequences such as drawing the ally into conflicts foreign to its interests. This vision, encapsulating the substance of the Gaullist conception of world affairs, found fervent thurifers in the military, and, until 1968, reflected the military doctrine that obsessive fear of the East was no longer justified; war could now spring from any point in the world. Consequently, the nation had to plan its military strategy according to a global paradigm; defense could no longer be targeted, it would have to be *tous azimuts*.[24]

For diverse reasons, however, such a policy appeared more and more untenable. Among other events, those of May 1968, the delayed development of the fixed ballistic missiles, the Soviet invasion of Czechoslovakia, which dashed French hopes of diluting the power of

NATO and Warsaw Pact blocs and of encouraging the construction of a pan-European entity, and the shift in West Germany's foreign policy revealed the lack of realism in French external policy, the danger of extreme isolationism from the Western alliance, and France's continued dependence on her Atlantic partners. From the end of Gaullist rule to Pompidou's presidency, declarations in favor of maintaining American troops in Europe, reducing animosity to U.S. investments in France, increasing interest in European cooperation, and improving relations with NATO signaled a change from the earlier foreign policy posture. Military doctrine, in denouncing the all-azimuths strategy as unrealistic, in advocating a return to a strategy of alliance, and, above all, in realigning itself with the view that the potential enemy was in the East, mirrored the change.[25]

But the pendulum never swung back completely. Though the perception of military threat was "normalized," though the idea of Anglo-French or European sectorial cooperation came to be regarded as *les choses possibles* as evidenced by French interest in the European Conference on Security and Cooperation, and though a minimum of concern for the Atlantic alliance and NATO were regarded as necessary, France, under the leadership of de Gaulle's successor, Georges Pompidou, did not give up the old Gaullist vision, as exemplified in the choice of defense and foreign ministers with personalities and ideologies patterned after the Gaullist tradition. Though the United States performed an important and welcome military function in the defense of Europe, it continued to be treated with a certain suspicion. And with mounting skepticism about the consequences of a Soviet-American détente (even though initiated by the very example of France), the perception of threats by superpowers remained visible. In a somewhat neurotic fashion, France now saw herself confronted by a threat from the coalescence of two superpowers rather than by a threat from only one superpower. World security, in the rhetoric of French national defense and foreign affairs specialists, was no longer threatened by a superpower encounter but rather by a two-fold superpower hegemony. The risks of collision were succeeded by the risks of collusion, or "superpower condominion." It is in this perspective that France's stubborn refusal to support MBFR talks, SALT negotiations, and any test-ban or nuclear proliferation treaties should be interpreted. As de Gaulle, who saw both NPT and the Test-Ban Treaty as efforts on the part of the big powers to disarm smaller countries, his successor considered every agreement and decision of this nature a "bloc deal" with a built-in discriminatory bias against small nations that would ultimately have a destabilizing effect on European security. Consequently, despite some change in attitude toward Atlantic cooperation, and despite a slight tendency toward "desanctuarization," post-Gaullist defense policy continued to emphasize the necessity and the value of an independent defense organization centered around a nuclear force that would be used solely for the protection of French territory.[26]

After the accession of Valery Giscard d'Estaing to the presidency in 1974, French foreign policy took a somewhat new orientation that subsequently affected the national defense posture. Orthodox Gaullists and Communist leaders who had heartily endorsed de Gaulle's external policy did not fail to denounce the new policy as sinful revisionism. The transformation of Franco-American relations in particular illustrated this change. The meetings at Ottawa, Martinique, and Rambouillet, for example, were milestone French-American compromises on issues ranging from the military organization of the Atlantic alliance to the management of the floating dollar exchange rate. Furthermore, French approval of the new Atlantic Charter, the appointment of a new liaison delegate to NATO general headquarters, and the joint French-U.S. military exercises at Canjuers could be viewed as evidences of French reentry into the Atlantic military alliance network.[27] Later, official declarations such as Chief of Staff General Mery's views on national defense as published in the quasi-official *Défense nationale* and President Giscard d'Estaing's speech at the Institut des hautes études de la Défense nationale stressing the need for a *stratégie élargie* (a forward strategy implying a tighter military cooperation with the armed forces of the United States and West Germany in particular) seemed to officially sanction France's renewed communion with the Atlantic orthodoxy.[28]

This interpretation, however, is a little excessive, at least for the period running from the beginning of 1974 to early 1976: it put an inordinate stress on the Atlanticist proclivities of the new external policy and overlooked continuing references to the independence of the country and of her defense organization. President Giscard d'Estaing's declarations after June 1974 offer some clarification.[29] This interpretation is also excessive because of its tendency to take as a frame of reference a very normative view of the Gaullist orthodoxy, an orthodoxy whose fierce anti-Atlanticism and myopic nationalism have been exaggerated.[30] One must take cognizance of de Gaulle's explicit statement that he was not seeking to disengage France from the Atlantic alliance. Pompidou also recognized that a minimum of military cooperation with the Atlantic partners was an unavoidable necessity. Therefore, it can be said that Giscardian foreign and defense policies were, until 1976, more in continuity with his predecessors' policies than they were in a situation of discontinuity. As before, emphasis was placed on a national defense based on nuclear deterrence and oriented solely toward the protection of the *hexagone*.[31] For the government this position was all the more justifiable in that the evolution of international relations left the country with ambivalent feelings. A lingering impression of détente, together with a perception of repolarization, made clear that "big ally" protection was less and less credible. In effect, the declarations of the American secretary of defense (for example, Secretary of Defense James Schlesinger's annual report to Congress in March 1974) convinced France that the United States, by advocating, for instance, more flexibility in the use of nuclear armament as well as a change in its targeting doctrine, would restrict its military power to the defense of indigenous interests. This was a posture that the United States felt all the freer to adopt as technically Europe became less vital for the operation of the American defense network. First, technological breakthroughs (such as the Trident class of nuclear submarines) had rendered extended overseas deployments less crucial since they allowed the undertaking of military actions from closer to the American soil and seas. Second, constraints resulting from budgetary considerations as well as the cost increase of the all-volunteer force and from political factors had already imposed limitations to the American deployment in Europe;[32] hence the growing perception in Europe of the illusory nature of the American protective umbrella.[33] In addition, the scars left by the Vietnamese War certainly rendered the United States extremely cautious on the matter of overseas involvement; criticisms made of the Ford administration's attempt to assist the pro-Western parties in the Angolan civil war indicated the difficulties the American administration would face in case of new external involvement. President Ford's trip to Europe in June 1975 was designed to reassure European allies of the credibility of the American defense umbrella, a credibility that had been badly shaken.

Other factors, such as the malaise created by the Soviet view of détente, the recent buildup of the Soviet armed forces, and, very importantly, the strong attachment of French society to national independence and the accompanying political pressures from its fiercest partisans, the Gaullists and the Communists, help to explain the government's continual paean to the idol of nuclear self-sufficiency. During his visit to the nuclear submarine *Le Terrible* on 7 and 8 November 1974, President Giscard d'Estaing clearly stated his belief in the need for an independent nuclear force. Throughout 1975 his commitment to this independent nuclear force grew even stronger.[34] At the army field maneuvers at Mourmelon held to commemorate the thirtieth anniversary of 8 May 1945, he affirmed: "In a world in which everyone struggles fiercely for independence, in which great events underscore the peoples' solitude, France must, given her capacities, insure her security entirely."[35] The prime minister's speech at the Mailly artillery training field during the presentation of a new unit of TNW Pluton equipment in February 1975 and his intervention during the May 1975 parliamentary debate on national defense offer additional evidence of the new regime's alignment with the previous pattern of external policy.[36] Later, in May 1976, Jacques Chirac was to declare: "No solidarity can prevent our country from keeping control over her defense, that is to say, her destiny. . . . There could be no question of French reintegration, under any form, with the military organization of the Atlantic pact."[37]

Thus, from 1961 to 1976, allowing for some significant changes in the formulation of foreign policy, there was a continuous concern for the enhancement of an independent defense organization founded on the principle of nuclear deterrence and oriented toward the maintenance of French sovereignty. However, the limited, though increasing, tendency toward "desanctuarization" and "strategic enlargement" somewhat confused the picture.

This summary is indeed very succinct. As stated earlier, the analysis was not aimed at describing the evolution of French foreign policy and its national defense aspects in detail. Rather, it sought to make apparent long-term continuities in order to evaluate very broadly the nature of the context in which the military establishment had to operate.

The question to which we will address ourselves in the following chapter concerns the effects of such a policy on the organization of national defense and the subsequent constraints on the French military establishment, particularly in regard to the latter's exposure to technological change.

Notes

1. Jean-Baptiste Duroselle, "Changes in French Foreign Policy since 1945," in *In Search of France: The Economy, Society, and Political System in the Twentieth Century,* edited by Stanley Hoffmann et al. (Cambridge, Mass.: Harvard University Press, 1963), pp. 342–46.

2. *See,* for example, Alphonse Juin, "Que devons-nous penser de la sécurité française," *Revue de Défense nationale* 13 (1957): 5–16 and Paul Ely,

"Notre politique militaire," *Revue de Défense nationale* 13 (1957): 1033–51. For a further discussion on this question, *see also* Guy de Carmoy, *Les Politiques étrangères de la France, 1944–1966* (Paris: La Table Ronde, 1967), part one; Claude Delmas, *L'O.T.A.N.* (Paris: Presses Universitaires de France, 1960); Alfred Grosser, *La IVe République et sa politique extérieure* (Paris: A. Colin, 1961); and L. Radoux, *La France et l'O.T.A.N.* (Paris: UEO, 1967).

3. *See* Raoul Girardet, *L'Histoire de l'idée coloniale en France de 1871 à 1962* (Paris: A. Fayard, 1972).

4. Tony Smith, "The French Colonial Consensus and People's War, 1946–1958," *Journal of Contemporary History* 9 (1974): 220–21.

5. As Raymond Aron aptly stated, "The weakening of France (as well as of Great Britain and other European powers) has contributed to the liberation of the Asian and African peoples, more than it has instigated it. The deep cause is that in imposing their ideas and their civilization, the Europeans justified the revolt of the colonies and thereby deprived themselves of the complacency of conquering people" (Raymond Aron, *L'Algérie et la République* [Paris: Plon, 1958], p. 83).

6. Grosser, *La IVe République et sa politique extérieure*, p. 250; de Carmoy, *Les Politiques étrangères de la France*, pp. 155ff.

7. Alfred Grosser, *La Politique extérieure de la Ve République* (Paris: Seuil, 1965), p. 19.

8. Maurice Keens-Soper, "Foreign Policy," in *France Today: Introductory Studies*, edited by J. E. Flower (London: Methuen, 1971), p. 104.

9. Smith, "The French Colonial Consensus and People's War," pp. 222ff.

10. The literature dealing with the theme of revolutionary warfare is voluminous. Among the leading writers in France on this theme are: L. M. Chassin, "Vers un encerclement de l'Occident," *Revue de Défense nationale* 12 (1956): 531–53; C. Lacheroy, "La Guerre révolutionnaire," in *La Défense nationale*, edited by Tony Albord et al. (Paris: Presses Universitaires de France, 1958), pp. 307–30; Colonel Nemo, "La Guerre dans le milieu social," *Revue de Défense nationale* 12 (1956): 605–23; Ximenes et al., "La Guerre révolutionnaire: données et aspects, methodes de raisonnement, parade et riposte," *Revue militaire d'information* (February–March 1957), special issue. For an analysis of the doctrine and its consequences, *see* Raoul Girardet, "Réflexions critiques sur la doctrine militaire française de la guerre subversive," *Revue des travaux de l'Académie des Sciences morales et politiques et comptes rendus de séances* 113 (1960): 233–45; and Peter Paret, *French Revolutionary Warfare from Indochina to Algeria: The Analysis of a Political Military Doctrine* (New York: Praeger, 1964).

11. Grosser, *La IVe République et sa politique extérieure*, p. 386; Smith, "The French Colonial Consensus and the People's War," pp. 228ff.

12. To dissect de Gaulle's Algerian policy and evaluate exactly how much was policy planning and how much was sheer improvisation is a thorny task. Many scholars are convinced that from the beginning, de Gaulle planned to achieve what was

actually accomplished, that is to say, to favor self-determination. However, as Herbert Lüthy pointed out, "This is an improbable hypothesis, and, above all, terribly unjust, for it supposes that de Gaulle willfully deceived and betrayed all those who carried him to power in 1958, but the reputation for being a man of unfathomable cunning did not displease him, and in any case he preferred it to the contrary hypothesis—truer but less grandiose—that, unable to do what he wished, he wished for what he could do" (Herbert Lüthy, "De Gaulle: Pose and Policy," *Foreign Affairs* 43 [1965], pp. 561–73). Stanley Hoffmann, who in connection with de Gaulle speaks of the *commedia dell'arte* in his keen and sympathetic portrayal of General de Gaulle, emphasizes the ambivalent nature of de Gaulle's political behavior, showing that "there was improvisation within the outlines of a script and with well-defined characters" (Stanley Hoffmann, *Decline or Renewal: France since the 1930s* [New York: Viking Press, 1974], p. 287). For another view of de Gaulle's political attitude *see* Brian Crozier, *De Gaulle* (London: Eyre, Methuen, 1973).

13. Carmoy, *Les Politiques étrangères de la France*, p. 234.

14. Charles de Gaulle, *Mémoires de guerre* (Paris: Plon, 1954–55), vol. 1, p. 70, as quoted by Duroselle, "Changes in French Foreign Policy," p. 353. De Gaulle's concern for national independence and France's greatness was rooted in both his personal and historic background (for example, his infatuation with independence was, to a large extent, a

reaction to his World War II predicament as a too dependent partner of the Anglo-Saxon allies, a position that he strongly resented). For a thorough analysis of this question, *see* Hoffmann, *Decline or Renewal*, and Grosser, *La Politique extérieure de la V* Republique*.

15. As quoted by Duroselle, "Changes in French Foreign Policy," p. 353.

16. *See also* A. Lamson, "L'Organisation de la défense nationale et des forces armées," *Revue politique et parlementaire* 58 (1956): 240–55. In this regard, Lamson wrote, "the function by which the State insures the maintenance of national independence is nothing more than national defense" (p. 240).

17. *See also* p. 42.

18. As Alfred Grosser reminds us, the idea of possessing an offensive force was central to General de Gaulle's conception of diplomacy; for de Gaulle, there was no effective diplomacy without the possession of an offensive weaponry. The weakness of French diplomatic power during the 1930s (especially at Munich) and the later French defeat can be accounted for by the fact that, with the exception of a narrow-minded defense strategy, there was no real military policy to accompany foreign policy. The force de frappe was largely a consequence of this reasoning (Grosser, *La Politique extérieure de la V* République*, p. 121). Several authors share this idea that possession of a deterrent force was mainly a diplomatic device that allowed participation in and supplied bargaining weight at the big powers club.

It is necessary to note that despite de Gaulle's obsessive concern for France's greatness through military power, this concern did not lead him to neglect other means of increasing France's prosperity. For example, even during the Algerian War, several measures were taken to balance France's staggering finances in order to make the French economy more competitive (for example, the 1958 devaluation). Moreover, the use of Common Market networks allowed for an increase of agricultural and industrial exports (*See* Hoffmann, *Decline or Renewal*, p. 294).

19. *See* Wolf Mendl, *Deterrence and Persuasion: The French Nuclear Armament in the Context of National Policy, 1945–1969* (New York: Praeger, 1970).

20. For a detailed account of the origins and development of the French nuclear program, beginning with the Gaillard government, *see* Charles Ailleret, *L'Aventure atomique française* (Paris: Grasset, 1968); idem, "La France et la puissance atomique," *Tendances* (March 1960); Robert Gilpin, *France in the Age of the Scientific State* (Princeton: Princeton University Press, 1968); Bertrand Goldschmidt, *L'Aventure atomique* (Paris: A. Fayard, 1962); Wilfred Kohl, *French Nuclear Diplomacy* (Princeton: Princeton University Press, 1971); Mendl, *Deterrence and Persuasion*; Lawrence Scheinman, *Atomic Energy Policy in France under the Fourth Republic* (Princeton: Princeton University Press, 1965).

21. Both the flexible response strategy and the multilateral nuclear force were rejected on the basis of their being an infringement on France's thirst for military and diplomatic autonomy. The multilateral nuclear force was viewed as too entangling a network, one that would have rendered the French nuclear force, its technological development, and its eventual employment too dependent upon the Allies, in particular upon American needs and willingness. The rather unequal partnership with the United States, especially in regard to the rate and scope of technological transfer from the United States, was an example that General de Gaulle emphasized in his denunciation of the multilateral nuclear force and in his rejection of the Nassau proposals.

As for the flexible response strategy, not only was it seen as a device to lessen French concern for independence and slow France's deployment of nuclear weaponry, but also as an effort by the United States to encourage a European effort toward conventional forces. This was precisely the type of force that France was in the process of reducing because of both the ending of the Algerian conflict and of the necessity of transferring financial allocations in her small military budget in favor of the nuclear strategic force.

Paradoxically, the flexible response strategy tended to reinforce France's decision to possess an independent nuclear force. In effect, because of the shift from a massive retaliation strategy to a flexible response strategy, the American military umbrella seemed, to European eyes, to have lost part of its credibility; flexible response strategy was perceived as a lessening of the American will to strike whenever European interests were at stake. For an official French reaction regarding this matter, *see* Charles Ailleret, "Opinion sur la théorie stratégique de la 'Flexible Response'," *Revue de défense nationale* 20 (1964): 323–40. For further comments, *see also* Edward Kolodziej, *French International Policy under de Gaulle and Pompidou* (Ithaca: Cornell University Press, 1974), and Lothar Ruehl, *La Politique militaire de la Vᵉ République* (Paris: Presses de la Fondation nationale des Sciences politiques, 1976).

22. Concerning the relations between France and NATO, *see also* Edgar S. Furniss, Jr., *France, Troubled Ally: de Gaulle's Heritage and Prospects* (New York: Harper and Brothers, 1960); Robert E. Osgood, *NATO: The Entangling Alliance* (Chicago: University of Chicago Press, 1962); and L. Radoux, *La France et l'O.T.A.N.*

23. Stanley Hoffmann, "Perceptions, Reality, and the Franco-American Conflict," *Journal of International Affairs* 21 (1967): 62.

24. *See* Charles Ailleret's famous article advocating a nuclear force capable of striking in any direction, "Défense dirigée ou défense 'tous azimuts,'" *Revue de Défense nationale* 23 (1967): 1923–32.

25. *See* Edmond Combeaux, "Défense tous azimuts? oui mais. . ." *Revue de Défense nationale* 24 (1968): 1600–1618. On page 1611 Combeaux is quite explicit when he writes, "the need for a permanent defense association between France and her neighbors is inescapable." Michel Fourquet, then chief of staff of the armed forces, developed a similar argument a few months later in "Emploi des différents systèmes de forces dans le cadre de la stratégie de dissuasion," *Revue de Défense nationale* 25 (1969): 757–67. For a discussion of these questions *see* Edward Kolodziej, "France Ensnared: French Strategic Policy and Bloc Politics after 1968," *Orbis* 16 (1972): 1085–108; Kohl, *French Nuclear Diplomacy*; and Ruehl, *La Politique militaire de la Vᵉ République.*

26. Kolodziej, *French International Policy under de Gaulle and Pompidou*; Wolf Mendl, "After de Gaulle: Continuity and Change in French Foreign Policy," *World Today*, January 1971, pp. 8–11.

27. This feeling is particularly acute among orthodox Gaullists, "leftist" Socialists, and Communists. For a thorough account of the French Left's attitude toward national defense, *see* Paul J. Friedrich, "Defense and the French Political Left," *Survival* 16 (1974): 165–71; idem, "L'Union de la gauche et la défense nationale," *Esprit* 43 (1975): 426–34.

28. Guy Méry, "Une armée pourquoi faire et comment?" *Défense nationale* 32 (June 1976): 11–34; and President Giscard d'Estaing's speech at the Institut des hautes études de la Défense nationale, published in extenso in *Le Monde*, 4 June 1976, pp. 14–15.

29. *Les Déclarations du président de la République sur la politique de défense et la politique militaire, juin 1976–décembre 1976* (Paris: Service d'Information et de Diffusion du Premier Ministre, 1977).

30. This has recently been confirmed by François de Rose, *La France et la défense de l'Europe* (Paris: Ed. du Seuil, 1976).

31. Contrary to former premier

Pierre Messmer's opinion, the new orientation advanced by General Méry's article could not be considered as a rupture with the past; on this point *see* Jacques Isnard, "Une Stratégie contestée," *Le Monde*, 3 June 1976.

32. Moreover, the accumulation of nuclear tactical weapons in the Warsaw Pact camp and the maintenance of huge quantities of TNWs by the United States in Europe (originally piled up in response to a possible conventional attack from the Warsaw Pact countries) was no longer necessary; at one point it was even considered dangerous. Hence the new idea of a return to a strategy of conventional dissuasion (made possible by the technological breakthroughs in the area of precision guided missiles); on this question *see* Alain C. Enthoven, "U.S. Forces in Europe, How Many? Doing What?" *Foreign Affairs* 53 (1975): 513–32.

33. Jacques Isnard, "Une Armée en quête de son identité," *Le Monde*, 11 July 1974, p. 10.

34. In this regard Joël Le Theule, defense *rapporteur* at the National Assembly, said at the end of 1974 that the currently implemented foreign policy was similar to that defined by President Giscard d'Estaing's predecessors; *see* Simon Serfaty, "The Fifth Republic under Giscard d'Estaing: Steadfast or Changing," *World Today*, March 1976, pp. 95–103. Raymond Aron also pointed out the continuity in the French doctrine: "The president [Giscard d'Estaing] does not break with his predecessors' doctrine, an integrated part of the Gaullist tradition . . . a doctrine all the more firmly established as the Communists have adopted it and the Socialists will soon do so" (*L'Express*, 21–27 November 1977, p. 106).

35. *Le Monde*, 9 May 1975, p. 5.

36. *Le Monde*, 23 May 1975; Jacques Chirac, "Au sujet des armes nucléaires tactiques françaises," *Défense nationale* 31 (May 1975): 11–16.

37. *Le Monde*, 23–24 May 1976, p. 6.

CHAPTER TWO ● OLD AND
NEW DEFENSE ROLES

The Imperial Role

The priorities that France chose to pursue after 1945 had important consequences for the posture of the military establishment. In the fifteen years or so following World War II, the missions confided to the military were primarily of two kinds, participating in the Western European security alliance and acting as a police force for the colonial empire. Interestingly, though in theory these missions were conceived of as equally essential, forming an indivisible ensemble—"the notion of security cannot be fragmented, it is a whole," wrote General Ely[1]—from a practical point of view, there was some degree of incompatibility between these two roles. By their nature the tasks to be performed in the fulfillment of these missions were almost mutually exclusive. For example, the fulfillment of the first could take place only on the Eastern front of Europe; that of the second was bound to take place somewhere overseas. The technical and strategic operational nature involved in the first task differed radically from that proposed by the second. The performance of the first could only be accomplished in collaboration with other components of the integrated alliance, whereas the performance of the second implied an autonomous, self-sufficient, and multifunctional military establishment.[2] Because of the insuperable difficulties that a multipurpose military establishment would raise and because of the size and resource limitations which prohibited the forming of two different military organizations, the simultaneous fulfillment of NATO-related missions and colonial missions appeared impossible: consequently, a choice had to be made. The pattern of perceived threats in the postwar era dictated the choice. Nationalist resistance to French domination appeared as the most immediate and extensive threat since it was considered as capable of jeopardizing the integrity of the empire, which was imperative to the enhancement of France's prestige. At the same time, France's approach to European security, including her perception of the communist threat, was too ambiguous to lead the country to involve itself wholeheartedly in the military activities of the alliance. It was argued, for instance, that should the Soviet Union attack Europe the conventional NATO shield would not be able to resist for very long. Hence French participation would make little difference. Thus the risk taken in peeling off the frontal structure of the shield by removing the French divisions was considered negligible. The only deterrent to Soviet aggression against the security of Western Europe, it was argued, would be America's ultimate weapon. The impression of security created by the absolute military superiority of the main actor in the alliance and by its doctrine of massive retaliation undoubtedly led a country like France to divert her forces for objectives not directly relevant to those of the alliance.[3] Besides, to a certain extent, action against liberation movements overseas could be advocated as being consistent with the objectives of the alliance.[4]

Therefore France resolved to dedicate the majority of her military activities and resources toward the colonial mission, the fulfillment of which appeared much more relevant to the country's priorities and much more urgent than the communist threat, given the gravity and the extent of overseas uprisings. Soon after the war, the French military establishment became largely an antisubversive force deeply committed to large-scale conflicts against powerful nationalist rebellions on Indochinese and Algerian soil. During the Indochinese War, in which France was involved as early as 1946, military pressures exerted by the Vietminh forces together with the political reluctance to increase the size of the expeditionary corps by sending drafted personnel resulted in the involvement of the greater part of the military establishment's professional elements.

The pace of the conflict and the strength of the resistance in Algeria, where France became involved soon after the Geneva Conference, the desire to avoid the humiliation of a second Dien Bien Phu, and the attempt to force the rebels to negotiate an early settlement led the French government to considerably increase the size of its military contingent as early as the first months of 1956. Most of the French military forces, even those attached to NATO-related missions, were sent to Algeria. In fact, the central part of the alliance in Germany was stripped of almost all French military units. Assessing the import of France's commitment overseas, Raymond Aron wrote: "In order to maintain herself in Indochina, France committed more military strength than had been needed to establish herself there. Never at any time in the past had she sent overseas an army as large as the one which is attempting to bring the task of pacification in Algeria to a successful conclusion. The attempt not to lose costs more in the twentieth century than the effort to win did a hundred years ago."[5]

The consequences of this posture were extremely serious, especially in regard to the military's exposure to technological change. It can be argued that by reducing her participation in the activities of the Western alliance to a minimum and by increasing her involvement in purely colonial objectives, France, to a large extent, slighted the modernization of her armed forces. At a time when military technology was undergoing revolutionary change, such a loose participation in the Western alliance blocked the French military from benefiting fully from the modernization that a closer participation would ultimately have brought. One could presume that, functioning under American leadership, in other words, under the leadership of a country in which the materialization as well as the transfer of technological outputs to the military was supposedly best accomplished, the alliance could have been a very important source of military modernization. A case in point was the implied growing technological parity among larger partners' armed forces as planned under the program of equipment normalization. Also, given the very nature of colonial warfare, it can be argued that French dedication to colonial-related roles without interruption, from 1946 in Indochina to 1961 in Algeria, further aggravated the military's alienation from technological modernization. In effect, one can argue that the type of warfare that colonial conflict entails is essentially preindustrial and paramilitary if not nonmilitary. Colonial conflicts, then, as compared to other, conventional forms of warfare, do not function as an impetus for technological modernization; to put it bluntly, colonial warfare, at least as conducted in Indochina and Algeria, was technically archaic in the sense that victory and other successful achievements did not depend greatly on the level of technology employed.[6] Colonial wars could be fought and won with any sort of armament. At times sophisticated equipment, particularly of the type pertinent for NATO-related missions, could even turn out to be a disadvantage: heavy tanks were powerless in the jungle, jets flew at too great a speed to be useful. Ideology and propaganda, the building of schools, the improvement of food production, the sympathy of the people were the critical weapons in this kind of war. In colonial warfare, consequently, the soldier was a schoolteacher, a policeman, a mason, a sanitation inspector; the time devoted to the manipulation of military hardware was but a small part of the soldier's life.

Colonial conflicts require, above all, considerable manpower investment. Technology is secondary. In Indochina, as in Algeria, the role of the navy and of the air force was marginal, as these services were employed strictly for logistic purposes, such as transportation and surveillance missions.[7] Motorized and armored army units sent to Algeria had to be dismembered before being sent overseas; their equipment, useless there, had to be stored. Much of it deteriorated due to lack of maintenance. Large mechanized corps and infantry divisions had to be divided into small partisanlike groups and guerrilla units. The few efforts made to modernize the military in the years following the Indochina War were hardly underway when they had to be abandoned or, at best, postponed to free more and more units for involvement in Algeria.

One could argue that this viewpoint is an exaggeration as, despite the colonial involvement, a few modernizing incentives always existed. After all, though loosely attached to the Atlantic organization, the French military establishment was not cut off from it, and remaining NATO-committed units could benefit from exposure to the alliance's plan for modernization and equipment normalization. In addition, though deeply committed to colonial warfare, the Fourth Republic had modernizing plans for its armed forces, such as its nuclear military program. Yet, even at these levels, it is difficult to see how modernization could have taken place in practice. Even if France had been more closely associated with the alliance, it is uncertain that her military establishment would have been exposed to high technological change. The alliance was an integrated organization based on a rigid and predefined functional division of labor. The members' military organizations were not juxtaposed one to another, rather they were integrated into a system in which each performed a specific task. The participants' armed forces, therefore, had no raison d'être except in regard to the alliance structure; they had no military purpose outside of concerted action. Especially important to this argument is the fact that distribution of tasks within the alliance—a distribution that depended upon each partner's actual military capability—took place at a time when France's capabilities were extremely limited. This explains why the French military was relegated to the performance of very conventional tasks, whereas Anglo-Saxon nations took over the highly technical roles such as long-range heavy bombing, naval surveillance, and the like. France provided the footsoldiers for the infantry of the alliance. From the standpoint of technological change, it is certain that the preparation and the performance of infantry-related roles did not constitute a highly modernizing environment. Such a role allocation was particularly detrimental for the technical branches of the military, the navy and the air force. It has been argued that the lack of an air force bombing capability lost the Indochina War.[8] Further impeding the development of a modernizing context were the conflicts between partners relating to the adoption of new armaments that often resulted in a delay or postponement in the introduction of more modern equipment.

As for the program of military nuclear development, it was at too experimental a stage to have any modernizing consequences. Moreover, in addition to the fact that its execution was somewhat overshadowed by the colonial involvement, the program of military atomic application undertaken by the Fourth Republic was not aimed at a deep nuclearization of the French armed forces as it was under the Fifth Republic. Therefore, even if it had been fully realized, it would not have had the modernizing technological effects that might have been expected. As pointed out earlier, it seems almost as if the possession of a nuclear military force was conceived as a device to secure, if not to force, the commitment of American military assistance. It was not seen as a means to enhance the credibility of the military power, nor was it an attempt to adapt the military establishment to the requisites of modern technological warfare. In short, French nuclear equipment appears to have been conceived of as a trigger whose role it was to insure the cooperation of the United States in case of conflict; because of the weakening of the American military hegemony, it was thought that the United States was no longer as committed as it had previously been to massive retaliation for the sake of European security.[9]

To a great extent, therefore, France's choices in external policy, and particularly with regard to the imperial domain, inadvertently contributed to the defining of a number of specific defense roles for her military establishment, roles that, it can be said, somewhat sheltered the military establishment from technological modernization precisely at a time when the scope of such modernization was overwhelming. Whereas Great Britain exploded its first nuclear bomb, whereas Germany, which provided the biggest contribution to the NATO central front, had more armored divisions than France, the French military had no other qualification than that of being the best antisubversive force in Europe.

In brief, due to what could be called its "quasi-alienation from technological change," the French military establishment remained a rather traditional institution from 1945 to 1960, dominated by a huge land force whose preponderance in the defense establishment generated interservice squabbles on the part of the technologically deprived air force and navy.

The Nuclear Role

After 1960, as noted earlier, French foreign and defense policies underwent considerable change. The settlement of the Algerian affair ended nearly a century of imperial hegemony and, consequently, all colonial military activities. In addition to removing the military from strictly traditional missions considered as not conducive to technological modernization, the reorganization of national defense based on the principle of nuclear deterrence propelled the French military establishment into an environment theoretically conducive to modernization. Yet, because of the nature of the defense deployment and of the diversity of the subsequent roles to be performed, the degree of exposure to modern technology varied greatly from service to service.

It was the ordinance of 7 January 1959 and the ensuing arrangements that framed the structure of French national defense and that specified the new roles of the armed forces. Despite subsequent changes, this organization remained basically the same throughout the period under discussion.

The objective of France's defense was to insure, at all times, under all circumstances, and against all forms of aggression, the security and the integrity of her territories, as well as the lives of her people. It also sought to respect international alliances, treaties, and agreements.[10] Given the fact France felt that, besides her vital interests localized in the home territory, she had to assume other responsibilities in Europe and overseas, the missions to be performed by her armed forces were of four kinds: the primary mission was to launch a nuclear counterstrike against any aggressor, a task designed to dissuade such offenses against French territory; second, linked to this first mission, was the defense and protection of the nation, her institutions, and military equipment; third, in order to organize the defense of her borders and to participate in the defense of Europe, the military was to lead operations beyond the frontiers; and, finally, the armies were to intervene overseas in order to defend French or allied territories. Put in another way, the security of the country depended upon a double capacity of deterrence: the capacity of massive nuclear retaliation and the capacity of defense of the home territory. In addition, and still part of the objectives of national defense, was the defense of French interests and influences outside the national territory, which implied the capacity to intervene in Europe, by which was meant the determination to retaliate as well as to participate in an interallies defense and the capacity to act outside the European con-

tinent, especially in territories under French sovereignty or in territories with which defense agreements had been signed.[11]

This new model, which anticipated the modern system of national
defense, established a functional organization of the services: this organization was derived not from their basic structure, but from the
conceptualization of their employment. The traditional interservice
divisions yielded precedence to new interservice functional structures. On the operational level, the four missions to be performed by
the armed forces formed a defense deployment in which the division
of labor operated among several *systèmes de forces* (hereafter translated as "systems of forces"): the four most important were the
Nuclear Strategic Force, the heart of the system, which was to ensure
the nuclear retaliation; the Security Forces, made up of aerial defense,
territory force, gendarmerie, and aeronaval forces, which were to
guarantee the protection of the political and military structures; the
Forces of Maneuver, which were to deal with the advance defense of
the border and which were also responsible for the capacity of intervention in Europe; and the Forces of Presence and Intervention,
which were to ensure the capacity of external, meaning overseas,
action.[12] There was a certain amount of integration since each of the
forces could cooperate with the others in the accomplishment of its
missions. Besides, because the defense operated according to the
paradigm of nuclear dissuasion, a certain degree of overlap between
the various systems of forces was seen as necessary. It is precisely for
this reason that in its conceptualization the organization of these
force systems sought to safeguard a balance between nuclear armament, both strategic and tactical, and conventional equipment. Pierre
Messmer, then defense minister, specified: "It is not possible to base
our military policy upon the possession of strategic nuclear weapons
alone. It is also necessary to get forces the use of which is simpler and
the triggering less cataclysmic: these are forces of intervention, our
second system of forces. . . . Their missions are to fight and hold in
check an enemy attacking France or her allies in a classic or nuclear
war."[13] In effect, such a balance was viewed as an indispensable
condition of the credibility and efficiency of nuclear strategy, as it
prevented, in case of conflict with another nuclear power, both capit-
ulation and utter destruction. The intermediary rungs below the
strategic nuclear level were necessary to prevent too rapid an escalation toward a massive nuclear encounter, while, at the same time,
allowing confrontation with an enemy operating beneath the nuclear
level. Referring to the tactical level, General Arnaud de Foïard wrote:
"Their utilization [of the tactical weapons] in battle allows, in effect,

the unleashing of a process which immediately confronts the opponent with the impossibility of reasonably continuing his aggression. The risk associated with the employment of tactical arms gives the opportunity to enhance, with credibility and independent of the level of the aggression, the threat of nuclear devastation."[14]

The point here is not to evaluate the logic or the efficiency of this organization but to derive from its syllogisms the type of context, particularly the type of technological context, in which the military found itself immersed. It is apparent that beginning in 1960, the French armies reassembled a system of various forces whose missions proceeded from the logic of modern warfare, as they were centered around the principle of nuclear deterrence. Therefore, it can be said that the military was, in theory, embedded in an environment highly conducive to technological change at every organizational level, because the successful achievement of its functions and the performance of its missions were irrevocably dependent on the modernization of structure and equipment. The primary source of modernization, the process of nuclearization, was also seen as one that would rapidly reach and penetrate all sectors of the French armed forces, at every level, and across all systems of forces. According to Messmer, "the distinction between nuclear and nonnuclear forces will become more and more artificial, for all our forces will progressively be equipped with nuclear armament and reorganized to insure at any time the security of these armaments, to employ them if necessary, and to exploit the effect of their use."[15]

True as it is in theory, this assessment calls for greater precision. As regards the degree of technological exposure, it can be said that the system of forces operating either at or close to the nuclear level would be most infused with modern technology, a degree of infusion that would decline gradually as the distance from the nuclear level widened. Thus, the forces of defense of the territories and the forces of overseas intervention were less exposed to advanced technology than were the strategic forces and the forces of maneuver. Likewise, within the forces of maneuver, the land battle corps was less exposed to advanced technology than the Aerial Tactical Force with its nuclear weaponry.

This variation in the degree of exposure to advanced technology tended to be accentuated by the French doctrine of force employment and by France's position with regard to the Atlantic military alliance. From 1962 to 1976 it was the principle of sanctuarization, itself a logical corollary of the primacy of national independence, which was the guiding paradigm for the employment of the military system of forces. Sanctuarization meant that the French nuclear force would be launched over an aggressor's towns and military installations only if the integrity of the French territory were threatened. As a consequence, there was a natural tendency to think that ruthless nuclear deterrence (that is, the use of the threat of sheer massive retaliation) was the best way to prevent aggression, since, whatever its destructive capacity, any nonnuclear weapon would be unable to match that of the most powerful potential enemy; also, massive nuclear retaliation, because of the "equalizing power" of the atomic fire, was seen as the ne plus ultra in security against any threat for it was seen as capable of inflicting damage exceeding any gains the aggressor would hope to make. The writings of General Gallois or of Alexandre Sanguinetti, *rapporteur* of the defense committee of the National Assembly, are representative of this line of thought. Sanguinetti even went so far as to deny the functions of subnuclear rungs of the military: "Time has come to warn the atomic enemy that we shall not accept any other form of combat but the total employment of nuclear weaponry when the stake of the struggle is our national territory and our people. This is deterrence."[16]

The official government position, however, was never this extreme. In face of, for example, the feasibility of indirect threats, with "limited stakes," conducted below the nuclear threshold, in other words, for fear that the nuclear defense would be bypassed as a Maginot line, it was felt that massive retaliation was too high a risk to run for the country; therefore, the development of forces operating below the strategic nuclear level, capable of intervening beyond the borders in order to dissuade an enemy preparing itself to use its conventional weaponry, was indispensable. This made possible the idea of an enlarged or forward strategy such as was developed after 1970 in which cooperation with allies became conceivable because it had limited objectives. The increasing sophistication of the nuclear arsenal and the development of nuclear potentialities at the tactical level also contributed to modifying earlier doctrinal conceptions. It is obvious that before 1965, having only a primitive atomic device, French defense leaders had no other choice than to conceive its use in the terms of massive retaliation. However, because of the preeminent concern for national independence with all its correlates of defense employment, and also because, as we shall see later on, of many delays in the development of nuclear force, it remained that the early vision of deterrence by the threat of massive retaliation as the exclusive panacea against multiple types of security threats continued to inspire French defense formulations. Even today, the thought that the protection of national interests rests on charging every conflict among nations with the possibility of swift escalation to nuclear war is not uncommon. General Gallois, one of the most prominent French strategists, who could hardly be accused of lacking discernment,[17] went so far as to advocate an intensive development of nuclear weaponry and the suppression of all other systems of force, except for a few thousand men to guard the equipment, in order to convince the Soviet Union that France was untouchable as she was capable of eventually destroying a significant number of Russian cities.[18] This again was an extreme vision of this strategy; yet it fed on a belief widely shared by French strategists. Even today many hold this view, though the "flexible response" argument is gaining on the *tout ou rien* approach. This is evident in official discourse; Giscard d'Estaing's March 1975 speech made this clear when he declared: "Being the third nuclear superpower strengthens the effectiveness of our deterrence by inducing eventual aggressors into escalating the nature of the conflict: instead of waging a conventional war, they would be forced to take . . . the risk of a nuclear war."[19] It is the attachment to national sovereignty then and the resulting avoidance of pledging her defense network for purposes that would restrict her freedom of choice and action that explain the lack of a more than succinctly defined doctrine of employment for the forces of maneuver. This probably also explains why their modernization and especially their nuclearization through the delivery of tactical nuclear weapons seem to have been somewhat neglected. The case of the Pluton system, the TNW with which the forces of maneuver were to be equipped, is a good example. One may wonder to what extent the slow development of this weapon, its delivery, and the ambivalence regarding its use were a direct result of the incompatibility of any armament system at the tactical level with France's refusal to think of herself as a nolens volens partner in a European conflict.[20] To be operational, given its range of 120 kilometers, the Pluton missile ought to be placed as far in advance as possible, the ideal location being the eastern borders of West Germany. This would mean that France would have to risk early entry into a conflict, a situation she has sought to avoid by withdrawing from the NATO defense network. Or, if she decided to delay using the weapon, thereby signifying her hesitation to the enemy, France would risk another situation in which the dissuasive power of her weapons would be useless. If the Pluton missiles were to remain on French soil, France could fire them into her allies' territory only with their authorization; this would imply a common and agreed upon strategy that could not function outside a common military organization.[21] One can understand then why, given the priority held by national independence, the defense of the country was conceived of as operational at the upper rungs, that is, at the strategic rungs of the nuclear scale.

It becomes clear then that because of the deployment doctrine derived from the axioms of the external policy, in other words, because of the basic ambivalence created by the issue of national independence and the subsequent autonomy of the French defense, those forces whose employment implied a modicum of cooperation were given less attention. These forces, situated below the nuclear level, escaped then the effects of full-fledged modernization and nuclearization programs that would have taken place had they been of primary importance to the country's protection.

These observations lead one to conclude that the degree of exposure to advanced technology, particularly to that created by the nuclearization process, varied from one system of forces to another. This discrepancy would have had little importance had each system of force remained a composite balance of each armed service. But this was not the case. After 1962, the French military organization was far from being a functionally integrated system of forces. Indeed, it operated according to traditional interservice divisions as evidenced by the maintenance of separate staffing administrations for each. Upon closer examination, it appeared that beyond the division of labor by system of forces, the old interservice division of labor continued to function. In this division of labor the navy and the air force tended to perform most of the functions at the nuclear level, both strategic and tactical, and the army those at the subnuclear level. Nuclear tactical missions were the sole responsibility of the air force even as late as 1973. Later, the army began to share some of these functions, yet because of the range of the Pluton missile, because of the small number of units available, and because of the ambiguity determining its use, extensive army participation in nuclear tactical functions continued to be hampered. Most of the activities of the army appeared to remain circumscribed by the performance of strictly conventional missions.

Thus, the observed discrepancy between the systems of forces, due to variations in their level of exposure to advanced technology, tended to coincide with a discrepancy between the services. As discussed in the next chapter, one important cause for these functional disparities was a financial and budgetary one. Other factors were also important. Two of these were closely linked to the essence of military nuclearization, particularly to the early period of its development. First, by reason of the degree of technological sophistication that it by definition entails, the process of nuclear military application could be started only within the framework of an already technically developed organization; the air force and, to a lesser extent, the navy were consequently the services most fitted for this application. These two services were already acculturated to nuclear ideology, so to speak. And during the time the army became embroiled in the Algerian conflict, the air force and the navy, whose functions in the conflict were less demanding, inevitably availed themselves of this circumstance to become the logical recipients of the Fourth Republic's program of nuclearization, however anemic this program might have been. It is also true that the nature of nuclear warfare, being transcontinental in scope, is largely at variance with the inherent pedestrian nature of the army; thus the support of the air force and the navy were a necessity. The army could, however, have fulfilled important functions in nuclear deterrence, such as managing and operating fixed ballistic missile units. Interestingly enough, when construction of the SSBM was undertaken, there was a question as to whether they should be put under the control of the army. For technical reasons, and undoubtedly for circumstances linked with interservice feuds, the air force was awarded control.

The second is related to the basic issue of reaction to change. An innovation such as the introduction of nuclear armament and all its resultant effects often ends in wider breaches between the main organizational components of an institution. There are two explanations for this; first, perceptual differences about the speculated outcome of the innovation create zones of resistance to change, and, second, the competition to receive the largest share of the allocation of the innovation furthers dissensions. Though antithetical, these reasons are not necessarily mutually exclusive. This was particularly true in the case of the nuclearization process. Each group perceived the process as a threat to traditional structures and, at the same time, as an inexhaustible source of advantages as diverse as funds and status. The introduction of atomic strategy and the adoption of the nuclear deterrence doctrine, originally designed as a device to foster interservice integration around a number of specific defense functions, thus had strong internal divisive effects that, paradoxically, consolidated the traditional interservice organization. Depicting the effects of the decision to undertake the nuclearization program, Admiral Antoine Sanguinetti wrote: "As soon as the doctrine of nuclear dissuasion was adopted, the various branches [of services] engaged in a merciless struggle regarding now limited funds, in order to retain as much as possible of their traditional structures, presenting these, by ingenious arguments, as being integral parts of the deterrence, thus as having the same priority."[22]

The first indication of tension appeared between the air force and the navy. Though air force officers were thought to regard the development of a nuclear force favorably, and though they played an important technical and doctrinal role in its development, one should not for all that ignore that navy officers also exhibited a keen interest in such equipment as early as the mid-1950s. The success of the American nuclear-powered submarine, the *Nautilus*, in its 1958 journey further convinced naval officers of the key role that their service would play in nuclear strategy. A series of important articles, most of them published in *Revue de Défense nationale*, shed some light on this matter. They reveal not only the extent of many naval officers' concern with nuclear doctrine, but also their conviction that the navy constituted the most appropriate medium for the optimal enhancement of atomic power in the context of nuclear strategy. The articles also stressed the navy's suitability for the multidimensionality, or the depth, of what would be the nuclear battlefield.[23] However, technological difficulties in the domain of atomic propulsion (the necessary enriched uranium 235 was not yet available) and in that of embarked delivery systems did not permit the immediate nuclearization of the navy. Thus, the air force instantly became the privileged recipient of the nuclear equipment. The sheer weight of the explosive device, the A-bomb, before its size could be reduced, favored the air force: aircraft could provide the only existing delivery system. Later arguments that the aircraft were outdated and that the future belonged to intercontinental missiles were countered by the air force argument that other nuclear powers, those already possessing SSBMs, still kept manned bomber fleets since bombers remained less vulnerable, especially when dispersed, than a group of silo-buried missiles. Moreover, bombers were easier to use.[24]

The navy–air force conflict flared up again in 1964 when the air force argued that any long-term emphasis on nuclear naval strategy would be a serious misallocation of strategic values, especially in respect to the future technological context of credible nuclear deterrence in which the primary role would be performed by satelliteborne missiles; the missile-launching submarine was a temporary strategic weapon, one that would serve only until the implementation of orbit-positioned weaponry.[25]

At this point, the army, barely extricated from its colonial involvement, and fearful of losing the attention it had enjoyed until then, claimed that it too could take part in the manipulation of the nuclear force. The army saw itself as the key element to be employed for the tactical purposes that were thought to be necessary to avoid the basing of French security on only one system of massive force. But, despite reassuring doctrinal declarations stating the primacy of the army in the dialectic of deterrence,[26] despite the promises of delivery of nuclear tactical equipment at the level of its intervention force component, it was not until the 1970s that the army's role as an element of the nuclear system was explicitly scheduled. The air force, seeking to maintain its preeminence in the new French defense organization, strongly opposed any tenet attributing an essential function to the army and criticized any enlarged interpretation of the nuclear strategic doctrine. In fact, the air force, through the intermediacy of its spokesman and chief, General André Martin, simply denied the utility of the army in nuclear dissuasion.[27]

For a long time the air force kept its supremacy over the nuclear defense system, at first with the Mirage IV nuclear bomber, then with the silo-buried SSBM. In 1972, when the nuclear submarine fleet became operational with the launching of the third submarine (the *Redoutable* and *Terrible* were already engaged in the performance of their missions)[28] thereby rendering more or less obsolete the manned strategic bombers, the air force lobbied to prolong the bombers' role in the nuclear strategic force.[29] Subsequent decisions to maintain the fleet of Mirage IV in service until 1980, and then 1985, despite increasing costs and technical difficulties raised by the aging of these aircraft, as well as the decision to proceed with the construction of a new bomber, the ACF, were without doubt related to these pressures.[30]

Moreover, the pursuit of the nuclear program, notably toward the miniaturization of nuclear explosives, provoked new dissensions between the army and the air force. The army was favorable to the elaboration of a miniaturized nuclear device (with the power of less than one kiloton) that would equip its artillery and infantry (referring here to the 155 shell and the *mininukes* mines) in the manner of what was done in the United States. But the air force tended to oppose such a program. Though it argued on strictly technical grounds, raising, for example, the issue of atomic proliferation, one is tempted to ask whether the air force was not trying in a way to resist the development of a new pattern of nuclear deployment in which its control and its role in general would be less important.

It would serve little purpose to further document these problems at this point. The instances discussed do, however, suggest how interservice tensions furthered the built-in imbalance in the organization of the different systems of force. It is certain that the preeminence won by the air force and later by the navy at the level of their doctrinal influence and of their position of command over the means of strategic nuclear deterrence contributed to reinforcing the weight of the strategic nuclear parameters in the force employment doctrine at the expense of the nuclear tactical and the conventional levels. In addition, the dissension between services, particularly between the air force and the army, furthered the dualism between the systems of forces above and below the nuclear threshold. But more importantly, it created a de facto interservice division of labor across these two areas, accentuating the imbalance initiated by the basic ambivalence of the continuing attachment to national independence and defense autonomy. This contributed to the erosion of the credibility of those forces whose existence could not be justified outside the framework of cooperative strategy. Thus, instead of being, as originally conceived, a technologically advanced institution, functionally integrated around a system of specific missions articulated around the principle of gradual nuclear dissuasion, the post-1960s French military establishment emerged as a dualistic organization. The main cleavage separated the army, on the one hand, from the navy and the air force, on the other; the latter two services obtained the biggest share of the nuclearization program and, therefore, the highest exposure to technological change. The army, because it assumed most of the conventional burden, found itself in a technological context that inevitably implied a lesser degree of exposure to modernization.

To some extent, these significant differences are not in themselves dramatic. After all, nuclearization is not the only source of technological change; it is not solely because it operated below the nuclear level that the army escaped modernization. Even today, a program aimed at the modernization of the conventional sector would constitute a technological upgrading. But, in the case of France, an unequal partition of resources among the various systems of force worsened these imbalances; due to the basic ambiguity of defense deployment below the nuclear level and because of budgetary restrictions, grave discrepancies in the diffusion of modern technology were introduced throughout the military establishment. This will be discussed in the next chapter.

Notes

1. Paul Ely, "Notre politique militaire," *Revue de Défense nationale* 13 (1957): 1034.

2. Bernard Chantebout gives several examples of such contradictions in *L'Organisation générale de la défense*

nationale en France depuis la fin de la seconde guerre mondiale (Paris: Librairie générale de Droit et de Jurisprudence, 1967), pp. 37–38.

3. When we speak of "an impression of security," we do not mean that France did not perceive the existence of the danger of collision between the West and the East; what is meant is that from the viewpoint of national defense, France felt that there could be no better military shield than U.S. protection. Toying with paradox, one could say that, with maximum protection being provided by the United States, European powers had little interest in building up their own defenses to match the military power of the Warsaw Pact nations, which, at some point, eliminated any risk of their being engaged in battle before the American military firepower could be set off. This, perhaps, explains why, despite U.S. pressures on its European partners, parity between the Atlantic conventional forces and those of the Warsaw Pact was never attained as had been originally planned during the 1952 NATO conference in Lisbon. In a way, the myth created around the actual military strength of the Warsaw Pact was a comfortable excuse for the Western European nations to rely entirely on American nuclear defense.

4. French Armed Forces Chief of Staff General Ely was explicit when he wrote about "our military policy which wholly fits into the framework of NATO" (Ely, "Notre politique militaire," p. 1043).

5. Raymond Aron, *Immuable et changeante: de la IVe à la Ve République* (Paris: Calmann-Lévy, 1959), p. 132.

6. As we shall frequently refer to this terminology, it should be clear that the qualification "archaic" (used by Guy Michelat and Jean-Pierre Thomas in "Contribution à l'étude de recrutement des écoles d'officiers de la Marine, 1945–1960," *Revue française de sociologie* 9 [1968]: 52) when applied to colonial warfare is not addressed to the historical and phenomenological content of such conflicts. For the historian and the political sociologist, colonial conflicts are modern phenomena indeed, but in the context of an organizational analysis of military institutions such a form of warfare can be defined as archaic in the sense that the values, and above all, the military technology involved were more in step with prewar traditions than they were in congruence with the new postwar trends.

7. At the end of the 1950s, more than 65 percent of the effectives in the army were in North Africa (essentially Algeria): almost fifteen divisions, 200 infantry regiments, forty-five armored regiments, and sixty-five artillery units. At the same time, only 30 percent of the air force and 23 percent of the navy personnel were garrisoned in North Africa. And, except for a *fusilier marins* regiment (equivalent to the U.S. Marines) operating on the Algerian battlefield, most of the navy effectives were assigned to two North African naval bases, Bizerte in Tunisia and Mers el Kebir in Algeria.

8. In his book on the Indochina experience, General Georges Catroux wrote, "Under the present Western system of defense, the French armed force has ceased to have its own bombing forces. This explains why when bombers were called to the battlefield, there was no coherent doc-

trine, no personnel and no qualified leadership" (*Deux actes du drame indochinois* [Paris: Plon, 1959], pp. 211–12, as quoted in Chantebout, *L'Organisation générale de la défense nationale en France*, p. 38).

9. This pattern of reasoning, it should be noted, has never been completely abandoned and can be found in the Fifth Republic's strategic thought. In the first years of the Gaullist era, for example, the trigger doctrine was viewed as giving, so to speak, credibility to the French nuclear weapon at its early stages of development; it was stated that, though not yet operational, the often scoffed-at *bombinette* was a credible deterrent because it could be used to set off the American atomic umbrella. Later, although the situation changed, the reasoning remained the same. Though the French nuclear force was now capable of powerful destructive effects, hence a credible deterrent on its own, the fact that it could be used to trigger U.S. defense was viewed as a further element reinforcing its basic deterrent powers. Even if, contrary to what might have happened earlier, the American atomic force were to remain untriggered, this very uncertainty, according to the French argument, had the advantage of boosting the deterrent capacity, and therefore the credibility of the French nuclear force. On this point, we can refer to André Beaufre, *Introduction à la stratégie* (Paris: A. Colin, 1963); idem, *Dissuasion et stratégie* (Paris: A. Colin, 1964); and Léo Hamon, "Puissance nucléaire et dissuasion: alliance et neutralité," *Revue de Défense nationale* 22 (1966): 234–57.

10. "Ordonnance n° 59-147 du 7 janvier 1959 portant organisation de la défense," *Journal officiel, lois et décrets*, 10 January 1959, pp. 691–94.

11. Service d'Information et de Relations Publiques des Armées, "Les Forces armées," *Notes d'information* 6 (1971): 2.

12. *Livre blanc sur la défense nationale* (Paris: CEDOCAR, 1972), vol. 1, pp. 11–26. Such a defense deployment was a slightly revised version of the deployment originally planned. In the early 1960s there were only three levels of defense, three systems of force performing three kinds of functions: the Strategic Nuclear Force, the Forces of Maneuver and Intervention, and the Operational Defense of the Territory. After 1970, the DOT was reorganized as the Forces of Security. The Forces of Maneuver and Intervention were divided into two distinct systems of force: the Forces of Maneuver and the Forces of Presence and External Intervention. In 1975, another modification was undertaken, although the basic organization remained the same.

The Strategic Nuclear Force is made up of the piloted Strategic Air Force (FAS), the Strategic Missiles Group (GMS), and the Oceanic Strategic Force (FOST). The Security Forces, whose mission it is to protect nuclear installations and to oppose enemy invasion, are composed of the Forces for the Defense of the Territory, the gendarmerie, the Defensive Air Force, and the Security Forces for the Maritime Areas. The Forces of Maneuver are composed of the First Army (stationed in France and Germany), naval units, and the Aerial Tactical Force (FATAC). The Forces of

Presence and Intervention are made up of units stationed in the southwest and in Brittany; their role is to intervene overseas when necessary and to serve as reserve units for the DOT.

For a detailed and more technical picture of the French defense system at the end of 1976, *see* the note on the organization of the French defense in Appendix A.

13. Pierre Messmer, "Notre politique militaire," *Revue de Défense nationale* 19 (1963): 748.

14. Paul Arnaud de Foïard, "Armement nucléaire tactique et dissuasion," *Défense nationale* 29 (October 1973): 68.

15. Pierre Messmer, "L'Atome, cause et moyen d'une politique militaire autonome," *Revue de Défense nationale* 24 (1968): 400.

16. Alexandre Sanguinetti, *La France et l'arme atomique* (Paris: R. Julliard, 1964), pp. 49–50; *see also* the writings of General P.-M. Gallois showing how the power of the atomic device insures peace while at the same time condemning all alliances. For a critique of such views, consult Roy C. Macridis, "The New French Maginot Line: A Note on French Strategy," *Journal of Political and Military Sociology* 2 (1974): 105–12.

17. For Raymond Aron's not unjustified critiques of General Gallois's theses, *see* his *Le Grand Débat: initiation à la stratégie atomique* (Paris: Calmann-Lévy, 1963).

18. Pierre-M. Gallois, *L'Adieu aux armées* (Paris: Albin Michel, 1976).

19. *Le Monde*, 27 March 1975, as quoted by Simon Serfaty, "The Fifth Republic under Giscard d'Estaing," *World Today*, March 1976, p. 97.

20. It is remarkable that it was only with the third military program law (1971–75) that the decision to equip the Forces of Maneuver with TNW was made. And it was not until April 1974 that the first Pluton system was introduced (to the 3rd artillery regiment, Mailly). Since then, it has been allocated in homeopathic doses. The second system was delivered in 1976 to the 15th regiment at Suippes, the third and the fourth were delivered in 1976 and 1977, respectively. This was less than forty units for two army corps and five divisions. For technical data on the Pluton, *see* the note on the organization of the French defense in Appendix A.

21. Lothar Ruehl, *La Politique militaire de la Ve République* (Paris: Presses de la Fondation nationale des Sciences politiques, 1976), p. 418.

22. Antoine Sanguinetti, "Une Autocritique de l'institution militaire," *Le Monde*, 19 September 1974, p. 10.

23. For instance the articles of Admiral Cabanier, "Le Sous-marin nucléaire français," *Revue de Défense nationale* 22 (1966): 595–605; Rear Admiral Lepotier, "La Stratégie sous-glacière," *Revue de Défense nationale* 16 (December 1960): 1931–48; idem, "La Force de dissuasion sous-marine," *Revue de Défense nationale* 18 (1962): 1666–82; Capitaine de Corvette Salzedo, "Les Moyens d'une force de dissuasion," *Revue de Défense nationale* 18 (1962): 82–90.

24. Another example of this kind of ambiguous attitude, born from a dual attachment to manned bombers and to ICBMs, was the case of the U.S. Air Force, as recently shown by Edmund Beard, *Developing the ICBM: A Study in Bureaucratic Politics* (New

York: Columbia University Press, 1976).

25. André Martin, "L'Armée de L'Air dans le contexte nucléaire," *Revue de Défense nationale* 20 (1964): 1499–1517.

26. General LePuloch, "L'Avenir de l'Armée de Terre," *Revue de Défense nationale* 20 (1964): 947–60.

27. Martin, "L'Armée de l'Air dans le contexte nucléaire"; for a good summary of these problems, *see* Ruehl, *La Politique militaire de la Ve République*, pp. 274–87.

28. The *Redoutable* and the *Terrible* were operational at the end of 1972. A third and a fourth unit (the *Foudroyant* and the *Indomptable*), launched in 1971 and 1973, respectively, were operable by 1974 and 1976. In October 1975, the construction of a fifth submarine (the *Tonnant*) was begun; plans called for its being set afloat in early 1978. In an October 1974 measure taken by the Defense Council, the construction of a sixth unit (not programmed originally) was decided upon; this construction was later canceled. For technical details on this system of force, *see* the note on the organization of the French defense in Appendix A.

29. The first and the second military program laws had anticipated that the Mirage IV system would be withdrawn from the Strategic Nuclear Force during the early 1970s; in

this respect, *see Avis présenté au nom de la Commission de la Défense nationale et des forces armées sur le projet de loi relatif à certains équipements militaires*, Doc. Assemblée nationale n° 882 (2nd session ordinaire 1960–61); *Avis présenté au nom de la Commission de la Défense nationale et des forces armées . . .* Doc. Assemblée nationale n° 1192 (1st session ordinaire 1964–65).

30. In 1975, 595 million francs ($110 million) were spent on the ACF program. The ACF is an "intervention aircraft" with fixed wings equipped with middle-range air-to-ground missiles. To be fully operational the plane must be outfitted with the Doppler-type radar scanning equipment. (Because the United States refused to sell the necessary radar equipment, construction of comparable equipment will delay the operability of the ACF until 1985). It is estimated that one ACF will cost 80 million francs ($15 million); this price is significantly higher than that of the MCRA model built by Panavia-Aircraft, an allied aerial cooperation established by Great Britain, Germany, and Italy (See *Avis présenté au nom de la Commission de la Défense nationale et des forces armées sur le projet de loi de finances pour 1975*, Doc. Assemblée nationale n° 1233, vol. 1 [1st session ordinaire, 1974–75], pp. 50–51).

CHAPTER THREE ● PERSONNEL, ARMS, AND BUDGET

In the light of the previous examination of French external policies, of the roles and missions these policies imposed on the military, and of the subsequent constraints implied by the performance of such roles and missions, two kinds of military establishments succeeded one another; the first was of a predominantly traditional nature, the second was of a more modern, though markedly dualistic, nature as a result of its uneven exposure to change.

The following general analysis of national defense budgeting policy will help clarify this emerging picture. The examination of the direction, nature, and volume of the resource allocations for the military constitutes a determinant variable for assessing the military establishment's situation in regard to factors affecting its format, and in particular its exposure to technological modernization. Before analyzing in detail the organizational effects created by the change in the level and the nature of expenditures, let us briefly survey the evolution of the French postwar defense budget, presenting an overview of the type and volume of the flow of resources available.

National Defense Budget Policy

A few observations can be made based upon the data in Table 3.1, which traces the share of national defense expenditures in the gross national product (GNP). First, two noticeable periods stand out. During the first period, 1945–60, the volume of defense expenditures represented more than a quarter of the total public spending and nearly 8 percent of the GNP.[1] In addition, throughout these fifteen years the amount of the defense budget varied from one year to another. It dropped from 13.3 percent of the GNP in 1945 to 5.4 percent in 1950, rose to 11.8 percent in 1952, and finally settled at around 5.6 percent in 1961. This relatively high proportion of defense allocations and their instability over time can be attributed to the combined demands of post–World War II developments, involvement in colonial conflicts, and Atlantic alliance military commitments.

In contrast to this first period, from 1960 to 1976 the defense budget

Table 3.1. Military Expenditures as a Percentage of Government Expenditures and Gross National Product, 1945–76

Year	Percentage of Governmental Expenditures	Percentage of GNP	Year	Percentage of Governmental Expenditures	Percentage of GNP
1945	40.7	13.3	1961	26.7	5.3
1946	26.4	7.7	1962	24.7	4.9
1947	28.2	5.8	1963	29.3	4.7
1948	28.6	5.4	1964	23.0	4.6
1949	20.6	5.8	1965	25.5	4.5
1950	18.3	5.4	1966	21.8	4.4
1951	35.5	8.0	1967	20.7	4.4
1952	36.3	11.8	1968	20.0	4.3
1953	27.8	11.4	1969	17.9	4.0
1954	30.0	7.5	1970	17.6	3.4
1955	26.0	6.3	1971	17.4	3.3
1956	28.6	7.4	1972	17.0	3.1
1957	26.8	7.0	1973	17.3	3.1
1958	25.3	6.1	1974	17.0	3.1
1959	28.8	5.8	1975	17.0	2.9
1960	28.5	5.6	1976	17.0	3.0

was characterized by a much lower relative size, on the one hand, and by a long-range regular decline (except between 1962 and 1965 and again between 1967 and 1971 when the figures fell sharply), on the other; in absolute figures, however, the defense budget increased from 37.7 to 45.8 billion francs, an absolute increase of 21.5 percent (1.5 percent in constant francs). This pattern of change in the defense budget during this period is attributable to two factors.

The stability of military expenditures was related to the changes adopted in the domain of national defense, more precisely to the adoption of a national defense paradigm functioning on the basis of nuclear deterrence. Such a pattern implied a defense model whose credibility was dependent upon a systematic accommodation to the dynamic of technological change. To achieve this required long-range planning and accurate evaluation and also demanded the securing of a stable allotment of the nation's financial resources. It was not so much the amount of the allocation itself that counted as it was the planned regularity of these resources. In this regard, the White Book on national defense stated: "The nature of strategic dissuasion itself, requiring a strict continuity of the deterrent effect, together with the very long duration of the development of the major defense equipment, imposes a great regularity of the resources which are appropriated for it."[2]

Second, in a modern industrial society, the growing difficulty of justifying spiraling military expenditures in relatively peaceful times, the increasing demands not only for an equal but for a higher share of national affluence, and the growing expectations for educational and social welfare constitute factors that tended to render sharp alterations in the balance between civil and military expenditures more and more illegitimate.

Soon after de Gaulle's coming to power, the government set itself to reforming the budgetary policy for national defense. It began by enforcing greater discipline in the vote for national defense spending so as to avoid the erratic practices that had characterized the voting on the national defense budget during the Fourth Republic, the continuation of which would have been a serious impediment to the shaping of a new national defense organization. This refers to the byzantine, punctilious approach of French parliamentarians toward each item of the overall budget and to the famous, but awkward, routine practices of the *douzièmes provisionnels*. Moreover, in order to restore the credibility to military expenditures and to counter a commonly held belief in their lack of productivity, the government, military officials, and other civil defense experts began to fully credit military expenses as instruments of economic stimulation, a practice that the succeeding administrations upheld. Each year, *rapporteurs* to the parliamentary national defense commissions commented lengthily on the matter.[3] Finally, the leaders of the Fifth Republic worked both to promote a stabilization of military spending and to secure an annual allocation that would fix an indicative ceiling for military expenses and yet permit enough flexibility to shape a quinquennial program of defense expenditures. Originally, national defense was scheduled to extract about 6 percent of the GNP and one-fourth of the public spending. In a semiofficial declaration, the defense minister predicted that, providing an annual increase of 4.7 percent in the GNP between 1960 and 1965 (from $61.13 billion to $73.48 billion) and then a 4 percent increase until 1970, the armed forces budget, which amounted to $3.48 billion in 1961, could be raised to $3.95 billion in 1965, and to $4.62 billion in 1969.[4]

But this is not what happened; instead of increasing, the share of defense expenditures in the GNP steadily decreased. Between 1968 and 1971, the fall in expenditures, amounting to nearly 1 percent, can be attributed to the growing appropriations for social and economic expenditures following the events of May 1968 and the Grenelle agreements. Although the 1972 White Book stated that the decrease observed after 1959 could not continue without mortgaging the development of French defense equipment, thereby mortgaging French security,[5] the decline continued until 1975, when defense spending accounted for less than 3 percent of the GNP. As shown in Table 3.2, the budget of the armed forces between 1971 and 1975 was among the lowest in the western hemisphere; in 1975, France occupied something like the forty-seventh rank among the world's nations with respect to the relative size of her defense spending.[6] It was only in 1976, probably due to the pressure from defense-minded parliamentarians and because of the necessity to reevaluate the material conditions of the career military, that the military budget increased again and reached a level comparable to that of 1965.[7]

Let us now examine more closely the manner in which national defense expenditures were allocated within the military establishment, as the analysis of such an allocation is critical to understanding the nature and evolution of the military.

The armed forces budget is made up of two types of expenditures. There are grants assignable to Title III, also called Ordinary Expenditures, which encompass allotments for personnel and operation. These are subdivided into four sections: Remunerations and Social Encumberances, Personnel Maintenance, Operation of Plants and Maintenance of Real Estate, and Subsidies and Various Expenditures. And there are allocations accruing to Title V, also labeled Capital

Table 3.2. Military Expenditures in Selected Western Nations as a Percentage of Gross National Product, 1952–72

Country	1952	1954	1956	1958	196
FRANCE	11.8	7.5	7.4	6.1	5.6
U.S.A.	13.6	11.6	9.8	10.0	8.9
U.K.	10.0	8.8	4.8	7.0	6.5
West Germany	5.8	4.0	3.6	3.0	4.0
Netherlands	5.6	6.0	5.7	4.7	4.1
Portugal	—	4.2	4.0	4.0	4.2
Sweden	4.4	4.9	4.7	4.7	4.8

Source: France: see Table 3.1; other countries: Stockholm International Peace Research Institute, *World Armaments and Disarmament: SIPRI Yearbook, 1974* (Stockholm: Almquist and Wiksell, 1974), pp. 208–13. Note that the SIPRI figures are slightly higher than the official figures used in Table 3.1.

Expenditures; these allocations are used for investment and equipment. They, in turn, are subdivided into Studies and Research,
Technical and Industrial Investments, Manufacture, and Infrastructure. Obviously the apportionment of funds into the various titles
and sections offers considerable insight as to how the military
actually deals with modernization. Indeed, it can be assumed that
budgetary allocations for personnel and operation (Title III) constitute routine allocations that have little effect on the actual format
of the military establishment, whereas those for equipment (Title
V) have the potential to greatly affect the military's structures,
since these allocations inevitably concern the injection of modern
technology.

   Using the data offered in Table 3.3 one sees that 1963–64 was the
watershed between two very distinct periods. From 1945 to 1962 Title
III allocations were preponderant: they constituted more than 60 percent of the total of the military budget. After 1962, this tendency
slowly reversed itself to the advantage of Title V, and by 1966 Title V
allocations again exceeded those for Title III. As nearly 70 percent of
the ordinary expenditures were exclusively devoted to personnel
(paying for salaries, social expenses, and maintenance),[8] this trend
confirms that between 1945 and 1963 the military establishment was
an army of men rather than of equipment. During this period, the
funds attributed to capital expenditures remained, to a large extent,
insufficient to permit swift technological change. After 1962, overall

962	1964	1966	1968	1970	1972
1.9	4.6	4.4	4.3	3.4	3.1
9.3	8.0	8.4	9.2	7.8	6.6
5.4	6.1	5.7	5.5	4.9	5.4
1.8	4.6	4.1	3.6	3.3	3.5
1.5	4.3	3.7	3.7	3.5	3.4
5.9	6.7	6.3	7.5	7.2	—
1.1	4.1	4.1	3.7	3.6	3.5

capital expenditures increased in absolute values, at least until 1969, and stabilized somewhat below 1969 values thereby giving the military new revenues for modernization. The increase in research and development (R and D) expenditures and in equipment-building outlays between 1960 and 1970 constitutes a good indication of the level of modernization achieved. For example, between 1960 and 1968 the R and D expenditures increased by an average of more than 15 percent, and between 1960 and 1964 by almost 29 percent; as for equipment-building expenditures, they rose at the rate of 4.3 percent between 1964 and 1970.[9] It should be noted, however, that after 1968 the annual portion of the armed forces budget assigned to Title III increased, mainly under the growing weight of expenditures for personnel, and again became larger than that of Title V. This new emphasis on ordinary expenditures in a nonexpandable budget was to some extent concomitant with a deemphasis of capital expenditures. As shown by Figure 3.1, the increasing expenditures for personnel were followed by a sharp decline in R and D spending (14.4 percent in 1969 and 1970; 5.3 percent in 1975) and in equipment-building expenditures (2.9 percent) after 1973.

Such changes were due to the long-postponed necessity for reevaluating the financial condition of career military personnel in the face of continuing inflationary costs of living (all the more negatively perceived by the military community as their basic remuneration remained relatively lower in comparison with that of the civilian community). The increase was also destined, in a period when the pres-

Table 3.3. Ordinary and Capital Military Expenditures, 1954–77 (percentages)

Year	Ordinary Expenditures	Capital Expenditures	Year	Ordinary Expenditures	Capital Expenditures
1954	64.0	36.0	1966	48.8	51.2
1955	69.0	31.0	1967	48.2	51.8
1956	71.9	29.1	1968	48.0	52.0
1957	73.4	26.6	1969	50.7	49.3
1958	75.6	24.4	1970	51.8	48.2
1959	62.3	37.7	1971	53.2	46.8
1960	64.3	35.7	1972	53.4	46.7
1961	65.8	34.2	1973	52.9	47.1
1962	67.6	32.4	1974	53.4	46.6
1963	57.8	42.2	1975	56.5	43.5
1964	54.1	45.9	1976	58.1	42.9
1965	50.1	49.9	1977	58.8	41.2

Figure 3.1. Defense Budget by Category of Expenditure, 1960–75 (in billions of francs)

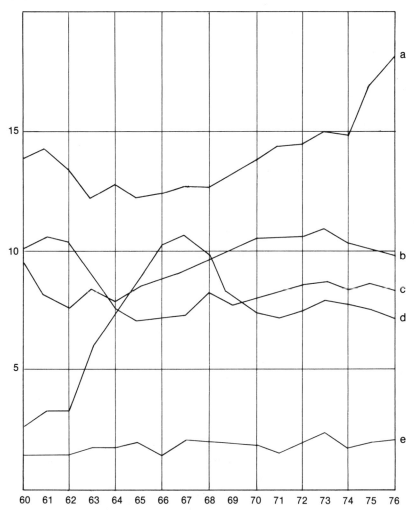

a. Salaries, social benefits
   (parts 1 and 3 of Title III)
b. Equipment (part 3 of Title V)
c. Operations (parts 2, 4, 5, 6, and
   7 of Title III)
d. R and D (part 1 of Title V)
e. Infrastructure (parts 2, 4,
   and 5 of Title V)

Source: Jean-Bernard Pinatel, ed., *L'Economie des forces*, p. 15.

tige of the military was on the decline, to attract and retain new personnel increasingly drawn to the generally brighter professional opportunities offered in the more competitive civil marketplace. And finally, spending for personnel was to augment the draftee's *prêt journalier*, particularly in regard to the minimum wage level, in order to pacify privates' restlessness and temptation to unionize.[10] Personnel expenditures increased at the annual rate of 3.5 percent from 1969 to 1975 and by almost 13 percent in 1975 and 1976. In the 1976 defense budget, ordinary expenditures accounted for 58.1 percent of the total spending, a figure not seen in a military budget since 1962.

This rapid survey permits us to form a preliminary series of conclusions. Between 1945 and 1960, the budget of the armed forces focused upon personnel expenditures rather than upon capital expenditures, which are often considered a basic impetus for modernization. Moreover, funds allocated for equipment were used to rebuild installations damaged during the war and to replace army equipment rapidly being worn out in the expanding colonial engagements. This period was followed by one that can be characterized by an increasing inelasticity of the defense budget, as well as by a steady decline in the armed force budgetary allocation with respect to the country's GNP. Consequently, it was in the framework of a nonexpandable overall budget that the compromise between personnel-oriented expenditures and equipment expenditures, two exigencies which then came into conflict, was going to operate. Before 1960, the orientation of defense policy decisions toward the colonial involvement of the armed forces required that a compromise be made in favor of personnel expenditures, as the type of warfare involved in Indochina and Algeria remained largely antithetic to new technology and was heavily dependent upon manpower investment. After 1960, the decision to accord national defense with nuclear deterrence principles required that the compromise be made in favor of equipment expenditures. But demands for higher personnel expenditures, following the demands for modernization, and to a certain extent because of them, rapidly grew more pressing. Given the impossibility of increasing the overall level of expenditures and the impracticability of meeting the two simultaneously, choices necessarily had to be made. It is to the question of how these compromises and choices were resolved and how they affected the pattern of constraints placed upon the military that we shall address ourselves now. (For the detailed estimates of defense expenditures between 1965 and 1977, on which the two following sections are based, *see* Appendix B.)

Personnel-intensive Budget, 1945–60

Between 1945 and 1960, the portion of grants allotted to ordinary expenditures in the military budget was fairly high, averaging nearly two-thirds of the entire military budget. Nineteen hundred fifty-eight marked the lowest level for capital expenditures; only 27 percent or so was spent for this category. This policy was the result of the nation's choices regarding her colonial position. By its very nature, colonial warfare required manpower investment rather than technological deployment; hence the burden of the war fell mainly on the shoulders of the army. Throughout almost fifteen years of colonial conflict, the so-called technical services performed only marginal functions, limited to logistical services such as transportation and observation.[11] Due to this funneling of resources toward the army and because of the marginality of their role, the navy and the air force remained untouched, so to speak, by the military technological revolution that was taking place at the time; this predicament was somewhat reinforced by the nature of the integration of the French armed forces into the NATO military division of labor.[12]

The pre-1960 air force provides a convincing example of this point. Between 1950 and 1960, at a time when aerial technology was making considerable progress, the average budgetary portion allocated to the air force seldom exceeded 23 percent of the total military budget, a figure lower than that that had been allocated during the 1936–39 period, when air force technology was not a major military concern. By comparison, between 1954 and 1956 the air force budgets of the United States and Great Britain exceeded one third of the total military expenditures of these nations (*see* Table 3.4).

In 1950, a year representative of the period under discussion, the total number of hours flown by French pilots was lower than it had been in 1949, and the 1949 figure was already 20 percent lower than that of 1948. Air force equipment consisted of a pathetic and ill-matched assemblage of combat aircraft. There were practically no bombers. The fleet was composed of almost sixty different models, 50 percent of which were of foreign manufacture. Given the budgetary restrictions imposed by the pursuit of the colonial engagements, any attempt at modernization fell short of its objectives. Preliminary research for the designing of a new combat airplane was found to be too ambitious, too unrealistic, and was therefore dropped (for example, the Matra project and the Flying Wing SE 1800). Laws passed on 19 August 1950, and 18 January 1951 were supposed to

Table 3.4. Air Force Expenditures as a Percentage of the Defense Budget, 1936–56

Country	1936	1938	1939	1946	1948	19!
France	20	22	30	21	17.4	1{
U.S.A.	—	—	—	—	—	—
U.K.	—	—	—	—	—	—

Sources: 1936–50: *Rapport fait au nom de la Commission des Finances sur le projet de loi et lettre rectificative au projet de loi relatif au développement des crédits affectés aux dépenses militaires de fonctionnement et d'investissement pour 1950*, Doc. Assemblée Nationale, 1950. Section Air; 1952–56: *Avis de la Commission de Défense nationale sur le projet de loi relatif au développement des crédits affectés aux dépenses militaires de fonctionnement*, Doc. Assemblée Nationale, n° 11245, 1950. Section Air.

launch an air force renaissance, but in the course of the next few years, these laws were bled of all innovative content. For the *Plan accéléré* of October 1950 and the *Plan de Paris*, which projected an air force fleet of 2,000 aircraft by 1956, *Plan X* was quickly substituted. *Plan X* reduced the projected aircraft to 1,000. Then *Plan XI*, calling for 1,300 airplanes by 1961, was passed. Eventually a series of new decisions, known as the *plan vert, plan jaune,* and *plan jaune bis,* postponed the building of the modern air fleet to a later date. The situation in the aeronautic industry was such that 10,000 layoffs were foreseen for 1961 and nearly 20,000 for 1964. Even the repairing of the nation's radar cover was slowed down. After 1955, the state of deterioration of the air force was such that a report prepared by a National Assembly economic commission questioned the advisability of continuing France's aerial participation in the NATO defense network given the obsolescence of her equipment.

The Indochinese and Algerian wars never acted as a stimulant to technological change. Quite the contrary, actually, because what was needed the most there were sturdy propeller-powered aircraft, capable of landing on short, rough airstrips and of performing low-speed surveillance missions. In other words, equipment based on pre–World War II technology, in contrast to that being developed after the war, was needed. It is noteworthy that it was the T6, engineered in 1942, powered by propeller and capable of a speed of 300 miles per hour, that was used for operation in Algeria. Actually, the colonial warfare requisites with regard to the use of aerial equipment were so odd and so much at variance with even rather conventional technology that the army sought to initiate its own air fleet adapted to its own

1952	1953	1954	1955	1956
21	21.8	24.2	24.7	27.0
—	—	33.0	37.9	44.2
—	—	33.2	31.6	—

needs and to the requirements of colonial warfare, and to dispense with the participation of the air force completely. One national defense minister even conjectured that, due to the parallel development of an aeronaval force and an army aviation unit, the existence of a separate air force might no longer be justified.[13]

The navy, too, was not spared the effects of the colonial conflicts. In addition to being significantly underbudgeted (the navy spending averaged between 15 and 18 percent of all military expenditures), the navy began the postwar era with a heavy handicap: it took from 1945 to 1949 to refloat the French naval yards, 85 percent of which had been destroyed during the war. In 1950, the global tonnage of the fleet reached only 285,000 tons, of which 96,000 tons were useless; the ideal tonnage would have been 365,000.[14] The *Jean-Bart*, which was set afloat in 1951, was outmoded before it went into service because what was to become the modern naval deployment was considerably lightened, and most capital ships and destroyers were to be replaced by aircraft carriers, helicopter carriers, submarines, and anti-aircraft light escort vessels. As shown in Table 3.5, compared to the American and British fleets, the structure of the French navy remained very traditional. In 1955, if obsolete ships and training vessels are deducted, the navy's total tonnage reached only 279,045 tons, and these were only nine large war ships: two line vessels, three aircraft carriers, and four cruisers. In 1960, of 312,456 total tons, 194,045 were between ten and thirty years of age. And, because of a cut in budgetary allocations, the construction of thirty-two new ships, nearly 97,000 tons, had to be interrupted. Navy spending was so limited that training programs were reduced to their absolute minimum. Between 1958 and 1963, the total tonnage of the navy declined by 31 percent, falling to 268,967 tons in 1963.[15]

It is needless to dwell on the case of the army itself. The style of combat undertaken in Indochina, and particularly in Algeria, required manpower more than any other resource. Army expenditures served mainly to support a large mass of men; in Indochina, military officials went so far as to argue that if the war was to be continued, the size of the expeditionary corps would have to be complemented by additional manpower. The idea of sending draftees was seriously considered. Most of the expenditures for equipment served to compensate for losses and for wear and tear on equipment used on the battlefield. The archaic nature of the combat did not encourage the development of any new sort of equipment. With the aggravation of the situation in Algeria in 1956 and the subsequent increasing needs for manpower, the limited forces that had until then been kept in France and Germany to be modernized as a part of the Western alliance structure were finally employed in Algeria. Thus between 1956 and 1958, three mechanized divisions were sent to Algeria and dismantled to fit the specific needs of the pacification mission. In 1960, there were only 50,000 army and 8,000 air force troops left in Germany. Projects aimed at reorganizing the army had to be postponed or abandoned. This was the case of a divisional structuring plan that hoped to substitute a modern division model based on the U.S. pattern of 1953 for the old "division 45" model still in operation. It was not until 1963 that the reform took place, by which time it was

Table 3.5. Comparative Structures of the British, American, and French Navies, 1950 (percentages)

	France	U.S.A.	U.K.
Line vessels	21	14	14
Aircraft carriers	13	36	21
Cruisers	31	18	22
Escort vessels			
first class	9	17	19
second class	21	8	19
Submarines	5	6.5	5

Source: *Avis présenté au nom de la Commission de la Défense nationale sur le projet de loi relatif au développement des crédits affectés aux dépenses militaires*, Doc. Assemblée nationale, n° 9884 (2nd session ordinaire, 1950), p. 44.

already outdated, particularly in regard to the context of nuclear deterrence.[16]

The cumulative effects of the colonial activities were added to the consequences of this troop transfer to the colonies. In Algeria, because of the kinds of missions that had to be completed, the degree of exposure to advanced technology was very low. Most divisions were actually transformed into administrative entities whose tasks consisted of patrolling and policing cities, surveying the eastern and western borders, and so on. And if human resources were plentiful, technological equipment was lacking. There was no mobile artillery; very few armored vehicles, tactical or transportation trucks, and heavy equipment; and antiaerial weapons were badly needed.

In a way, the colonial involvement and the subsequent budgetary allocations contributed to what was viewed by many as the disorganization of the army. In 1957, as a protest against what they considered the sacrifice of the modernization of the army in North Africa, Chief of the General Staff General Guillaume and another division general, General Duffour, resigned their commissions.[17] There is little doubt that the colonial budget helped to destroy all efforts aimed at reconstructing a new army and, to quote Jean Feller, "to exclude France from the international competition opened since the beginning of the Cold War."[18]

Then, because it remained estranged from technological change by reason of the personnel-oriented nature of its resources and at the same time committed to the nonmodernizing functions of colonial conflicts, the French military establishment continued until the early 1960s to exhibit the morphology of a traditional military institution, a morphology very similar to that of the prewar period. It was still, for example, a highly pluralistic organization. It consisted, on the one hand, of an overswollen army (averaging 765,000 men during this period and peaking at 830,000 men in 1957), which was involved in a somewhat archaic type of warfare and, on the other hand, of an underbudgeted air force and navy, which, though inherently technical services, were only tangentially affected by technological change. On the whole, in the decade and a half following World War II, the French military found itself plunged into an environment that, at least technologically, was not very different from that of prewar times—a milieu, hence, likely to favor the persistence, rather than the alteration, of those traditional mass army features that had previously characterized the military establishment.

Capital-intensive Budget

General de Gaulle's famous speeches, at the War College on 3 November 1959, Verdun on 28 June 1961, and Strasbourg on 11 November of that same year, lifted the curtain on a new epoch for the French military establishment. This period was marked by the termination of the overseas missions, by a withdrawal into the *héxagone*, and, above all, by the technological and nuclear modernization of the military organization. For a landscape of marshy jungles and sunburnt *djebels*, a glowing universe of electronic precision and atomic strategy on a global scale was substituted. The redefinition of the national defense structures, including the reliance on the strategy of nuclear dissuasion, were, as we recall, to favor the emergence of a homogenous military establishment composed of specific systems of forces, all functionally integrated with respect to the objectives to be performed, all structurally balanced with respect to both nuclear and conventional deployment.

But in reality, the military establishment that rose in the dawn of the 1960s and grew during the 1970s was quite different from the ideal type that had been conceived during the elaboration of the new national defense scheme, or from that still described in the official rhetoric. As stated, because of the interplay of interservice tensions, the inherent division of labor along structural lines, and the unbalanced allocation involving the nuclear aspects of the defense universe, the army emerged as the dominant component of the conventional dimension of the defense organization below the nuclear level, whereas the air force and the navy became the dominant components of the strategic dimensions and operated essentially at the nuclear level.

Budgetary practices tended to accentuate these discrepancies, and as such, to reinforce disparities in the level of exposure to technological modernization, thereby contributing to the continued structural dualism of the contemporary military establishment.

Once France decided to "go nuclear," it was obvious that capital expenditures allocated to the building of nuclear armament would be given priority—a priority all the more pressing because France was starting her program of atomic military application from scratch, so to speak. Because of the United States' concern with nuclear proliferation, France had to "rediscover," undertake, and build both the atomic explosive and delivery system by herself. Once the basic nuclear chemistry was known, factories for the production of plutonium, uranium 235, hexaflouride of uranium, and deuterium had to be built; nuclear reactors and tritium plants had to be set up.[19] And given the peculiarity of nuclear technology, particularly its high threshold of obsolescence, the maintenance, which in this context means the modernization, of the equipment inevitably required a constant and regular inflow of capital investment in order not to jeopardize its operational credibility.

It was to achieve these objectives, the building of a nuclear force and the reorganization of the military establishment rendered necessary by the redefinition of its roles, that a procession of quinquennial blueprints, the *lois de programme militaire* (hereafter translated as "laws of military program"), were promulgated after 1960. These plans were considered indispensable for the efficient remapping of the French armed forces, and particularly for the nuclearization program, after the colonial disengagement.

Though not all the plans covered the entire range of capital allotments—the first one covered only 38 percent of the total capital expenditures; the second one, 68.6 percent—the laws of military program constitute an appropriate instrument for determining the flow of expenditures between the various services, the priority-holding sectors, and for establishing the normative frame against which modifications of previously planned allotments can be contrasted.

In principle, the main objective of these programs concerned the reorganization and modernization of all sectors of the defense deployment; the modernization of the systems of force below the nuclear level as well as the construction of the nuclear force itself were carefully planned in order to avoid internal discrepancies in the operationality of the various rungs of the defense deployment. Yet the spending authorizations for equipment in the laws of program revealed that it was upon nuclearization that these programs focused, at least until 1971. The plans seemingly were patterned by the intention to provide the most feasible framework for a rapid development of the process of nuclear modernization; for example, they sought to minimize the use of atomic intermediary generations. All in all, the content of these programs could be summarized thusly: the program law, covering 1960 to 1964, focused upon research in basic nuclear devices (such as in the field of isotope separation) and in nuclear military equipment (such as propellant and delivery systems). It scheduled the testing and construction of the first generation of atomic bombs and the building of the first generation of delivery devices, the manned Mirage IV aircraft. The second program law, covering 1965 to 1970, arranged for the completion of the Mirage system and, above all, put into work the second generation of atomic weaponry, namely the fixed intermediate-range ballistic missiles, of the SSBM type.

Furthermore, research concerning thermonuclear technology and nuclear-powered missile-launching submarines had been undertaken. Finally, the third law of military program, for 1971 to 1975, concerned itself with the enlargement of the naval nuclear force and its environment, the development of tactical atomic weaponry, and research programs for new warheads with MIRV devices to equip the silo-buried and submarine-embarked missile systems.[20]

An analysis of the quantitative amount of authorized expenditures makes clearer the relative importance of the nuclear investments over these years. The allocation defined by the first law of program for the Strategic Nuclear Force (FNS), 6.348 billion francs, constituted 51 percent of the total funds allocated to the program (11.750 billion francs) and 20 percent of the whole budgetary envelope for equipment expenditures between 1960 and 1964. The second law of program controlled a volume of 54.898 billion francs, 50 percent of which was allocated for nuclear-oriented expenditures; this represented 35 percent of the entire budget (81.8 billion francs) for the period. It was only with the third law of military program, which, contrasted with the two preceding ones, covered the total allotment planned for capital expenditures from 1971 to 1975, that the nonnuclear sector received more monies than the nuclear sector; spending authorizations reached 62.611 billion francs for the nonnuclear sector compared with 30.889 billion francs for the FNS and tactical nuclear armament.

Further indication of the importance of the nuclear sector is the fact that the percentage of coverage of the actual expenditures (*crédits de paiement*) over the planned authorized expenditures (*autorisations de programme*) was always higher for nuclear items than for nonnuclear ones. For example, in the second law of program, actual expenditures for the FNS constituted 89.2 percent of those authorized, whereas they reached only 69.3 percent for the nonnuclear sector. In the third law of program, these percentages were respectively 98.4 percent and 83 percent.[21]

All this is only one side of the argument. Had the level of the allotments remained as originally planned, this slightly built-in imbalance between the nuclear and the nonnuclear sectors, that is between the army, on one side, and the navy and air force, on the other, would not have been too serious, especially after 1970. But the data related to the implementation of the laws of program show that the actual volume of expenditures alloted to the nuclear sector was always much higher than planned at the beginning. And, because the overall budget was fixed, the volume of funds allotted to the nonnuclear sector and its supporting services had to be reduced. Study of the execution of the laws of program shows that since 1960 the nuclear force continuously absorbed a significantly larger share of the capital resources, the volume of which continued to rise (program authorizations for the first law increased by 56 percent compared to their initial value; those for the second law by 6 percent).[22] For example, whereas the volume of planned authorized expenditures for the nuclear force under the first law of program amounted to 6.348 billion francs, they actually reached almost 7.5 billion.[23] Many experts consider even this figure too low; they estimate the actual overall expenditures at close to 10 billion francs.[24] Thus, the funds alloted to the nuclear force reached 63.3 percent instead of the 54 percent initially planned; that amounted to more than one-fourth of the total capital expenditures. Similar observations can be made for the following quinquennial laws. Authorized expenditures for the atomic sector established by the second law were increased by 3.308 billion francs; the FNS thus received 56 percent of the total against the 51 percent originally planned. As for the third law of program, whose objectives were directed toward developing and modernizing the nonnuclear sector, the level of authorized spending for the FNS, originally fixed at 30 percent of the total, was increased to nearly 40 percent of this total.

Finally, as an additional note confirming the privileged place occupied by the nuclear sector, one ought to emphasize that the initial program authorizations for the FNS were always covered by the actual allotments, whereas this was not true for the nonnuclear sectors, where a significant difference often existed. As an example, it suffices to compare the amount of authorized versus actual capital expenditures; this comparison between actual and planned expenditures accruing to the FNS and to the modernization of the conventional armament, the most important nonnuclear item and the largest entry under capital expenditures after 1970, is enlightening, as illustrated in Table 3.6. These observations suggest that not only was there a greater emphasis on the development of the FNS than on the other forces, even after 1964, but also that this priority seemed to have coincided with, if not been the cause of, the compression of resources at the nonnuclear level. Thus, the attempt at equalizing resources for the nuclear and nonnuclear sectors after 1965 failed; in practice the equilibrium had broken in favor of the FNS by the end of the second law of program.

It is not our purpose here to elaborate on the factors that might have accounted for the swelling of the resources allotted to the nuclear force. Errors of evaluation, both technical and financial, inflation, and, perhaps at the beginning, a too optimistic belief in the myth of

Table 3.6. Authorized and Actual Expenditures for the Major
Nuclear and Nonnuclear Programs as a Percentage of Capital
Expenditures, 1970–75

	1970	1971	1974	1975
Nuclear force				
Authorized expenditures	33.5	28.3	28.5	29.0
Actual expenditures	37.2	34.2	31.2	32.0
Modernization of conventional equipment				
Authorized expenditures	33.3	33.0	34.3	31.8
Actual expenditures	31.0	29.0	31.2	30.8

the low cost of nuclear military equipment[25] constitute some of the
most important variables in relation to this matter. The case of the
major isotope separation plant located at Pierrelatte is an example.
Costing 3.5 times more than the anticipated price (evaluated initially at 1.5 billion francs, then at 3.5 billion in 1962 by Pierre Messmer)
it became the most expensive and controversial industrial installation
ever undertaken in France. But it was not an isolated instance. The
Mirage IV system, initially priced at 1 billion francs, eventually cost
1.3 billion; to this sum it was later necessary to add 600 million francs
to cover the expense of maintenance beyond the term (to 1980) originally fixed for its use (1970). Because of unforseen technological obstacles, the construction of the silo-buried ICBM delivery systems
took more time and more investment than originally planned. Authorized expenditures for the special studies and systems, for example, have been increased by 187 percent by the end of the first quinquennial plan. Moving the nuclear testing station to the Mururora
Islands and the necessary shift from atmospheric to underground testing added further strains to the program of nuclear development.[26]

A second series of difficulties was linked to inaccuracies in financial
planning. The second law of program, for instance, assumed that
prices would remain stable, and as a consequence no provisions were
made for an automatic revalorization of the allotments in case of an
increase. Since the rate of growth adopted was 5 percent of the GNP,
during the implementation of the third law of program the problems
were even more serious, for the estimates took into consideration
very imperfectly the price changes—this even before the outset of the
1973–74 world economic crisis. For example, although the plan did

integrate into its evaluation a price increase of 5 percent for armaments and 3 percent for other expenses, a rate higher than that provided for by the Sixth Economic Plan, the spending estimates of the third program law remained far below reality as the level of prices of the GNP rose 5.2 percent in 1970, 4.8 percent in 1971, and 5.6 percent in 1972. And, despite a reevaluation made by new computations of the revised plan of 1972, and despite an increase in the level of the annual programmed expenditures authorized by the yearly *Loi de finance*, the overall loss for national defense was fairly high. For example, in order to absorb the cost of inflation, the programmed expenditures for 1975 alone, which had been pegged at 22 billion francs after the 1972 revision and later at 24 billion, should have amounted to 28 billion francs. A total of more than 8 billion francs was lost, 11 percent of the allotments accruing for the last three years of the third plan.

One of the key elements in the asymmetry between cost estimates and cost invoices was not so much the underappreciation of the actual level of inflation or of the price change but an underestimation of the increase in price of military equipment itself; this rate of increase always tended to be higher than that for other commodities. And this "price drift," which was not taken into account by the government in the course of the elaboration of military planning, was very important. According to recent computations, the price increase reached an average of 8 percent per year between 1945 and 1970; that amounted to double the average national growth of 4 percent per year.[27]

On the whole the nuclear force cost the country a very large sum: the chairman of the National Assembly's defense commission estimated that between 1960 and 1972 it cost 50 billion francs. Other estimates for 1955–75 evaluate the cost of the FNS at around 70 billion.[28] The firmly held doctrinal conviction that nuclear weaponry plays a key role in defense strategy and the early investments that induced a pursuit of the nuclear program until it reached what could be considered an appropriate level of credibility and operationality led to this inordinate emphasis on the nuclear sector—an emphasis that had detrimental consequences for the development of other components of the defense system. Given the fact that after 1960 the defense budget was rather narrow, as well as inelastic, it is evident that all increases in the nuclear sector were made at the expense of the nonnuclear ones. Additional constraints unrelated to this imbalance in favor of the FNS imposed further strains upon the nonnuclear components of the defense system. As mentioned previously, the actual level of resources (*crédits de paiement*) never matched the authorized level of resources (*autorisations de programme*) in the non-nuclear sectors; the former were always lower. Though in principle these discrepancies did not technically constitute a loss, as the balances were to be credited for later use, it remained that they constituted serious constraints; they led to the postponement of one or more projects. Yet, this was not true for the nuclear sector; here the authorized expenditures were generally covered, if not overcredited (see Table 3.6). Thus, the strains produced by these financial discrepancies were entirely borne by the nonnuclear areas of the program. And these residual balances concerned large sums. At the start of the first law of program in 1960, there already was an accumulated balance amounting to 8 billion francs. The balance due at the beginning of the second law of program was 19 billion, and by the beginning of the 1970s there was a debt of 24.7 billion francs. During the execution of the third law of program the annual coverage of authorized expenditures averaged about 80 percent (84 percent in 1971, 79 percent in 1972, 81 percent in 1973, 92 percent in 1974, and 79 percent in 1975); thus a total of 42.737 billion francs had not yet been allocated to defense. Most of these monies were diverted from the nonnuclear sector. To these two factors, a third ought to be added. The unforeseen exponential increase in the cost of classical equipment between 1960 and 1976 necessitated making a choice that led to the postponement and abandonment of various projects originally scheduled.[29]

Throughout the decade and a half following the reorganization of the French national defense in the early 1960s, there was a significant imbalance in the flow of resources across the various systems of forces that compose the defense network. Students of the Fifth Republic defense policies, as well as numerous *rapporteurs* for the defense commissions at the National Assembly and the Senate, consistently pointed out the gravity of the consequences that the emphasis on the nuclear force had on such other systems of forces as the Forces of Maneuver and the Operational Defense of the Territory. "What strikes me the most in the French situation is the state of weakness of her conventional defense"; this lapidary yet realistic view, attributed to German Chancellor Helmut Schmidt by President Giscard d'Estaing, sums up the thought of most defense specialists in France.[30] Thus this inequal partition of capital resources throughout the military institution resulted in creating around it a heterogenous modernizing environment. In other words, the distribution of resources reinforced the discrepancies in the level of exposure to technological change between the two sectors. Above all, and beyond this sectorial dualism, an interservice dualism emerged: the navy and air force, constituting the backbone of the Strategic Nuclear Force, found themselves in a highly modernized environment, whereas the army did not.

It is no coincidence, then, if an interservice comparison of equipment-building expenditures for the 1965–73 period revealed that allocations to the navy and the air force were, even in the absolute, higher than those for the army. This situation was all the worse in that, even before reduction and changes in budgetary allotments had to be made, at a time when, for example, the equipment-building expenditures for the army were the highest, the funds available to the army were, to a great extent, diverted from modernizing objectives. In effect, while resources allocated to the air force and to the navy were, from the beginning of the nuclearization program, used for the achievement of their intended objectives, until 1964 the resources allocated to the army were used to absorb the costs entailed by the colonial disengagement. This included the repatriation of men and equipment, the adjustment of salaries, and the reduction of effectives. In 1962 more than half of the army was still involved in Algeria. This was the case of a good many of the effectives of the Second Corps of the First Army, who were originally supposed to be stationed in Germany as a component of the Forces of Maneuver. Until 1965, the army found itself separated from the technologically modernizing stream because of the aftereffects of the colonial wars. It was only after 1965 that the army was ready for modernization surgery. And though the second and the third quinquennial programs sought to balance the allocations between the nuclear force and the modernization of conventional forces, reductions were made at the expense of the latter and resources were transferred away from the army. After 1969, when it again became necessary to increase ordinary expenditures without modifying the overall envelope, there were fewer resources available that could be mobilized to compensate for the loss of capital allocations for the army. This difference in the flow of modernization-oriented resources, the capital expenditures, between services is clearly demonstrated in Figure 3.2. The graphs, presenting the evolution of the five most important categories of expenditures for each service, show that between 1960 and 1975 capital spending, notably industrial investments and fabrications, were always higher than ordinary expenditures in the navy and the air force and lower in the army. Moreover, the examination shows that during the decade and a half following 1960, the volume of capital spending across services, in relative as well as absolute terms, was larger in the navy and the air force, despite an increase in fabrication and industrial investment expenditures in the army after 1969. Between 1965 and 1970, a period when capital expenditures outweighed

Figure 3.2. Defense Budget by Category of Expenditure and Service, 1960–76 (in billions of francs)

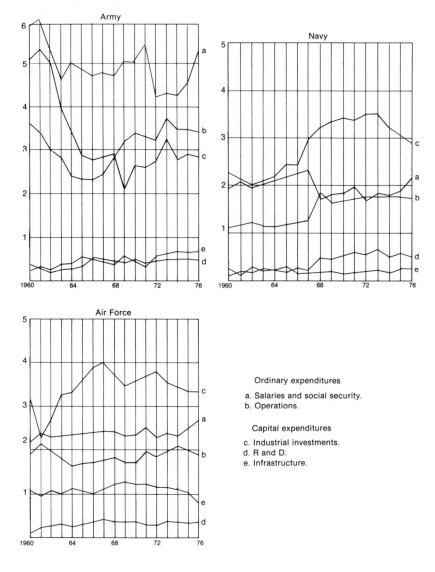

Ordinary expenditures

a. Salaries and social security.
b. Operations.

Capital expenditures

c. Industrial investments.
d. R and D.
e. Infrastructure.

Source: Jean-Bernard Pinatel, ed., *L'Economie des forces*, pp. 155–57.

ordinary expenditures on the whole, the former remained lower than the latter in the army. After 1970, when the volume of ordinary expenditures again exceeded that of capital expenditures, the latter always stayed higher than the former, as illustrated in Table 3.7, in the navy and the air force.

It is remarkable that, even in absolute values, the mass of capital spending allotted to the navy, the smallest of the three services, remained almost equal to that of the army, the largest of the three services.

One should note in passing that the importance of the resource attributed to the Common Services, the *section commune* according to French budgetary terminology, is actually due to the fact that many of the resources allocated for the Strategic Nuclear Force were, for a few years, classified under this section. This being said, and given the fact that the navy and the air force were the major recipients of FNS resources, one sees that the importance of the allotments received by these services was higher than appears from a study of the annual defense budget in its conventional presentation.

The parliamentary reports concerned with defense matters add supplementary evidence to this interservice imbalance. The complaints and warnings issued by defense *rapporteurs* clearly expose the extent of the army's technological underdevelopment in the 1960s and the early 1970s. We have already alluded to the state of backwardness of the French ground forces during the colonial wars and to how the Algerian War contributed to delaying a first attempt at reorganization along the lines of a new division pattern. This reform, which was originally an essential model for optimizing the use of conventional equipment, was not achieved until the mid-1960s, by which time it had become somewhat incongruent with the parameter of nuclear deterrence. And even then it was never fully implemented. The new division, for example, included only two out of three squadrons in the armored regiments, five to six sections out of twelve in the mechanized infantry regiments, fourteen out of twenty-four sections in the motorized infantry regiments, and one group out of two in artillery regiments. The equipment, moreover, was very heterogenous: in addition to the newly delivered heavy AMX tanks, one also found a number of old American M-48 tanks. Discrepancies between the divisions stationed in Germany and those assigned to French territory remained numerous despite a 1965 attempt to balance them. The second reorganization of the army, planned in 1967, consisted of replacing the old "division 59" model with a new one.[31] The reorganization progressed so slowly that it was not until 1976–77 that it neared completion, with five mechanized divi-

Table 3.7. Capital and Ordinary Military Expenditures by Service, 1970–75

	1970		1971		1972	
	(In Francs)	%	(In Francs)	%	(In Francs)	%
Ordinary expenditures	14,111,926	51.91	15,333,567	53.14	16,613,426	53.3
Common services	4,195,005	15.43	4,445,997	15.41	6,199,969	19.9
Air force	2,630,916	9.68	2,897,547	10.04	2,973,883	9.5
Army	5,031,271	18.51	5,529,324	19.16	4,956,978	15.9
Navy	2,254,734	8.29	2,460,699	8.53	2,482,596	7.9
Gendarmerie	—	—	—	—	—	—
Capital expenditures	13,076,000	48.09	13,521,662	46.86	14,514,550	46.6
Common services	4,359,000	16.03	4,613,080	15.99	4,663,550	14.9
Air force	3,410,000	12.54	3,375,000	11.70	3,735,000	12.0
Army	2,839,300	10.44	2,774,300	9.61	3,055,000	9.8
Navy	2,467,700	9.08	2,759,282	9.56	3,061,000	9.8
Gendarmerie	—	—	—	—	—	—
Total	27,187,926	100.00	28,855,229	100.00	31,127,976	100.0

sions. In the early 1970s, there were only five motorized brigades, instead of the fifteen mechanized brigades originally called for. The army had only 500 modern combat vehicles whereas it should have had 4,000. In other words, a number far below that called for by the defense minister's computations: 1,500 tanks, 3,500 armored vehicles for troop transportation, 400 self-propelled cannons, 900 helicopters, and tactical nuclear weapons.[32] By 1976 the modernization through the dissemination of new equipment had progressed so slowly that it lagged behind even the most pessimistic projections, and France found herself with perhaps the poorest conventional equipment among powers of similar strength: 190 helicopters (120 Puma and 70 Alouette III), 190 self-propelled 105 millimeter cannons, 450 Milan antitank missiles, 2,500 various military vehicles (transportation, reconnaissance), 1,000 light AMX-13 tanks, and only 850 operational heavy AMX-30 tanks. Not only did Israel possess an incomparably better fleet of heavy tanks, but also West Germany with 3,000 tanks, Italy with 1,500, East Germany with 1,500, Czechoslovakia with 2,500, and Poland with 3,000 tanks. Moreover, the manufacture of new equipment and its delivery were such that the army was simultaneously in possession of old and new equipment; often, when new equipment arrived, the old had to be decommissioned. That was the case with the AMX-13 tanks (AMX-13 VTT on the one hand and the new AMX-10P and AMX-30 on the

1973		1974		1975	
n Francs)	%	(In Francs)	%	(In Francs)	%
8,300,000	52.59	20,797,073	54.06	24,484,419	55.92
4,082,699	11.73	4,426,370	11.51	5,936,817	13.56
3,336,841	9.59	3,931,828	10.22	4,372,612	9.99
5,519,258	15.86	6,299,006	16.37	7,148,044	16.32
2,706,365	7.78	3,087,417	8.03	3,508,764	8.01
2,654,837	7.63	3,052,452	7.93	3,518,182	8.03
5,500,000	47.41	17,674,000	45.94	19,301,952	44.08
5,092,000	14.63	5,532,000	14.38	6,080,913	13.89
4,937,900	11.31	4,298,670	11.17	4,637,900	10.59
4,685,600	10.58	4,028,560	10.47	4,481,000	10.23
4,389,900	9.74	3,369,900	8.76	3,632,739	8.30
395,600	1.14	444,870	1.16	469,400	1.07
,800,000	100.00	38,471,073	100.00	43,786,371	100.00

other), the tactical UNIMOG trucks (the first were delivered in 1955, the last in 1975), helicopters, and so on. This high degree of heterogeneity in army equipment required the simultaneous use of different specialist repair teams and the stockpiling of several kinds of replacement parts; this resulted in an increase in operation and maintenance costs, an increase that had to be extracted from equipment expenditures. Finally, in some cases, unforeseen technical problems also delayed the delivery of modern materiel; such was the case of the AMX-30 bridge thrower and the AMX tank in its offensive version.[33] As for the introduction of nuclear technology in the army, it is not necessary to dwell on it at length. We have already seen how the introduction of the Pluton system was delayed until 1974 and how, since then, it has been allocated very sparsely, thus preventing the creation of poles of advanced technology that could have spread within the various segments of the army.

In the light of these observations about the imbalance in the flow of budgetary resources within the military establishment and in particular between the nuclear and the nonnuclear sectors, it is difficult not to conclude that the army was underexposed to technological modernization either because impetus for such a modernization was delayed or because it was too fragmentary. Reduced flows of resources at the nonnuclear level also affected the navy and the air force. In 1973, for example, the air force was still utilizing a great number of fifteen- to twenty-year-old aircraft (110 Mystère IV, 45 SMB, 45 Vautour, 45 F-100) as well as newer but outmoded or limited capability ones (e.g., the Mirage IIIC with its radar and in-flight refueling deficiencies).[34] In the navy, the antiquated state of many conventional ships (the thirty-year-old cruiser *Colbert*, and the fleet escorts *Duperré* and *La Galissonnière*), the weariness of the Fleet Air Arm (using thirty-five outmoded American F8E Crusaders and fifty-five of the now aging Etendard IV in 1975), the declining tonnage of the logistic fleet (four petroleum supply tankers, five logistical support ships, no electronic support lightships, and no ammunition supply ships in 1975), and the abandonment of the objectives set forth by the naval plan of 1972 illustrate the precariousness of the situation below the nuclear level. But, even if some segments of the air force or the navy were not as highly exposed to intense technological modernization, these services as the dominant vectors of the technologically advanced Strategic Nuclear Force, have, on the whole, become permeated with change. For the army, on the other hand, the possibility of being exposed to change by contiguity with the sophisticated services, as would have been the case if the systems below the nuclear level in the navy and the air force had not been neglected, disappeared. The reduction of the flow of technological change below the nuclear level in the navy and the air force prevented their playing the role of transmitter of modern technology for the forces associated with them such as the army.

Thus, it was, according to General Bigeard, "a tour de force to have managed to constitute the strategic force while maintaining the traditional forces," but if maintenance means modernization, the tour de force, as Ruehl put it, "remained to be accomplished."[35]

To complete this picture, it should be said that the emergent technological dualism between the French military services created by the internal organization of the defense system and by the discrepancies in resource allocation was, in a way, self-perpetuating. The imbalance in the allocation of resources, with its emphasis on the nuclear sectors and the deemphasis on nonnuclear sectors, has contributed to eroding the nonnuclear operational capabilities of the military establishment. This in turn has affected the original imbalance introduced in the defense division of labor by the adherence of the official doctrine to the nuclear dimension of defense. Though no empirical proof can be advanced, it is possible to hypothesize that, confronted with the slow deterioration of the nonnuclear capabilities of the military, official strategic thought tended, even in the mid-1970s, to consider the lower, nonnuclear rungs in the escalatory ladder as secondary and to favor the idea of a swift escalation to the nuclear rungs should the sanctuary be attacked by any kind of military means. Sanctuarization, on the one hand, and deterrence by threat of massive retaliation, on the other—these two underlying tenets of the French defense doctrine were undoubtedly the result of a rationally engineered choice, particularly in the early 1960s, but their persistence afterward was also the product of the technical reasons discussed above. It is likely that during the 1960s and early 1970s the much-complained-about fact that the planned developmental level of the Forces of Maneuver was never achieved resulted in the constriction of the operational availability of the whole system, thereby contributing to the regression of the strategic conception as a credible component of the French defense system below the nuclear threshold. This underlying bias in favor of the nuclear forces tended to minimize the importance of development of the nonnuclear sectors and thus eliminated any objection to decreasing the flow of resources to these sectors. In effect, the erratic transfer of technological modernization toward the nonnuclear sectors of the defense considerably affected the operational readiness of those services called upon to operate at this level; this in turn made them less important in the defense system and less important in the allocation of funds.

Notes

1. One must recall that assistance from the allied powers helped France in her military efforts and therefore reduced her military financial burden. The table on p. 80 lists the amount of financial assistance received from various sources from 1951 to 1958.

2. *Livre blanc sur la défense nationale*, vol. 1, p. 57.

3. The literature dealing with the question of the economic effects of military expenditures is extensive. In the case of France, the following studies are particularly helpful: Henri Aujac, "L'Efficacité militaire et les structures économiques, sociales et politiques," *Revue économique* 22 (1971): 561–84; Jean Barbery, "L'Impact industriel du IIIe plan militaire," *Revue de Défense nationale* 27 (1971):

1755–72; Claude Lachaux, "Economie et défense," *Défense nationale* 32 (April 1976): 29–46; Marceau Long, "L'Incidence des dépenses des armées sur l'économie," *Revue de Défense nationale* 24 (1968): 987–1000; Jean-Bernard Pinatel, "Les Effets de la politique et des dépenses militaires sur la croissance: le cas français, 1965–1972" (Doctoral dissertation, Ecole pratique des hautes études, VIe section, Paris, 1974); Pierre Routside, "Budgets militaires et équilibre national," *Revue de Défense nationale* 19 (1963): 951–65.

4. Pierre Messmer, "L'Armée de demain," *Revue des deux mondes*, 15 February 1962, pp. 481–93.

5. *Livre blanc sur la défense nationale*, vol. 1, p. 59.

6. As a percent of GNP; see *Military*

	1951	1952	1953	1954	1955	1956	1957	1958
Foreign assistance included in the budget (millions of francs)	5	61	95	166	148	85	33	23
Percentage of the budget	—	4.8	7.3	10.4	11.7	5.6	2.1	1.6
Foreign assistance not included in the budget (millions of francs)	207	298	380	361	151	98	69	30
U.S.A.[a] (millions of francs)	—	—	—	246	97	72	44	30
Germany (millions of francs)	—	—	—	115	54	26	25	—
Total foreign assistance	212	358	475	527	299	183	102	53
Percentage foreign assistance	20.5	23.0	28.4	22.3	11.8	6.4	4.5	2.0

Sources: For 1951–53, Jean Godard, "La Contribution alliée aux charges militaires de la France," *Revue de Défense nationale* 12 (1956): 443–44; for 1954–58, "Le Coût de l'armée et les moyens à sa disposition: 1954–1958," (Paris: Ministère des armées, 1959), pp. 11 and 22.
[a]Edgar S. Furniss indicates that between 1954 and 1958, the United States helped France in at least four different ways: "There was direct military aid and financial assistance, with a large international loan coming too late to help the beleaguered Pflimlin government. Equipment supposedly destined for Western Defense wound up in Algeria; without the United States being able, whether or not it had wished to do so, to prevent the diversion. The United States, by keeping a large number of American troops in West Germany, rescued France from the dilemma created by concentrating its forces in North Africa while at the same time masquerading as a leader of NATO. Equally significant in the long run, the United States, backed up by Great Britain, forced France to agree that Germany should be permitted to rearm. A Bonn-Washington axis thus filled the void left by the Fourth Republic's departure for Algeria" (Edgar S. Furniss, *De Gaulle and the French Army: A Crisis in Civil-Military Relations* [New York: Twentieth Century Fund, 1964], pp. 182–83).

Balance 1974–75 and *1975–76* (London: International Institute for Strategic Studies, 1976); Stockholm International Peace Research Institute, *World Armaments and Disarmament: SIPRI Yearbook 1975* (Stockholm: Almquist and Wiksell, 1975); Antoine Sanguinetti, "Produit national brut et budget de la défense," *Le Monde*, 13 February 1975, pp. 1 and 7; David Greenwood, "The Defence Efforts of France, West Germany and the United Kingdom," *ASIDES* 1 (October 1973).

7. To many this decline in military expenditures appeared problematic, if not intolerable. For example, in 1975, a political group related to the former Gaullist party, the *Groupe de réflexion et de proposition*, decided to oppose the upcoming military budgets if they were below 4 percent of the GNP in 1976 and 5 percent in 1977. Interestingly enough, the first official words of the new defense minister, Yvon Bourges, indicated that the 1976 defense budget would be greater than 3 percent of the GNP since he believed that any figure under 3 percent would be insufficient in regard to the development of the French military program (*Le Monde*, 23 May 1973, pp. 14–15). Finally, it must be noted that the new quin-

quennial military program for 1977–82, "Rapport sur la programmation des dépenses militaires et des équipements des forces armées pour la période 1977–1982," stipulated an increase in the defense budget from 17 percent of the public expenditures to 20 percent by 1982; that would be an increase of nearly 4 percent of the GNP (Service d'Information et de Relations publiques des Armées, "Les Armées françaises de demain: programmation 1977–1982," *Dossier d'information* 49 [October 1976]).

8. The table below shows the importance of the proportion of personnel-directed expenditures in the category of ordinary military expenditures (Title III) between 1960 and 1972.

9. Jean-Bernard Pinatel, ed., *L'Economie des forces* (Paris: Fondation pour les études de Défense nationale, 1976), pp. 13–18.

10. *See* Chapter 5.

11. *See* note 7, Chapter 2.

12. *See* Chapter 2, pages 37–38.

13. *Rapport fait au nom de la Commission des Finances sur le projet de loi relatif au développement des crédits affectés au Ministère de la défense nationale et des forces armées pour l'exercice 1955–1956,* Doc. Assemblée nationale, no. 1128, 3rd part (1st session ordinaire, 1955).

14. At this time the United States Navy had 3,974,000 tons plus 227,000 tons under construction; the British Navy, 1,317,000 tons and 224,000 under construction; the Soviet Navy, 400,000 tons with 146,000 tons under construction. *See Avis présenté au nom de la Commission de Défense nationale sur le projet de loi relatif au développement des crédits affectés aux dépenses militaires,* Doc. Assemblée nationale, no. 9884 (1st session ordinaire, 1950). Moreover, in 1950, 3,000 tons were decommissioned; in 1954, three cruisers (the *Bertin, Fantasque,* and *Terrible*) were disarmed. And finally, in 1960, 47,000 were decommissioned.

15. *Avis présenté au nom de la Commission de Défense nationale et des forces armées sur le projet de loi de finance 1960,* Doc. Assemblée nationale, no. 365 (1st session ordinaire, 1959–60). *Rapport fait au nom de la Commission de Défense nationale et des forces armées sur le projet de loi de finance pour 1963,* Doc. Assemblée nationale, no. 25, appendixes 40 and 41 (1st session ordinaire, 1963–64).

16. For greater detail on this point, see Lothar Ruehl, *La Politique militaire de la Ve République* (Paris: Presses de la Fondation nationale des Sciences politiques, 1976), pp. 330–32.

Title III	1960	1965	1968	1969	1970	1971	1972
Personnel expenditures	73.0	72.7	69.7	72.6	72.3	72.7	72.3
Salaries	57.9	62.9	60.0	63.7	63.5	64.1	63.8
Maintenance	15.1	9.8	9.7	8.9	8.8	8.6	8.5
Non-personnel expenditures	27.0	27.1	32.4	27.4	27.8	27.3	27.7
Operation and maintenance	23.9	23.5	28.8	23.8	24.0	23.3	23.3
Subsidy	3.1	3.8	3.6	3.6	3.8	4.0	4.4
	100	100	100	100	100	100	100

Source: *Livre blanc sur la défense nationale,* p. 61.

17. Ibid, p. 330.

18. Jean Feller, *Le Dossier de l'armée française: la guerre de "cinquante ans,"* 1914–1962 (Paris: Librairie académique Perrin, 1966), p. 464.

19. For example, the United States refused to authorize the licensing of American equipment for French nuclear development. This refusal can be explained by the American fear of setting a precedent for the proliferation of nuclear armament (*see* the McNamara speech at Ann Arbor in June 1962). After 1962, the United States declared that it was ready to participate in the construction of nuclear armament in Europe (the United States offered, for example, to provide France with Polaris missiles) only to the extent that this armament remained integrated within the Atlantic defense network (for example, the Nassau proposals). The Nassau proposals were rejected by de Gaulle in January 1963. *See* Wilfred Kohl, *French Nuclear Diplomacy* (Princeton: Princeton University Press, 1971), pp. 229 ff.

20. "Loi de programme no. 60-1305 du 8 décembre 1960 relative à certains équipements militaires," *Journal officiel, lois et décrets*, 10 December 1960, p. 11076; "Loi de programme no. 64-1270 du 23 décembre 1964 relative à certains équipements militaires," *Journal officiel*, 24 December 1964, p. 11500; "Loi de programme no. 70-1058 du 19 novembre 1970 relative aux équipements militaires de la période 1971–1975," *Journal officiel*, 20 November 1970, p. 10659.

21. The *autorisations de programme* (authorized expenditures or programmed expenditures) are the upper limit of the total funds that the

ministers are authorized to commit to an investment. The *crédits de paiement* (actual expenditures) constitute the upper limit of the funds that can be ordered for payment or that can be paid during any one fiscal year to meet the cost of commitments entered into within the framework of the corresponding *autorisations de programme* (article of the Organic Law as quoted by Guy Lord, *The French Budgetary Process* [Berkeley: University of California Press, 1973], p. 28).

22. In the first law of program, planned authorizations amounted to 11.79 billion francs, with 6.348 (53.8%) for the FNS and 5.442 (46.2%) for uses other than the FNS; but actual authorizations came to 18.437 billion francs, with 12.281 (66.6%) for the FNS and 6.156 (33.4%) for uses other than the FNS. In the second law of program, planned authorizations reached 54.898 billion francs, with 27.383 (49.8%) for the FNS and 27.515 (50.2%) for other uses, but actual authorizations, which totaled 58.208 billion francs, came to 31.203 (54%) and 27.005 (46%), respectively.

23. This figure includes 3.99 billion francs for special studies, 1.2 for military implementations at the Atomic Studies Center, 770 million for delivery systems, 225 for propulsion, 225 for explosive, 55 for military contributions to space studies, and one billion for the Mirage IV fleet.

24. Ruehl, *La Politique militaire de la Ve République*, p. 268.

25. For a logical argument concerning the economic advantages of atomic armament, *see* Charles Ailleret, "L'Arme atomique, arme à bon marché," *Revue de Défense nationale* 10 (1954): 315–25. This argument was

repeated by former defense ministers, Michel Debré and Pierre Messmer. On 13 May 1963, Georges Pompidou also declared that "Firepower being the same, the atomic force is the most economic of all modern weaponry."

26. The tests were then conducted at Faugataufa on Touamatou Island. The price increase caused by this move was due to the fact that in addition to the cost of constructing the installations (an expensive proposition given the problems created by the drilling of the test well through volcanic and coral layers), underground tests are estimated to be three to four times as costly as regular atmospheric tests; on this point see Avis présenté au nom de la Commission de Défense nationale et des forces armées sur le projet de loi de finance pour 1974, Doc. Assemblée nationale, no. 684 (1st session ordinaire, 1973–74); and Défense nationale 31 (May 1975): 145–48.

27. Bertrand Bonavita, "Progrès matériel et politique militaire," Défense nationale 33 (November 1977): 93.

28. Ruehl, La Politique militaire de la Ve République, p. 368.

29. The logic of this increase in the price of conventional weaponry is detailed in Pinatel, ed., L'Economie des forces, pp. 77–86.

30. Interview given by President Giscard d'Estaing to Figaro, 12 November 1975.

31. The "division 67" type was conceived as a unit of three mechanized brigades. The battle corps, or the forces of maneuver, would be composed of fifteen brigades, each with one regiment of AMX 30 tanks, a large allotment of antitank devices (Milan type), one artillery regiment with self-propelled 155 millimeter cannons and a total manpower of 3,600 men.

32. Messmer, "L'Armée de demain"; for a more severe criticism of the weakness of the conventional defenses and of the army in particular see General Georges-Picot, "Pour une défense nationale," Le Monde, 25, 26, 28, and 29 September 1970.

33. Avis présenté au nom de la Commission de Défense nationale et des forces armées sur le projet de loi de finance, Doc. Assemblée nationale, no. 2588 (1st session ordinaire 1972–73), vol. 2, pp. 36–37.

34. Ibid, p. 33. It should be stated here, though it is not our purpose to evaluate the strategic consequences of such budgetary policy, that the reduction in the allocations for classic propulsion (gasoline, fuel, kerosene) correlated with that of flying time considerably affected training opportunities and trial flights. Moreover, the economies practiced in the domain of the infrastructure, which led to the closing of a number of bases, and the savings looked for in the reduction of standby readiness further jeopardized strategic deployment and, as a consequence, increased the vulnerability of existing equipment. The Mirage IV fleet was once stationed on nine bases (Cambrai, Creil, Saint-Dizier, Luxeuil, Avord, Orange, Istres, Cazeaux, and Mont-de-Marsan); by 1976 it was based on only six. And the eleven KC 35 refueling aircraft usually dispersed between Mont-de-Marsan, Avord, and Istres were gathered together at Istres; see Le Monde, 8 March 1975.

35. Ruehl, La Politique militaire de la Ve République, p. 340.

CONCLUSION TO PART ONE

The Basic Paradigm of French Military Dualism

A brief summary of our findings will provide the basic paradigm that will serve as the framework for the analysis in this study.

Until the early 1960s, France's primary military objectives were concentrated toward the maintenance of her imperial hegemony, threatened first on the Far Eastern front and then on the North African front by rising nationalist rebellions. Though the entire armed forces were not directly committed to the colonial wars, they were, nonetheless, considerably affected by these struggles. A consequence of major importance was that the French military institution was sheltered from the modernizing effect of the technological change that was occurring during that time. The army, which had been the main protagonist in the colonial conflicts, was kept from technological modernization simply because of the preindustrial nature of colonial warfare; the pedestrian nature of the colonial strategy was such that the transfer of modern technology would have had little effect on the outcome of the conflict. The air force and navy suffered from the financial effects of colonial war: because of the channeling of funds in favor of the army, all opportunities for undertaking major modernizing programs were halted. The consequences of this situation were particularly detrimental since it was precisely at this time that naval and aerial technologies were undergoing tremendous change.

The unevenness of the pattern of budgetary appropriation within the military constituted a tangible indication of the circumstances under which the army, involved in a preindustrial conflict, received priority to the detriment of the navy and air force. In addition, ordinary expenditures (for personnel and operations) amounted to one and a half times, if not two times, as much as capital expenditures (for equipment).

Thus, because the entire military establishment found itself immersed in an environment characterized by low technological modernization—technological modernization being the main source of organizational change—it can be assumed that the French military establishment continued to exhibit most of its pre–World War II characteristics; it remained arrayed with the main accoutrements of what is usually identified as an institution patterned along the mass armed forces model.

The beginning of the 1960s marked the onset of a new era. The termination of colonial involvement and, above all, the decision to subscribe to a nuclear military posture suddenly threw the French military establishment into a new environment, a highly technological, modernizing environment. But, in practice, technological diffusion in the military institution remained uneven for various reasons. For example, budgetary limitations and unexpected costs and expenses were such that technological change below the nuclear level was minimal. The inflationary costs of modern equipment and increasing demands for personnel spending in conjunction with the priority given to the construction and development of the nuclear force compelled the government, caught in the constraints of a limited defense budget, to sacrifice the modernization of all equipment for missions not directly relevant to nuclear deterrence, most of which were performed by the army. Therefore, it can be said, very schematically, that only the air force and the navy, which were in charge of most of the nuclear missions, were "technologically exposed." The army, on the other hand, remained in a technological context similar to that of the previous fifteen years. Because of the unsophisticated nature of the equipment manipulated by the army, and due to the postponement and delay of its modernization, the missions the army was expected to fulfill in the framework of the new national defense deployment were much more in the style of the missions it performed before 1960, and as such could be viewed as less integrated with the deterrence logic (see Figure P1.1).

From these observations it can be inferred that the professional and organizational profile of the contemporary military establishment is highly dualistic, sheltering the navy and the air force, closely modeled along the force-in-being pattern, and the army, still resembling the classic mass armed forces system.

This basic paradigm constitutes the theoretical background of the following reflections about some aspects of the organizational, professional, and social dimensions that we have considered most relevant to this descriptive study of the post–World War II French military establishment.

Figure P1.1. Armed Forces in the Defense Structure and Their Levels of Exposure to Technological Change

Nature of the Defense Deployment	Nature of the Systems of Forces	Relative Participatory Weight of Each Service in Relation to the Various Levels of Defense Deployment			Level of Exposure to Technological Modernization
		Army	Navy	Air Force	
Strategic Nuclear Level	Strategic Nuclear Force	Support and Surveillance	Oceanic Strategic Force	Aerial Strategic Force	High
Tactical Level	Tactical Nuclear Force	Pluton Regiments	Fleet Air Arm	Aerial Tactical Force	High/Medium
Conventional Level	Forces of Maneuver / Forces of Security / Forces of Presence and Intervention	Divisional units and general reserves	Multipurpose maritime forces and maritime defense forces	Aerial defense forces and air transport	Medium
					Low

PART TWO ● THE ORGANIZATIONAL DIMENSION OF THE FRENCH MILITARY ESTABLISHMENT

INTRODUCTION

In their organizational aspects, macrosociological studies dealing with long-term changes that have affected Western military institutions over the last centuries have focused upon a number of variables such as the size of the armed forces, the level of citizen participation, and the nature of the internal military structure. The classic mass army model, which typified the military institution that developed at the end of the nineteenth century, was defined as an organization centering on full-fledged military participation by the citizenry, with a large number of effectives that could be further expanded in time of war by national mobilization, performing rather standardized tasks, and depending on career personnel for the training and administration of the mobilized forces. It is in reference to these variables that recent change affecting Western military organizations, usually referred to as the decline of the mass army, has been assessed.[1] More specifically, this mutation can be characterized at the manpower level by a decrease in overall personnel strength (more acute in the army than in the other services), an attenuation of fluctuations in the number of effectives between times of peace and crisis, and a stabilization of the global volume of forces. At the level of national mobilization this change took the form of a decrease in the degree of popular participation in the military and in military mobilization capabilities, both in times of peace and war, a reduction of the citizen's active and reserve duties, an increasing selectivity in conscription, and an increasing differentiation of the citizen's service. At the structural level a growing heterogeneity and complexity in the internal division of labor within the organization, as shown by the continuing median inflation of the rank structure, the change in occupational distribution between line, staff, and technician personnel, and the increasing recruitment of civilian and female personnel, reflected this mutation.

It is noticeable that in regard to previous trends born during the transformation of neofeudal military institutions into mass armed forces, and the latter's subsequent evolution, the two first characteristics mark a reversal in trends, whereas the third constitutes a continuation, rather an accentuation, of the previous tendency.

It is in regard to these sets of features and to the transformation they underwent that this analysis of the changing organizational dimensions of the French military establishment over the last three decades will be conducted. The first chapter focuses on the evolution of the size of the French armed forces, and then on the changes in the nature of the internal division of labor, mainly through a study of the rank structure. The next chapter concerns itself with the important question of citizen mobilization and participation in the military, with, given its historical centrality in France, a special emphasis on conscription.

Notes

1. For an earlier discussion of these changes, *see* Morris Janowitz, "The Decline of the Mass-Army," *Military Review* 50 (1972): 10–16. This article was followed by a series of papers seeking to develop the theoretical basis of this mutation and to assess, with precision, its nature, scope, and organizational consequences; *see*, in particular, Morris Janowitz, "The All-Volunteer Force as a Socio-Political Problem," *Social Problems* 22 (1975): 432–49; Jacques Van Doorn, "The Decline of the Mass Army in the West: General Reflections," *Armed Forces and Society* 1 (1975): 147–58; and G. David Curry, "A Comparative Analysis of Military Institutions in Developed Nations" (Ph.D. dissertation, University of Chicago, 1976).

CHAPTER FOUR ● MANPOWER AND ORGANIZATION

Trends in Manpower

In order to identify accurately the recent phases of the evolution in the size pattern of the French armed forces and to determine their nature and scope, it seems appropriate to place this question in a framework of long-term perspective and to examine the various phases through which this pattern has evolved in the past.

Long-term Trends prior to World War II

In broad diachronic perspective, including the two and a half centuries preceding World War II, two characteristics concerning the size of the French military establishment emerge with clarity. As Figure 4.1 shows, there was an increasingly erratic pattern of fluctuation in military manpower between times of peace and times of war, especially after the second half of the nineteenth century. Concealed behind these oscillations was a steady increase in the overall personnel strength of the military.

A cursory observation of the evolution of the size of the French military indicates that the differences between peacetime and wartime strength during the seventeenth, eighteenth, and the beginning of the nineteenth century were definitely less pronounced than that characterizing later periods. Under Louis XIV, peacetime effectives in corrected figures[1] averaged around 130,000 men yearly and wartime effectives around 200,000 to 270,000 men. In 1672, on the eve of the war with Holland, the army numbered roughly 110,000 men; in 1674, when the war was at its height, the army had about 190,000 men. During the War of the Spanish Succession, 1701–13, the annual strength was probably raised to between 260,000 and 280,000 men. Of these, 120,000 to 140,000 were among the effectives at the start of the hostilities. There was an estimated yearly recruitment of about 52,000 men for replacement and manpower increase. In the course of the war, the king sought nearly 655,000 men: 167,000 for the infantry, the artillery, and light troops, 28,860 for the cavalry, and 455,000 for replacement (foreign units being included).[2]

Figure 4.1. Fluctuations in Military Manpower, 1600–1945

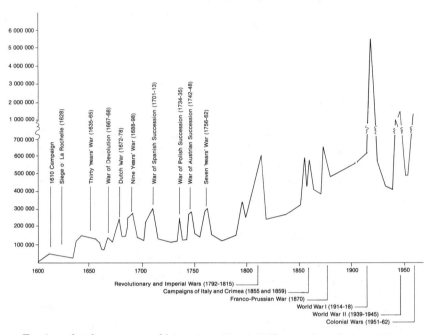

During the first years of his reign, Louis XV completed the military reforms undertaken by his grandfather. There was also a slight decline in personnel strength: in 1717, peacetime effectives numbered 110,000 men. Later, however, the number of effectives increased again: 125,000 men in 1738; 145,000 in 1763. As for wartime manpower, it followed a similar rising and falling pattern. But it never surpassed the size reached during Louis XIV's reign. In corrected figures, the annual average number of wartime troops rose to 250,000 men (in 1735) during the War of Polish Succession (1734–35), to 264,571 (in 1746) during the War of the Austrian Succession (1742–48), and to 290,000 (in 1760) during the Seven Years' War (1756–62). The yearly level of mobilization for replacement and manpower increase was 42,500 between 1734 and 1735, 49,285 between 1742 and 1748, and 40,000 between 1756 and 1762.[3]

During the wars following the Revolution, the army shifted from a peacetime strength of 150,000 men in 1792 to a wartime strength of 350,000 in 1794. It was during the Napoleonic era that fluctuations became important: 350,000 men in 1800; 400,000 in 1805; and 600,000 in 1812. However, the level of mobilization, as pointed out by Gustave Vallée, was never as high as it could have been or was generally believed to be.[4] Between 1799 and 1806, only 35 percent of the eligible men were called up. Between 1806 and 1810, the figure fell to 29 percent, and then rose to 41 percent between 1811 and 1813.

Having fallen to an annual average of between 240,000 and 270,000 men under the Restoration, the figure rose to between 300,000 and 350,000 men under the Republic and the Second Empire, and then increased sharply to nearly 600,000 during the war with Italy (588,857 in 1855) and the Crimean War. It fell again to an average of 410,000 during the 1860s (420,850 in 1863; 391,397 in 1866) and then reached a new height of 650,000 men during the Franco-Prussian War.

Then comes a period of large-scale oscillations: from a yearly average of about 570,000 men in the early 1900s (554,219 in 1901; 585,704 in 1909), the figure rose to more than five million men during the war (5,692,000 men in 1917). After World War I, army personnel dropped sharply to 571,000 men in 1923 and then to 426,000 in 1930, only to jump again, on the eve of the defeat of June 1940, to nearly a million men.

This brief overview shows that together with a pattern of increasing fluctuation in manpower between wartime and peacetime, there was a steady overall growth of the average size of the French military. Such an increase correlates with the extension of citizen military participation that materialized after 1870 with the rising universalism and egalitarianism of conscription and with the recourse to full-fledged mobilization in times of war. It was also a result of what has been called the "ratchet effect"; that is to say the inability of the military to return to its prewar personnel strength after mobilization.[5] Figure 4.1 demonstrates that after each conflict except World War I the total manpower of the French armed forces never fell below the premobilization figure.

This changing pattern in the evolution of military effectives mirrored important organizational development. The growth and increasing variations in personnel strength over time clearly indicated the displacement of the old neofeudal, self-contained organization by a mobilization- and conscription-based mass army.

Post–World War II Trends

From 1945 to the early 1960s, the basic characteristics of the evolution in personnel strength observed prior to the war appear to have maintained themselves. Until 1964, for example, oscillations in size were frequent. The global size of the French military establishment fell from 1,200,000 men in 1945 to 490,000 in 1947. Afterwards, it increased again until it reached 1,153,000 men in 1957; in 1959 it fell again to 1,019,400. After a slight increase in 1960–61, when they numbered 1,100,000, the effectives of the French military dropped to 675,439 in 1964. What is remarkable is that the amplitude of the fluctuations was diminishing. And, considering recent evaluations, it appears that the volume of effectives should not, in case of future crisis, fluctuate to a higher level as they would once have; it is likely that French military strength would not increase beyond 900,000 men in a crisis. As for long-term growth, it reversed itself after the end of the 1950s. Between 1957 and 1966, the size of the French armed forces declined to 580,995 men; thereafter it stabilized at an annual average of about 550,000 men. (Computations made on the basis of the budgetary effectives, those in "arms and services" excluding the common services, corroborate these trends, though the peak of the curve was reached in 1959–60. See Figure 4.2.) Let us note in passing that the number of effectives actually continued to decline and that this decrease is likely to go on in the future (a decrease of 30,000 men is called for in the new military program for 1977–82). An effect of stability is created by the relative increase of the gendarmerie.

From the viewpoint of personnel strength, one could thus argue that the format of the French military establishment was entering a new phase in which there was a shift away from the traditional model of the mass armed forces. The fact that the decrease in strength was sharper in the ground forces tends to confirm this hypothesis.

The level of strength at which the size of the military stabilized for a decade and a half would seem to indicate that the organizational format of the armed forces continued to keep some of the features of the mass model. The study of the question of citizen mobilization, which will be undertaken in Chapter 5, will prove this point.

An interservice examination, moreover, reveals that, though its size significantly declined, it is the army that continued to present the mass model characteristics. The two other services, whose strength remained somewhat lower and more stable over time, exhibit the characteristics of the force-in-being format (see Figure 4.3). This dualism will appear with more clarity in the analysis of the internal division of labor and rank structure.

Division of Labor and Rank Structure

Among the various elements related to the structural aspects of the military establishment, the nature of the internal division of labor is

Figure 4.2. Fluctuations in Military Manpower, 1945–76 (in 100,000)

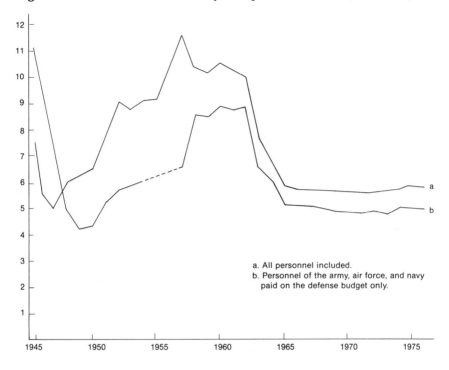

a. All personnel included.
b. Personnel of the army, air force, and navy paid on the defense budget only.

Sources: a) Table C.3 in Appendix C; b) Table C.4 in Appendix C.

Note: The variation in the difference between the two curves is due to changes in the size of the Common Section (not computed in curve b), which are the result of various modifications of the content of this section.

the indicator most commonly referred to; other indicators include the degree of civilianization, ratio of combat to noncombat personnel, and so on.

The nature and the evolution of the division of labor in the military is, from an empirical standpoint, somewhat difficult to assess. However, in the light of various works undertaken on the topic by sociologists concerned with the military and other complex organizations, it appears that the hierarchical structure, or, more specifically, the distribution of personnel throughout this structure, constitutes the most operational variable with respect to such an assessment.

Figure 4.3. Fluctuations in Army, Air Force, and Navy Manpower, 1946–76

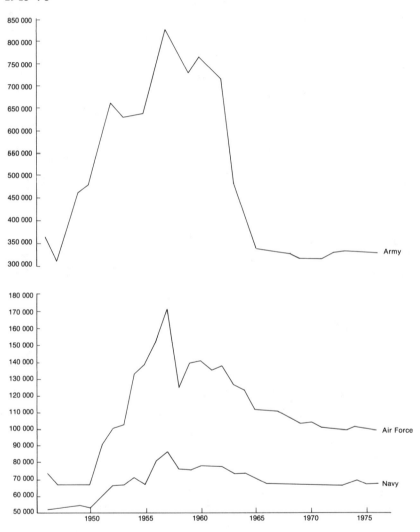

Source: See Table C.3 in Appendix C.

To set up an appropriate frame of reference for the discussion that follows, a few theoretical observations seem in order. Even a casual overview of the organization of the armies that collided with each other on the European battlefields from the sixteenth to the end of the nineteenth centuries reveals the extreme simplicity of their structures. In a way, the main structural characteristic of neofeudal and protomass military organizations was the homogeneity of their internal division of labor, which implied that "the military rank system was a continuous pyramid, with direct and clear cut lines of authority from the top to the bottom."[6] In such an organization, most of the effectives were unskilled or semiqualified men who were expected to execute a number of standardized tasks. These troops were commanded by a small group of officers, the high-ranking stratum being invested with decision-making power, the remainder being given the mission of leading and coordinating the activities of the troops. For centuries, such a pattern of organization was functionally relevant to the type of missions performed by military institutions. Until the end of the nineteenth century, the conduct of war did not require a great deal of specialization. Over time, adequate knowledge and appropriate skills could be acquired through training offered within the framework of the institution. The pace and the amplitude of technological change were such that, in the end, individual accommodation to these changes was always possible. Promotion was based on age and on length of service; it depended only upon natural attrition (retirement or death).

But this type of structure was rapidly modified: first, under the effect of the progressive inflation of effectives (thereby encouraging the creation of new administrative tasks); second, under the effect of an increasing dependency of the entire military upon technical services whose structural format, originally more complex (because of the diversification of roles set up for optimal use of the technological resources at hand), had served as a model for the shaping of the internal organization of the entire military; and third, later, under the effect of the technological modernization in the domain of warfare and of armament. Thus, once standardized tasks grew more and more specialized, diversified, and complex, at the same time demands for unskilled labor declined sharply. Technical and managerial expertise, formerly subordinate to line skills, became crucial to the military. In order to further the execution of such increasingly complex and diversified functions, a new division of labor emerged. This division was all the more significant in that new patterns of promotion (one in which forced attrition replaced natural attrition) set up to cope with recruitment and retention problems and with rising career expectations led to expanding career opportunities for the military personnel. The new division of labor, as a result, had a profound impact on military rank structure. The officer corps and the NCO group were significantly enlarged. In proportion, the number of lower enlisted ranks—now solely made up of those who had not yet completed their training—was reduced. The shape of the officers' and NCOs' organizational structure—traditionally pyramidal—was modified greatly. As Kurt Lang pointed out: "The development of managerial and technical expertise has stimulated a pattern of organizational growth by which the middle ranks have expanded more rapidly than the rest. The grade distribution has had to accommodate to the new roles and specialties that have grown up within the military, many of which have their counterpart in civilian institutions. As a result, the rank structure ceases to be a direct expression of a simple hierarchical authority structure." [7]

In actuality, the formerly monolithic military structure split into a twofold organization. And instead of being articulated around a single pyramid of command with rapidly narrowing echelons, the military institutions patterned under the advanced mass armed force model now had two rank distributions, one for privates and NCOs, a second for officers. Both distributions, given the increasing importance of the roles in the intermediate ranks, followed a diamond-shaped diagram.

Because it entailed the manipulation of highly advanced equipment, in other words, because it was even more dependent on managerial and technical resources than were the mass armed forces, the force-in-being organization was even more greatly affected by the tendencies just described. At the noncommissioned personnel level, the absence of draftees and the possibilities for rapid promotion after basic training (resulting from increasingly lenient recruitment and retention policies) further reduced the basis of the hierarchy and further swelled the intermediate ranks. Interestingly, one notices that with the shift from the advanced form of the mass armed forces model toward the force-in-being pattern, the bulging which affected the median rungs in the organization seemed to move up in the hierarchy, until it reached the lower echelons of the senior officer ranks.

Consequently, the shift from one model of military organization to another resulted in the long-term increase of the internal heterogeneity that was marked by an inflation of the median ranks of the structure of the officer corps, on the one hand, and of the enlistees and NCO corps, on the other. This proclivity was all the more pronounced in those branches and services most highly exposed to technological change.

These observations being made, let us turn our attention to the rank structure of the French military establishment. Given the nature of the time span, one should not expect to see emerging any clearcut manifestations of change such as those described in the preliminary remarks. If the material forms in the structural change that took place during the shift from the neofeudal type of military organization toward the mass armed forces type were tangibly manifest, those relative to the shift from the mass army model to the force-in-being posture were less so, because they were a continuation of the previous trends. Only with the aid of highly sophisticated statistical methods would it be possible to measure these changes. And, though the diachronic dimension of this study is based on three decades, such a time span is too limited, in regards to this kind of change, for structural changes develop gradually over many decades.

Despite this, definite signs of change can be discerned. To help clarify these changes, they will occasionally be placed into a longer diachronic perspective, one going back to the late nineteenth and early twentieth centuries.

General View of the Rank Distribution

A macroanalytical examination of the rank distribution will highlight some of the most conspicuous traits of its evolution. In view of the figures of Table 4.1 regarding the ratio of officers, NCOs, and privates in the structure, the first observation that can be made is that the proportion of privates has declined over time and that of NCOs has risen.

A closer inspection across services, however, reveals a difference between the army, on the one hand, and the air force and the navy, on the other. In the army the proportion of officers, which remained lower than in the two other services, seems also to have followed a more erratic pattern of evolution, whereas it has grown more regularly in the navy and air force. Another difference between the services concerns the NCO group. In the navy and the air force, the size of this group grew faster than it did in the army. Consequently, it constituted a larger share of the modern services.

These data indicate a number of noteworthy preliminary details about the French military establishment's internal structure. The relative stability of the size of the officer corps in the navy and air force, for example, is a sign of the modernization of the organization of

Table 4.1. Percentages of Officers, NCOs, and Privates by Service, 1949–76[a]

	1949	1953	1957	1960	1964	1968	1972	1976
Army								
Officers	6.4	4.7	6.0	4.9	7.4	8.8	6.7	6.0
NCOs	18.7	16.0	19.3	14.8	21.2	20.3	20.0	21.3
Privates	74.9	79.1	74.6	80.2	71.3	70.8	73.3	72.6
Air Force								
Officers	7.5	5.2	5.8	6.2	7.3	7.7	7.7	7.2
NCOs	37.3	26.9	35.2	35.8	41.3	44.9	45.2	46.6
Privates	54.2	67.6	59.0	58.0	51.4	47.3	47.1	46.1
Navy								
Officers	7.0	5.9	5.8	6.3	7.0	7.1	6.8	6.4
NCOs	25.7	26.1	27.2	26.8	29.8	30.1	33.4	39.7
Privates	67.0	67.9	66.9	66.9	63.1	62.8	59.7	53.8

[a]Percentages may not total one hundred percent due to rounding.

these two services; it has been observed that the upper part of the rank distribution is generally stable in advanced, complex bureaucratic institutions. The air force officer corps is exemplary in this regard as the number of officers remained fairly stable between the early 1950s and 1974 (it only varied from 6,400 men in 1954 to 7,300 in 1974) following a sharp increase of from 2,380 to 6,400 men between 1936 and 1954, the period during which the air force was in the process of becoming a complex modern organization.[8] Concomitantly, the enlargement of noncommissioned personnel strength reflects the growing need for managerial and technical skills that characterizes all organizations relying on modern technology.

In contrast, the instability of the army officer corps, particularly until 1960, which incidentally reflected the involvement of this service in the military operations of the colonial wars, and the relatively small size of the NCO group and the large number of privates constitute the main features of an organization usually associated with traditional bureaucratic structures and relying primarily on unskilled or semiskilled labor.

Even in the most advanced organizations, there are a residual number of tasks, hence roles, that do not require any special degree of qualification to be performed. For this reason the number of seamen in the navy remained important. If this situation was less visible in the air force, where the proportion of privates was relatively small, it could be attributed to the use of civilian manpower for these tasks. The navy was less able to rely as heavily upon civilians because many of these tasks had to be performed at sea.

Figure 4.4, presenting a rough rank structure of each service for 1953 and 1972, summarizes the changes that took place over the three decades from 1945 to 1976. These graphs demonstrate that the basic rank distribution of the army, which was modified little over time, presents the shape generally associated with the mass armed forces model—a large base with rapidly dwindling upper rungs. The air force, on the contrary, has a basic structure that has changed considerably: the size of the NCO corps has grown to equal that of the privates. The navy's rank distribution seems to hold an intermediate position between the other two services. A close look, however, shows that

Figure 4.4. Rank Structure of the Military by Service and Category of Personnel, 1953 and 1976

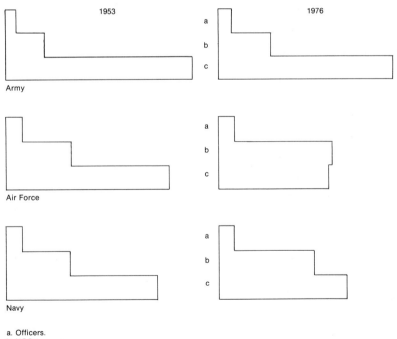

a. Officers.
b. NCOs.
c. Privates.

the navy shared most of the air force's characteristics; these are the characteristics of the force-in-being model.

To complete these observations, a detailed examination of the officer corps rank distribution and of the NCOs' and enlistees' structure is in order.

Rank Structure of the Officer Corps

According to the data in Table 4.2, which gives the percentage of each rank of officers, the proportion of junior officers declined after a series of fluctuations between 1949 and 1960. Seemingly, this was to the advantage of the senior officers, for the proportion of general officers, though varying erratically, did not change significantly.

Read from an interservice perspective, the data point out further differences. First, the navy had the highest and most stable proportion of general officers, the air force the smallest, and the army the most unstable. Yet in every service, the ratio of division generals over brigade generals (vice admirals over rear admirals in the navy) remained the same. Second, the proportion of senior officers was similar in the air force and the army, but was much larger in the navy. Third, although the strength of the junior officer group was higher in the air force than in the other two services, it tended to decline more sharply after 1960. In the long run, the proportion of junior air force officers fell from 87.2 percent in 1926 to 67.7 percent in 1976, to the advantage of senior officers, whose proportionate strength grew from 12.6 percent in 1926 to 31.3 percent in 1976.[9]

A detailed inquiry of the grade evolution of the officer hierarchy would add little of interest, as each rank conforms, more or less, to the overall pattern observed for each main type of officer. In each service, but particularly in the army and the air force, the ranks of major and lieutenant colonel expanded more rapidly than did the average for all senior officers. Among junior officers, the proportion of vessel lieutenants in the navy decreased, whereas that of ensigns, especially first class ensigns, tended to grow. In the air force and the army, the percentage of lieutenants and second lieutenants declined and that of captains grew; yet it is in the air force that the increase in the relative strength of captains was the sharpest.

This evolution is summarized in Figure 4.5. Each bar represents the relative proportion of personnel in the officer hierarchy for the selected years, 1949 and 1976.

Examining these graphs, it is possible to visualize more clearly the differences in the internal structures of the officers corps in each service. Obviously, the hierarchical organization of the technical services became less pyramidal than that of the army, reflecting the lesser exposure of the army to technological modernization. In the air force, the lower ranks of junior officers narrowed considerably, to the advantage of the ranks of captain and major. In the navy, all ranks of junior officers shrunk and the bulging of the hierarchy occurred in the ranks of frigate captain and corvette captain.

It should be added that if, in practice, the two patterns of organizational structure, the mass armed forces model and the force-in-being model, did not appear with as much contrast as might have been expected, given the unequal degree of exposure to modernization between the army and the other two services, this was due to the interaction of additional factors related to in-service specifics that counteracted the expected effects of the exposure to change.

The relatively important size of the general officer group, as well as of the upper rungs of the senior officers in the navy, exemplified a reinforcement of the basic tendency—that is, the sliding up of the bulge in the middle ranks, found in technical services, due to specifically inservice factors. To some extent this was caused by the fact that in the navy, as opposed to the other two services, the total proportion of officers having graduated from a military academy was much higher. Because officers from military academies had a greater chance of reaching the upper echelons of the hierarchy, it was normal that in the navy these ranks were more populated than in the army or in the air force, in which the proportion of officers from the academies was lower.[10] Also, the navy, though technologically developed, remained the prestigious service. Consequently, considerations of status were still important, and promotion to the higher ranks might have been a response to the demand for status satisfaction.

If in the rank structure of the navy the basic trend was reinforced, in the rank structure of the army the basic tendency, the persistence of the pyramidal model, seemed to be counteracted by inservice particularism. If the bulging of middle ranks—captains, majors, and lieutenant colonels—was an expected organizational manifestation in the navy and the air force (due to their being intrinsically technical and modern services and, since 1960, the repositories of advanced nuclear technology), one may wonder why the same phenomenon occurred in the army. To this a number of answers can be proposed. First, for many officers, notably for those who came out of the ranks, and they constitute an important proportion of the officer corps, the grade of major or lieutenant colonel constituted the upper limit of their military career. Given the types of tasks usually performed in the army,

Table 4.2. Rank Structure of the Officer Corps by Service, 1949–76 (percentages) [a]

Rank Distribution		1949		
Army–Air Force	Navy	Army	Air Force	Nav
Division general	Vice admiral	0.3	0.2	0.
Brigade general	Rear admiral	0.6	0.3	0.
Total: General officers		0.9	0.5	1.
Colonel	Vessel captain	3.3	1.6	3.
Lieutenant colonel	Frigate captain	5.0	3.8	8.
Major	Corvette captain	14.0	10.8	15.
Total: Senior officers		22.3	16.2	27.
Captain	Vessel lieutenant	30.6	29.5	36.
Lieutenant	Ensign, 1st class	36.6	18.4	28.
2nd Lieutenant	Ensign, 2nd class	9.6	35.4	7.
Total: Junior officers		76.8	83.3	71

Rank Distribution		1964		
Army–Air Force	Navy	Army	Air Force	Na
Division general	Vice admiral	0.2	0.1	0
Brigade general	Rear admiral	0.5	0.4	0
Total: General officers		0.7	0.5	1
Colonel	Vessel captain	3.4	2.3	3
Lieutenant colonel	Frigate captain	5.8	5.0	8
Major	Corvette captain	16.6	13.3	1
Total: Senior officers		25.8	20.6	28
Captain	Vessel lieutenant	36.8	37.5	29
Lieutenant	Ensign, 1st class	36.7	41.4	2
2nd Lieutenant	Ensign, 2nd class	—	—	18
Total: Junior officers		73.5	78.9	7

Source: These percentages have been calculated on the basis of the *effectifs budgétai* *moyens* published in the appendix on national defense in the annual *Loi de finance*. computations were made on the basis of the effectives in "arms and services," chap 31–11 and 31–12, that is, on the basis of all personnel actually in active duty and p by the national defense budget. For more detail see Table C.3 in Appendix C.

[a] Percentages may not total one hundred percent due to rounding.

	1953			1957			1960	
Army	Air Force	Navy	Army	Air Force	Navy	Army	Air Force	Navy
0.3	0.2	0.5	0.2	0.2	0.5	0.2	0.2	0.2
0.5	0.3	0.9	0.5	0.4	0.9	0.4	0.3	0.5
0.8	0.5	1.4	0.7	0.6	1.4	0.6	0.5	0.7
3.4	2.4	4.4	2.9	2.2	4.5	2.7	1.7	2.8
5.3	5.4	9.4	4.9	4.9	9.8	4.5	4.1	7.5
14.1	14.7	15.9	13.8	13.6	15.0	11.6	11.4	14.8
22.8	22.5	29.7	21.7	20.7	29.3	18.8	17.2	25.1
31.7	38.5	34.4	34.4	38.6	34.9	33.3	35.9	30.0
34.7	38.4	25.9	43.1	40.1	26.8	47.3	46.5	24.6
—	—	8.6	—	—	8.2	—	—	19.4
76.4	76.9	68.9	77.5	78.7	68.9	80.6	82.4	74.0

	1968			1972			1976	
Army	Air Force	Navy	Army	Air Force	Navy	Army	Air Force	Navy
0.2	0.2	0.4	0.3	0.2	0.3	0.3	0.2	0.3
0.5	0.5	0.7	0.6	0.5	0.8	0.6	0.5	0.8
0.7	0.7	1.1	0.9	0.7	1.1	0.9	0.7	1.1
3.6	2.4	3.8	4.1	3.2	4.4	4.2	3.6	4.7
5.0	5.3	9.2	6.8	6.7	10.5	7.0	7.7	11.1
17.3	13.7	16.5	18.5	16.7	17.3	18.9	17.8	18.3
25.9	21.4	29.5	29.4	26.6	32.2	30.1	29.1	34.1
37.7	38.4	30.5	33.6	35.2	30.8	34.0	35.3	32.2
34.7	27.6	22.4	36.0	25.8	21.9	35.0	26.8	24.1
—	11.9	16.5	—	11.7	14.0	—	8.1	8.4
72.4	77.9	69.4	69.6	72.7	66.7	69.0	70.2	64.7

Figure 4.5. Rank Structure of the Army, Air Force, and Navy Officer Corps, 1949 and 1976

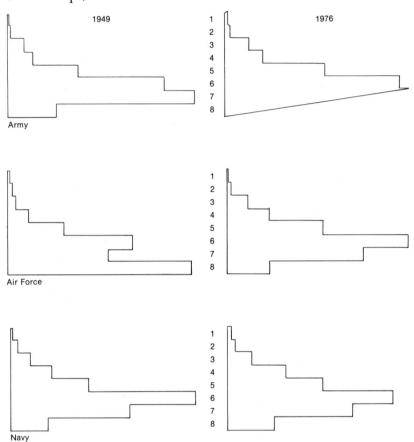

1) Division general/Vice admiral, 2) Brigadier general/Rear admiral, 3) Colonel/ Vessel captain, 4) Lieutenant colonel/Frigate captain, 5) Major/Corvette captain, 6) Captain/Vessel lieutenant, 7) Lieutenant/Ensign, 1st class, 8) Second lieutenant/ Ensign, 2nd class.

the skills of these officers were less transferable to the civilian labor market than were those of their naval and air force colleagues; hence army majors and lieutenant colonels tended to stay in the service longer, waiting until they could retire with full advantages and benefits.

Second, the increasing proportion of army majors, lieutenant colonels, and, more recently, colonels was also a sequel to the dynamics of commissioning that took place during the colonial wars. In effect, because these conflicts, like all types of subversive and guerrilla warfare, were fought by younger soldiers, it was necessary to call for a larger number of lieutenants as soon as the Indochinese War began. It was not a coincidence that this war was sometimes called the "lieutenants' war." The Algerian engagement only accelerated the process. The rather high increase in the proportion of lieutenants between 1953 and 1960, from 44.7 percent to 47.3 percent, confirmed this trend. Thus the lieutenants and the captains of the Indochinese swamps became the captains and majors of the Algerian *djebels*, where they were joined by more lieutenants. Between 1957 and 1964 the proportion of captains shifted from 34 to 37 percent. After the colonial wars ended, these still-young officers had to be assured a decent career. It was then these lieutenants and captains who enlarged the ranks of senior officers after 1964.

And finally, if there were not more clearcut distinctions between the officer corps of the army and of the navy and the air force, despite the intrinsic and deep differences between these services, it is essentially because the officer corps rank structure is less reflective of such differences, like variations in exposure to technological change. This is a current phenomenon in contemporary organizations. In many large-scale modern bureaucracies, especially those in which modern and traditional organizations coexist, there is a tendency toward structural uniformity of the hierarchical distributions, particularly at the highest levels.

The following study of the noncommissioned personnel rank structure will help to further illustrate the dichotomous nature of the internal division of labor in the French military establishment.

Rank Structure of Noncommissioned Personnel

Table 4.3 helps analyze the second organizational subgroup in the military institution. It is readily apparent that, over time, the proportion of NCOs increased, while that of privates dropped significantly. This was a result of the growing managerial complexity of the organizational structure of noncommissioned personnel. Again, important differences between services emerge upon closer examination of the data. From an interservice standpoint, it appears that in the technical services—the navy and air force—the middle ranks of the NCO/private hierarchical distribution, notably junior NCOs and corporals, were more highly developed than in the army. In these services, this section of the structure tended to grow over time whereas the contrary seemed to be the tendency in the army.

There were two small, but noteworthy, differences between the rank structures of the air force NCO/private group and that of the naval petty officer/seaman group. In the navy, the proportion of senior NCOs was narrow, from two to three times smaller than in the air force, yet the proportion of quartermasters was somewhat larger than the proportion of corporals in the air force. Also, if in both services the proportion of privates was relatively equal, one notices that in the air force the number of second class privates, the lowest military rank, was much higher than that of first class privates. In the navy, the opposite was true, particularly after 1964, when the number of third and second class seamen dropped, to the advantage of first class seamen.

The differences between the army and the two technical services are all the more conspicuous when the inspection is made in a diachronic perspective. The series of bar graphs in Figure 4.6 illustrate that over the last thirty years there has been little change in the army NCO/private organization, whereas that of the navy petty officer/seaman and of the air force NCO/private have been modified considerably. In the army, the only noticeable change is a slight decrease in the dispersion of the hierarchical pyramid with a significant enlargement in the proportion of senior NCOs. But the ratio between the strength of contiguous ranks did not fluctuate much. On the whole, the rank structure of each category has kept the traditional pyramidal shape.

In the navy and the air force, the situation is radically different. As early as 1949 definite signs of median bulging had appeared and after 1960 became particularly important. In each main personnel category, the upper ranks increased at the expense of the lower, to the point that the latter grew relatively smaller than the former, contributing to strengthening the flasklike silhouette of the overall rank structure.

Consequently, in comparison to the situation found in the officer corps, interservice discrepancies in the NCO/private organizational structure were more pronounced and reflected more acutely the differences in the level of exposure to technological modernization. Most of the various aberrant characteristics occurring in the evolution of the rank structure, aberrant with regard to the expected pattern, are again the result of particularities indigenous to each service that interfered with the effect of technological modernization. In the army, for example, two of these abnormalities were the swelling of the senior NCO population and, after 1960, the thinning out of the pyramid above the rank of private. Such a pattern of growth was the consequence of circumstances related to colonial wars and to the nature of the rate of enlistment and retention in the service. Overall, the pattern of enlistment throughout the three decades under study shows a large increase during a period roughly corresponding to involvement in colonial conflicts, followed by a steady decline. This reversal in the rate of enlistments caused the thinning out of the structure of noncommissioned personnel, for after 1962 the bulk of those who enlisted during the wars were promoted up the ladder without being replaced by a similar inflow of enlistees. And because of their contribution to the wars, which created a need to insure them with a regular army career, and because of their rapid promotion to the upper ranks, coupled with the poor civilian transferability of their skills, there was little possibility for their moving outside of the structure of the military institution. This dynamic was reinforced by the decline in the retention rate of enlistees. One notes, for example, that, probably because of their heightened sensitivity to the relative deterioration of enlistee conditions of service, marked by precariousness of status, slow promotion, financial insecurity, and so on, the younger and often the more capable enlistees were led to leave the service sooner than anticipated. After 1968, the average length of service for an NCO had dropped by two years, falling to a low of eight and a half years in the early 1970s. This explains the narrowing of the noncommissioned personnel structure at the upper levels of the junior NCO ranks. Those who remained in the military, being too old or unqualified to find a job in the civilian labor force or to be selected for promotion in the officer corps, were promoted to senior NCOs; these ranks were thus swollen by those who stayed in the military until they reached retirement.

Some of the small anomalies in the NCO/private rank structure of the air force and navy can be explained similarly. For instance, the apparently narrow overhead in noncommissioned naval personnel is simply due to the fact that promotion in the navy is slower than in the other services. Hence, the increase of enlistment noted before 1960 has not yet resulted in the enlargement of these ranks. As shown by the graph of the naval noncommissioned personnel in Figure 4.6, such an enlargement took place at the lower echelons among junior

Table 4.3. Rank Structure of Enlisted Personnel by Service, 1949–76 (percentages)[a]

Rank Distribution Army–Air Force	Navy	Army	1949 Air Force	Nav
Officer cadet	Midshipman	—	8.2	—
Chief Adjutant	*Maître principal*	2.6		0.
Adjutant		2.9	8.2	3.
total: Senior NCOs		5.5	16.4	3.
Sergeant major	*Maître*	1.1	—	7.
Chief sergeant	*Second-maître*, 1st class	4.1	11.9	6.
Sergeant	*Second-maître*, 2nd class	9.2	11.9	9.
total: Junior NCOs		14.4	23.8	23
Chief corporal	*Quartier-maître*, 1st class	6.0	3.9	12
Corporal	*Quartier-maître*, 2nd class	11.5	7.7	13.
total: Corporals		17.5	11.6	26
Private, 1st class	Seaman, 1st class	13.2	48.1	6
Private, 2nd class	Seaman, 2nd class	49.3		18
	Seaman, 3rd class	—	—	21
total: Privates		62.5	48.1	45

Rank Distribution Army–Air Force	Navy	Army	1964 Air Force	Na
Officer cadet	Midshipman	0.3	5.7	
Chief adjutant	*Maître principal*	3.4		
Adjutant		3.8	6.8	
total: Senior NCOs		7.5	12.5	
Sergeant major	*Maître*	1.5	—	1
Chief sergeant	*Second-maître*, 1st class	4.5	12.8	
Sergeant	*Second-maître*, 2nd class	9.4	19.3	
total: Junior NCOs		15.4	32.1	2
Chief corporal	*Quartier-maître*, 1st class	5.3	5.4	
Corporal	*Quartier-maître*, 2nd class	10.3	6.6	
total: Corporals		15.6	12.0	2
Private, 1st class	Seaman, 1st class	11.0	43.3	
Private, 2nd class	Seaman, 2nd class	50.5		
	Seaman, 3rd class	—	—	
total: Privates		61.5	43.3	

Source: see Table 4.2.
[a]Percentages may not total one hundred percent due to rounding.

rmy	1953 Air Force	Navy	Army	1957 Air Force	Navy	Army	1960 Air Force	Navy
0.8	5.6	—	0.7	5.6	—	0.4	5.1	1.0
1.9		0.8	2.8		1.0	1.8	—	—
2.4	4.3	3.4	3.2	4.5	3.5	2.1	4.6	3.5
5.1	9.9	4.2	6.7	10.1	4.5	4.3	9.7	4.5
1.0	—	7.3	1.4	—	6.9	0.9	—	7.2
2.8	5.6	7.0	4.0	6.9	7.4	3.7	7.2	7.4
8.0	12.8	9.3	8.4	20.4	9.9	6.5	21.3	9.4
1.8	18.4	23.6	13.8	27.2	24.2	11.1	28.5	24.0
5.3	5.1	12.4	6.2	6.1	12.8	8.3	5.5	11.9
0.3	10.2	15.5	11.5	7.8	14.9	15.6	6.6	16.0
5.6	15.3	27.9	17.7	13.9	27.7	23.9	12.1	27.9
3.0	56.4	6.3	13.1	48.8	—	16.1	49.7	7.9
4.4		19.5	48.5		43.4	44.2		23.2
—	—	18.3	—	—	—	—	—	12.5
7.4	56.4	44.1	61.6	48.8	43.4	60.3	49.7	43.6

my	1968 Air Force	Navy	Army	1972 Air Force	Navy	Army	1976 Air Force	Navy
.7	0.6	0.2	1.1	0.8	0.8	1.2	1.2	1.3
.8	6.2	1.5	3.7	7.4	2.2	3.8	8.1	4.3
.2	7.4	4.7	4.1	8.4	4.8	4.6	9.5	8.3
.7	14.2	6.4	8.9	16.6	7.8	9.6	18.8	13.9
.0	—	10.9	0.7	—	9.9	—	—	13.8
.3	14.0	7.8	4.1	13.7	10.9	4.5	13.2	14.6
.2	20.5	7.3	7.8	18.7	6.9	8.3	18.3	
.5	34.5	26.0	12.6	32.4	27.7	12.8	31.5	28.4
.5	5.1	15.1	6.8	4.1	12.7	7.3	4.3	7.7
.4	7.0	11.9	11.9	7.5	11.8	11.7	7.0	11.4
9	12.1	27.0	18.7	11.6	24.5	19.0	11.3	19.1
9	8.4	30.3	7.1	8.9	29.8	6.7	9.5	28.6
9	30.7	10.2	52.7	30.4	10.1	51.5	28.7	9.8
-	—	—	—	—	—	—	—	—
8	39.1	40.5	59.8	39.3	29.9	58.2	38.2	38.4

Figure 4.6. Rank Structure of the Army, Air Force, and Navy Enlisted Personnel, 1949 and 1976

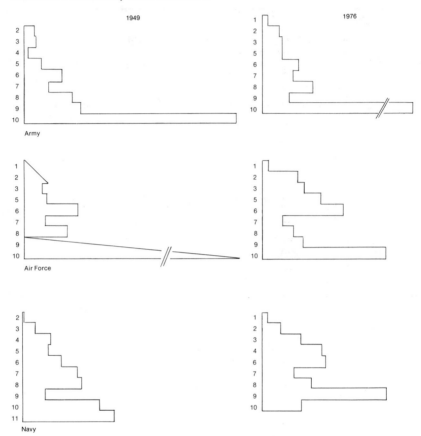

1) Officer cadet/Midshipman, 2) Chief adjutant/*Maître-principal* (Master chief P.O.), 3) Adjutant/*Premier-maître* (Master chief P.O.), 4) Sergeant major/*Maître* (Senior chief P.O.), 5) Chief sergeant/*Second-maître*, 1st class (Chief P.O.), 6) Sergeant/*Second-maître*, 2nd class (P.O., 1st class), 7) Chief corporal/*Quartier maître*, 1st class (P.O., 2nd class), 8) *Quartier maître*, 2nd class (P.O., 3rd class), 9) Private, 1st class/Seaman, 1st class, 10) Private, 2nd class/Seaman, 2nd class, 11) Seaman, 3rd class.

NCOs. Besides, this narrowness in the senior ranks of naval petty officers was compensated by the importance of the proportion of second class ensigns in the officer corps.

In the air force, the only unexpected aspect in the development of the structure of noncommissioned personnel was the large number of privates. This was due to the fact that, of the two technical services, the air force was the only one to absorb a significant proportion of draftees, who, given the declining length of service time and thus a decreased chance of receiving an adequate training, had less and less opportunity to rise above the rank of corporal. Between 1960 and 1976, the relative strength of drafted personnel reached 37.5 percent of the air force manpower; at the same time, this strength constituted only 25 percent of the naval effectives. As for the general inflation occurring at the level of senior NCO rank, it was the result of a tendency common to any complex organization whose overhead continually expands. But it was also the result of the rapid promotion policy practiced by the air force: by offering brighter career prospects, the air force hoped to retain in the service its best young NCOs, who might otherwise be tempted by more attractive opportunities in civilian life.

Such are the observations that can be made about the internal division of labor in the French military, looking at the evolution of its rank structure. A more extensive picture could certainly have been obtained, notably from the viewpoint of internal differentiation, had changes in the various categories of personnel been examined. Such an assessment is usually approached through an evaluation of the ratio of combat to noncombat personnel. This ratio, in effect, offers a complementary, interesting indication with respect to a functional definition of the nature of the division of labor and beyond it to the nature of the organizational format of the military. In the context of classic models of military organizations, such as the mass army, the military archetype has been the combat soldier and his superior, the heroic leader. All personnel engaged in noncombat functions were subsidiary. In the modern forms of military institutions, the reverse situation can be observed. As in the marketplace of industrial societies, tertiary activities in the armed forces have developed and the specialist has precedence over the warrior. The competence of the specialist is exercised over a great number of tasks. To a great extent, it is upon him rather than upon the line soldier that the outcome of the battle depends, for the efficacy of the military essentially relies upon technological rather than upon human resources.[11] Moreover, the rise of deterrence strategy reinforced this trend as deterrence is the antithesis of combat at the same time that its credibility is intrinsically bound to the immediate availability of sophisticated armament.

Unfortunately, in the case of the French military, such information is not readily available across services. The various entries that can be found in budgetary documents, the main source for statistical material, cannot be utilized for such a purpose since they correspond to classifications of a purely budgetary nature and have no functional or organizational significance. One also has to be content with a rather ill-assorted set of data. Yet these tend to confirm our previous observation about the organizational dichotomy that emerged from an analysis of the rank structure. For example, the functional distribution of noncommissioned personnel in the army followed the old "arms and services" pattern centering on specifically military-oriented tasks or on various duties related to the maintenance of the premises, the daily life and work, as well as the control of nonprofessional personnel. This indicates a rather homogenous division of labor, one in which multiskilled ability prevailed over technical specialization, a pattern common to less technologically advanced organizations. In the air force and the navy, on the contrary, the distribution of personnel, which was articulated upon a wide range of technical specialties, mostly of an industrial and managerial nature with a direct equivalent in the civilian labor market, suggested the kind of division of labor found in most modern complex organizations. The case of the air force officer corps, for which systematic statistical evidence exists, illustrates further the decreasing importance of the combat soldier in comparison to the so-called specialist and the growing complexity of the internal division of labor. This latter trend materialized at several levels: first, in the growth of the number of categories of officers; second, in the growth of those categories removed from combat functions; and third, in the increase of personnel employed in these latter capacities. Among the five categories of officers that emerged after 1935 (there had been only three before)—the corps of flying officers, officer engineers, officer managers and accountants of the administrative services, air base personnel, and *commissaires*—only the first can be considered combat oriented. The proportion of flying officers decreased after 1933, from 90 to 70 percent (1940) to a stable average of 41 percent (after 1954). Meanwhile, the proportion of officer engineers shifted from 7 percent in 1933 to 34 percent after 1954, and that of officers involved in administrative and other managerial tasks from 3 percent in 1933 to 33 percent after 1954. (See Table 4.4) [12]

These facts about the air force officer corps confirm the tendency of

Table 4.4. Occupational Structure of the Air Force Officer Corps, 1924–74

Year	Total Officers	Flying Officers		Engineering Officers		Administrative Officers		Other	
		Number	Percentage	Number	Percentage	Number	Percentage	Number	Percentage
1924	1,660	1,413	85.1	27	1.6	107	6.4	113	6.8
1933	2,003	1,804	90.2	143	7.1	53	2.6	3	—
1939	2,763	1,939	70.2	347	12.6	477	17.3	—	—
1948	5,197	2,277	43.8	1,358	26.1	1,562	30.1	—	—
1954	6,390	2,645	41.4	1,634	25.6	2,091	32.7	20	0.3
1962	7,019	2,770	39.5	1,828	26.0	2,420	34.5	—	—
1968	7,361	2,927	39.8	1,935	26.3	2,499	33.9	—	—
1974	7,269	2,965	40.8	1,831	25.2	2,473	34.0	—	—

Source: Gaxie, "Morphologie de l'Armée de l'Air," p. 43.

this service toward organizational complexity. The internal division of labor also indicates that it was as early as the beginning of the 1950s that the air force began to take the shape of what is regarded as a modern advanced organization.

To conclude, there was a clear distinction between the organizational structure of the army, on the one hand, and the air force and the navy, on the other, at both the level of the officer corps and of the NCO/private rank structure. The structural organization of the army corresponded most closely to the ideal pyramidal structure usually associated with the traditional mass military organization. The structure of the navy and the air force clearly stemmed from a more advanced model of the type found in all organizations exposed to highly technological modernization.

Notes

1. Given the questionable validity of the official figures for effectives in the armies of the *ancien régime*, it was necessary to adjust their value in order to obtain figures that are closer to reality. It was a custom among officers of that time to deliberately falsify reports on personnel strength given to army inspectors and comptrollers. Moreover, the figures often included effectives not physically present, such as disabled soldiers, noncombatants, and foreigners. The peacetime strength, by contrast, is a fairly agreed upon figure, and it has thus been possible, using the adjusted evaluation of mobilized effectives for replacement and manpower increases, to estimate with some degree of accuracy the wartime strength.

2. These estimates were made by André Corvisier in his major work, *L'Armée française de la fin du XVIIᵉ siècle au ministère Choiseul: le soldat*, 2 vols. (Paris: Presses Universitaires de France, 1964), pp. 157–58, based on his own computation and upon Lt.-Col. Belhomme's estimates in *Histoire de l'infanterie en France*, volume 3 (Paris, 1893–1902).

3. Corvisier, *L'Armée française de la fin du XVIIᵉ siècle au ministère Choiseul*, pp. 157–58.

4. Gustave Vallée, *En marge de l'épopée: population et conscription, 1798–1814* (Rodez: Imprimerie P. Carrère, 1939), pp. 10–12.

5. The term is from Bruce Russet, *What Price Vigilance: The Burden of National Defense* (New Haven: Yale University Press, 1970). *See also* G. David Curry, "A Comparative Analysis of Military Institutions in Developed Nations" (Ph.D. dissertation, University of Chicago, 1976), pp. 16–20.

6. Morris Janowitz and Roger Little, *Sociology and the Military Establishment* (New York: Russell Sage Foundation, 1965), p. 35.

7. Kurt Lang, "Technology and the

Career Management in the Military Establishment," in *The New Military: Changing Patterns of Organization*, edited by Morris Janowitz (New York: John Wiley, 1967), p. 67.

8. D. Gaxie, "Morphologie de l'Armée de l'Air: les officiers (1924–1976)," in *Recueil d'articles et d'études*, edited by Service historique de l'Armée de l'Air (Vincennes, 1977), p. 39.

9. Ibid, p. 50.

10. On this point, *see* Chapter 8.

11. Harold Wool, *The Military Specialist: Skilled Manpower for the Armed Forces* (Baltimore: The Johns Hopkins Press, 1968); Kurt Lang "Trends in Military Occupational Structure and Their Political Implications," *Journal of Political and Military Sociology* 1 (1973): 1–18.

12. Gaxie, "Morphologie de l'Armée de l'Air," p. 50.

CHAPTER FIVE ● CITIZEN
PARTICIPATION IN THE MILITARY

Inspired by the principle of the nation in arms that systematized the revolutionary idea of *levée en masse*, the mass armed forces model that typified the French military was based upon the availability of citizens for participation in the defense of the nation. This participation, which took place through conscription in times of peace and through mobilization in times of war, was made operational by the institutionalization of a system of obligations that linked the citizen to the service of the state for a period encompassing most of his adult life. The historical development of the mass armed forces, which can be measured by the degree of universalism of conscription and by the importance of reserve forces available for mobilization, was thus correlated with the extension of the military obligations of the citizen. Originating with the great military laws promulgated after the Revolution, first the Gouvion Saint-Cyr, Soult, and Niel Laws, then the Laws of 1872, 1889, and 1905, this evolution, which culminated with the legislative reforms of the 1920s, followed a new path after World War II.

Citizen Military Participation in Transition

Until the early 1960s, the theory and the practice of military manpower organization closely followed the prewar pattern derived from the classic mass armed forces model. Conscription and reserve systems remained the crux of the military organization. An analysis of reforms related to the armed forces clearly shows the concerns of legislators to carry on the historic tradition of the nation in arms. The law of November 1950,[1] for example, reiterating principles already defined by a March 1928 law, reconfirmed the perenniality of universal and egalitarian military service, the length of which was fixed at eighteen months. But compulsory military service was only one aspect of citizen participation in the military. Reserve duty was the other. Besides the active service, the French citizen was liable for three years of active reserve duty, followed by sixteen years in the first line reserve and then eight years in the regular reserve. As before World War II, the French citizen's military duty extended over a period of twenty-eight years—that is, until the age of fifty. After that he could still be called up for nonmilitary defense duties until he reached the age of sixty. The frequent reliance on reserve forces until 1962 (in the second half of the 1950s, more than 220,000 men were called up to "beef up" the French forces in Algeria), the fairly high degree of egalitarianism and universalism of citizen participation in the military as evidenced by the extremely low rate of exemption from active service (see Table 5.1), and the increase of the length of active service from eighteen to twenty-four and then to thirty months after 1957 show the extent to which the classic model of the mass armed forces was being put into application.

However, judged by emerging trends in the pattern of citizen military participation, through both conscription and mobilization, the old model of military organization was greatly modified after the early 1960s and there was a drift away from the traditional mobilization-based armed forces. Legislation and its subsequent effects on conscription and reserve military power are explicit in this respect. Al-

Table 5.1. Exemptions and Deferments by the Conseil de Révision, 1955–64

Year	Population Examined	Number Exempted	Percentage Exempted	Number of Deferments	Percentage of Deferments
1955	293,217	13,632	4.64	21,674	7.41
1956	320,751	18,214	5.65	25,195	7.86
1957	312,056	15,642	5.01	34,638	11.10
1958	285,254	10,468	3.66	36,745	12.89
1959	312,902	13,526	4.32	39,589	13.65
1960	278,576	11,828	4.24	34,952	12.55
1961	262,654	8,800	3.35	35,693	13.60
1962	288,832	8,983	3.11	48,893	16.91
1963	309,017	9,677	3.13	58,817	19.04
1964	298,010	8,927	3.00	62,580	21.00
Total	2,961,269	119,062	4.04	398,776	13.46

Source: Claude Vimont and Jacques Baudot, "Etude des caractéristiques sanitaires et sociales des jeunes du contingent," *Population* 18 (1963): 517 and 523.
Note: The Conseil de révision, a sort of selection council, was the first phase in the selection of future draftees. Until 1971, the time at which it was abolished, the *conseil*, meeting in the chief town of every district, made a preliminary selection of those who were not fit to bear arms as well as of those qualifying for student deferments. Those declared by the *conseil* as "fit for service" were called up to selection centers (created in 1954 as mobile centers, there are now eleven throughout the territory) several years later. All personnel data of the future draftees, who are intensively examined and tested, are collected in these centers. Before 1954, this second screening was undertaken directly after induction into the military. In general, 80 percent of the selective process took place during the first step. Since 1971, the entire selection process takes place in the eleven centers during what is called "*les trois jours*." (Actually, the selection procedure lasts only one and a half days.)

though the ordinance of 7 January 1959 did not affect the global reach of the French citizen's duties, it did cut, for the first time, the duration of his military obligation.[2] By 1959, the length of these military duties had been reduced to seventeen years: sixteen months in active service, three and a half years in the active reserve, and twelve years in the regular reserve. The law of 9 July 1965 did not greatly alter these measures, but the laws of 9 July 1970 and 10 June 1971 further shortened the duration of military service;[3] henceforth the citizen's military obligation ended at the age of thirty-five.[4] Table 5.2 sums up this evolution in the reduction of military obligations in France.

A more extensive examination also reveals a reduction of duties relative to active service, concomitantly with a modification of the nature of these duties. Fixed at twenty-four months during the Algerian War, the length of active military service was reduced to eighteen months in March 1963, and then to sixteen months by the Law of 9 July 1965.[5] After 1967, although there was no formal reduction, the National Assembly passed an amendment, proposed by the National Defense Commission, authorizing the government to discharge a fraction of the contingent four months before the normal expiration of their obligation. Finally, with the law of 9 July 1970, active military service was cut to twelve months, one of the shortest periods of service in Europe.

The adulteration of the universal and egalitarian character of conscription was another indication of the decline of this institution in France and, beyond that, of the mass army model. To some extent, the introduction of legal status for conscientious objectors on 20 December 1963 was the first element of change, symbolic perhaps, yet significant, as conscientious objection had been outlawed in France since the Restoration.[6] But it was after 1965 that the most tangible changes appeared. The introduction into the framework of the so-called national service, through the ordinance of January 1959 and the

Table 5.2. Length of Military Obligations of the French Citizen, 1950–75

Year of Reform	Active Military Service (months)	Active Military Reserve (years)	Regular Military Reserve (years)	Age Limit for Military Service	Age Limit for National Defense Duty
November 1950	18	3.0	23.5	48	60
January 1959	18	3.5	14.0	37	60
July 1965	16	3.6	13.5	37	60
June 1971	12	4.0	13.0	35	50

law of July 1965, of three alternative forms of paramilitary and non-military active service—the services of defense, technical aid, and cooperation—contributed to the erosion of the universal nature of conscription.[7] The deterioration of the egalitarian character of con-scription, a second crucial aspect of the classic conception of military duty in the context of the mass army by which a socially isomorphic segment of the population is represented in the military, was another element of change. The laws of July 1965 first instituted a reform whereby new categories of individuals—those whose father, mother, brother, or sister had died for the *patrie* or in the line of military duty, those who supported a family, and those residing in a foreign country or holding dual citizenship—could be exempted from ser-vice.[8] This reform resulted in a greater number of disqualifications from active service, formerly limited to medical disabilities. Between 1967 and 1969, the number of exemptions for social or familial reasons tripled; after 1969, it climbed from 15,000 to almost 25,000 per year. By the mid-1970s the annual average of dispensations had reached 7 percent. Even at the level of medical exemptions, where the criteria for disqualification were more objective, exemptions multiplied steadily. And the discrepancy between the level of exemptions practiced and the actual rate of morbidity was such that the principle of egalitarian-ism was on the point of losing its significance. In 1960 barely 8 per-cent of the draft-liable youth were granted exemptions; this percent-age rose to 20.5 in 1965, and to almost 25 in 1976.[9] The deferment policy followed after 1967, until it was abandoned in 1973, also in-creased the degree of selectivity of conscription. After the decree of 25 January 1967 was passed, conditions for granting student deferments, already lenient, were further liberalized.[10] Whereas only 8 percent of the contingent had benefited from deferments in 1950, in 1966, that proportion rose to 26 percent. In 1970, there was a total of 351,000 de-ferments (115,000 for 1970, plus 236,000 from earlier periods). At such a rate, there would have been 466,000 deferments in 1977 had not deferments been suppressed.[11]

Thus, within the course of a dozen years, conscription cloaked the forms of a selective and differentiated military service. As a result, the level of citizen participation in the military was considerably af-fected. In 1975, only 4.8 percent of the male population aged between eighteen and forty-five was under arms; fifteen years before that, al-most 14 percent of the male population had served in the armed forces. The change in the Military Participation Ratio (MPR)—used here as the percentage of people involved with the military in pro-portion to the total labor force—after 1960 illustrates this trend: the

MPR fell from 5.4 in 1958 (one of the highest levels in Europe) to 2.9 in 1966 and 2.5 in the mid-1970s. Historical and national comparisons show that the level of the mid-1970s MPR was almost the same as the figure relative to the time preceding the development of the mass armed forces and that it was practically equal to the figure found in the United States (2.48 in 1973; 2.20 in 1976) where the all-volunteer force format had been in effect for several years.

Furthermore, with the decline of citizen participation, the principle of mobilization, which was at the heart of the organizational logic of the mass armed forces, lost a great deal of its importance. The global volume of the reserve force sharply decreased because the age liable to be called for military service (both active and reserve) fell from fifty to thirty-five and the number of exemptions from active service increased. And all personnel called up in the services of defense, technical aid, and cooperation were excused from reserve duty. In addition, because of a reduction in the length of time served and because of reductions of the military positions in which draftees served, conscription played a lesser role in the military training of the citizen. Consequently, conscription had little effect on the preparation of qualified reserve personnel capable of serving efficiently in a military force that operated in a milieu, given the rapidity of technological change, of constant modification. In part this explains why the navy and the air force would, in case of emergency, mobilize only a small reserve. Even in the army, which apparently continued to operate according to the tradition of mobilization, changes were noticeable. The constraints imposed by the updating of reserve training and the problems raised by their integration, for example, made unfeasible any mass mobilization plan. Mobilization became more selective and, despite recent reforms seeking to revitalize the mobilizable reserve, it has become more so. How could it be otherwise with training periods whose sole objective was simply to crank up the mechanics of mobilization and which were limited to a few days (two for the infantry, five or six for the technical branches) every two or three years? Army mobilization capacities illustrated the degree of selectivity of this institution. According to one estimate, in the early 1970s the army could have mobilized only a quarter of the number of men who were mobilized in 1939.[12] The number of men liable for recall in the mid-1970s was only 340,000 from an instructed reserve pool of nearly four million men.[13] A comparative analysis clearly shows that the French case seemed closer to the force-in-being model as it existed in the United Kingdom or in the United States than to the classic mobilization-based organizations found in Israel, Yugoslavia, Switzerland, and even Germany, in which the part played by reserve forces in case of mobilization would have been significantly higher than 50 percent.[14]

Thus the decline of citizen military participation and of the centrality of mobilization, and the reduction and the selectivity of conscription were further critical elements in the accentuation of the force-in-being nature of the French military system.

The Perenniality of Conscription

A closer and more careful analysis of the French military organization, however, sheds some light on the limitation of these trends and on the persistence of mass army sequels in the contemporary military establishment. Let us briefly examine this point and look at a few instances.

First, to a certain extent, one is tempted to say that the classic mobilizing pattern traditionally at work in the mass armies was preserved in the case of France, at least in principle. Even though the total length of a citizen's military obligations was reduced from twenty-eight to seventeen years, he was still liable to be called for reserve duties in the service of defense until he reached the age of fifty. It must be stressed that, though the tasks to be performed were essentially of a nonmilitary nature, they were an inseparable part of national defense. Thus, the mobilized citizen was subject to the control and the authority of the military establishment. All personnel linked to the service of defense were in every respect considered as military, and any lapse from regulations, duties, or discipline was punished according to military standards. In a way, therefore, the authority of the military remained pervasive and covered the entire reserve force —that is, all men from the age of eighteen to fifty.[15]

But this is not the main point. One may argue that what is important is not so much the scope of military authority as the size of the mobilizable and administrable reserve force, which, as noted, was smaller than it had been. The format of the conscripted force and the nature of active military service appeared to be the tangible elements of the remnant of mass army features in the French military. Although the proportion of draftees who entered the military decreased slightly (it has evolved from 70 percent in the immediate postwar era to 55 percent in 1976: 65 percent in the army alone), in the long run their visibility remained relatively important.[16] During the last ten years, statistical evidence highlights not only the importance of the representation of draftees in the composition of French military manpower but also its stability (see Table 5.3). Furthermore, contrary to what is usually thought, the presence of conscripted personnel in the three main services and in the various systems of forces constituting French defense deployment was never negligible, even in those services, such as the Nuclear Strategic Force, in which one might have expected a lower number of draftees given the high level of technological sophistication at which they operate (see Table 5.4). It is interesting that draftees were not only assigned to the fulfillment of housekeeping or *valet d'arme* tasks. According to official figures, in the army four out of five draftees served in combat formations and direct support units; in 1974 this amounted to 171,371 men (80.5 percent of the contingent).[17] Later, and perhaps more accurate, figures placed 74 percent of the manpower in combat and direct support units, 16 percent in the infrastructure, and 10 percent in military schools.[18]

In addition, the extent of the development of new forms of active paramilitary or nonmilitary services and the development of selectivity in the regular military service, both of which alter the principle of universalism, on the one hand, and that of egalitarianism, on the other, as generally practiced in a military organization of a mass army nature, was surprisingly limited. For example, from 1963 until April 1965 only 4,879 men served in the technical aid and cooperation services; during this time, 8,724 posts were available—that is, 56 percent of the posts offered were filled and an average of less than 1 percent of the contingent served in these posts.[19] In 1975, of the more than

Table 5.3. French Military Manpower, 1968–76

	1968	1969	1970	1971
Army (total)	330,421	323,727	323,653	322,16
% draftee	63.2	64.1	64.0	63.4
Air force (total)	107,584	104,380	104,332	102,21
% draftee	37.0	36.3	36.2	37.0
Navy (total)	68,998	68,320	68,440	67,96
% draftee	23.6	23.8	23.5	24.0
Armed forces (total)	507,003	496,427	496,425	492,3
% draftee	52.3	52.7	53.0	52.5

Source: These figures were computed from the annual decrees on the budgetary eff tives of the military personnel of the armed forces (*Décret portant répartition des effecti budgétaires du personnel militaire des armées*) published by the *Journal officiel*.

410,000 men liable for military duty, only 9,000, that is, 2.1 percent, served in the technical aid (0.5 percent), the cooperation (1.4 percent), and the defense (0.2 percent) services.[20] Though the trend was upward, military service per se still constituted the essential component of national service.[21] A similar observation can be made about the increasing level of exemptions from service, for when "relativized" (taking into account additional factors and using a comparative perspective) this increase was, in the end, limited. And regarded in the light of the meteoric rise in size of the annual draft-liable age group from 257,790 men in 1961 to 307,700 in 1965 and to 430,000 in 1976, the level of selectivity was not as high as it appeared at first.[22] Besides, the trend in selectivity actually seemed to stabilize from 1968 to 1975: the yearly rate of service disqualifications remained between 23 and 26 percent. And yet, with the draft-reduction reforms, the annual volume of draftees incorporated was maintained at a slightly higher level than before these reforms, as it had grown from 210,000 men a year in 1970 to nearly 290,000 men in 1975. Although the level of mobilization had reached 3.8 per thousand under the law of eighteen months, under the law of one year it grew to 6.2 per thousand. Finally, the abolition of deferments, though revived in 1973 in milder form,[23] can be perceived as an attempt to restore the equal liability of all for military duty and to end what could be considered a nondemocratic means of selection.

A brief examination of the legislative background of recruitment

1972	1973	1974	1975	1976
26,982	331,617	338,459	331,522	331,495
64.3	65.0	65.3	65.2	65.1
1,175	100,966	104,983	102,078	101,606
38.0	38.1	37.0	37.9	38.1
7,833	68,382	70,267	68,315	68,273
24.0	24.0	25.0	24.1	24.1
5,990	500,065	513,709	501,915	501,374
53.4	54.0	54.4	54.1	54.1

Table 5.4. Proportion of Draftees in the "Systems of Forces," 1976

		Forces of Maneuver		
	Strategic Nuclear Force (1974)	Battle Corps (Army)	Tactical Squadron (Air Force)	High Se? Fleet (Navy)
Percentage	32.5	69.7	38.1	27
Number	18,714	115,000	14,060	8,425

policy during the 1960s and early 1970s reveals that the maintenance of conscription, more precisely, the maintenance of the military service's principles of universality and egalitarianism, was always at the forefront of the legislators' preoccupations when reform became necessary; at no time was the question of actually ending universal military service discussed.[24] For example, the creation of the complex policy that substituted the national service for the narrower military service was conceived of by many as a device to preserve the tradition of universal and egalitarian conscription. The new forms of service were seen as ways to absorb excess draftees who, for technical and budgetary reasons, could no longer be inducted into the military without having to increase the disqualification rate to a level that would have contributed to the belief that a selective service was being organized.[25] It is interesting that the number of assignments in the alternative services always remained limited, almost as if it was felt that their use should not be abused. This is not completely coincidental, if, as discussed, the actual number of assignments in those services remained lower than the number of positions available. Besides, to reestablish some kind of equality, as the burden of serving in the alternative services was somewhat lighter, the length of duty was always higher, from sixteen to twenty-four months. Returning to the topic of the degree of selectivity and completing this exercise in "fact relativization," one should realize, as a matter of synchronic comparison, that a few years before the draft was terminated in the United States the exemption rate was more than 50 percent—at least 40 percent on medical grounds. Throughout the 1960s, the exemption rate in Italy also averaged around 50 percent, 35 percent on medical grounds and 15 percent on social grounds. In the Netherlands it was 60 percent, in Belgium, 50 percent, and in West Germany, 44 percent. Even some Eastern European countries had exemption levels higher than

Forces of Security		
Army	Air Force	Navy
34.1	64	24
9,000	53,220	12,450

France's: for example, 37 percent in the USSR and 60 percent in Poland.[26]

If other evidence were necessary to show France's prudence in reforming her conscription policies and her care in limiting alterations of the classic format and principle of universal military service, the study of conscientious objection would shed further light on the subject. It could be argued that the fact that conscientious objection was finally recognized indicated a diminishing concern for universal conscription; but this does not seem to have been the case. First, the idea and the project of conscientious objection status were admitted with considerable hesitation and not until the end of 1963; such a status had already been in existence for at least four decades in most European countries. Actually, the main motivation guiding both the formulation and the vote on the bill was primarily humanitarian and aimed at introducing greater justice in conscientious objectors' penal treatment, which, until this time, had been astonishingly brutal: they were treated as common offenders.[27] But, on the whole, not very much changed. The status voted in December 1963 remained a legislation *d'exception* essentially directed toward deterring conscientious objection actions.[28] In addition to facing a complex procedure for obtaining this classification and to fulfilling a very restricted list of conditions for eligibility, the conscientious objector, after being legally recognized, had to serve in special assignments for twice as long as active military service would have involved. After the 1963 decree, very little was done to further liberalize the conditions of the conscientious objector or to lessen the exceptionalness and the rigidity of his status. Indeed, with the promulgation of the decree of 17 August 1962, also known as the Decree of Brégançon, instigated by Michel Debré, there was a stiffening of the conditions of service of the conscientious objector.[29] And, although the number of conscientious objectors increased in absolute numbers after 1964, it stayed very small: between January 1964 and February 1970, only 1,053 requests were submitted for approval; that amounted to a yearly average of 170. After that there was a slight increase, from 190 in 1970 to 221 in 1971. Considered in the light of the increasing size of the annual age-sets, such a growth had very little significance—nothing comparable, at any rate, to the German figures: in Germany the number of conscientious objectors grew from 5,963 in 1967 to 33,792 in 1972, the level at which it then stabilized.[30]

In conclusion, the contemporary French military establishment a decade and a half after World War II was no longer the archetype of the mass army model. However, there is no doubt that it still exhibited some of the characteristics by which such a model is recognized. Reliance on universal conscription as a source of manpower procurement, one of the most tangible and persistent of the mass army features, continued even after 1970. After all, France, which in 1975 was ranked fourteenth in size of population (52,590,000 inhabitants) and thirty-fourth in surface area (212,659 square miles) among the world's nations, was one of the largest military powers, behind only the Soviet Union, the United States, China, and India (and today perhaps also behind South Korea and Iran). In contrast, Germany, with a population of ten million more inhabitants, had a military organization smaller than the French by some 100,000 men. Among Western European nations, France had the greatest concentration of manpower, a concentration that seemed higher than that of the United States and the Soviet Union.

Until the 1960s, a military organization espousing the contours of the traditional mass army structure could be justified by the technical circumstances created by the type of missions with which the French military was charged, the style of warfare (colonial involvement) it practiced, and by the state of permanent premobilization created by the cold war. Indeed, given the nature of strategic and technological changes the military underwent and the advent of peaceful coexistence and detente between the superpowers and their allies, it is astonishing that so many traditional characteristics persisted. Certainly the reorganization of national defense along the line of nuclear deterrence strategy and the renouncement of further imperial commitments, at least in the classical style of colonial hegemony, were factors that called for a smaller and more highly technological force. And in regard to the objectives and the system of deployment (the strategy of territorial sanctuarization in vogue until June 1976)[31] of French national defense, the massive profile of the Forces of Maneuver and Intervention, for example, became questionable. It seems certain that, even if one did not staunchly adhere to the radical strategy of the type developed by General Gallois, who went so far as to refute the usefulness of any system of forces operating below the nuclear level,[32] the format under which these forces were supposed to intervene was perhaps neither the best nor the most operative; adversaries of what has come to be known as the strategy of the *gros bataillons* grew more numerous every day. One should point out, for instance, that although in theory four out of five men called up to serve in the army were assigned to combat units or direct logistic services, more than 50 percent of the contingent ended up, whether in combat units or not, in overstaffed and overcrowded nonmilitary assignments.[33] With such swollen infrastructures and with the heavy and complex system of incorporation imposed by the existence of conscription, it was estimated that the operational efficiency of most army units barely reached 50 percent.

Yet universal conscription remained the privileged formula for manpower procurement in France; in the National Assembly, partisans of an all-volunteer force, such as Alexandre Sanguinetti and Aymeric Simon-Lorrière, or of a quasi-volunteer force, such as General Stehlin, received no support.[34] Only a few years ago, in a discussion before the National Assembly on the defense budget, one could still hear the defense minister, quoting Jean Jaurès, end his speech by saying, "Gentlemen, a conclusion imposes itself: the only possible solution is a conscript-army based upon universal military service." He went on to announce his decision to set up, for 1974 and 1975, a plan to improve the democratic nature of the military service: "First of all, I want to make the national service more just. To do so, I plan to reinforce its egalitarian and universal character."[35]

At this juncture, therefore, the question that naturally comes to mind is why compulsory universal conscription was continuously utilized in France. The first response can be derived from the general observations made in the first part of this analysis. Unequal exposure to technological modernization, particularly low in the army, delayed the evolution from the mass armed forces posture toward the force-in-being model; hence some features of the earlier model remained. This explanation, though partly true, is incomplete. Perhaps it explains why conscription was maintained in the army as the army was the service that, from 1960 to the mid-1970s, had the least exposure to technological modernization. Yet conscription, though to a lesser extent, also existed in the technologically advanced navy and air force. In 1976, draftees made up 32.5 percent of the manpower contingent in the Strategic Nuclear Force. Other factors, therefore, must be taken into account to understand the retention of universal conscription.

Conscription and Economic Constraints

As the study of the oral and written rhetoric which adorns the conscription-related legislative corpus shows, the reasons invoked to justify the existence of the universal draft in France tended, in general, to feed on a system of syllogisms derived directly from the revolutionary ideology that, besides claiming that mass participation in national defense was the only guarantee of its credibility and efficiency, linked the popular bearing of arms, citizenship, and democracy into a very special relationship.[36] In this respect, the pages in the White Book concerning military service or on *le service national* in the colorful brochure put out by the public relations service of the armed forces (SIRPA) are illuminating. "The maintenance of conscription remains the essential pledge of the efficiency of our dissuasion."[37] Elsewhere, formulas like "the brewing of the social origins, professions, and regional backgrounds," "fundamental solidarities," and "the knotting of durable friendships" praised the functions of social integration performed by the service, which are also seen as a source of social mobility and democratization favoring the underprivileged. For example: "Indeed, the armed forces have neither the vocation nor the means to substitute themselves for National Education and for Employment Services, but they intervene in a man's life in such a way that they play an important role in the area of social promotion. They are in a position to start useful educational projects of professional reconversion, they can even play the role of 'revealer' to the advantage of those that misfortune or the rigors of a sometimes unjust industrial society bring to the service too little equipped to face the life ahead."[38]

However, in addition to the bona fide revolutionary convictions of the partisans of conscription, there is no doubt that beyond the shadow of this Jacobin phraseology, more pragmatic factors committing the French political class to the retention of the draft were at work.

The first and most rational explanation for the keeping of universal conscription that comes to mind is the economic one. It is also the most frequently proposed argument. "The military service is a great economic saving for the nation," declared General Vanbremeersch, then army underchief of staff, in a television interview.[39] Stated in other words, the conscript army was considered a preferable format of military organization simply because it was cheaper than any other, particularly an all-volunteer force. Great Britain, for example, with a force structure smaller by 200,000 men than that of France, spent almost 2 percent more of its gross national product on the military. Though not often discussed, analysis of the accounts of parliamentary commissions for national defense reveals that the economic considerations were not totally ignored: many evaluations proving that volunteer or quasi-volunteer systems would make the burden of defense significantly heavier were made.[40] Therefore the cost of a conscript army, simply because it was a form of manpower procurement that escaped the law of the labor market, as compared with the costs of an all-volunteer or quasi-volunteer force capable of performing equivalent defense functions, was the least expensive system of recruitment. And studying the budget figures, it is indeed difficult to see how France could possibly have abandoned conscription without an enormous financial effort. Recent estimates show that for the army alone the cost increase, computed on the basis of a strength similar to the current model, would evolve from $2.75 billion with one year of service, to $2.87 billion with an eight-month military service, to $3.09 billion with six-month service, and finally to $3.4 billion for an all-volunteer army.[41] Completing these observations, data in Table 5.5 provide further estimates of the cost of a 470,000 man all-volunteer armed force compared to a 500,000 man conscript-based armed force.

But, to be completely accurate, these estimates should actually be doubled, if not tripled. They ought to take into consideration the costs necessary for increasing the inflow of personnel, in other words, for increasing the level of enlistments and reenlistments. In effect, according to most evaluations, an all-volunteer force similar in size to the existing pattern would call for a yearly enlistment inflow of 95,000 men for the three services (75,000 for the army alone), and a quasi-volunteer force, an enlistment inflow of 60,000 men (47,000 for the army).[42] Considering the average rate of enlistment of the fifteen years from 1960 to 1975 (around 25,000 men) and the exceptional paucity of reenlistments, a policy demanding an annual rate three to five times higher than the previous one would obviously presuppose a very large increase in national defense spending. In reality, such an effort would have to be all the greater since the military would have to match an increasingly competitive civilian labor market for the recruitment of qualified personnel. Should unskilled and semiqualified personnel be hired, the military would have to spend more on initial training, technical formation, and equipment. In addition, whatever the alternative chosen, salaries, fringe benefits, retirement compensa-

Table 5.5. Comparative Costs of All-Volunteer and Conscript
Armed Forces in Dollars (5F = $1)

| | | All-Volunteer (470,000 Men) | |
	Strength	Cost per Capita	Overall Cost (in Millions of
Officers	32,000	22,430	720
NCOs (drafted)	135,000	14,270	1,920
Chief-corporals	30,000	9,860	300
Privates (drafted)	273,000	5,760	1,630
Total	470,000		4,570

Source: "Conscription ou armée de métier," p. 16.

tion, and the like would necessarily have to be improved, since, in the context of widespread welfare and declining poverty, the social groups with low economic expectations that had previously served in the military tended to disappear.

According to official estimates, in order to increase the flow of enlistments to 83,000 men a year, it would be necessary to raise salaries well above the minimum wage, to $400 a month; to pay a substantial enlistment bonus of $2,000; and to ensure professional training at the end of the service period, estimated at $2,000 per person. The total cost would run to $5.5 billion, nearly $2 billion more than the cost for the conscripted armed forces.[43]

Given the economic circumstances of the last two decades, such a policy could hardly have been implemented. Since the early 1960s, France, like all industrial welfare states, has been faced with the classic dilemma of rising domestic demands for a greater share of the national revenues in a context of limited available resources.[44] Such a predicament resulted in a reduction of all expenditures perceived as either nonproductive or irrelevant to immediate public expectations. In the context of the post-colonial war period ending the French imperial role, and in the context of growing international détente, there was little justification for high military expenditures. This explains

| | Conscript Armed Forces (500,000 Men) | |
| | Cost per Capita | Overall Cost (in Millions of $) |
strength		
32,000	22,430	720
123,000	14,270	1,800
12,000	3,760	
20,000	9,860	200
45,000	5,100	230
68,000	3,000	800
00,000		3,750

why the level of national defense spending as a share of the GNP and of public expenditures consistently declined during the 1960s and 1970s (see Table 3.1). In addition, because of the Fifth Republic's commitment to a strategy of nuclear deterrence and subsequently to the operational development of an independent atomic force, there was very little possibility of channeling funds from capital-equipment expenditures (see Table 3.3) to personnel costs that could help increase the number of enlistments should an all-volunteer force formula be adopted. Since 1970, those transfers of funds which have been realized through a deemphasis on capital expenditures have been absorbed to compensate for inflation, deteriorating material conditions, and the financial status of career personnel.[45] Hence, given the volume of resources available for national defense and the priorities reserved for nuclear development, conscription was, from the standpoint of marginal economic thinking, the best form of manpower procurement. As one author pointed out, conscription, in the end, makes possible a higher volume of expenditures on equipment than does an all-volunteer force.[46]

At this point, however, one wonders to what extent the economic factor, often presented as the rationale behind the maintenance of conscription in France, was a determining element. It seems somewhat questionable to consider conscription as the cheapest form of manpower recruitment available. Conscription appeared inexpensive only by comparison with the cost of an all-volunteer or a quasi-volunteer force of the same size and same organizational pattern as the conscript army, irrespective of whether such a pattern was the best possible for the objectives that the French national defense tried to achieve. In other words, if evaluated in a cost-efficiency perspective rather than in a cost-benefit analysis—the latter is the framework within which the problem is usually approached—there is no valid proof that a conscript army was the most economical form of military organization. Twenty years ago a conscript army was an economical military organization even from the viewpoint of cost efficiency. The mass conscript army, in effect, was functionally adapted to the types of objectives that the French military establishment was required to attain. The military tasks related to the NATO defense commitment, defined, it will be recalled, on the basis of a cross-national division of military labor in which the French army was mainly confined to infantrylike missions, as well as the tasks related to colonial engagements were both compatible with a large conventional military organization in which manpower was more important than equipment and technology. But after 1960, and one need not be a great strategist to realize this, the military deployment resulting from the new military objectives and patterns of threat perception, on the one hand, and the strategic and technological means devised to achieve these objectives, on the other, were completely different from what they had been. And even though conventional missions, especially below the nuclear level, remained to be performed, such missions could be performed by a smaller military establishment whose cost could be lowered should conscription be used on a selective level, as, on a universal basis, the manpower resources would necessarily exceed the need, or would presuppose a great deal of structural modification. This would have meant that the marginal advantage gained by employing conscripted manpower would have been lost in the accommodation of a great number of men and in an organizational expansion that would have added nothing to overall efficiency; it might even have jeopardized it.

But this is only one side of the argument. The other is that the intrinsic cost of conscripted personnel increased considerably. Undoubtedly, compulsory enrollment always permitted recruitment of manpower for a lower price than that existing on the national labor market, yet the price to be paid during the decades following the 1950s could not, obviously, be that paid during earlier periods. Accommodated in spartan quarters and offered cartons of Gauloises, the *quart de place* in transportation, and a ludicrous monthly allowance, the conscript of the past cost the military little more than what was spent for strictly military purposes. Later, however, mainly because of the changes taking place in the social structure and because of the aspirations of new generations of draftees, such austere conditions became intolerable.

In the last twenty years, the drafted population shifted from a predominantly rural and semiliterate base to a predominantly educated and urbanized one. The proportion of draftees with a high school education quadrupled (from 10 to 40 percent); the proportion of those holding baccalaureates and university degrees increased from 6 to 25 percent. The social structure of the draftees also altered significantly as a result of the change that affected the French community. Between 1954 and 1975, the population of urban areas (towns with more than 25,000 inhabitants) increased tremendously: in 1975, for example, the concentration of population in towns with more than 50,000 inhabitants reached 25,200,112 people, and 29,359,406, that is, 56.1 percent of the population, lived in urban centers with more than 20,000 inhabitants.[47] At the same time, the proportion of rural-oriented occupations in the French population fell from 26.7 to 10.1 percent. And the concentration of laborers, employees, and small entrepreneurs rose from 50 to 66.2 percent. The volume of the secondary and the tertiary sectors changed significantly (from 36.2 to 39.1 percent for the secondary sector and from 36.4 to 50.8 percent for the tertiary).[48] At every level of society the standard of living improved considerably and the level of socioeconomic expectation was consequently enhanced. Thus, not only were a greater number of draftees educated men, but also a greater number came from milieus with high expectations or from milieus that had recently been involved in intensive actions for the improvement of their well-being.[49] It was obvious that new generations of draftees would not accept the conditions under which their predecessors had lived, conditions that, it should be mentioned, tended to worsen with every passing day. After all, twenty years earlier the barracks had been twenty years younger, and to many the lack of central heating and private showers had not been important. The five dollars per month, a few cigarettes, and a liquor discount at the *foyer du soldat* no longer satisfied the basic expectations of even the most patriotic recruit. Therefore, it became necessary to improve the living and economic conditions of draftees. Between 1960 and 1975, the draftee's pay rose significantly: representing less than 20 percent of the minimum wage in 1960, it rose to nearly 37 percent by 1975. Although the draftee's allowance remained appallingly low ($1.30 per day in 1976—very low compared to what draftees in other European military institutions received), the overall cost of such increases was enormous. Every increase also implied a readjustment of the entire salary scale above the rank of private. The April 1975 raise cost the state 400 million francs, about $96 million.[50] Between 1965 and 1975 the per capita annual cost of drafted personnel grew from $1,200 to almost $3,100.[51]

One could further multiply the arguments about the relative importance of the budgetary weight of conscription, notably by mentioning its "hidden costs." For example, it could be said that conscript manpower constituted a labor force whose potential productivity was kept out of the economic market. In actuality, conscript manpower was an economic strain on the labor market: being low-salaried, conscripts were in almost every case economically dependent on their relatives. A smaller, all-volunteer force would perhaps have reduced all these inconveniences. The volunteer, receiving a normal salary, would not have been dependent on other sources of support for a living. And, entering the military establishment for a longer period of time, the volunteer's training costs would have been lower and more easily redeemable. Conscripted personnel, consequently, could no longer be realistically considered as a cheap labor force. And, based on a universal and egalitarian military service, the conscript armed forces probably cost almost as much as an all-volunteer force capable of the same performance.

However, if the cost of an all-volunteer force is evaluated, as is often the case, on the basis of a force structure similar to that obtained with the use of the universal draft, there is indeed a sizable difference in cost between the two models. But comparisons made in such a manner, though common, have little validity. In many ways, former defense minister Pierre Messmer, a new partisan of the all-volunteer model, was correct when he argued that proliferation of effectives does not add to the capacity of the military institution; on the contrary, their weight can be seriously detrimental.[52]

In short, the economic factor is a variable that must be taken into account when explaining the maintenance of the conscript military organization even after 1960. Though the price of conscription increased tremendously, especially when computed on a cost-efficiency basis, the draft-based armed force remained somewhat less expensive than an all-volunteer force. But, especially after 1960, in contrast to earlier periods, the economic factor no longer weighed enough to be assigned a conspicuous causal priority with respect to France's reliance on the draft system. More significant causes are to be sought elsewhere.

Conscription and the Left

If, despite strategic, technical, and even economic problems, universal conscription was continued, this was probably for political purposes. One is actually tempted to insist on the importance of such reasons. Indeed, in a political context that was increasingly animated by what can be called, for our purposes, a Left and Right polarization, and in the light of the French political tradition, in which the military had always been an important component of the political stakes fought for by rival factions, such a hypothesis seems to be well founded. More specifically, one could suggest that the widespread support for conscription shown by the French political community was perhaps linked to the fact that each side of this community saw the defense of conscription as a device to promote its respective political objectives and to secure existing achievements from reciprocal encroachments.

For clarity, one could say that the French political community's commitment to the maintenance of the draft was due to the cumulative effect of two distinct currents of thought that roughly corresponded to those of the ideologies of the Right and the Left. The attitude of the Left, however, appeared to be the more crucial; therefore, it will be the central focus of the discussion. As far as the Right was concerned, though many variations of the argument existed, its basic reason for continuing to support the draft lay in the fact that the draft performed a useful function of socialization. Conscription was considered as a vestibule agency through which the acculturation of the youth into the values of the liberal bourgeois democracy was accomplished. This, it should be noted, was not the view of nineteenth-century rightist political philosophy, which tended to consider military service as a means to "put a gun on the shoulder of every Socialist." The contemporary conservative approach, also guided by political concerns, developed much later, at a time when the Right, forced to admit conscription as a military necessity, became aware of the nationalist logic of conscription and of its subsequent usefulness in undermining the influence of internationalist and socialist ideologies. This feeling was still an important part of conservative political thinking, which conceived of military service as an instrument for eradicating various leftist influences and philosophies considered unrealistic and tendentious. To be precise, from a conservative point of view, the function of military service was not primarily aimed toward the socialization of the conscript-citizen to a specific set of values (as was generally argued by leftist critics); rather, it was by shaping the individual and by accustoming him to respect authority that the military served to prevent the eventual development of contentious tendencies after the conscript returned to the civil community. In other words, the role of military service was to inure the citizen and enable him to face and accept necessary hardship upon his return to civilian life. Military service was viewed as a school of social maturation. Any content analysis of the motivations that guided Gaullist defense ministers in their conscription reforms—here the name of Michel Debré naturally comes to mind—would reveal the importance of such a conception.[53] Moreover, it appears that in response to what the bourgeoisie in general tended to consider a crisis of civilization and an era of disintegration of traditional values the role of military service became, for the conservatives, all the more important since other agencies of socialization no longer seemed successful in propagating traditional norms and styles of social behavior among the younger generations. For example, in a conservative newspaper, one could read that the army must be a substitute for family and religion, which were failing in their obligations to bring the necessary moral and civil nourishment to French youth.[54]

Besides this widely shared belief in the integrating and maturing function of conscription and in its role as a means of perpetuating a particular model of social status quo, the Right's commitment to the principle of universal conscription was also based on more pragmatic considerations. It is possible that universal military service was maintained for the simple reason that it fulfilled a set of socioeconomic regulatory functions that remedied converging socioeconomic disequilibria that would ultimately have constituted a source of discontent with the existing ruling majority. It is difficult to show much evidence on this point and avoid being speculative. But there is no doubt that the maintenance of universal conscription helped prevent an excessive flooding of the economic market and concomitantly held down the unemployment rate. For a ruling party whose legitimacy was being increasingly threatened, both in and out of the institutional arena, in a society where political and social struggles tended to polarize rapidly, the control of an important part of the active population under military law was an advantageous means of social control. In a sense, universal military service was, for the class exercising power, an important device of economic and social stabilization, as well as of political engineering.[55]

Despite all this, the Right never had a particularly strong sociological and ideological attachment to the idea of universal conscription. The Right, viewing conscription as a commodity rather than a principle, was more accommodating to the idea of a volunteer military establishment than was the Left. Therefore, in regard to any explanatory model concerning the existence of conscription during the 1960s and 1970s, the attitude of the Right did not constitute the paramount variable that the leftist adherence to the draft did.

For the Right, military service seemed to be an appropriate political device for the endurance and stabilization of a social system in which it had vested interests. However, for the Left, universal conscription was an element of the guarantee by which the political and social domination of the bourgeois ruling class could be limited and the rights and interests of the working class protected. It was also interpreted as an institution through which military adventurism could be controlled if not avoided. The Left's commitment to the principle of universal conscription was thus less inspired by the intrinsic quality of conscription, as was the case for the Right, than by the perceived dangers of an all-volunteer force.

Though the nature of the leftist defense of conscription thus appears ambivalent, it was not, for all that, weak. Because of this particularism and because the Left in France became a political force of great importance after World War II, the nature of leftist opposition to an all-volunteer force model deserves to be discussed in more detail.

Opposition to the all-volunteer force and subsequent support for the conscript-army model have long been notorious elements in the development of the Left's sociopolitical thought and praxis. In 1866, during parliamentary debates on an imperial-sponsored bill known as the Niel project (to become the Niel Law in 1868),[56] a flurry of Republican projects of military organization ranging from spontaneous *levée en masse* to genuine conscript armies came under discussion. The debates stirred up a great deal of interest for the revolutionary style of military organization and set the path that Republican politicians followed in the decades after 1870.[57] Throughout the Third Republic, the Left fought continuously for the promotion of a military institution derived from the nation-in-arms pattern, while castigating conservative proclivities for the *armée de caserne*.[58] In the late years of the Republic, one of the most illustrious victims of the leftist dedication to the nation in arms was Lieutenant Colonel de Gaulle. His 1934 proposal calling for the creation of a professional armored military,[59] despite a brilliant and appealing presentation of the necessity for systematic mechanization, was harshly attacked for linking "the growth of French armored forces to the appearance of a professional army."[60]

The rejection by the Left of the all-volunteer force formula can be best understood as a component of leftist antimilitarism, itself an element of a wider opposition to capitalism and imperialism and also an element of the defense of working-class sociopolitical enfranchisement. Though there is a great deal of variation about it, militarism is usually referred to as, to quote Alfred Vagts, "a vast array of custom, interest, prestige, actions and thought associated with armies and wars and yet transcending true military purposes."[61] Yet for the Left this definition is more specifically qualified. Militarism is viewed as an excrescence of the internal logic of capitalism. The search for new markets and new sources of raw materials made necessary by sharpening economic competition leads to global expansion policies and, with the attendant international tension, to the building up of the instruments of conquest and war, and then to involvement in wars of aggression and colonization. But this is only one aspect of the militarist phenomenon. Militarism manifests a still more dubious face, "the militarism against the internal enemy," to quote Karl Liebknecht.[62] Undue emphasis on military preponderance imposes heavy burdens on the people by infringing on the development of their well-being. Also, in the context of increasing contradictions of the capitalist system and class polarization, this emphasis incites the bourgeois ruling class to make domestic use of its standing forces to suppress the working class's struggle or to maintain itself in power. Referring to particular instances of ruthless domestic military use in France, Belgium, and Italy, Karl Marx wrote, "The militaristic governments which are always ready to attack each other, march to the battle field shoulder to shoulder in their crusade against the proletariat, their common enemy."[63] It is in this context, therefore, that the Left's devotion to conscription grew stronger. Indeed, the positive effect of conscription on the liberation of the individual or the advent of revolution was not ignored by leftist theoreticians—"Contrary to appearances, compulsory military service surpasses general franchise as a democratic agency," wrote Friedrich Engels, who, after 1870, argued also that revolution would be facilitated by the working class's acceptance of universal military service. But it was essentially in the conventional class struggle and anticapitalist perspective that commitment to conscription emerged. The conscript army made up of peace-loving citizens prevented the launching of aggressive wars, as it would not allow itself to be used for other purposes than the defense of the sacred soil of the *patrie*, the purpose for which conscription was believed to be the best format. The mass army, seen by antimilitarist Republicans as unfit for imperialist wars, served as an invincible tool against external aggression. To use Jules Simon's formula, it was "an army of citizens which would be invincible on its home soil but incapable of launching a war abroad."[64] And to exemplify the argument, one always contrasts the victories of the 1793 *Levée en masse* and the World War conscript armies with the defeat and military adventurism of the Second Empire's quasi-professional guards. Thus de Gaulle's proposal was unacceptable because the mechanized armored force was believed to be efficient only in the framework of military offensive; therefore, it was a "menace to peace" in the words of Socialist leader Léon Blum.[65]

More importantly, the conscript army undoubtedly represented a means of alleviating "inward militarist tendencies." For moderate Republicans, the conscript army constituted the form of military organization most congruent with the needs of democracy and least disharmonious with the democratic functioning of social and political institutions. But for the bulk of the Left, reasoning within a class-struggle framework, the point of having a conscript army was to make it more difficult for the ruling bourgeoisie to rely on military coercion for domestic purposes: draftees would probably be less prepared to turn their weapons against the working class than would be a professional. This was to be the case during the domestic military operations in Dunkirk, Montceau-les-Mines, Longwy, Le Creusot, and Beziers, to name but a few instances in which class-conscious soldiers refused to shoot into a crowd of strikers.[66] Perhaps it is not a coincidence that the leftist inclination toward a nation in arms grew concomitantly with the conservative tradition of relying on the military to enforce law and order, particularly when faced with disturbances originating from the Left. By the time of World War I, the prophecy of an 1830s commentator—"Formerly, freedom made itself a soldier, [but] order will be a soldier too."[67]—had become a gloomy reality. The brutality of the 20,000-man force of the duc d'Aumale in Lyons in December 1831, the massacre of the rue Transnonnain in Paris in 1834, the bloody army repressions in June 1848 and, above all, during the somber days of 1871 were the first of numerous examples of order-maintenance activities that kept the French military on the alert during the Third Republic, from the Midi (1907) to the center (1900–1907), from Paris suburbs (1908) to the North (1911–13), against wine growers, factory workers, and miners.[68] In this regard, France was quite exceptional. As one author, referring to the role of the army in 1848 and 1871, stated, "Only in France did the regular army reconquer the capital like an enemy fortress."[69] And if the Left remained more sensitive to this issue, it was because this inward militaristic tendency was felt to be facilitated somewhat by the traditional antirepublicanism and reactionary outlook of army career personnel. When Jules Guesde wrote, toward the end of the nineteenth century, "The army does not look toward the frontiers but toward the factory. . . . Its unique objective is the defense of the capitalist and governing bourgeoisie,"[70] he was expressing the rampant fear of the Left that is still acutely felt today when the same statement is applied to the *armée de guerre civile.*[71]

This brief glance at the ideological genesis of the Left's beliefs about the appropriate format for the military puts into perspective leftist military expectations that continued to feed on the same kind of belief, particularly the leftist opposition to the all-volunteer model. The military was still regarded as an intricate element of society's *rapport de forces*, an element of the state apparatus, held in the hands of the ruling bourgeoisie for the protection of its hegemony and used against the legitimate demands of the people. In the course of the last few years, for example, the Left, Socialists as well as Communists, frequently voiced their fear of the government. They accused the government, as *L'Humanité* puts it, of "using the army to maintain the domination of the social groups attached to the privileges of wealth," and of what Georges Marchais, the general secretary of the Communist party, considered as the recurrent *tradition versaillaise* of the ruling class.[72] This fear was all the greater, as there were many indications in the professional military's attitude that led people to believe that it would not necessarily be neutral. The Socialist weekly, *L'Unité*, stated, "It is obvious that today the army is not the army of the people. To safeguard its privilege, isn't a large part of the military hierarchy ready to designate as its enemy the people from which it was born and which it is its mission to defend?"[73]

This fear of "inward militarism" expressed by the entire Left, though felt in different degrees by each of its factions, was not completely unjustified. It is true that, after the creation of the Garde mobile, a special branch of the gendarmerie charged with maintaining internal order, in July 1921 and of the Compagnies républicaines de securité, which succeeded the Groupes mobiles de réserve created in 1941, the regular army was practically exempted from any task related to keeping domestic order.[74] However, all ambiguities were not cleared up. Legally, the military could still be called upon to perform such operations; after all, in reductio ad absurdum, the Algerian War was an operation of order maintenance. Furthermore, the definition and the qualification of the modern military establishment's missions, both in peacetime and in time of internal emergency, as they were perceived by the Left, still presented many equivocations. First, as the logical result of the goal-conversion process that all modern military institutions in a deterrence-oriented environment were undergoing, the number of paramilitary and nonmilitary tasks in which military manpower and resources were being used tended to multiply. Hence, they included more and more relatively ordinary activities, and the procedure that commanded their execution tended to become less exceptional and the nature of the control more casual. Though such a tendency was a normal and logical moment in the evolution of modern military deployment, it was a serious source of concern for the Left. With the multiplication of the eventualities in which the military could intervene, the chances for its becoming involved in the task of order maintenance or, more seriously, in tasks whose nature could have affected the pattern of political dialectic (that is, interfering in the "normal" evolution of the class struggle) were increasing. For the Left, nonmilitary functions undertaken by the military, except in very special emergencies, were never "politically neutral." At first, indeed, the use of military manpower in the management of heavy traffic during holidays or of military vehicles during public transportation breakdowns seemed a legitimate peacetime use of the military. Yet, even if the former was so, the legitimacy of the latter was more doubtful, especially when the breakdown was the result of a strike. Therefore, when the military was called to replace striking workers, as actually happened for public transportation, sanitation worker, and air controller strikes, it fulfilled a politically oriented task that was not very different from those it had performed a century before when it pushed the workers back into the factories. It interfered with the workers' exercise of rights and jeopardized the possibility that their demands would be met. When strikers were replaced by military personnel, the workers were robbed of the leverage of the strike and their bargaining position was weakened. For this reason leftist representatives frequently tried to introduce amendments during parliamentary debates that specified the nature of military missions and limited them to those strictly relevant to national defense.

A second ambiguity related to the peacetime deployment of the military was added to the first; it concerns the nature of national defense-related missions and the philosophy behind them. After World

War II, as a result of changes in the technology of warfare, rigid battlefronts and strictly defined lines of defense no longer existed; enemy penetration of and implantation in the territory was a danger which now had to be faced shortly after the first hours of battle. Therefore, it became necessary to conceive a military deployment capable of meeting the enemy not only at the borders of the nation's territory, but also within it, and to give the military the appropriate means, both technical and institutional, to prepare itself to perform these missions. This was the rationale behind the creation of such military formations as the Défense en surface and the Défense intérieure du territoire (DIT; the internal defense of the territory) during the Fourth Republic and the Défense opérationnelle du territoire (DOT; the operational defense of the territory) during the Fifth Republic. Though technically different from one another with respect to the scope of the military authority involved, the putting into practice and the procedure of control both had basically the same objective: to take every measure to prevent and fight the internal infiltration of enemy forces. Inevitably, such a mission implied some degree of involvement of the military in diverse actions more or less related to the keeping of internal order. Though such an objective was in itself extraneous to national defense, it was legitimate since it was technically relevant to national defense. For example, the Decree of 24 February 1962 stipulated that the government could, during international tensions, be authorized to use the DOT to maintain public order, thereby considerably enlarging the prerogatives of the military authority.[75]

Furthermore—and it is at this point that the rationale of the Left's distrust for this type of deployment operated—because of the nature of the postwar pattern of threats that made the Eastern Socialist powers, and communism in general, the main enemies of every Western country's security, the danger to security was naturally viewed as twofold. Danger could come not only from beyond the Elbe but also from within the national boundaries, from among the nationals themselves, because some adversaries of the regimes shared the ideology of the external enemy. Thus the internal and external enemies could be either the same entity or two different ones. In the former case, the control of the internal enemy by military organizations of the internal defense type would be legitimate, for such a use would be relevant to the defense against the external enemy. Thus strategic circumstances might eventually contribute to legitimizing the domestic use of military manpower and resources. On the other hand, because of the nature of the ideology that imbues the national defense and all missions considered relevant to it, such a use would inevitably be somewhat contaminated by a bias in favor of the defense of a certain type of order against a certain type of threat. In this regard, the goals of the Défense en surface and DIT were hardly disguised. As Bernard Chantebout stated, "they [the Défense en surface and DIT] were aimed at least as much at the defense of the republican regime as at that of the territory itself."[76] In addition, dubious metaphors such as the "implanted enemy," "the Fifth Column," and the "internal adversary," used by the military as well as by civilian officials to refer to targets of internal military defense missions, were implicit indications of the identity of this internal enemy, particularly in the ambivalent context of the cold war and of colonial conflicts perceived in terms of the defense of the West against communism.

Though the goals of DOT (established in 1962) were, in theory, at least, more politically impartial in the sense that the internal struggle against the infiltrated external enemy was restored as its basic objective, in practice DOT still intended to fulfill specific political purposes. André Fanton, then secretary for national defense, did not hide the fact that DOT would be used to prevent the occurrence of internal disorders such as those of May 1968. Besides such declarations, proposals written by high-ranking officers and presented in official publications such as *Défense nationale* and *Forces armées françaises* as well as the development of training sessions in anti–urban subversion techniques—as manifested by the content of several field exercises and the topics of discussion at the War College seminars—indicated the military's readiness to participate in the restoration of public order in cases of "internal disorder" or "of threats of illegal or dangerous paralysis of public services."[77] Together with the discovery of military intelligence activities, legally undertaken within the framework of the internal defense organization against not only the extreme Left but also the Communist and Socialist parties and the major labor unions, very little doubt remained either about the ultimate objectives of DOT or about the ideology of the military. A defense specialist at *Le Monde* wrote: "Then, does not the activity undertaken by military intelligence services indicate a clear choice made by the armies for the defense of a predefined model of society and didn't Robert Galley (former minister of national defense) want to confirm this option recently in qualifying the army as 'the last recourse of a liberal society,' should the established order be threatened."[78]

As shown, the Left was not totally unjustified in its fear of being the major target of internal defense organizations or of what has been called the "State of defense"[79] that it viewed as being set up for purely domestic and political purposes; nor was it totally unjustified in its accusation that the government was preparing the military, as the leaders of the Communist party put it, "to confront the active mass of the French people, treated as a potential enemy." Whatever the exact intentions of the government or the opinions of the military, they were always sufficiently ambiguous to lead even the most moderate segment of the Left to perceive the military organization as a possible source of inward militarism and sufficiently ambivalent not to contradict the leftist ideological proclivity to conceive of the military, in a class-struggle perspective, as an organization of "preparation for the defense of the bourgeois state, that is, to civil war."[80] In this context then, a conscript army was seen by the Left as the appropriate format of military organization. Thus, besides attacking any measures perceived as encouraging domestic use of the army (such as the 1959 ordinance),[81] the Left throughout the Fifth Republic sought to defeat any attempt leading toward the emergence of an all-volunteer force and consistently supported compulsory universal conscription. Although conscription was no panacea, with its regular influx of citizens it was viewed as the only means to undermine any political actions by or any political uses of the military. In that sense, the French Left was Tocquevillian; the Left was as convinced as was the author of *Democracy in America* that "in democracies it is the private soldiers who remain most like civilians; it is on them that national habits have the firmest hold and public opinion the strongest influence. It is especially through the soldiers that one may well hope to inspire a democratic army with the same love of liberty and respect for law as has been infused into the nation itself."[82] And in this regard, it was usually argued that it was draftee disobedience to insurgent officers' orders that was accountable for the failure of the attempted coup in Algeria in April 1961, further feeding the belief that conscription was indeed a guarantee of a democratic military posture.[83] If draftees were capable of preventing military adventurism, they should also be unwilling to let themselves be used for undemocratic political purposes such as order maintenance. And it was not a coincidence that the government always sought (this was particularly true under the Fourth Republic) to avoid inducting draftees into units in charge of domestic missions; later, though draftees were allowed to serve in the gendarmerie, they could not participate in order-maintaining operations. Therefore, by advocating the maintenance of universal compulsory military service rather than other, more rational, forms of service such as civil service, paramilitary service, or even some form of military separated from the career personnel—a proposal frequently advocated by antimilitarist and extreme Left groups—it was the Left's purpose to ensure that the entire military organization would be permeated by drafted personnel. This would multiply the chances that, if the military were to be used internally, class-conscious draftees could help to paralyze and perhaps dissuade this kind of use.

It is in the light of such beliefs that one must understand the systematic opposition of Communists and Socialists to government-initiated military service reforms, such as the 1965 and the 1970 bills, viewed as being used to "accustom the minds to the exclusive constitution of an all-volunteer force," to quote a Socialist commentator.[84] But it is in the light of these same beliefs that one ought also to understand the Communists' and Socialists' early negative response to conscientious objection[85] and to later condemnations of antidraft and antimilitarist demonstrations originated by the extreme Left, despite the desire of the leaders of the traditional Left not to lose touch with the youth, who were increasingly attracted by the antimilitarist rhetoric of the extreme Left. For the traditional Left, these demonstrations, which the Communists once mocked as "puerile and demagogic," were dangerous, as they could provide the opportunity sought by the government to put an end to the draft and to institute an all-volunteer force, the ideal tool of internal militarism. This was clearly expressed in the following declarations: Charles Hernu, a member of the executive committee of the Socialist party and chairman of the Conventions pour l'armée nouvelle, declared: "The Socialist Party would not think of sympathizing with antimilitarist demonstrations which cannot but turn against France in due time, hence against the Left, and play into the hands of those who seek to put an end to national conscription."[86] The general secretary of the French Communist party youth, Jean-Michel Catala, asserted on 20 September 1974: "We will never tolerate any activity which could discredit the very principle of the necessity of a national army to defend the national territory. . . . To abolish the military service would, indeed, reduce the French armed forces to a body of mercenaries ready to protect the interests of the highest bidder or ready to organize itself into a faction against the nation."[87] Thus, the only forms of draft-related protests supported by the Left were precisely those with corporate orientations, those that demanded that the living conditions and human rights of the draftees be improved, because by giving in to those demands, the military service became a more tolerable, hence acceptable, institution. And proposals such as *Le Soldat-citoyen* or the Communist-originated *Pour un statut démocratique du soldat-citoyen* were merely attempts to reconcile the necessity of retaining national conscription with the incremental and legitimate expectations of the draftees.[88]

It should be noted, before concluding this section, that besides strictly ideological reasons, support for conscription from both the Left and the Right might also have been based on more pragmatic grounds. This seems to have been all the more true for local politicians, particularly for those in areas in which important military installations and garrisons were established. These areas were generally nonindustrial ones in which the military constituted an important source of wealth for the local population. The suppression of conscription, resulting in a reduction in size of the military establishment would have had as a principal consequence the closing down of many garrisons or other military training camps, and would thus have had tangible detrimental economic effects for these regions.

This study would not be complete if one did not emphasize that the French political commitment to military service has always been, to a certain degree at least, consistent with the expectations of the national collective consciousness. Between the military community and the civil society, there has always been some amount of consensus about this formula of military organization, and though it no longer arouses unanimity about its existence (but had it ever?), one can say that in France, more than in any other Western European country, the public approach to military service is far from being antagonistic. Such observations deserve to be commented on briefly; we shall examine the attitude of professional military personnel regarding conscription before commenting on the views of the civil community.

Conscription and the Professional Soldier

The attitude of the French military establishment has rarely been given full consideration. Too often the assumption crediting the military with an explicit preference for the all-volunteer organizational format prevailed. Nothing, however, could be more doubtful. Military journals and other documentation on the opinion of French professional soldiers revealed clearly that partisans of the all-volunteer force were less numerous than presumed. A 1973 opinion poll taken by the Institut français d'Opinion publique (IFOP) indicated that 72 percent of officers polled were in favor of conscription; only 19 percent were against it.[89] In another survey, conducted among cadets attending the

Ecole spéciale militaire, 66 percent of the Saint-Cyriens (direct recruitment) and 87 percent of the Interarms Military School students (semidirect recruitment among NCOs) supported compulsory universal military service and 9 percent and 3 percent, respectively, a selective service. Attachment to conscription can be further demonstrated in that 90 percent of the EMIA cadets and 85.3 percent of the Saint-Cyriens interviewed believed that something was lacking in the formation of a man who had not completed his military service.[90]

It is common to attribute the career military's adherence to the conscript-army model to its strategic conceptions of warfare or to military staffs' doctrinal bent for "big batallions." Such a view is misleading, for it is doubtful that professional soldiers would have been unaware of the operational inadequacies of such a formula of military organization and would therefore have based their national defense conceptions upon it. It is also common to view the career soldiers' attachment to conscription in ideological terms. The military establishment, particularly its officer corps, is seen as culturally conservative, hence committed to conscription for reasons similar to those advocated by the Right. Military service was supported because it was an instrument favoring the social reproduction of the traditional liberal model of society, all the more useful in time of crisis. To cite General Maurin, former armed forces chief of staff: "The fact that the crisis of civilization that we are undergoing materializes through the almost general abandonment of old values, by an explosion of freedom in which everything is possible, in which any constraint is rejected, necessitates as a counterpart, the preservation of the traditional structure in the country."[91]

Moreover, for many officers, as for partisans of the Right, military service had to be maintained because it served to compensate for visions of the world and ideologies detrimental to the current ones. Writing as if he considered the military institution as the unique bearer of "humanism and of the exclusivity of moral rectitude," General Jacques Beauvallet stated, "The formative value of the military service . . . is particularly important at a time when youth runs the risk of conceiving, by reason of the philosophies that it is taught, an unrealistic or tendentious vision of the world."[92] Although not totally ill-founded, the approach that views the professional military's faith in universal conscription as a function of his ideological proclivities— conservative proclivities, to be precise—is only a poor approximation of reality. The causes of this attachment were numerous and diversified, sometimes foreign to one another. All, however, were conducive to the reinforcement of the commitment of career personnel to keeping the military service in existence. There were professional and psychological as well as political and technical reasons.

These reasons were related, first, to the serviceman's traditional cognitive approach to its profession. A particular characteristic of the French military, and particularly of French officers, was the tendency to derive a sense of purposefulness not only from its role as defender of the nation against external military encroachment, but also from its participation in the shaping and the propagation of the national system of values through the civic education of the nation's youth. It would take too long to retrace the origin of such a belief, rooted in both the revolutionary tradition that made the army the protector and the propagator of ideologies and in the practices of the Third Republic, which, for various reasons,[93] consecrated the army as the agency responsible for spreading the Republican values—a mission that the military sometimes took too much to heart, especially when it sought to bring the civil community into accord with its own social project. In the latter respect, the nature of the role and the activities with which the Armistice army or later the forces in Algeria felt invested is revealing.[94]

The nature and the content of the values diffused by the military and the question of whether the military acted as the agent of the state or under its own responsibility, although important, are not of paramount interest to this study. What is of interest is the fact that such a tradition led the military to derive its sense of professional purpose from the accomplishment of that mission. In other words, such a mission was at the bottom of a deeply held conviction that it was the purpose of the military not merely to assume responsibility for the security of the nation, but to participate in establishing the nation's system of values and in instilling it in the community. Naturally, without conscription, the realization of this professional role would not have been possible—hence the devotion of the military to universal military service. Conscription was institutionally reconfirmed in the postwar era because it was in part a response to "the demand of the French military that it be assigned an intimate relationship with the French youth."[95] Similarly, conscription was preserved in the aftermath of the colonial conflicts because, once again, the military clung to its role of social apostolate. "To continue (or to undertake) the formation of the young generations in the qualities of their characters and in devotion to the public good" was seen as one of the four main missions of the military for the 1960s and 1970s, in the words of General Valluy.[96] When General Beauvallet emphatically expressed his opinion of the military service, praising its *vertu forma-trice*, its maturing function, he echoed the sense of an old tradition—a tradition inherited from a Lyautey or a Weygand, in whose minds the military was "the guide and the tutor" and the source of moral and intellectual regeneration.[97] The tradition was carried on by younger officers, one of whom recently wrote: "Trustees of the civism, we also feel it is necessary to share it with the men we have the mission to train. . . . This is why, for us, compulsory universal military service . . . must be maintained, even if its length is reduced, even if the complexity of the new equipment requires that a greater number of posts be attended by specialists who of necessity are enlistees."[98] And it is not a coincidence that the aforementioned survey revealed that in 1973 94.6 percent of the EMIA and 88 percent of the Saint-Cyr students interviewed agreed that one of the missions of the military was to ensure the civic and moral education of French youth.[99] Consequently, the entry of the military establishment into the modern era of strategic deterrence, the technological environment of which required highly specialized servicing, the system of threats of which could hardly be handled by nonprofessionals, and the effects of which eroded the functionality of a conscript organizational deployment did not, for all that, affect the career personnel's attachment to universal military service.

As a final note, we may also wonder whether to a certain extent the ambiguity of the security-related mission, resulting from both the nature of the deterrence posture (which negates the primacy of war) and the somewhat ill-defined state of the strategic conceptions of the national defense, did not affect the military professional's perceptions of his defense role. As a consequence, it may have reinforced the officer's attachment to the more tangible elements of the profession, such as the social role, capable of nourishing its search for purposefulness.

Second, the reasons for the officer's desire to see conscription maintained are of a psychological nature. Though producing evidence on that point is not an easy task, it can be hypothesized that, for many professional soldiers, the existence of drafted personnel constituted a means to bridge the gap separating the military from the rest of society. By arousing the nation's interest, conscription prevented social isolation. In effect, a century of nation-in-arms practices led the career military to relate its existence to a sense of oneness with the rest of the nation, and therefore made it ill at ease in isolation from society. In addition, periods during which the military found itself isolated from the nation turned out to be bitter experiences for its servants. Most writing by officers throughout the 1940s and 1950s reveals how acutely developed were their feelings of self-estrangement and how acutely they resented the nation's lack of interest in their activities. The common "stabbed in the back" explanation for the loss of the Indochina War was a typical expression of such a syndrome. The decision taken to involve draftees in the Algerian War was certainly meant to increase manpower deployment, but it was probably also a response to military expectations for the symbolic involvement of the nation in the undertaking. Though one must be careful in the manipulation of such an argument, we can say that if conscription continued to be defended by the military, it was because it was seen as a way to limit the alienating effects inevitably produced by the progressive "technologization" and the bureaucratic complexity of the military institution.[100]

Third, there are political factors for that adherence to conscription. To a great extent, the assimilation of conscripted personnel into the military institution contributed, by symbolizing the nation, to justifying the actions of the professional soldiers as well as serving to glorify them. There is no doubt that the army-nation rhetoric professed by the military cadres of the postwar era was not foreign to their desire to see the reputation of the profession restored—cleansed, so to speak, of its ambiguous role in 1940 and of its association with the Vichy regime. Moreover, the claim for conscription, particularly when made in connection with the educational mission, had even more explicit political purposes such as the indoctrination of society and its deliverance from foreign ideological evils. The revolutionary war engineers made this clear in the 1950s. On the other hand, conscription seemed necessary, for it could serve as an endorsement of any action taken by the armed forces. This was the case in 1958. During the spring of 1958, it was pointed out that the military forces in revolt in Algeria and in France did not feel that they had violated any law. On the contrary, they felt that their actions were legitimate, for they fulfilled the aspirations and the *volonté générale* of the nation; the presence of draftees in their ranks legitimized their deeds.[101] Thus, the army-nation provided the most militant soldiers with an alibi for the righteousness of their conduct.

Finally, there were technical and materialistic factors for the military professional's reluctance toward the establishment of the all-volunteer force. The army is an interesting case in point. In addition to the reasons already cited, the army seemed to have motives of its own for wanting military service maintained. Conscription provided a means of limiting the decline of national and political attention that had affected the army after 1962. It also limited the extent of the institutional shake-up following the ending of France's imperial pretenses, for which the army had been a most prestigious tool, and the shifting of organizational priorities in favor of the navy and the air force, demanded by the new program of nuclearizing national defense. Certainly for a great majority of army officers (after nearly fifteen uninterrupted years of colonial wars, their numbers were quite important), the colonial disengagement and the change in the interservice budgetary appropriation pattern resulting in the reduction of the army's strength had been a gloomy threat to their careers. As there was no doubt that the establishment of an all-volunteer force would have resulted in a drastic reduction of total manpower by at least 150,000 men, two-thirds of which would have come from the army alone, thereby thinning out the middle and upper parts of the hierarchy, it is likely that the French officers' bent for conscription was motivated by the fear of a severe *dégagement des cadres*. It is not our purpose to question the veracity of the officers' defense of the draft, an argument that held that an all-volunteer force, which would cause the termination of six of the sixteen army divisions, the disarming of two or three dozen ships, and the closing of one harbor and of several air force bases, would have disastrous strategic consequences for the nation's security. This was certainly true, but one cannot ignore the more corporatist interests that were also at stake. The conscript mass armed force had provided jobs and professional security for many officers who were too young to retire and who were not qualified to be reintegrated into the civilian labor force. As one major bluntly put it, "The importance of the effectives makes the importance of the generals." [102]

Also, for a good number of officers, particularly those in the nonspecialized branches, the conception of the military profession was still a nontechnical one. Interactions in the military could not be like those in complex industrial bureaucracies. Writings by many army officers about the military profession revealed a pervasive clinging to a neofeudal vision of military life. In this vision, the exercise of command, together with field exercises, prevailed over staff and technical tasks—it was a vision in which human interactions and direct contact with men were seen as the basic elements of the profession. Enhanced between 1945 and 1960 by the nonindustrial nature of colonial warfare, such a conception of professionalism did not disappear afterward. A 1973 analysis of the career motivations of Saint-Cyr cadets showed very little difference from those of preceding decades; the interest in human relations and in leadership were still the most conspicuous incentives for the Saint-Cyriens's military vocation. In light of the findings, one can better understand any officer's reluctance about an all-volunteer force. Such a format would have placed the focus on technology, skills, more impersonal interactions, and would have offered fewer opportunities for satisfying career expectations based on human relations, leadership, and the like. And it is probable that "for these officers," as one author said, "the military service offers the most appropriate means to contain the effect of the technological evolution."[103]

In conclusion, there were a great number of reasons that, albeit very different in nature and content, had a part in the formation of a fairly important consensus among the professional military concerning the issue of retaining the draft. Only a few of these reasons have been discussed. A more exhaustive list would have included such things as the officers' fear that if an all-volunteer force of mostly privates and NCOs were built, it would be of too mediocre a caliber. Also there was the fear that the number of enlistments would be too small because, as proven by experience, financial incentives were no panacea for solving the two-fold question of the quantity and quality of military manpower.[104]

Conscription and Public Opinion

Surprisingly, the civil community's commitment to conscription was no less tangible, though an exact appreciation of the strength of the commitment and of its evolution is more difficult to assess.[105] In France, paradoxically, the institution of conscription did not appear to be as violently questioned as it was in other Western societies during the last fifteen years. One could say that, despite appearances, after World War II compulsory universal conscription remained a fairly agreed-upon institution.[106] This was particularly true until 1960. Draft-related actions such as the "manifesto of the 121" and the *jeune resistance* movement received scant support or explicit negative responses from the French community, even from those segments, such as the Communists, most opposed to the regime's colonial policy. And both organizers and followers of these movements, as well as conscientious objectors, continuously sought to avoid any misunderstandings about their actions; their activities were not to be interpreted as a rejection of universal conscription.[107]

The privileged place that the military service occupied on the community's social cultural horizon, exemplified by the key role it played in the life development of the adolescent, as revealed by many a social survey,[108] helps explain society's deeply entrenched commitment to conscription until the early 1960s. Yet the military was not seen only as an appropriate channel for the maturation of the adolescent and of his emergence into adulthood; it was also, consciously or not, viewed as the proper agency for assisting in the blossoming of the citizen's consciousness. In a way, it was still perceived as being an integral part of the accession to national consciousness. Requests by French youths from overseas *départements* to complete their military duty like any French citizen, even at the price of being sent to Algeria, exemplified this viewpoint. From 1962 through the early 1970s, despite noticeable disagreements over the length and the conditions of service—according to two opinion polls, in 1963, 72 percent, and in 1967, 62 percent of the population were partisans of a reduction of the length of service—opposition to serving in the armed forces remained limited. For example, the same surveys indicated that in 1963, 9 percent, and in 1967, 11 percent of the respondents favored the abolition of military service. The commitment to the idea of the national draft was also reiterated in a 1969 opinion poll: 72 percent of the French population favored a national service for women.[109]

To accurately measure the exact degree of public attachment to conscription after the 1960s is more problematic. First, from a microdiachronic point of view, although there are rather erratic fluctuations that can be observed, it is possible to say that there seems to have been a sharp decline in adherence to the idea of universal conscription in 1972–73. This was followed by as sharp an increase in 1975–76. Second, when it comes to precise statistical evaluation, it is extremely difficult to give an accurate estimate of this attachment to conscription since the variations from one poll to another were so extreme. To the question "Do you wish France to depend on a defense based on universal military service or on a volunteer force?" the IFOP polls found that in 1973, 31 percent of the interviewees were in favor of conscription and 53 percent favored an all-volunteer force; this proportion changed to 45 and 42 percent, respectively, in 1975. However, to a similar question, SOFRES polls showed that responses in favor of military service increased from 64 percent in 1973 to 70 percent in 1976 and the figures relative to partisans of the all-volunteer force declined from 29 to 17 percent.[110] On the whole, however, and this is confirmed by cross analysis, it appears that beyond such variations in estimates, the weight of public attachment to military service was not greatly modified, especially when seen from a long-term perspective.

When it came to the attitudes of the younger groups, however, particularly of those liable to be drafted in the near future or those just discharged from duty, attachment to military service was less evident, particularly during the years from 1965 to 1976. Draft-related protests undertaken by high school students in spring 1973 and by draftees in 1974 and 1975 seemed to contradict the idea that there was a latent consensus about conscription. A 1968 opinion poll taken among young men between the ages of fifteen and twenty revealed that, if given the choice between military service and a civilian form of service, 70 percent of the respondents would have preferred the latter; only 28 percent would have chosen military service. Another IFOP poll, conducted in May 1973 among four hundred newly discharged draftees (less than three months), presented a clear-cut antagonism to military service. For example, 74 percent of the respondents thought they had wasted their time, and 78 percent thought that the defense of the country could best be ensured by an all-volunteer force. Another survey, by the same agency, covering a national sample, confirmed these trends: of those aged between fifteen and nineteen, only 25 percent were in favor of military service and 63 percent preferred an all-volunteer force. Of those between twenty and twenty-four years, 21 percent favored conscription, 60 percent an all-volunteer force. Twenty-nine percent of those between twenty-five and thirty-four chose conscription, 53 percent an all-volunteer force.[111] Though one might expect more antagonism against conscription from the young than from the population as a whole, one should not draw hasty conclusions from such figures, as they do not necessarily constitute reliable proof of rampant antagonism against the principle of conscription. In some ways such figures are misleading. Much depends on the time that has elapsed between the completion of the respondent's military service and the taking of the poll. For example, it is agreed that the attachment to conscription before World War I and World War II or even in 1960 was well established, but there is no doubt that the feeling of wasting one's time in service or of the pettiness of many tasks and military rituals was just as pervasive in 1940 as in 1970. It is a well-known fact that in the period immediately preceding and following military service, the level of agreement with its principles sharply declines. In a 1968 survey conducted among young men between fifteen and twenty years of age, the question, "Do you think that the military service is useful to the forming of a man?" had these varying responses: 75 percent of those between fifteen and sixteen said yes, 63 percent of the seventeen- and eighteen-year-olds said yes, and 50 percent of those between nineteen and twenty responded affirmatively. Among women, the decline in the number of affirmative responses for the same age-sets was less pronounced—83 percent to 78 percent.[112] The same phenomenon can be observed elsewhere. A German survey conducted in the early 1970s (1972–75) showed a similar trend.[113] These figures do not measure the level of acceptability of the service as much as they measure a temporary animosity toward the interference of the service with personal plans. Often the figures tend to reverse themselves after the completion of military service. Opinions from a 1973 poll illustrate such a recurrence. To a question concerning the indispensability of military service in a man's life, 72 percent of the young men interviewed replied positively. Yet closer to the time of induction, their conviction declined to 51 percent, reaching 47 percent immediately after their service. Two years later, 72 percent of the interviewees agreed upon the indispensability of the service.[114] One sees that, in reality, youth's attitude to military service was far from being a negative one, when considered in a broader perspective than that based on interviews with men who were immediately draftliable or recently discharged.

Responses also depended on the kinds of questions that were asked. Most young people gave negative answers to questions based on a "do you like it or not" pattern; but if open-ended questions were asked there is plenty of specific detail to show that there was more consensus. In 1970 a majority (70 percent) indicated that they had pleasant memories of their time in service; 75 percent felt that they had acquired a better knowledge of others. More important, this survey showed that 76 percent of those who had completed their service agreed that it favored useful social interaction; 47 percent felt the service provided professional training; and 50 percent of the recently discharged draftees agreed on the indispensability of military service in the formation of a man. On the whole, even if the level of the acceptability of military service was lower among the younger generations, a significant number of young people were still attached to conscription; a tendency that, after a decline until 1973, was reinforced after January 1976, when 51 percent of young people aged between eighteen and twenty-four and 63 percent of those between twenty-five and thirty-four agreed with the idea of maintaining compulsory military service.[115]

These data, though extremely disparate and somewhat fragile, are of interest for two reasons. First, they show, much as one can argue that there was a decline in the acceptability of military service, particularly among the younger generation, the opposition to conscription was not as vehement in France as in other countries. In Germany, for example, only 44 percent of the young between eighteen and twenty-four and only 56 percent of the total population favored conscription (1972–75). A more critical indicator, the number of conscientious objectors in Germany, rose until 1973; after that it stabilized at about 35,000 a year. In 1972, 29 percent of the young people with primary and intermediate education stated that they would refuse to complete their military service and would try to evade it. This figure reached 39 percent among secondary school students.[116] In France, though the number of conscientious objectors increased in absolute terms after 1964, it remained extremely small, too low, in any case, to serve as proof of the existence of a large scale delegitimization of the draft. Between January 1964 and February 1970 only 1,053 requests for conscientious objector classification were submitted for approval; that came to a yearly average of 170. The number increased from 190 requests in 1970 to 221 in 1971; yet considered in light of the increase in the size of age-cohorts liable to the draft, this growth had little significance. As regards draft evasion, here again the figures were comparatively low: 1,149 in 1965, 1,906 in 1968, 950 in 1970. Whereas one would have expected an increase following May 1968, one is forced to notice that even barricade leaders, Nanterre *enragés*, completed their military duty and this with more equanimity than their attitude would have led one to think. During the turmoil of the spring 1973 draft-related demonstrations, not one of the men called to service failed to appear.

Second, a closer inspection of the nature of public sentiment toward the draft revealed that commitment to conscription after World War II tended to feed upon the same kinds of beliefs as before. The public continued to perceive the military service as an agency of social integration, education, professional promotion, and maturation. This was observed in the 1950s, as well as in the early 1970s. A survey conducted in 1970 showed that 84 percent of the respondents stated that military service favored social encounters, 60 percent that it provided useful professional qualifications. In a SOFRES poll taken in January 1977, 80 percent of the interviewees agreed (54 percent strongly, 26 percent mildly) that military service significantly contributed to the formation and the maturation of young men.[117] To a large extent this explains why official rhetoric continuously focused upon these functions of military service, although in reality the role of the service in their accomplishment remained secondary. It has been estimated that less than 5 percent of all draftees were able to complete their schooling during service.

As for the sociopolitical structure of the public support of military service, it seems that—at least insofar as can be inferred from the scant data available for the late 1960s—greater attachment was found among the working and the rural classes, though the support of other classes was not lacking. Asked the question "Do you think the military service is useful to a man's formation?" 74 percent of the young men aged between fifteen and twenty who came from a rural background and 78 percent of those from a working-class origin answered positively; 67 percent of those from the other classes responded in the affirmative.

Of particular interest to this study, especially in the context of the observations made in the fourth section of this chapter, is that, classified by political opinion, support for conscription was stronger among individuals of conservative opinion. The aforementioned survey showed that positive responses to the same question were about 12 percent higher for those whose political preferences verged on rightist parties than for those whose political preferences were for leftist parties.[118] The IFOP survey of May 1973, conducted among young men who had just completed their military service, indirectly confirmed this tendency since higher negative responses were found among respondents holding leftist political opinions. In the same year, on a nationwide level, respondents sympathizing with the Left seemed less attached to conscription than others and correlatively were more favorable to an all-volunteer force model: 54 percent of the Reformers, 53 percent of the Socialists, and 57 percent of the Communists preferred that France's defense be based on an all-volunteer armed force. Later evidence tended to corroborate this trend, though the figures indicated were lower than those of 1973 (probably because general commitment to conscription increased after 1974 and because the 1973 estimates were IFOP figures, which always seem extreme when compared with those arrived at by other polls). In January 1976, 67 percent of the Communists' supporters and 66 percent of the Socialists' supporters interviewed favored maintaining conscription; 82 percent of those affiliated with the *majorité* favored its maintenance. Only 10 percent of the latter were partisans of the creation of an all-volunteer force, whereas 25 percent of the Socialists' followers and 21 percent of the Communists' followers were in its favor.[119] Though it is risky to draw definite conclusions from such sketchy data, it can be said that there was some sort of inverse relationship between the public's attitude toward conscription and that of the political elite. Though this opposition is now developing in the Right with more and more leaders championing an all-volunteer force, it is sharper in the Left. But, this phenomenon is not new. Discrepancies between the "real country" and the "legal country" have long been observed. Regarding this, two remarks deserve to be made. In the first place, the importance of the differences in degree of attachment to military service held by leftist and rightist blocs of the public should not be exaggerated. If one ignores the 1973 IFOP figures, the differences never exceeded 10 percent either in the mid-1960s or the mid-1970s. Second, the discrepancies between the elite's and the public's attitudes had a political logic that had nothing to do with the form of the military. In effect, the opposition to conscription among leftist sympathizers actually expressed an opposition to something that was defended by the *majorité*, to which the Left was hostile. Furthermore, it is possible that purely circumstantial events interfered with great effect: possibly the extreme figures for 1973 and the wide rejection of the conscript model by the Left were more symptomatic of the widespread discontent with the Debré Law, which put an end to student deferments and which was perceived as an encroachment of the "right to study," than of an extreme change in opinion regarding conscription. It is a fact that during the discussion of the proposed Debré Law, the Communists, through spokesman Pierre Villon, opposed the law. They held that the suppression of deferments would affect most severely the students from the working class who generally undertook their studies at a much later time in life than did students from other social categories. If military service interrupted their education, they would have fewer opportunities to resume their studies after service than would students from other classes.

All in all, the problem of assessing the exact nature of the public's attitude toward the draft is agonizingly complex. Over the long run there seemed to be a decline in public acceptance of compulsory military service. The April 1973 draft-related demonstrations, which took place in the streets of Paris and then flared up in many of the nation's cities, and the draftee dissent that echoed throughout French barracks after 1974, the *sursis ou pas, on n'ira pas* painted on streamers, the "down with the army" shoutings, the *appel des cents*, the raised-fist parades and wildcat affiliations with labor unions, seemed to confirm such a view. But this view, based on a sort of "beginning of the end" vision, is simplistic and far from depicting accurately the complexity of these social phenomena. A careful analysis of these events reveals that this apparently collective draft-related dissidence is a rather multifaceted phenomenon involving a collection of loosely related, if not mutually estranged, groups of ill-assorted actors pursuing diverse objectives. Paradoxically, a common factor has been that none of these groups set out deliberately to abolish the draft. At least ten groups were involved in these demonstrations; among the most visible were the Groupe d'insoumission totale, the Collectif de lutte antimilitariste, the Front de lutte antiautoritaire, and the Mouvement antiautoritaire. A good half dozen newspapers and more or less regularly published leaflets were circulated such as the *Crosse en l'air*, *Le Parisien déchaîné*, and *Rompons les rangs*. Discarding the particular case of conscientious objection, three different components made up this apparently draft-related movement: an antiauthoritarian ingredient, an antimilitarist ingredient, and an economic or materialistic ingredient. In reality, each wave of protest was an intricate mixture of these three, with one or two different components dominating. Some were new, such as the amenities-related protest; others, such as antimilitarism, were simply resurgences of old perennial proclivities. Analysis of these movements leads to the conclusion that their dynamics did not feed on any deep anticonscription feelings. Only a small minority—the ultras—in the ranks of the Ligue trotskyste de France, Combat communiste, and the Programme communiste bordiguiste within the antimilitarist movement were against conscription; even they opposed conscription solely because they advocated the total suppression of the military institution. The core of the antimilitarist movement, associated with the Ligue communiste révolutionnaire, Lutte ouvrière, and the Organisation communiste internationaliste, were more "girondist" and tended, like the parliamentary Left, to see the draft as a lesser evil than an all-volunteer force that could constitute a ready-made instrument for domestic repression. They advocated that the contingent be protected as much as possible from what they saw as the pernicious grip of the military establishment, and that it be reduced to the sole apprenticeship of military skills. In a way, compared to the famous hours of the *gueules de vaches* or the *sou du soldat*, the various attempts at encouraging desertions and demoralizing draftees, and the other fierce Republican manifestations of hatred toward the military and its institutions, present forms of antimilitarism looked rather edulcorated.

As for draftee unrest, another facet of this draft-related movement (though sometimes initiated by antimilitarists' maneuvers), it is clear that the catalyst was purely "corporatist," that is, aimed at an improvement of the draftees' economic and legal conditions of service. There was indeed a great deal of anticonscriptionism and even antimilitarism in the *appel des cents* and in the Draguignan and Karlsruhe demonstrations, memorable cases of draftee unrest, but the primary goals of these demonstrations were aimed at protecting draftees from the arbitrary and brutal behavior of NCOs and at requesting higher allowances, better conditions of living, more regularity in the granting of furloughs, and so on.[120] Paradoxically, in relation to conscription, this type of protest was self-encapsulating; with the improvement of conditions, the roots of discontent tended to wither away.

Perhaps only those demonstrations initiated by high school and university students, such as those that took place in the spring of 1973, could be taken as signs of a change in the younger generation's approach toward military service. Yet, this is not certain. In light of the sociopolitical context of the post-Gaullist period, in which many expected a sharper break with the Gaullist tradition of heavy-handed presidential leadership, it is possible that opposition to the Debré law, the avowed purpose of these demonstrations, was just another way of expressing an increasingly resentful disappointment with the practices of the regime. Perhaps the demonstrations were simply another visage of a pervasive "antinomian" behavior—to use a qualificative suggested by Edward Shils[121]—that had already materialized in other collective attacks upon the *système*'s most traditional institutions: the university, the school, welfare organizations, and every other "*enfermements*" to refer to a fashionable neologism. In spring 1973 the latent disappointment among the younger generations was all the more exacerbated by the fact that the legislative elections returned a Gaullist majority, which might not have happened if the government had not blocked all attempts to lower the voting age to eighteen. The cataclysmic nature of the dissent inevitably tended to underscore the dimensions and the significance of the protest. In a society where, as Stanley Hoffmann said, "the protest is the norm,"[122] where relationships between the state and its citizens frequently degenerate into fugitive yet ferocious clashes between a sacred authority and "delinquent communities," to borrow Jesse Pitts's concept,[123] where intellectual intransigencies, ideological purity, and excessive moralism turn competition into conflict, cooperation into distrust, the external configuration of the society's life ought not to be taken at face value. Thus, as far as the attitude of the civil community toward the institution of military service is concerned, social manifestations, public behavior, and so on were relatively fragile indicators and were, to some extent misleading. Would one consider the legitimacy of compulsory taxation in decline from observing the grumbling reluctance with which French citizens pay their taxes, their exhilaration every time they successfully evade the scrutiny of the fiscal administration, or on the basis of an endemic antitax or tax-related resentment? Certainly not. Though the comparison is technically questionable, it shows, however, the complexity of any task aimed at unraveling the "true nature" of the latent collective feeling for public institutions in France. Moreover, in dealing with the draft-related protests, there is always a tendency to treat them as new patterns of attitude, as marking a change from previous positions of opinion. A diachronic observation of social events since the creation of universal military service a hundred or so years ago would demonstrate that, except during times of emergency, a great deal of animosity was expressed toward conscription. Pacifism and antimilitarism have always been latent attitudes among Frenchmen, and going to serve under the colors was never a thrilling moment for most of them. The usual presumption of public enthusiasm for military service is derived from short moments of nationalist fervor and patriotic zeal. However, we do not seek to deny the existence of a recent decline in the citizen's veneration for traditional public institutions and a concomitant decline of the legitimacy of such institutions; this would be unrealistic. We have simply attempted to suggest that in France, the public perception of military service was, until recently, positive, and even after the onset of the 1970s, it did not deteriorate as much as various events seemed to suggest. The succession of demonstrations that were, in one way or another, stirred up by military-related matters, were specific, if not anomic, manifestations of modifications in the nature and the rate of social change. Certainly, these modifications had some effect upon the way in which French youth responded to conscription and to other societal demands; yet they did not drastically affect the level of acceptability of military service, at least not to the extent manifested in other Western societies.

To conclude, given the transformation and the modernization of the technological environment surrounding the French military establishment, notably that created by the nuclearization of the national defense, a modification of the format of the military establishment could logically have been expected, particularly in the form of an attenuation, if not an abandonment, of at least the more conspicuous traits of citizen mobilization. As early as 1965, General Ailleret pointed out that one crucial effect of the adoption of nuclear weaponry would be to render an armed force based on the traditional mobilization model of military deployment more and more obsolete. "The most recent development in the evolution of armaments is truly a revolution, one not at all comparable in the upheavals that it brings to warfare with all the preceding progress in techniques of killing and destroying: it is the nuclear revolution which calls into question the idea of mass armed forces."[124]

But, as shown, numerous factors related to French society contributed to slowing down this evolution. Some were of a budgetary nature, others were linked to the beliefs held by military career personnel. The most important, however, seemed to be those related to the political culture of the nation—to the historical attachment of the Left to conscription, on the one hand, and to the relative tolerance of the public for a system that was perceived through its revolutionary origins, on the other. If, indeed, this series of variables has a significant weight in regard to the perenniality of the traditional prenuclear model of military organization, it is, for all that, not comprehensive. Geographic factors, for example, certainly had some effect. What André Mesnard called the "geographical fatality in the path of invasions"[125] contributed to a consolidation in the collective consciousness of the feeling that numbers, if they cannot stop the enemy, will in the long run overcome the enemy's pressure. But though continuity with past practices was striking in this domain, signs of change abounded and more and more factors held to be relevant for the maintenance of the traditional style of mobilization lost their importance.

Notes

1. "Loi n° 50-1478 du 30 novembre 1950 portant à dix-huit mois la durée du service militaire actif," *Journal officiel, lois et décrets*, 1 December 1950, p. 12151.

2. "Ordonnance n° 59–147 du 7 janvier 1959 portant organisation de la défense," *Journal officiel, lois et décrets*, 10 January 1959, pp. 691–94.

3. "Loi n° 65-550 du 9 juillet 1965 relative au recrutement en vue de l'accomplissement du service national," *Journal officiel, lois et décrets*, 10 July 1965, pp. 5917–20; "Loi n° 70-596 du 9 juillet 1970 relative au service national," *Journal officiel, lois et décrets*, 10 July 1970, pp. 6461–63. All these reforms concerning the national service have been collected into a new codification: "Loi n° 71-424 du 10 juin 1971 portant code du service national," *Journal officiel, lois et décrets*, 12 June 1971, pp. 5659–69; for comments on the new code, *see* Georges Marey, "Le Service national et le code du service national," *Revue militaire générale* 1 (1972): 31–48.

4. At the age of thirty-five, the citizen was transferred to the reserve forces of the so-called Service de défense, created by the ordinance of 1959. The idea of a service of defense had been conceived for the first time in 1955 by the general secretariat of the national defense. The creation of the service of defense, which, with the military service, formed the national service, mirrored the "globalization" in the conception of national defense, due to an adaptation of the defense to the conditions of modern technological warfare in which the distinction between the military and the civil universe tended to blur. This explains why the service of defense accompanied a system of forces corresponding to the non-military needs of national defense.

5. It should be noted that there was no legislative modification of the

draft between 1950 and 1965. The change in the length of military service during this period, rendered necessary by the military engagement in Algeria, was made possible by applying the Decree of 20 March 1939, authorizing the minister of national defense, in certain circumstances and without any mobilization order, to temporarily retain in active duty classes, or fractions of classes, of conscripts having fulfilled their obligations, or even to recall those in active and normal reserve.

6. "Loi n° 63-1255 du 21 décembre 1963 relative à certaines modifications d'accomplissement des obligations imposées par la loi sur le recrutement," *Journal officiel, lois et décrets*, 22 December 1963, pp. 11456–57; now Section III of the law of 10 June 1971, *Journal officiel*, pp. 5662–63.

7. These reforms were undertaken within the framework of the national service, which, after the ordinance of 1959, was substituted for the traditional notion of military service; for a more detailed discussion about this concept, *see* P. Genevey, "Le Service national," *Revue de Défense nationale* 15 (1959): 395–401. The service of defense, as already mentioned, encompassed a system of tasks corresponding to the nonmilitary needs of national defense. The ordinance of 1959 stipulated that only a part of the active service period could be completed in the service of defense. It is the law of July 1965 that allowed the entire active service to be completed therein. The service of the cooperation and the service of technical aid have been in de facto existence since 1961. The objective of the service of technical aid is to contribute to the

economic development of French overseas territories and *départements*. The service of cooperation proceeds by a similar logic, though more culturally oriented, in favor of foreign countries requesting such aid.

8. These figures were collected in *Avis présenté au nom de la Commission de Défense nationale et des forces armées sur le projet de loi de finance pour 1970*, Doc. Assemblée nationale (2nd session ordinaire, 1969–70), vol. 1, p. 22; *Le Monde*, 21 March 1973, p. 9; André Loyer, "Les Mécanismes de la conscription en France en 1976," *Défense nationale* 32 (October 1976): 38; and the chronicle of Gérard Vaillant in *Défense nationale* 33 (December 1977): 160.

9. Bernard Tricot, "Dossier pour la réforme du recrutement," *Revue de Défense nationale* 21 (1965): 982; Loyer, "Les Mécanismes de la conscription," pp. 38–39.

10. "Décret n° 67-71 du 25 janvier 1967," *Journal officiel, lois et décrets*, 27 January 1967, pp. 990–92.

11. *See* Georges Marey, "Le Service national et le code du service national," Part 1, *Revue militaire générale* 10 (1971): 662.

12. Basteau, "Réserves et mobilisation," *Revue de Défense nationale* 27 (1971): 1451–63.

13. General Gilliot, "Pourquoi la France s'en tient à l'armée de conscription," in *Le Système militaire français: Bilans, problèmes et perspectives*, edited by Jean-Pierre Marichy (Toulouse: Université des Sciences sociales, 1977), p. 54.

14. Anthony S. Bennell, "European Reserve Forces: England, France, and West Germany," in *Supplementary Military Forces: Re-*

serves, Militias, and Auxiliaries, edited by Louis A. Zurcher, Jr. and Gwyn Harries-Jenkins (Beverly Hills, Ca.: Sage Publications, 1978), p. 59.

15. This is an interesting issue, which cannot be studied in depth at this time. For a discussion of the role of the military and its power in time of mobilization, *see* Bernard Chantebout, *L'Organisation générale de la défense nationale en France depuis la fin de la seconde guerre mondiale* (Paris: Librairie générale de Droit et de Jurisprudence, 1967), pp. 369–70.

16. It should be pointed out that, contrary to what is usually thought, the French military establishment has always had a fairly high proportion of career personnel; therefore, relatively speaking, the proportion of draftees who entered the institution in the 1970s has a more important significance than is conveyed at first glance.

17. For the remainder, 13,743 (6.4 percent) served in the central administration, operational, and territorial commanding staffs; 18,816 (8.7 percent) in logistic units; 8,208 (3.8 percent) in service equipment units; 1,351 (0.5 percent) in research units; *see Le Monde*, 29–30 December 1974. The accuracy of these figures has been questioned, especially by the defense specialists of the Socialist party, who assign only 70,000 draftees to combat units; *see also* Antoine Sanguinetti's critique of the French military establishment in his *Le Fracas des armes* (Paris: Hachette, 1975).

18. General Costa de Beauregard, in *Bulletin d'information du Comité Défense-Armée-Nation* 5 (1977); referred to in *Le Monde*, 12 March 1977, p. 12.

19. Tricot, "Dossier pour la réforme du recrutement," p. 984.

20. Vaillant, *Défense nationale* 32 (March 1976): 173.

21. This is explicitly stated in the White Book on national defense: "As is natural, the military service remains, consequently, the essential component of the national service" (*Livre blanc sur la défense nationale* [Paris: CEDOGAR, 1972], vol. 1, p. 30).

22. On this point, *see* "Démographie et conscription," *Armées d'aujourd'hui* 8 (March 1976): 24–25.

23. "Loi n° 73-625 du 10 juillet 1973 modifiant certaines dispositions du code du service national," *Journal officiel, lois et décrets*, 11 July 1973, pp. 7486–87.

24. In other words, all reforms concerning manpower recruitment undertaken after 1950 were proposed without the principle of compulsory universal military service being questioned at all.

25. Indeed, it is not difficult to see that the new system of *dispenses*, though resulting in the disqualification of a higher percentage of draftees, was nevertheless presented in such a way as to be fairer and more congruent with the principle of equality. This was explicitly stated in the bill. The new exemptions, in effect, were justified on the grounds that they were compensations given to those who had already been handicapped (war orphans, for example) or those who were faced with exceptional burdens (sole supporters of families): "the exemption does not create the inequality [but] it reestablishes the equality of duty," as was stated in a preparatory document

concerning this reform; *see* Tricot, "Dossier pour la réforme du recrutement," p. 971.

26. Relatively speaking, therefore, the figures discussed here ought not to be taken at face value and serve to indicate that the French military service is seriously selective. When they denounce the nonegalitarian and selective nature of the state of recruitment, many critics—be they supporters of universal conscription or defenders of an all-volunteer force—implicitly assume that in the past the draft system was egalitarian and universal. Even at the high tides of Napoleonic fever, in the aftermath of the famous 1905 law, or in the interwar period, inequality was rampant. Paradoxically, during the hundred or so years of the existence of the principle of universal military service, the last three decades have perhaps been the *least* inegalitarian. For a view focusing somewhat misleadingly on the high level of selectivity of the French military service, *see* Jérome Dumoulin, "La France: l'armée et la nation," *Le Figaro*, 31 March 1976, p. 2; Alexandre Sanguinetti, "Stratégie directe et stratégie indirecte," *Le Monde*, 15 May 1976, pp. 1, 11. Sanguinetti, for example, pretends that "we have come back to the Gouvion Saint-Cyr law of 1818, that is to say to the drawing of lots." Such a comparison is quite inaccurate. In 1976, 70 percent of the contingent was incorporated into the military and 3 percent into other services (gendarmerie included). Consequently, about 73 percent of the contingent was called up for national defense duty. Let us recall, for the sake of the argument,

that under the terms of the Gouvion Saint-Cyr law, only between 20,000 and 30,000 men served in the military—less than 30 percent of the contingent.

27. Until 1958, conscientious objectors could be sentenced to prison for many years. (In theory, those persisting in their refusal to serve could be imprisoned until the age of forty-nine.) After 1958, they were condemned to eighteen months of imprisonment; the sentence was renewable every time they refused to serve. However, the total length of imprisonment could not exceed five years (three years after 1962). Moreover, conscientious objectors were barred from certain categories of occupations, particularly in public and local administration, and they were not eligible for political and administrative appointments. (Actually, conscientious objectors faced great difficulties in being employed anywhere because of their penal records.)

28. It is interesting to note that conscientious objection was recognized in France by the *Convention* of 19 August 1793 exempting from military duty "all citizens whose denomination and moral beliefs forbid the bearing of arms." Maintained during the Napoleonic period, the principle of conscientious objection was abandoned under the Restoration. It was not until World War II that the question came under discussion again. Yet all attempts at solving the problem (in 1949, in 1956, and then in 1962) failed. The bill of December 1963, proposed for deliberation in July 1963, was the object of tumultuous debates: there were forty

amendments. The text was adopted by a narrow majority of only 204 votes. After several shuttles between the National Assembly and the Senate (which defeated the bill several times), the bill was finally approved on December 11. For details, *see* Pierre Sablières, "Le Statut légal de l'objection de conscience en France" (Ph.D. dissertation, Paris, 1971); Jean-Pierre Cattelain, *L'Objection de conscience* (Paris: Presses Universitaires de France, 1973).

29. After 1972, conscientious objectors found themselves more isolated and constrained to perform, under quasi-military discipline, tasks totally irrelevant to their humanitarian and altruistic aspirations; *see* Michel Castaing, "Les Hors-la-loi de l'antimilitarisme," *La Monde*, 6 February 1974, pp. 1, 10; Cattelain, *L'Objection de conscience*, p. 62.

30. Federal Minister of Defense, *White Paper 1975/1976: The Security of the Federal Republic of Germany and the Development of the Federal Armed Forces* (Bonn: Press and Information Office of the Government of the Federal Republic of Germany, 1976), p. 162. After the law of 13 July 1977 suppressing all jury examinations of the authenticity of the motives given by conscientious objectors, the number of applicants jumped to 130,000. This reform was suspended in January 1978 by the federal constitutional court at Karlsruhe.

31. *See* Chapter 2.

32. Pierre-M. Gallois, *L'Adieu aux armées* (Paris: Albin Michel, 1976); *see also* Gérard Vaillant, "Forces nucléaires et conscription: un divorce inévitable?" *Défense nationale* 32 (June 1976): 123–30.

33. *See* note 17.

34. Partisans of an all-volunteer or quasi-volunteer force have always formed a small minority. Their opinions are generally personal and do not represent the official view of the political group or party to which they belong. Such was the case of a few *rapporteurs*, such as General Stehlin, and some members or former members of the *majorité*, such as Alexandre Sanguinetti, Michel Jobert, and Pierre Messmer. Moreover, one notes that they favored an all-volunteer force in the strictest sense very rarely; rather, they were proponents of a quasi-volunteer force with some kind of civil national service. Alexandre Sanguinetti, who was a fervent partisan of the all-volunteer force, once declared, "This being said, I shall never request the abrogration of the *An VI* law allowing *patrie* to call up its children for its defense." About these proposals, *see* Alexandre Sanguinetti, *La France et l'arme atomique* (Paris: R. Julliard, 1964): Pierre Stehlin, "Contre le service militaire pour un service civique," *Preuves* 8 (1971): 110–15.

35. *Défense nationale* 30 (January 1974): 167; *Le Monde*, 10 November 1973, pp. 5–7.

36. A symbolic materialization of the relationship between citizenship and conscription, a relation that was at the crux of the social and political development of nineteenth-century Western democracies, can be found in the fact that young draftees, having accomplished their military duty before the age of twenty-one, became full citizens with civic and political rights; *see Livre blanc sur la défense nationale*, p. 38. The voting age was

lowered to eighteen in 1974. On the relationship between conscription and democracy, *see* Herman Benkema, "The Social and Political Aspects of Conscription: Europe's Experience," in *War as a Social Institution*, edited by J. D. Clarkson and T. C. Cochran (New York: Columbia University Press, 1941); Morris Janowitz, "Military Institutions and Citizenship in Western Societies," *Armed Forces and Society* 2 (1976): 185–204.

37. *Livre blanc sur la défense nationale*, p. 28.

38. Ibid., p. 34.

39. On 14 May 1974, reported in *Le Monde*, 16 May 1974.

40. For details about such evaluations, *see Avis présenté au nom de la Commission de l'économie générale et du plan sur le projet de loi relatif au recrutement en vue de l'accomplissement du service national*, Doc. Assemblée nationale, n° 1381 (2nd session ordinaire, 1964–65), pp. 8–13; Tricot, "Dossier pour la réforme du recrutement," pp. 976–77, 984; Gilbert Koenig, "Affectation des ressources et systèmes de conscription en France," *Revue économique* 24 (1973): 65–108; Vaillant, *Défense nationale* 32 (March 1976): 175–78; Gilliot, "Pourquoi la France s'en tient à l'armée de conscription."

41. "Conscription ou armée de métier: réponses aux questions sur le service national," *Armées d'aujourd'hui* 19 (April 1977): 16.

42. Vaillant, *Défense nationale* 32 (March 1976): 17.

43. "Conscription ou armée de métier," p. 17.

44. *See* Edward L. Morse, *Foreign Policy and Interdependence in Gaullist France* (Princeton: Princeton University Press, 1973), especially Chapter 4, pp. 147–203.

45. A reading of the annual reports and *avis* of the national defense and armed forces commission of the National Assembly or the Senate upon the occasion of the vote on the national defense budget would shed more light upon these problems.

46. Claude Lachaux, "Economie et défense," *Défense nationale* 32 (April 1976): 29–46.

47. Jacqueline Beaujeu-Garnier, *La population française après le recensement de 1975* (Paris: Gallimard, 1976), pp. 135–36.

48. Ibid., p. 170; Jean-Paul Courtheaux, "Population active," *Population et avenir* 525 (1975).

49. This was the case of the working class; *see*, for example, Richard F. Hamilton, *Affluence and the French Worker in the Fourth Republic* (Princeton: Princeton University Press, 1967).

50. *Le Monde*, 6 March 1975, p. 10. In May 1976 a French private received $40 per month; a corporal, $50; and a sergeant, $60. By comparison, the *de luxe* Dutch draftee, since the Vredeling reforms, was the best paid ($182 per month), then came the German conscript ($60), the Swedish ($60 the first three months, then $81), the Belgian (with $56 the first six months, and $74 after that), and the French, followed by the Italian conscript ($16.20) and the Spanish ($4.20).

51. Vaillant, *Défense nationale* 32 (March 1976): 175–76.

52. Pierre Messmer and Jean-Pierre Chevènement, *Le Service militaire* (Paris: Balland, 1977).

53. The *Livre blanc*, originated by

Michel Debré, is a typical example of this conception.

54. *Carrefour*, 9 April 1969, p. 5.

55. For example, it is difficult not to consider the famous Debré law of 1970 abolishing student deferments as a device of political engineering, especially when it is analyzed in relation to the problems of higher education in France. With the democratization of education, the increasing numbers of baccalaureate holders, and the simplification of access to the universities, the density of the student population was substantially augmented without a parallel modification of the economic structures or of the labor market. Further, the old but still-living tradition of the university diploma, a symbol of assured social mobility supported by the socio-educational prejudices of the general public and future employers, contributed to the serious growth of this phenomenon. Thus, the abolition of student deferments and the arbitrary setting of the induction age at eighteen to twenty-one years appeared to be a means by which the state could direct the mass of high school students and first- or second-year students out of universities. But what seems to have inflamed the suspicion of the students about government sincerity when dealing with conscription was the institution by the Ministry of National Education of a Diploma of General University Studies (*diplome d'études universitaires générales*, or DEUG), to be presented upon completion of the first two years of university study. The fact that such a diploma would be obtained at about age twenty-one, the upper age limit for induction, led

one to suspect that this procedure was a new method of regulating the number of students. It could also be viewed as a measure for deterring the pursuit of a longer course of study, for, as careful observation showed, after a year's interruption, the number of students reenrolling was quite low. As has been noted, the two logical dates for induction were set either before entry into the university or before the second cycle of university studies, that is, before the two most populated periods of the university cycle. This led people to think that the civil authorities were not insensitive to these problems. This double measure—the abolition of deferments and the institution of the DEUG—as a fortuitous or calculated coincidence, therefore made military service into an instrument for university "selection"—an evil concept, it goes without saying, for the partisans of complete democracy in education. On this point, *see* Jacques Robert, "La Sélection par le service," *Le Monde*, March 1973.

56. For details, *see* Arpad Kovacs, "French Military Institutions before the Franco-Prussian War," *American Historical Review* 51 (1946): 217–35; A. Becheyras, "La Question militaire à la veille de la guerre de 1870," *La Revue critique* 21 (1913): 386–402.

57. On this point, *see* the excellent analysis by Richard D. Challener, *The French Theory of the Nation in Arms: 1866–1939* (New York: Russsell and Russell, 1965).

58. Ibid.; and Arpad Kovacs, "French Military Legislation in the Third Republic: 1871–1940," *Military Affairs* 13 (1949): 1–13; Joseph Monteilhet, *Les Institutions militaires*

de la France, 1814–1932 (Paris: Félix Alcan, 1932).

59. Charles de Gaulle, *Vers l'armée de métier*, translated into English as *The Army of the Future* (London: Hutchinson, 1940).

60. Robert A. Doughty, "De Gaulle's Concept of a Mobile, Professional Army: Genesis of the French Defeat," *Parameters* 4 (1974): 28.

61. Alfred Vagts, *A History of Militarism* (New York: Meridian Books, 1959), p. 13.

62. Karl Liebknecht, *Militarismus und Antimilitarismus*, translated into English as *Militarism and Antimilitarism* (Cambridge: Rivers Press, 1973), pp. 22–23.

63. Karl Marx, "Vierter jährlicher Bericht des generalrats der internationalen Arbeiterassoziation," *Werke*, vol. 16 (Berlin: Ost, 1964), p. 321. Quoted from Shinkichi Eto, "The Concept of 'Militarism' in Marxism-Leninism and Maoism," in *Military and State in Modern Asia*, edited by Harold Z. Schiffrin (Jerusalem: Jerusalem Academic Press, 1976), p. 89.

64. Jules Simon was the leader of the Republicans before 1870. He is quoted from Raoul Girardet, *La Société militaire dans la France contemporaine, 1816–1939* (Paris: Plon, 1953), pp. 42–43.

65. Doughty, "De Gaulle's Concept of a Mobile, Professional Army," p. 26.

66. It must be noted in passing that after the events that occurred in 1907 in southeastern France when the 17th infantry regiment of Agde was called up to reestablish public order during the vinicultural crisis, conscripts were called up to serve outside the area of their origin or residence. At Beziers, many soldiers refused to obey orders to fire at demonstrators because they had a parent or a relative involved in the strike. In the 1970s, interestingly enough, an effort has been made to reverse the previous habits. It was decided, for instance, that the average distance between the place of assignment and the place of residence should not exceed 400 kilometers. And among draftees from the Atlantic or the Mediterranean coasts, only volunteers serve in units posted in Germany, which are made up of draftees from the eastern (41 percent) and the mideastern (32 percent) regions of the country. In 1976, the geographical distribution of the conscripted force looked as shown on p. 172.

67. Quoted in Girardet, *La Société militaire*, p. 28, from J. Ambert, *Essais en faveur de l'armée* (1839).

68. For details about this matter, *see* Girardet, *La Société militaire*; David B. Ralston, *The Army of the Republic: The Place of the Military in the Political Evolution of France, 1871–1914* (Cambridge, Mass.: MIT Press, 1967); Leo Loubère, "Left-Wing Radicals, Strikes, and the Military, 1880–1907," *French Historical Studies* 3 (1963): 93–105.

69. Robert O. Paxton, *Parades and Politics at Vichy: The French Officer Corps under Marshal Pétain* (Princeton: Princeton University Press, 1966), pp. 14–15.

70. Quoted in Challener, *The French Theory of the Nation in Arms*, note 40.

71. Formula currently and repeatedly used in all types of leftist literature, Socialist as well as ultra-

	Assignment			
Origins	West and Mediterranean	Mideastern/Western (north to south)	Eastern	Germany
West and Mediterranean	53%	30%	14%	3%
Mideastern/Western (north to south)		39%	29%	32%
Eastern		59%		41%

Left; for an interesting view of the problem, *see* Louis de Villefosse, "Armée nationale ou armée de guerre civile," *Esprit* 18 (1950): 732–48.

72. Speech given at the 22nd Congress of the French Communist party; *see Cahiers du Communisme* (February–March 1976); and in the same issue *see also* Louis Baillot, "L'armée et la voie démocratique au Socialisme," pp. 187–90.

73. *L'Unité*, 1–7 February 1974, pp. 1–2.

74. For more details about the organization of the forces of internal order *see* Jean-Louis Loubet del Bayle, Lucien Mandeville, and Alain Picard, "Les Forces de maintien de l'ordre en France," *Défense nationale* 33 (July 1977): 59–76.

75. "Décret n° 62-207 du 24 février 1962 relatif à l'organisation de la défense opérationelle du territoire," *Journal officiel, lois et décrets*, 25 February 1962, p. 1900.

76. Chantebout, *L'Organisation générale de la défense nationale en France depuis la fin de la seconde guerre mondiale*, p. 323.

77. *See*, for example, Jacques Beauvallet, "Cybernétique de défense et secrétariat général de la dé-

fense nationale," *Défense nationale* 29 (August–September 1973): 3–28; *see also* his more explicit position in *Forces armées françaises* 18 (January–February 1974); Bernard Usureau, "Défense civile et stratégie de dissuasion," *Défense nationale* 29 (August–September 1973): 41–52. In an article, "L'Armée vue du dedans, reflexions d'un appelé après un an de service national," *Esprit* 43 (1975): 413–18, Bernard Kitou reported that in a classified document, the army staff requested that military units be trained further in antisubversion warfare in urban areas (p. 417).

78. Jacques Isnard, "Quand l'armée se renseigne sur l'adversaire intérieur," *Le Monde*, 17 October 1973, p. 16. In a speech before an assembly of reserve officers on May 13, 1973, in Lille, Defense Minister Robert Galley declared that "the military remains the only recourse of our liberal society." *See also*, Antoine Sanguinetti, *Le Monde*, 19 June 1976, p. 26; Claude Bourdet, "La France et son armée," *Politique aujourd'hui*, January–February 1976, pp. 110–11.

79. Dominique Arrivé, Marie Laffranque, and Bernard Vanderville, *L'Etat de défense: économie, société et répression* (Paris: Maspero, 1970).

80. From *Frontière, Les Cahiers du CERES*, September 1973.

81. One can read in the common program of the government elaborated by the Socialists and the Communists: "The ordinance of January 7, 1959, will be abrogated and the laws necessary to the organization of the national defense, to the remodeling of its organs of direction and administration and to the parliamentary control on National Defense, will be adopted" (*Programme commun de gouvernement du parti communiste et du parti socialiste; 27 juin 1962* [Paris: Editions Sociales, 1972], p. 172).

82. Alexis de Tocqueville, *De la démocratie en Amérique*, translated into English as *Democracy in America*, trans. George Lawrence and ed. J. P. Mayer (Garden City, N.Y.: Doubleday, Anchor Books, 1969), p. 652.

83. Regarding the role of the draftees in the failure of the Algiers putsch of April 1961, *see* Christian Herbert, "Quatre journées d'avril en Algérie," *La Nef*, July–September 1961, pp. 112–22; for a view that questions the draftees' role *see* Walter Kerr, "The French Army in Trouble," *Foreign Affairs* 40 (1961): 89–94.

84. Pierre Métayer, "Le Réforme du service militaire: une loi antidémocratique," *La Revue socialiste*, October 1965, p. 238.

85. One should recall that as early as 1949, the Socialists (SFIO) opposed a project (elaborated by André Philip) proposing the creation of a sort of civil service for conscientious objectors. Interestingly enough, even today, though the Left defends objectors against unnecessary repression, it tends to avoid any excessive liberalism and, as one author stated, "remains faithful to the *entrisme* in the military and fears that too rapid an extension of conscientious objection would lead to the establishment of an all-volunteer force," Cattelain, *L'Objection de conscience*, p. 75.

86. *Le Monde*, 15 January 1975, p. 9. On 20 February 1975, Charles Hernu once again declared, "We Socialists reject antimilitarism and any form of irresponsible actions and demand a real military service of six months."

87. *Le Monde*, 22–23 September 1974.

88. Charles Hernu, *Le Soldat-citoyen: essai sur la sécurité de la France* (Paris: Flammarion, 1975); Jean-Pierre Chevènement, "La Volonté du peuple est la suprême dissuasion," *Le Monde*, 9 November 1973; as for the Communist proposal, *see* "Un Statut démocratique du soldat-citoyen et pour une défense nationale au service de l'indépendance nationale et de la paix," *L'Humanité*, 21 September 1974.

A similar attitude was also observed in Italy, as shown by Angelo Panebianco, "La Politica militare de PCI e del PSI," *Citta E Regione* 2 (February 1976): 49–64.

89. *Le Point*, 29 January 1973.

90. François Helluy, "Les Jeunes officiers de l'Armée de Terre: une étude psycho-sociologique," EMSST thesis, Centre de Sociologie de la Défense nationale, 1974, pp. 74 and, in Appendix, 19; among the rare comments written in favor of the all-volunteer model by officers, *see* Sanval [pseud.], "Pour l'armée de métier," *Le Monde*, 6, 7, and 8 January 1976.

91. François Maurin, "Pérennité et

nécessité de la défense," *Défense nationale* 29 (July 1973); also quoted in Jean Boulègue, "Société militaire et crise de société," *Esprit* 43 (1975): 373.

92. *Forces armées françaises* 18 (January–February 1974); the sentence in quotation marks preceding Beauvallet's words is from Jacques Isnard's commentary on the Beauvallet article, *Le Monde*, 24 January 1974, p. 24.

93. This idea of investing the military with such a mission was born during the aftermath of the Franco-Prussian War and the Commune. It was thought of as a device whereby a new sense of national unity could be forged. But it had other sources as well. In making the officers teach Republican ideals to young draftees, the Republican government attempted to force the military to behave in conformity with the very values it was teaching.

94. Actually, the cases of the Armistice army as well as that of the army in Algeria were deviant only to the extent that the doctrine they sought to impose on the civil community was no longer feeding on the old Republican ideal. But paradoxically, the attitude and the behavior technically adhered to the logic of the Third Republic's vision of the role of the military. On this point, *see* Paxton, *Parades and Politics*; Philip C. F. Bankwitz, *Maxime Weygand and Civil-Military Relations in Modern France* (Cambridge, Mass.: Harvard University Press, 1967).

95. Edgar S. Furniss, Jr., *De Gaulle and the French Army: A Crisis in the Civil-Military Relations* (New York: Twentieth Century Fund, 1964), pp. 164–65.

96. Jean Valluy, "L'Armée française

en 1961," *Revue des deux mondes*, 15 June 1961, p. 589; quoted in Paxton, *Parades and Politics*, 431.

97. In this regard, *see* two interesting articles; Philip C. F. Bankwitz, "Maxime Weygand and the Army-Nation Concept in the Modern French Army," *French Historical Studies* 2 (1961): 157–88, and Robert Soucy, "France—Veterans' Politics Between the Wars," in *The War Generation: Veterans of the First World War*, edited by Stephen A. Ward (Port Washington, N.Y.: Kennikat, 1975), pp. 59–103.

98. E. Walter, "Notre enthousiasme," *Revue de Défense nationale* 26 (1970): 764–66.

99. Helluy, "Les jeunes officiers de l'Armée de Terre," p. 19, in Appendix.

100. The reading of military journal editorials, such as those in *Défense nationale*, *Le Casoar*, *Forces armées françaises*, and so on, and of many other writings by army officers would shed more light on the rampant reluctance or distrust concerning elaborate technology and the rise of "push-button warfare." Not so long ago, in the early 1960s, General Valluy, for example, denounced the danger of having too technologized an army; on this point, *see* Boulègue, "Société militaire et crise de société," *Esprit* 43 (1975): 366–69; Furniss, *De Gaulle and the French Army*, p 168. *See also*, Chapter 6.

101. Boulègue, "Société militaire crise de société," p. 382.

102. *Le Point*, 12 April 1976, p. 77.

103. Boulègue, "Société militaire et crise de société," p. 367; for further details on the question of career motivations, *see* Chapter 6.

104. A recent survey revealed that with a monthly allowance of $210, the number of enlistments would reach 50,000 men (25,000 more than under the present system), with an allowance of $310, it could be 65,000, and 75,000 men with a monthly salary of $500. It appears that with an increase in salary (in addition to room and board, professional training, and promotion to the rank of corporal after three years) from $210 to $500 the proportion of those who would enlist would only increase from 8 percent to 15 percent, and those who might enlist would increase by one percent from 9 to 10 percent ("Conscription ou armée de metier," p. 19).

105. These difficulties were discussed in a series of articles published in *Défense nationale* 33 (August–September 1977): 21–72.

106. On this question of the legitimacy of the armed forces *see* the articles by Lawrence Martin and Stanley Hoffmann in "Force in Modern Societies," *Adelphi Papers* 102 (Winter 1973); Gwyn Harries-Jenkins and Jacques Van Doorn, eds., *The Military and the Problem of Legitimacy* (Beverly Hills, Ca.: Sage Publications, 1976).

107. The objective of such movements was aimed to attract public interest and to arouse debates over the Algerian War. If the attack was directed against the army it was only insofar as the army was viewed as the secular arm of an unjust colonial domination. The principle of conscription always remained outside the debates. When André Philip and Pierre Mendès-France, leaders of the Socialist Unified party, defended a group of *insoumis* prosecuted for draft evasion, they specified that the party, as well as they themselves, did not approve of draft evasion, even though they sympathized with one's refusal to participate in the repression. *Le Monde*, 6 September 1960 and 4 October 1962.

108. Viviane Isambert-Jamati, "Remarques sur le service militaire," *Revue française de Sociologie* 2 (1961): 100–105.

109. *Sondages* 25 (n° 3 1963): 104; ibid. 29 (n° 4 1967): 60; ibid. 32 (n° 1-2 1970): 165.

110. Jean-Marc Lech, "L'Evolution de l'opinion des Français sur la défense à travers les sondages de 1972 à 1976," *Défense nationale* 33 (August–September 1977): 47–56; *Valeurs actuelles*, 19–25 January 1976.

111. *Sondages* 30 (n° 4 1968): 19; "Le Service militaire pourquoi faire?" *France-Soir*, 6–9 June 1973; Lech, "L'Evolution de l'opinion des Français," p. 51.

112. *Sondages* 30 (n° 4 1968): 19.

113. Federal Minister of Defense, *White Paper 1975/1976*.

114. Commission Armées-Jeunesse.

115. *Valeurs actuelles*, SOFRES poll (January 1976).

116. Federal Minister of Defense, *White Paper 1975/1976*; Wehrstruktur-Kommission der Bundesregierung, *Die Wehrstruktur in der Bundesrepublik Deutschland* (Bonn, 1972–73), pp. 143–44.

117. This poll also confirmed the stability of the attachment of French society to military service; this was illustrated again in another poll taken in November 1976, which indicated that 72 percent of the population

interviewed found military service useful or indispensable; *see La Croix*, 29 November 1976.

118. *Sondages* 30 (n° 4 1968): 19.

119. "Le Service militaire pourquoi faire?"; Lech, "L'Evolution de l'opinion des Français," p. 50; *Valeurs actuelles* (January 1976).

120. This refers to a series of events that took place after 1973. The *appel des cents* was a petition requesting a number of reforms for the material well-being of the conscript; the petition was prepared by a committee of a hundred privates and sent to the two candidates in the 1974 presidential race. Widely circulated, this petition received thousands of signatures and was the object of a great deal of publicity. However, this was not the only form of draftee unrest. A few instances among numerous cases: in 1974 draftees belonging to the units stationed in Draguignan and in January 1975 draftees stationed in Karlsruhe undertook demonstrations in the streets of these towns; in November 1975 a group of conscripts went so far as to affiliate a soldier committee with the CFDT, a section of the labor union federation.

121. Edward Shils, "Plenitude and Scarcity: The Anatomy of an International Cultural Crisis," in *The Intellectuals and the Powers and other Essays* (Chicago: University of Chicago Press, 1972), pp. 265 ff.

122. Stanley Hoffmann, "Protest in Modern France," in *The Revolution in World Politics*, edited by Morton A. Kaplan (New York: John Wiley, 1962), p. 69. On this point, *see also* Bernard E. Brown, *Protest in Paris* (Morristown, N.J.: General Learning Press, 1974).

123. Jesse R. Pitts, "Continuity and Change in Bourgeois France," in *In Search of France*, edited by Stanley Hoffmann et al. (Cambridge, Mass.: Harvard University Press, 1963); *see also* Jesse R. Pitts, "La Communauté délinquante," *Esprit* 38 (1970): 69–81.

124. Charles Ailleret, "Evolution nécessaire de nos structures militaires," *Revue de Défense nationale* 21 (1965): 947.

125. André Mesnard, "National Security and France," *The Annals of the American Academy of Political and Social Sciences* 241 (1945): 160–66.

PART THREE ● THE PROFESSIONAL DIMENSION OF THE FRENCH MILITARY ESTABLISHMENT

INTRODUCTION

Two particular aspects of the professional dimension of the military institution will be studied in detail: the career motivations and conceptions, on the one hand, and the discipline, on the other. The first chapter attempts to define and describe the main patterns of motivation and conception of career among the various categories of military personnel that can be observed, and assesses their respective importance over time, across services, and throughout ranks. The second chapter covers an analysis of organizational authority and discipline, in other words, the patterns of relationships between the men of different ranks, and tries to identify the changes in the way these relations were organized.

Indeed, the choice of these two particular questions as the object of analysis has been guided partly by the density of the information available, but above all by the fact that these two variables constitute powerful indicators for the definition of the professional profile of the military institution. Why men enter the military, how they conceive of their career, and how they relate with those above and below them are, in effect, a set of questions the answers of which highlight such a profile and its evolution during the last few decades.

CHAPTER SIX ● CAREER
MOTIVATIONS AND CONCEPTIONS

For a long time, military life has been conceived of as a special state—a *stand* to borrow from Weberian vocabulary—and a military career as a sacred endeavor. The career of arms was seen as a social role to be spiritually and physically embraced as a religious *sacerdoce*, even sometimes as if it were a source of salvation. "If the bullets have led to the death of many bodies, in how many souls have they brought a new life?" asked Paul de Molènes in *Les Soirées du bordj*, praising the virtue of military life. The military profession was viewed as a condition of living implying complete self-sacrifice and disregard for material rewards. Like those who entered the church, those who entered the military were driven by vocation, by the conscious feeling of being called, as the Latin root *vocare* and the German *beruf* (described by Max Weber in his seminal *Protestantische Etik und der Geist des Kapitalismus*) imply. The following words, written in 1938 by a French general about the officer's career, encapsulate this traditional approach to the military profession: "To be an officer is not to exercise a trade, it is the fulfillment of a sacerdotal engagement. He who is not convinced of this is only a 'wearer of bars.' . . . Apostle of the cult of the *patrie*, the officer worthy of such title must as a prelude to possible sacrifice on the battlefield completely give himself up to the noble duties of his function." [1]

Together with vocation, tradition and "militarism" have been the key components of military career motivations. Tradition was an especially important source of career commitment in the preindustrial military. Members of a specific segment of society often had to serve in the king's armies because of the demands of tradition. This was the case of the sword nobility in feudal Europe and during the *ancien régime*. It was especially true in societies where military service by the nobility was quasi-institutionalized, as in Prussia and Russia, or strongly enforced by social usages, as in Poland and Sweden. Yet with the centralization of the state and the emergence of a national consciousness through the idea of citizenry that materialized with the rise of modern revolutionary nationalism, the tradition of service modified; it became less mechanical and one served no longer because of social or legal norms but because of personal choice. And as early as the beginning of the nineteenth century the ideal of service, or service to the *patrie*, stood as an important motivational source of military recruitment.

With the organizational expansion of the military institution and its increasing war-ready deployment, these motivations had often "militarized," that is, become deeply impregnated with such tendencies as drive for glory, desire for command, and love of combat and risk.

These motives, whether based on vocational, self-sacrificing drives or on strictly militaristic aims, were functionally relevant to achieving the primary goal of the military—war-making. In other words, they constituted a sufficient and, one is tempted to say, necessary condition for effectiveness and strategic productivity in the conduct of war. Based upon heroism, self-sacrifice, drive for danger, and disregard for death, these motivations were in harmony with the nature of warfare and the objectives of the military organization.

However, with technological changes, including the development of the mass armed forces under the impact of full industrialism, hence with the transformation of military professionalism under the impact of specialization and expertise, career motivations "secularized," although former patterns of motivations did not completely disappear. Motives appeared more "civilianized" and technologically oriented. In terms of career conception, the emphasis was put on expertise and technical or managerial specialization rather than on the idea of public service. Such a trend continued and was even accentuated with the decline of the mass armed forces format. For example, with the nuclear revolution, vocational, traditional, and, to a lesser extent, militaristic motives turned out to be not only poorly functional, but also incongruous with the context produced by a nuclear strategy. Reliance upon the nuclear deterrence paradigm in the conduct and regulation of international relations reduced the possibility of major or minor armed conflicts to the point that combat is no longer the ultimate aim of the military. To some extent, the use of force would mean the failure of this deterrence strategy. Thus, traditional patterns of motivation such as military vocation and militarism, based on readiness for self sacrifice and conceived in the belief of the inevitability of armed encounters, became increasingly outmoded in respect to the new organizational purpose of a modern military institution, an institution whose rationale was the preservation of peace with a minimum use of force. Consequently, vocational and militaristic elements in the matrix of motivations gave way to more rational and secularized ones. This is especially evident among individuals recruited for the more technologically developed and civilianlike services, for these services are the ones most closely associated with the manipulation of nuclear equipment. Interesting in this respect is the fact that as a result of the continuing emphasis on expertise and job responsibility and of a change in the social values of the parent society due to the development of welfarist, hedonistic attitudes and enhanced sensitivity to material affluence, career expectations took on new forms. They became more reward oriented, in the sense that, among the professional military, claims for status and demands for improved material and professional conditions were being phrased less in terms of responsibility and expertise and more in those of personal well-being. Job motivations grew more careerist; job security and material welfare emerged as new incentives for embracing a military career.

Such a pattern of change in career motivations and in the nature of these motivations is highly idealized. In actuality different types of motivations are to be found together with one probably being dominant. In his study of the American professional soldier, Morris Janowitz pointed out that with the development of the mass army, there was a shift in which motivations based on the "missionary zeal" slowly lost precedence before more careerist ones; emphasis was also shifted from a career conception based on public service to one focusing on expertise.[2] Recent studies show that, in the context of the rise of an all-volunteer force model, these trends took new forms. Charles Moskos, for example, argued that in the American all-volunteer force the concept of the military career was again being modified. He pointed out that given the changing nature of expectations, especially increasing demands for material gratifications, working conditions, "equal pay for equal work," comparability with civilian employment, and so on, the military career became simply another occupation as it moved away from traditional patterns derived from the calling, or professional, models.[3]

Though reliable empirical data are frustratingly scant,[4] similar forms of change can be traced in the French military. Yet it must be stated that, given the absence of systematic evidence, this study will focus on dominant types and shifts in these types of career motivation and conception among French soldiers.

Changing Patterns of Career Motivation

Until the early 1960s, the dominant pattern of career motivation was clearly of a very traditional nature, particularly among officers. Interviews with officers who entered the military during the decade following World War II showed rather well the continuing importance of military vocation and tradition. There was also a continued attachment to values such as patriotism and a taste for command and discipline, although these were mixed with more secularized motivations such as desire for action and travel and, to a lesser extent, an expressed technical interest among officers entering the air force and the navy. For many, and this was more pronounced among officers recruited from military academies than among those commissioned from the ranks, the military career was seen as a lifetime *sacerdoce* and a quasi-sacred mission. Defense of the *patrie* and the search for glory were viewed as the only valuable motives for a man's career. And, as pictured in military literature, shaped by military academy instructors, and fancied by French novelists, the lieutenant of the 1950s could have been the twin of his prewar predecessor. And if Psychari or Bournazel were no longer the main sources of professional inspiration for the young lieutenant of the postwar period, the authors most likely to be found on his bookshelf were their direct descendants. More than one young officer found his "Damascus path" reading de Lattre, Weygand, or Juin; more than one dreamed of that "trail which leads nowhere . . . the trail where one dies like that. . . ," and prayed, "O God, help me to die greatly on this trail," to use Bigeard's celebrated metaphor of the military life.[5] To a great extent, the career motivations found among groups usually considered the most traditional, such as the paratroopers, whose mentality fed on the "rejection of materialism, the exaltation of asceticism, violence and risk, of action for action's sake,"[6] were, in reality, hardly exaggerated deviations from the collective French military model for this time. Referring to the dominant model of military men of the late 1950s, Jean Planchais wrote: "In the United States, the symbol of the modern soldier is the helmeted pilot in his 'anti-g' flying suit. . . . In France, it is the muscular tanned paratrooper, the man 'painted' to blend in with the jungle, with his chiefs living the same life and sharing the same dangers, disdaining bureaucrats and intellectuals."[7]

A survey conducted in 1961 among 1,250 candidates at the military academies helped to confirm the preceding observations. When asked to classify the factors having influenced their decision to embrace a military career by order of importance, respondents' replies were distributed according to the pattern summarized in Table 6.1.

What is important to note is that this general distribution varied only slightly according to the type of service chosen as the locus of the career. The motivation pattern of Saint-Cyr candidates closely followed this distribution. Dominant attitudes of the Saint-Cyr candi-

Table 6.1. Career Motivations of Military Academy Candidates, 1960 (ranked)

Primary motivations	1	Patriotic ideal
		Leadership
	3	Travel
	4	Risk
		Fraternity in arms
Secondary motivations	6	Glory attached to the profession
	7	Recruitment advertising
		Familial tradition
Elements not influencing	9	Technical specialization
the decision	10	Employment security
	11	Difficulty with other civilian school examinations
	12	Circumstances independent of the candidate's will
	13	Advice from teacher

Source: Centre d'Etudes et d'Instruction psychologiques de l'Armée de l'Air, "Attitudes et motivation des candidats aux grandes écoles militaires," *Revue française de Sociologie* 2 (1961): 140.

dates were expressed through three motivations: the search for an ideal, which indicated the existence of a strong vocation; militarism; and a taste for combat, generally placed in opposition to a taste for technology.[8] It was also noticed that militarist proclivities in the motivation patterns of Saint-Cyr candidates were more pronounced among those who took the "humanities" options for the entrance examination (history or languages); those taking the "sciences" options seemed more open to the prospect of technical specialization. On the whole, however, differences remain insignificant. For example, the majority of candidates expressed a preference for serving in those branches of the armed services with the lowest technical level. Artillery, engineering, and communications were generally neglected, whereas the marines, the cavalry, and the naval infantry were the most-favored branches. "Whatever the nuances [between these groups of Saint-Cyr candidates], it remains that it is still to the officer's traditional archetype that the great majority of the future Saint-Cyriens refer."[9]

Though among the naval academy candidates, "desire for travel" came first and "patriotic ideal" fourth, their pattern of motivations did not deviate greatly from the general model or even from the model of the army academy candidates. Technical motives such as "desire for technical specialization" ranked tenth.[10] Another survey concerning naval academy officers recruited between 1945 and 1960 underlined this trend since a significant number of militaristic/vocational motivations were noted.[11]

Only among air force academy candidates were the motivations different. "Patriotic ideal," for example, ranked sixth, whereas such factors as "desire for technical specialization" came third. "Desire for travel" ranked first. Yet, on the whole, there is little doubt that it was the traditional militaristic pattern that dominated officers recruited from the military academies. As the authors of the detailed survey on military academy candidates summarized: "The great military virtues remain the essential confessed element of the orientation toward the profession of arms. . . . The future evolution of the armed forces toward a more and more important technical specialization does not seem to concern most of the young men looking forward to a military career."[12]

Further analysis of the officer of the postwar decade indicates that he approached the military career as a special endeavor and related the functions to be performed as an officer to the final goal of the military institution. In other words, he consciously identified with the ultimate mission of the armed forces, combat. Because his reference system was the military institution, he fully embraced military norms of behavior, both inside and outside the institution, and developed a strong feeling of being different from the other working members of the parent society.

It has not been possible to collect any systematic data about other segments of the officer corps, particularly those who were not recruited from the military academies, or about NCOs and enlistees. Tangential inquiries, however, through in-service publications and informal interviews did not lead to any observations significantly different from what could have been inferred from the preceding discussion. Among officers, whether they were recruited through officer schools for NCOs or whether they came up from the ranks, the dominant pattern of motivation remained of a vocational or militaristic nature. Career motivation indicated that the military trade was viewed as a calling rather than a profession per se, although perhaps with less intensity than among officers recruited from the military academies.

As for the NCOs, all that can be said is that across services a greater difference can be noted in their attitudes than in that of the officers. In the army, militaristic motivations were prevalent, whereas in the navy and the air force, antiroutine (search for opportunities to perform activities that cannot be performed in the civilian world) or technically oriented motivations had some importance. In the latter services, the professional conception of career prevailed over the vocational conception in some cases.

On the whole, though, the ubiquity of the militaristic/vocational pattern during the 1950s cannot be denied. Yet, to be completely accurate, while our goal is to attempt to uncover dominant patterns of motivation, it should be added that indirect investigations reveal that a small margin of career military, in the army in particular, appeared to have entered the military for purely careerist motives, the search for a protected niche. The fact that a good number of officers and NCOs come from social sectors that remained outside postwar socioeconomic changes and thus found it difficult, if not impossible, to adjust to the new social system, partially explains the existence of such careerist outlooks. But this focusing upon what has been called "military poujadisme"[13] must not be exaggerated. And in the end, one can assume, without reshaping reality too much, that careerist and technically oriented motives were, during the decade and a half following World War II, of secondary importance, overshadowed by the traditional pattern with its emphasis on vocation and militarism. To a great extent the continuous involvement of the French military in colonial conflict between 1945 and 1961, a type of conflict that was by nature pretechnological in which traditional and heroic styles of warfare prevailed, helps to explain the importance of the military vocation and militaristic career motives. These, it can be argued, were the most relevant to this type of military commitment.

Entering the 1960s, one witnessed a significant change in the career motivation pattern and in the general approach toward the profession of arms. Instead of being homogeneous, the emerging model of motivations and career representations of the postcolonial military establishment was somewhat pluralistic. However, a distinction must be made between the officer corps and the noncommissioned personnel, as two different patterns can be observed. First, the military vocation as a form of career guide was on the decline, though it was still a salient characteristic of the army officers. A significant, albeit indirect, measure of this trend is the age at which the decision to embrace the military profession was made, since the younger the decision was made, the higher the likelihood for a strong vocation. According to a 1971 survey, 41 percent of the army officers interviewed, compared to 23 percent of the air force officers, claimed that they decided to enter the military during their childhood. Forty percent of the air force officers, however, compared to 24 percent of the army officers, decided to stay in the armed forces at the time (26 percent against 13 percent) or after (14 percent against 11 percent) they entered the profession.[14]

Second, a closer examination of the nature of officer motivation across services tends to confirm this emerging dichotomy between the army and the other services. This is illustrated by Table 6.2 in which a number of major career motivations have been ranked for each of the three services. The figures demonstrate that militaristic motivations were still prevalent in the army, whereas civilian-oriented motivations predominated in the navy and the air force. The dichotomy is particularly striking between the army and the air force. Tradition and vocation ranked first in the army, second in the navy, and fifth in the air force. Patriotic ideals ranked second in the army but fourth in the other two services. But in both the navy and the air force, what can be called anti-routine-oriented motives ranked first. The fact that technology-oriented reasons ranked only third was probably due to the times. Had the survey been taken one or two years later, it is likely that technical-professional reasons would have taken precedence, at least in the air force, where the process of nuclearization started before it did in the navy. At the end of the 1960s, the traditional forms of motivation were clearly dominant in the army; the navy and the air force were patterned more on the professional model. An analysis of literary output in the army, notably of contributions dealing with the question of career motivations, and the like, confirms this observation. Most army journals emphasized the ideal of service and praised the military virtues that animated the modern

Table 6.2. Career Motivations of Officers by Service, 1966–68 (ranked from 1 to 7 in descending importance)

Motivation	Army	Navy	Air Force
Militaristic			
Tradition	1	2	5
Patriotic ideal	2	4	4
Discipline and order	3	7	6
Civilian-like			
Risk and action	4	5	1
Life-style	5	1	2
Technology	7	3	3
No other opportunities	6	6	7

Source: Adapted from Bureau d'Etudes et de Recherches en Sciences humaines appliquées, "Les Français, l'armée et la force de frappe" (mimeographed, Paris: Institut des Sciences humaines appliquées, 1966–68), p. 24.

officer. Army officers recruited from Saint-Cyr expressed this view even more strongly. Navy and air force literature, on the contrary, usually focused on the professionalism of the officer—professional consciousness, efficiency, and expertise.

For example, a comparative reading of periodicals published by alumni of the military academies shows that whereas it is hardly mentioned or written about in air force and naval journals, the ideas of vocation and of readiness for self-sacrifice were still to be found in most contributions in the Saint-Cyr review, *Le Casoar*, as the key motivational elements of a military career. Paradoxically, such views were not at all the idiosyncratic *apanage* of old-fashioned stiff-necked cavaliers or nostalgic self-styled "colonial" centurions. They were held by most army officers. One could still read, from the pen of General Beaufre, who in addition to being a prominent intellectual figure was among the first proponents of the nuclearization of the French military: "An officer cannot fulfill his duty unless he has the calling. This vocation draws its strength from interest in military affairs, devotion to the public good, but especially from the acceptance of the supreme sacrifice in the name of a traditional ethic, going back to chivalry."[15]

A recent study based on the content analysis of editorials and articles published in *Le Casoar* between 1962 and 1973 demonstrated the extent of such beliefs, and particularly the perennial concern with the necessity of being "called." A sentence such as "The soldier's career is a vocation . . . an entry into an order for combat and toward sacrifice" is but one among an endless number of variations around the same theme.[16] These observations were corroborated by an empirical survey undertaken in 1973 among Saint-Cyr and Interarms School cadets, in which 90 percent of the Saint-Cyriens and 94 percent of the students at the EMIA responded that they were ready to sacrifice their lives for their country.[17] The same survey, moreover, provided further evidence about the importance of traditional career motives, especially when these were compared to motivations based on scientific or technical interests. The career motivations of the Saint-Cyriens, who continued to constitute the core of the army elite, still resembled, to a great extent, those of past generations (see Table 6.3).

Though the evidence collected is somewhat poorer than for the officer corps, it is at least possible to fathom some of the more salient features of noncommissioned personnel's patterns of career motivation. Perhaps the main point is that, in contrast to the French officer corps, the NCO and enlistee career motivation presented a greater homogeneity across the services. With the possible exception of the least technical services of the army, a large proportion of NCOs and

Table 6.3. Career Motivations of Saint-Cyr and EMIA Cadets, 1973 (percentages)

Motivation	Saint-Cyr	EMIA
Human relations	93	93
Leadership	92	89
Patriotic ideal	87	77
Familial tradition	67	62
Technical and scientific interest	40	48
No other possibilities	20	19

Source: François Helluy, "Les Jeunes Officiers de l'Armée de Terre," p. 72.

enlistees joined the military with professional expectations. This trend, which was more pronounced in the air force and the navy, became a recurrent pattern in the army, too. For example, figures concerning the army NCOs in 1969 indicate that only 40 percent of the new NCOs who joined the army after 1961 enlisted for what can be interpreted as militaristic (patriotism, desire for combat) or quasi-militaristic motives (the need for action, risk), whereas this proportion averaged to 60 percent among NCOs who enlisted in the 1950s.[18]

In all services, the major reasons given for enlisting were technical or professional, that is, a desire to learn or to perfect a skill. A survey concerning enlistees in all services (see Table 6.4) indicated this disposition, though one can see that in the navy and, to a lesser extent, in the army, motivations based on the search for an active life were important. Among NCOs, the trend seemed even stronger, particularly among those who had attended special schools for NCOs. Table 6.5 illustrates the prevalence of professional and technical motivations among army NCO candidates at the time of enlistment and when they chose a particular branch of service.

Before continuing this discussion, it should be said that, though dominant, the traditional/militaristic pattern in the army officer corps and the technical/professional pattern in the rest of the armed forces were not the only observable patterns. A more extensive examination of the data and further inquiries, through interviews with officers and enlisted personnel, revealed the existence of a residual, yet nonnegligible, form of motivation. References to action, risk, travel, human relations, lifestyle, and security appeared as distinct motivational elements in making a career choice. To some extent, such motivations were actually inseparable outgrowths of the two dominant observed

Table 6.4. Career Motivations of Enlistees by Service, 1975 (percentages)

Motivation	Army	Navy	Air Force
Professional/technical	43.1	41.0	88.2
Life of action	16.7	46.3	8.3
Military vocation	14.8	7.9	—
Economic	8.3	5.3	3.5
Negative motives	3.5	—	—
Other	13.6	—	—

Source: Philippe Marchand, "Ceux qui s'engagent," *Armées d'aujourd'hui* 17 (January–February 1977): 50–51.

Table 6.5. Career Motivations of Army NCO Candidates, 1968 (percentages)

Motivation in the Choice of the Military Career			Motivation in the Choice of the Branch of Service	
	Primary	Secondary		
Professional/technical	45.2	25.8	Professional/technical	60
Failure	16.0	12.4	Sport, lifestyle	11.6
Sport, risk, travel	14.9	20.8	Social mobility	8.5
Military vocation	7.9	6.8	Combat, risk	6.1
Atmosphere, life-style	5.7	15.2	Leadership	4.1
Social, economic	4.3	6.4	Atmosphere	3.6
Other	6.0	11.0	Travel	3.6
			Security	0.3
			Other	1.3

Source: Henri Pillot, "L'Elève sous-officier d'active: motivation et personalité" (EMSST thesis, Paris, 1968).

types. Action and risk can be forms of militaristic motivations, for example. Conversely, it often happened that motivations such as desire for employment security were correlates of the technical/professional system of career motivations; the technician, the professional, even if he liked his work does not necessarily disdain the material gratifications attached to it. In general, however, one is tempted to raise the question of whether the existence of such motivations did not proceed from a specific dynamic. During many interviews, themes like "need for action and risk," "need for security," search for "human relations," and "fraternal community" were frequently voiced without any reference to a strong sense of vocation, militarism, or any especially marked technical/professional orientation. One gets the distinct impression that these men were impelled to enter the military not because they were really attracted by the career, but because they were pushed into it. The military career was "chosen" as if it were a refuge. Interestingly, this orientation can be found in two categories of individuals. Some of them, particularly those who expressed a strong need for action and risk, viewed the military career as the place where a number of activities that could not be conducted in the civilian world could be performed, including piloting, parachuting, and mountain climbing. As for motivations centering around a search for "human relations," "desire for security," and the like, it is suggested that for another segment of personnel the military career was seen as a refuge—interestingly, often as a refuge from the civilian world. Indirect questioning and informal discussions underline this. Joining the military was an escape from a world that was often perceived as increasingly impersonal, individualistic, and competitive. Whether such a "choice" was voluntary (that is, refusal to go on in the civil world) or purely passive (that is, incapacity to adjust to it) remains to be determined.

This twofold pattern of motivation is a very old one. From its beginning the military sheltered a special type of individual, one in search of an opportunity to ease an irrepressible need for action, or one in search of a secure place. Over the years this residual proportion of individuals has remained stable. What seemed to change was the ratio of those seeking action over those seeking shelter. The former type is not as evident in the modern military. Formerly, those with a strong urge for action and risk could always find an appropriate niche in the military: joining the navy was always an occasion for extensive travel; joining the paratroopers after World War II guaranteed an active and risk-filled life. In the late 1960s and 1970s, this was no longer true. It was rare for an individual to have to join the Chasseur alpins in order to satisfy a passion for skiing or mountain climbing; it was no longer necessary to become a paratrooper or an air force combat pilot to satiate one's passion for parachuting or doing stunts with high-performance aircraft. Most of these activities could now be pursued in the civilian world with fewer difficulties than twenty years earlier. It is, then, careerist proclivities that came to prevail. This seemed particularly true for NCOs and enlistees. In 1972, 10 percent of the responses by army enlistees indicated motivations based on desire to travel and need for action, whereas desires for independence and an escape from failure and/or family, accounted for almost 20 percent of the response. Interestingly, this type of motivation was characteristic not only of those joining routine branches of the services but, to some extent, of those joining active militaristic branches, such as the paratroopers.[19]

Among officers, this tendency was less pronounced. When they did not embrace a military career for vocational/militaristic purposes (the majority of army cases) or for professional/technical purposes (navy and air force), the future officers joined to satisfy an aspiration for a different life and for role singularization. The paratroopers and the Foreign Legion thus offered shelter to potential *baroudeurs* and *têtes brulées*. This does not mean, however, that more prosaic reasons or careerist tendencies were absent from the officers' career motives. Table 6.3 shows that 20 percent of the Saint-Cyriens admitted that they decided to embrace a military career because they had no other possibilities. Such a response can be interpreted in several ways. The first hypothesis has to do with a peculiarity of nonuniversity students' practices concerning the conduct of their scholarship following the baccalaureate. Among those choosing to follow the *grandes écoles* curriculum instead of entering the university, it was common to take simultaneous entrance examinations to several schools, including the military academies. By so doing students sought to minimize the risk of failure (the age limit being rather low, it was not always possible for all of them to take the exam more than twice) by increasing their chances to enter one of these schools, although many planned to enter a particular school. Students trying to enter engineering or business schools also prepared for Saint-Cyr. More often, students who hoped to pass the air force academy examination also applied for Saint-Cyr. Since the Saint-Cyr examination was probably the easiest one of all *grandes écoles* examinations, students who failed the more difficult ones found themselves admitted to Saint-Cyr without making a decision to enter an army career.

A second hypothesis is that a small number of individuals sought entrance to Saint-Cyr for careerist reasons, that is, a search for a protective environment and a noncompetitive system of gratification. This would be a form of what we referred to earlier as "military poujadism." Though less pronounced than it was before the 1960s, this possibility should not be ruled out. Finally, as among NCOs, probably more than one Saint-Cyrien found himself drifting into a military career. However, the proportion of officers belonging to this category was probably very small, probably smaller than among NCOs and enlistees.

Changing Patterns of Career Conception

The pluralization of the pattern of career motivations of regular personnel and the visibility of the various types of career motivations within the services and across the ranks were paralleled by similar trends at the level of the career conception. Before the 1960s, there had been a great homogeneity across services and across ranks in attitudes toward a military career. During the 1960s, heterogeneity or pluralism was more characteristic. The boundaries of differentiation coincided indeed with those separating the patterns of career motivations, at least insofar as we continue to reason in terms of a dominant ideal type. Yet, as we shall see, subtypes can be identified in one of the dominant patterns.

The first pattern of career conception is that which could be observed in most sectors of the French armed forces in the years following World War II. Thereafter, it turned out to be mostly a feature of army officers; after the early 1960s it was mainly among army officers and particularly among officers recruited from Saint-Cyr that the military career was viewed as a lifetime engagement of self in the service of an ideal or a cause—the defense of the *patrie*. The perceived and conscious purpose of the career, as well as of the functions accomplished in the course of this career, were thus intimately linked with the ultimate aims of the institution, with which there was a strong identification. The defense function was seen in terms of war-making and war, a phenomenon that 65 percent of the Saint-Cyriens continued to see as inevitable, even in 1973. Self-sacrifice and disregard for material well-being were paramount features of such a career conception. Most surveys or interviews with army officers indicated their readiness to sacrifice themselves for the defense of their country. The reactions aroused by the publication of an article in *Défense nationale* in 1971 pointing out that the traditional notion of military vocation, built on the dialectic between war and peace, had become incompatible with the institutional goal of a defense based on deterrence, were extremely revealing.[20] And it was not merely coincidental that in 1973, three Saint-Cyriens out of four still expressed their opposition to such a view.[21] There was also an almost obsessive preoccupation with death and self-sacrifice, especially true among Saint-Cyriens. One aforementioned survey covering *Le Casoar*'s thematic content pointed out this quasi-romantic infatuation with the idea of a heroic death and the glorification of all acts leading to self-sacrifice.[22] The concept of service went even further as it led the soldier not only to sacrifice his life but also, as General Beaufre has said, "to deal with the mediocrity of daily life and in particular with the modest size of the salaries, especially as compared to what could be earned in civilian life."[23] Concern for technology and all values related to industrialism, management, or organization was at a minimum, as if these were viewed as detrimental to the military institution. Typical of this feeling was General Valluy's 1962 criticism of Pierre Messmer's conception of the modern military as an establishment made up of engineers (the officers) and foremen and skilled workers (NCOs and enlistees). Such a model or organization was seen by Valluy as somewhat servile and even dangerous, and he added, "One could fear that an excessive specialization would spread throughout the whole institution and disintegrate it."[24] This attitude persisted over time: in 1973, only 27 percent of the Interarms School students and 24 percent of the Saint-Cyriens thought that management and organization were inherent elements of the military profession, whereas 63 percent and 75 percent, respectively, considered that patriotism, combativity, and discipline were the proper values of a military profession.[25]

Self-sacrifice, together with faithfulness, devotion to the corps, and its members, and antiindustrialism were components of a vision of the military career that was rooted in a conception of the military institution that can only be understood by referring to the classic concept of gemeinschaft: "[The military institution] is a collective being which has its soul, its laws, its loves, and its hatreds, and one that cannot be amputated without rendering the whole ill."[26] These words, recently written by an army officer, encapsulated almost perfectly the peculiarity of this vision of the military, one that is still shared widely among army officers.

This attitude toward the military career, held predominantly by army officers, was overshadowed by a second model of career conception found essentially among air force and navy officers, and among a great majority of noncommissioned personnel across the three services. Yet there was a great deal of difference between the two categories of men. The military career was seen primarily in professional terms, as the place for the exercise of a skill. Concern for the ultimate role of the military was absent, although the officer's career conception tended also to transcend, somewhat, the immediate objectives of their function, or the activities performed, and to relate to the overall missions of the institution. This restrictive and pragmatic approach toward the profession was particularly acute among air force NCOs and navy petty officers. For example, the preparation and maintenance of a squadron of Mirages or a maneuver at sea was rarely seen as a participation in the national defense or as important to the nation's security. The reference group was not the unit or the corps of assignment, but rather the fellow technicians specialized in the same skills. Identification thus occurred at the level of the job subculture and, in some circumstances, even regardless of national considerations. In his study of naval petty officers, Jack Garcette observed: "[Their] comaraderie is greater with the foreign navies' personnel who are in the same specialties than with the other members of the French services involved in the defense mission."[27] A survey conducted among army NCO candidates in 1968 demonstrated this lack of attachment for the corps and the concomitant concern for exercising a technical specialty: nearly 70 percent of the interviewees indicated that they would gladly accept a transfer if the conditions for the use of their skills were good.[28] But what made the difference between officers and enlistees was that to the majority of the latter the idea of a long-term military career was almost inconceivable. A military career was seen as a fleeting moment in a longer professional trajectory that continued to and ended in civilian life. This tendency, clearly noticeable among NCOs, was more acute in the air force and the navy than in the army. A survey showed that 41 percent of the interviewed naval petty officers and 35 percent of the air force NCOs did not plan to pursue a military career for more than ten years, and 31 percent for no longer than fifteen years. In the army it was slightly different though the overall trend was identical: the same survey showed that 24 percent had decided on a short-term career, whereas only 23 percent decided to go on until the age limit, and the remainder were undecided. In 1968, for example, 35 percent of the army NCO candidates declared that they had entered the army to acquire a skill with the view of being able to find employment in the civilian marketplace. Only 16 percent saw their career as a means to become an officer.[29] After the mid-1960s, one of the major problems faced by the armed forces, and a source of concern for the defense administration, was the extremely high turnover and rate of attrition among NCOs.[30]

Though officers in general, and naval ones particularly, seemed to have a longer-term vision of their career, they did not necessarily see this career as a lifetime engagement; only the fact that retirement before completing twenty-five years of service raised financial and administrative problems tended to limit early retirements. But the smoothness of the transition to a professional civilian world observed among retired air force and navy officers highlighted not only that they were well prepared to embrace a second career, but also that their commitment to a military career was not as firm as that of many army officers.

Concomitantly, it was observed that most military men in the air force and the navy, as well as a majority of army NCOs, showed a greater indifference toward the norms of the institution. Loyalty to the service or to the institution was kept to a minimum; most tasks extraneous to the specialties, largely military tasks, were completed with little interest and were often considered as irrelevant *corvées*. The only area of normative concern focused primarily on the norms that were immediately relevant to the exercise of a function, most of them pertaining to a reference system located outside the military, in the industrial-managerial world. In this regard, Garcette wrote, "The more the specialty is nonmilitary in essence, the more it conforms to the standards of the industrial society and considers the traditional form of military life as too heavy."[31] It was essentially in terms of job proficiency, collective responsibility, and loyalty to a standard of competence, rather than in terms of service or engagement, that the career was being regarded. Inevitably, because the reference-value system was that of the industrial professional society, career claims were made in terms of material well-being and gratification. The extent of the shift in recruitment strategies, with its new themes, gave an indication of the ubiquity of such a pattern of career conception. A single glance at recruiting propaganda is enlightening in this regard, as mottos like "become an expert" and "be an engineer" succeeded those emphasizing manhood and patriotism. Posters depicting the square-jawed fusilier coldly flinging a hand grenade against a background of combat-engaged men, surrounded by various explosions had become a collector's item. The walls of recruiting stations were now covered by pictures of white-clad, bespectacled analysts sitting at computer consoles. Leaflets outlined in detail all the technical treasures of the armed forces and carefully chronicled the material conditions of a military life, the financial advantages, and miscellaneous amenities.

In addition to these two types of career conceptions, a residual model recurrently visible across services and ranks can be identified. It can best be described by contrasting it with the other two models. In this third case the military career was not regarded as a service for a cause or an ideal, nor was it the locus for the exercise of a professional skill. Indeed, there was little or no identification with the institution and its norms. Yet, as noted by Thomas, in some cases, mainly among special branches such as the paratroopers, combat pilots, and commandos, there existed a very strong attachment to the immediate community formed by those practicing the same activities. "These people will challenge the general norms of the institution, but adhere to the non-written code of the restricted community."[32] Service-related tasks were looked upon as menial. Activities such as piloting or parachuting were generally disconnected from their military ends. As Garcette wrote referring to airborne soldiers, "The paratroop specialty leads to an emphasis on individual prowess and self-enhancement to the detriment of its military goal."[33]

In some cases only a refuge was sought. A military career was regarded solely as some sort of sinecure providing both psychological and occupational security. Though it was expected that this pattern of career conception would be held by enlistees and NCOs in routine-secure army branches employing either unskilled or unspecialized personnel, Thomas's survey indicated that it also surfaced in the air force and the navy in their least technical branches.

As just outlined, these different patterns of career motivation and career conception actually constitute ideal dominant types—ideal dominant types that emerge from a macroanalysis. Given the paucity of empirical evidence, it was difficult to proceed otherwise. In reality, as one can easily imagine, the types of motivation or career conception were more composite. The same argument goes for the institutional areas in which these patterns of career motivations and career conceptions were observed. It is certain that all army officers were not motivated by vocation, nor did they all conceive of the military career as an engagement in the service of the defense of the *patrie*; Table 6.3 shows that, in 1973, technically oriented motivations, indicating a professional rather than a vocational conception of career, were actually more frequently observed among the Interarms School students (48 percent) than among the Saint-Cyriens (40 percent). Conversely, it is doubtful that all naval officers were engineers concerned only with their jobs; certainly a sense of vocation also animated them. To some extent, then, each service, each unit, was a microcosm in which the different trends could be observed. For example, among air force NCOs, if technical/professional outlooks dominated among those employed in highly technical tasks, it can be said that militaristic outlooks predominated in military-related specialties.

This being said, it remained that, from a less myopic standpoint (across services), it can be observed that army officers were dominantly vocation- and military-oriented, whereas naval and air force officers and the majority of the enlisted men were more professionally oriented. In addition, a residual pattern—the refuge syndrome—was constantly visible in each service. The schema presented in Figure 6.1 summarizes this series of remarks.

Career Motivations and Conceptions in Perspective

Recast in a more conceptualized but more familiar frame of reference, the change in career motivations and conceptions, as just described, clearly suggests a trend away from the idea of the military career as a calling and a move toward the idea of the military career as a profession, and as we shall see, even as an occupation. This was particularly true in the technical services. But before investigating the most recent developments in the evolution of the career motivation pattern, a few words about the logic of the shift from vocational to professional motives seem in order.

Exposure to modernization is the major factor associated with this trend and it is not a coincidence that the professional model became the dominant feature of air force and naval careers. Conversely, if among army officers the pattern of career motivation and career conception remained similar to that observed in earlier periods, it was to a great extent due to the fact that the post-1960 environment had changed little from that of pre-1960. But, if such an assumption is correct, one may wonder why these patterns of motivation and career

Figure 6.1. Dominant Patterns of Career Motivations and Conceptions in the Military

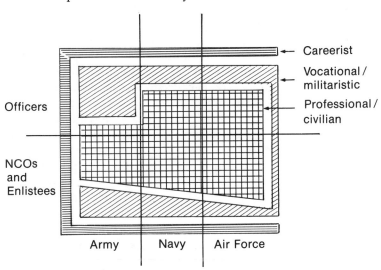

conception generally found in association with a highly modernizing environment can be traced among army enlistees. Several hypotheses can be advanced. First, by opposition to the situation in the officer corps, the particularism linked with each service was less pronounced in the enlistee corps, which favored the spreading of a common style of behavior. A major factor is that the enlistees' structure was perhaps that part of the whole organization susceptible to change, even if the overall level of exposure to change was weak; hence it attracted a number of individuals with a professionalized set of expectations.

In the navy and air force the changes in job structure at the level of the enlistee corps were tremendous after 1960. The exposure to modernization, with the technological constraints it imposed, was such that the old, traditional internal organization was completely transformed. It became more complex and highly diversified, changing into a new system made up of dozens of technical specialties. A specialty constituted the locus of the exercise of a specific skill. Though directly relevant to the functioning of the service unit, these skills were conceived in industrial rather than in military terms. Most of the traditional military tasks usually fulfilled by NCOs became limited and, at the same time, more complex. For example, tasks related to "garrison service" or "internal service," that is, the maintenance of discipline and order, disappeared, since the NCOs' traditional role as cadres for draftees became obsolete because the technology involved in the services prevented large-scale use of unskilled manpower from the draft. Given their increasing complexity, tasks of the "general service," such as operation and service, were now handled by civilians in the air force or by skilled managers. These tasks had become specialties requiring a good deal of technical competence. Thus a quasi-civilian and modernized environment was created at this level of the military organization, an environment unfavorable to the recruitment of nonspecialists or individuals with militaristic expectations.

This was less true in the army. Because that service was not as exposed to modernization, structural changes could not be as sweeping and the old structures still operated, and the traditional tasks related to the Service général, Service de garnison, and Service intérieur remained important. And as there was little specialization, army enlistees were, in theory, polyvalent manpower. But despite low technological exposure, some transformation took place, creating within the enlistee rank structure an environment favorable to the recruitment of a profession-oriented manpower. This was particularly evident as it concerned managerial tasks. The functions related to the Service général, such as stockpiling or transportation maintenance, among the oldest in the service, were inevitably modified as they became more complex; subsequently they required more qualified manpower. The personnel assigned to these tasks joined the military on the basis of technical and professional motivations, as the practice of such functions was a source of training that could be negotiated in the civilian marketplace later. Functions linked with the field service (Service de campagne) also became quasi-specialties. Such was the case with radio communication. However, the old tasks of the garrison service and the internal service (discipline and military training) still permitted the recruitment of nontechnical or militaristic-motivated personnel. Thus, because technological change was unevenly diffused throughout the organization, some sectors of it remained traditional. Certain branches continued to function without the need for technical specialization and thus tended to serve as an appropriate shelter for those individuals in need of psychological or professional security or those motivated by militaristic expectations.

Interestingly, the trend away from a career conception based on calling appears to have developed even beyond the professional view and to have entered a new phase similar to that recently observed in several Western military establishments. With this phase, the military career was seen less as a profession than as an occupation in the sense that "priority inheres in self-interest rather than in the task itself or in the employing organization."[34] Though evidence is not plentiful, enough exists to confirm this new evolution in the case of the French military. Table 6.6, for example, illustrates the relative importance of economic factors in the air force NCOs' career motivations across three technical branches in the mid-1960s. The trend seems further corroborated by the analysis of the second main motivation for enlistments in the air force in 1975 (Table 6.7). Moreover, since the early 1970s, in effect, one can observe a growing concern among regular military personnel about the material conditions of their career expressed in a rising consciousness about what is seen as the relative degradation of these conditions in the armed forces. The reading of the various service magazines over the last five years shows well this inclination, which actually has also been discussed in the national daily and weekly newspapers. Military personnel appeared to be less restrained in expressing their material grievances and criticizing the long-standing features of military life. And many tended to see themselves as no longer deterred by such taboos as unionization, taboos from which they thought the military should be exempted, given the impotence of the traditional devices for the protection and enhancement of their interests (inspections and reports on the attitudes of the troops), a syndrome that a group of officers with undisguised sympathy called the "trade-unionist temptation."[35]

It is true indeed that after 1965 living conditions had deteriorated. Comparative evolution of the indexed value for salaries between military and civil service personnel (at equivalent ranks) showed that between 1948 and 1972 the latter's salaries increased faster than the military's. Figure 6.2 dealing with the comparative change in the purchasing power of salaried civilians, NCOs, and officers between 1964 and 1972 further illustrates this tendency. Hence, to some extent, less rewarding career profiles and an absence of programs for financial improvement (the military career was one of the few in which it was not possible to double the entry-level salary after twenty years of service) justified this increasing preoccupation with material conditions.

But, it should be mentioned that, comparatively, the resources of military personnel and of civilians at corresponding occupational

Table 6.6. Career Motivations of Air Force NCOs (percentages)

Motivation	Detectors	Mechanics	Pilots
Military vocation	8.6	13.0	7.2
Life of action	13.8	14.1	18.6
Travel	29.1	29.6	19.3
Employment security	28.5	40.8	27.8
Economic	46.7	51.9	43.1
Professional/technical	75.1	64.9	62.4

Source: Survey reported in LeJeune, "Les Sous-officiers," p. 27.

Table 6.7. Career Motivations of Air Force Enlistees, 1975 (percentages)

	Primary motivation	Secondary motivation
Professional/technical	88.2	10.0
Life of action	8.3	22.5
Salary	3.5	54.0
Enlistment bonus	—	13.5

Source: Marchand, "Ceux qui s'engagent," p. 51.

Figure 6.2. Military Personnel Purchasing Power

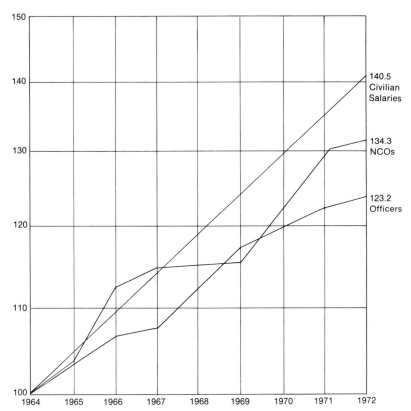

Source: Jean-Paul Mourot, *Rapport d'information fait au nom de la Commission de Défense Nationale et des forces armées sur la condition militaire en 1974,* Doc. Assemblée Nationale n° 945 (2ème session ordinaire 1973–74), p. 15.

ranks have been highly unequal for years and in the postwar decade the situation of the military was already rather mediocre. In this respect, the data provided by Girardet and his associates about army officers' living conditions in the 1950s are enlightening.[36] Thus even if it is probable that the state of deterioration was slightly higher in the 1960s and 1970s than in the 1950s, on the whole, it is clear that from 1950 on, these conditions were continuously precarious. Therefore, the fact that in the 1950s these conditions did not call forth any voiced feelings of relative deprivation or a reaction of the type that took place recently was in itself an indication of the change of attitude regarding the military career. Formerly such conditions of life had been considered as normal, or at least as something that had to be accepted, but later they were seen as less bearable and even perceived as degrading. As a major at the cavalry school of Saumur put it: "A quarter of a century ago, an officer did not ride on gold, but this relative poorness was well accepted, for it did not, as today, give the impression of any social *déclassement.*"[37] Hence, one can hypothesize that, as the conditions of life did not greatly change, it was then attitudes toward the career that modified. And the growing concern for material well-being of military personnel, such as that expressed during the discussions of the defense budget or in the publications of documents such as the *Rapport Mourot,* and the extent of governmental reforms that materialized with the creation of the Conseil supérieur de la fonction militaire (an advisory board whose goal it is to represent and defend military interests), with the 1974 plan for the improvement of military conditions and with the new statutes for the various military corps, for instance, are highly significant. For they not only constituted an indication of the increasing importance of military personnel demands, but also the implicit recognition of this new attitude toward career, now judged as an established, if not entirely acceptable, pattern of behavior in the military.

The emergence of this new phase in the evolution of career conception in the French military was the result of a complex logic. It was at first a natural extension of the professional approach to a military career. There is little doubt that at a certain stage of its development, the professional outlook tends to be accompanied by occupational concerns. After all, a profession is only an "occupation more professionalized than other occupations."[38] Preoccupations with expertise, standards of competence and craftsmanship, ethics, and so on, are, sooner or later, blended with some elements of aspirations toward security, material well-being, equality in remuneration, and so on. In addition, the professional conception of career, especially in the technical services, implies a continuous reference beyond the boundaries of the military, in the industrial social system. Inevitably, then, such a disposition increased the serviceman's awareness of new norms and new patterns of behavior, which in turn shaped his expectations and comportment. Hence, by looking outside the military for the appropriate standards of professional competence, the serviceman was led, little by little, to evaluate his own material condition against that of his civilian peers, a process whose consequences can best be understood in reference to the classic phenomena of rising expectations and relative deprivation. This tendency occurred at the very moment the dominant values and accepted style of behavior in the industrial marketplace were shifting away from concerns with the working organization and the tasks to be performed to an emphasis on the members and their material interest. Not surprisingly, then, French military personnel became conscious of their working situation and wages, and became increasingly absorbed with the protection and enhancement of their personal welfare; this, all the more, as they realized the import of discrepancies between military and civilian living conditions. Because of a higher degree of convergence, this trend was more developed in the technical services. It was not a coincidence if, as noted by Garcette in his survey of NCOs, the relationship between rising consciousness of industrial norms and attention to the protection of servicemen's interests, even under the trade-union form, was stronger in the air force.[39]

One may further wonder to what extent recent changes in draftee attitudes influenced this shift in the regular personnel's approach to a military career. After 1973, in effect, French draftees found themselves continuously involved in laborlike corporatist actions. And by petitioning, demonstrating, setting up soldier committees, and even unionizing, they have succeeded in obtaining significant improvements in their conditions of service. In this regard, the famous *appel des cents*, the uprisings at Draguignan and at Karlsruhe (to name two well-known cases), and the various soldier committees throughout the country, exemplified the extent of draftee activism.[40] It is not unlikely then that these actions increased the regular personnel's awareness of their material situation and led them to resort to similar forms of grievances to enhance it. Thus, the draftees' own material preoccupations and styles of behavior derived from the civilian arena, and their probable impact on the attitudes of the regular personnel have further contributed to accelerate the process by which the new norms of the civilian marketplace penetrated the military.

Finally, it should be added that, once engaged, this trend, by which occupation-related matters displaced profession-related concerns in the military personnel's career conceptions, is self-perpetuating. Because of a dynamic similar to that of relative deprivation, discontent remained rampant despite all the reforms undertaken to improve the conditions of service. Pay increases, attempts to compete with wages and working conditions in the civilian world, and the simplification of military salary structures, including the integration of indemnities, bonuses, and the like, with the central wage, made the military career more amenable to "envious comparison," to use Tocqueville's words. This increasing degree of comparability resulted in the military career's being more and more evaluated in terms of the conditions of employment and rates of reward found in similar civilian occupations. Gwyn Harries-Jenkins's reflections on the case of the British armed forces where a similar syndrome developed encapsulate what seemed to be happening in France:

> Here, the emphasis consistently placed on pay comparability and on the high degree of convergence between military and civilian specialties, has encouraged the emergence of a sense of relative deprivation. Individuals, rather than looking upon the military task as a unique exercise of specialist skills in which job satisfaction is derived from task performance, have tended to evaluate their function against the conditions of employment enjoyed by their perceived civilian counterparts. Other servicemen experience a sense of frustration and dissatisfaction when they conclude that society is not prepared to give them the degree of public recognition which is afforded to other professional groups.[41]

This incursion into the professional dimension of the military establishment highlights quite clearly that, at least in regard to career motivations and conceptions, there was an evolution from a rather homogenous professional vision of the military toward a more pluralistic one—one in which professional and occupational motivations coexisted with more traditional ones. Such coexistence, with, in particular, the rising dominance of new patterns of career conceptions, has certainly contributed to the increasing malaise felt among holders of the traditional vision, with, as could be expected, a particular intensity in the army. In its milder form, this strain was manifested by a recurring longing for the illustrious "good old days"—"We had our heroes, the Guynemers, the Leclercs; we envy them for having been able to lead a life totally in full bloom, sometimes even until death, during an exalted period for our arms. The present prospects appear more lusterless; we feel ourselves caught in a picture painted in tones of gray"[42]—or by a deep concern for the military identity— "It is not by . . . blending into society and renouncing its personality and vocation that the military will succeed in imposing itself."[43] But often, beyond this nostalgic cleaving to the old image of military life, the malaise took the form of sharp criticism, if not aggressive rejection, of the new military professionalism. "The military institution is not a factory, nor is it an agglomeration of experts which one can divide at will," wrote one critic.[44] And Captain Delas's well-publicized diatribe against the evils of the factory-barracks was another expression of this lingering opposition to modern technical styles of professionalism, and reflected the refusal to consider the military establishment as the appropriate shelter for such forms of professionalism.[45]

Finally, when Pierre Sergent, another tenacious champion of the old professional style, wrote, "No one embraces the military career to get social security. . . . In entering Saint-Cyr one makes a vow of poverty. No adolescent chooses the career of arms for the mess-tin. An officer has always disdained money,"[46] he simply was not describing the post-1960s reality but, rather, was expressing his own disenchantment; perhaps he was even exorcising the irresistible emergence of the "occupational mentality" in the French military establishment.

Notes

1. General Maurin, *L'Armée moderne* (Paris: Flammarion, 1938), p. 167.

2. Morris Janowitz, *The Professional Soldier: A Social and Political Portrait* (Glencoe: The Free Press, 1960), pp. 108–23.

3. Charles C. Moskos, Jr., "The All-Volunteer Military: Calling, Profession, or Occupation?" *Parameters* 7 (1977): 3.

4. This analysis is based on informal interviews and, more often, on interviewees' choices between a selected number of predefined types of career motivations. These types of motivations, it should be pointed out, constitute an idealized expression of the dominant motivation; in reality, the choice of a career is the result of a complex system of factors. The problem indeed is that the answers were not always valid expressions of reality. As revealed by cross-interviewing, sometimes the answer given was only an ex post artifact, because the deeper, actual motives were consciously or unconsciously covered up or adorned with more socially acceptable motives. For example, an apparently genuine military vocation might be an a posteriori justification for less "noble" motives (or at least perceived as such by the

interviewee), such as failure in an examination or unexpected financial drawbacks in the family. Therefore, when a study of this type is being undertaken, skepticism is a useful tool and could help to avoid misinterpretation of some career determinism. For example, in seeking to define the career motivations of military academy graduates, one notes how often the vocation or the desire to serve the nation tends to reoccur; yet, further interviews show that beyond these motives are more prosaic factors that also contribute to the military vocation. This is particularly true for those graduates who have prepared, in addition to the military academy examinations, other examinations enabling them to enter the civil *grandes écoles*. In effect, it is customary for students desiring to prepare the *grandes écoles* curriculum (*see* Chapter 7) to take several entrance examinations at the same time in order to maximize their chances of passing. The less bright or less lucky students fail to pass the most difficult examinations, those leading to the civilian schools, but are often able to pass the less difficult exams of the military academies. Thus one can understand why many of these students prefer to justify their presence in the military by invoking a vocation or an acceptable motivation rather than the failure to enter another career.

Actually, for each category of military personnel, one faces a specific problem in attempting to define career motivations. Among NCOs and, above all, enlistees, the difficulties are caused by the fact that in most cases the interviewees were very young when they entered the military profession and consequently

did not have well-structured career goals. The motivations they give later may well be reconstructed ones.

This being said, the data can be considered, on the whole, as a valid instrument of analysis, particularly when used to determine less the exact proportion of the various models of career motivation than changes over time.

5. Marcel Bigeard, *Sans fin* (Paris: La Pensée moderne, 1957) quoted in Jean Feller, *Le Dossier de l'armée française: la guerre de "cinquante ans,"* *1914–1962* (Paris: Librairie académique Perrin, 1966), p. 447.

6. John E. Talbott, "The Myth and Reality of the Paratrooper in the Algerian War," *Armed Forces and Society* 3 (1976): 75.

7. Jean Planchais, "Crise de modernisme dans l'armée," *Revue française de Sociologie* 2 (1961): 121.

8. Raoul Girardet and Jean-Pierre Thomas, "Problèmes de recrutement," in *La Crise militaire française, 1945–1962: aspects sociologiques et idéologiques*, edited by Raoul Girardet (Paris: A. Colin, 1964), p. 53.

9. Ibid., p. 54.

10. Centre d'Etudes et d'Instruction psychologiques de l'Armée de l'Air (CEIPAA), "Attitudes et motivation des candidats aux grandes écoles militaires," *Revue française de Sociologie* 2 (1961): 141.

11. Guy Michelat and Jean-Pierre Thomas, "Contribution à l'étude du recrutement des écoles d'officiers de la Marine," *Revue française de Sociologie* 9 (1968): 66.

12. CEIPAA, "Attitudes et motivation des candidats aux grandes écoles militaires," p. 141.

13. For more details on this point *see* the comments about the social structure of the military in Chapter 8,

particularly pp. 279–88 and note 31.

14. From a survey conducted in 1971 by the Center of Military Studies and Sociology (CESM).

15. André Beaufre, "Officier, pour quel office? la vocation militaire et la tradition," *Le Casoar* 43 (1971): 11.

16. Rémy Ponton, "Le Thème de la vocation dans le système de valeurs des Saint-Cyriens d'après les éditoriaux et les chroniques du Casoar, 1962–73," *Le Casoar* 58 (1975): 72–73.

17. François Helluy, "Les Jeunes Officiers de l'Armée de Terre" (EMSST thesis, Centre de Sociologie de la Défense nationale, 1974), p. 78 and Appendix, p. 15.

18. Jack Garcette, "Les Conséquences de la spécialisation du sous-officier sur le recrutement et la conception du métier," in Les Militaires et leur formation (Paris: SPEI éditeur, 1972), p. 61.

19. For more details on this survey about army enlistees, *see* CESM, "Evolution sociologique et psychologique des engagés dans l'armée de terre," mimeographed (1975). It is unnecessary to point out that the great predictability offered by the military norms, the existence of tightly knit primary groups, and so on, make the military institution an adequate locus for the satisfaction of basic individual needs such as security or self-esteem. Moreover, the manhood/masculinity element of military activities offers further psychological elements of support for those who have been deprived of an identifiable father figure during their early life. It is not strange if, as we shall see in Chapter 7, almost a fourth of the enlisted population came from "disturbed families" (orphans, illegitimate children, sons of divorced parents). The fact that this type of individual was often found in stress-based units such as the paratroopers, commandos, frogmen, combat pilots, and so on, can be explained by the ego-strengthening effects of the activities performed in these units. On the sociology of risk-seeking activities, *see* R. Lopez-Reyes, *Power and Immortality* (New York: Exposition Press, 1971); for an interesting approach to this question in the military environment, *see also* Gideon Aran, "Parachuting," *American Journal of Sociology* 80 (1974): 124–52.

20. This refers to Jean-Paul Moreigne, "Officiers, pour quel office?" *Revue de Défense nationale* 27 (1971): 718–27.

21. Helluy, "Les Jeunes Officiers de l'Armée de Terre," p. 68.

22. Ponton, "Le Thème de la vocation dans le système de valeurs des Saint-Cyriens d'après les éditoriaux et les chroniques du Casoar."

23. Beaufre, "Officier, pour quel 'office,' la vocation militaire et la tradition."

24. Jean Valluy, "Réflexions sur l'armée de demain," *Revue des deux mondes*, 15 July 1962, pp. 161–71. This article was a comment on the then defense minister Pierre Messmer's proposal, "L'Armée de demain," *Revue des deux mondes*, 15 February 1962, pp. 481–93. In regard to this question *see also* Chapter 5, note 100.

25. Helluy, "Les Jeunes Officiers de l'Armée de Terre," Appendix, p. 15.

26. Colonel Proudhom, "Anthropos," *L'Armée* 88 (June 1969): 40.

27. Garcette, "Les Conséquences de la spécialisation du sous-officier," p. 62.

28. Henri Pillot, "L'Elève sous-officier d'active: motivation et personalité" (EMSST thesis, Paris, 1968).

29. Bernard Lejeune, "Les Sous-officiers: exemple de schéma directeur relatif aux carrières des sous-officiers dans les trois armées" (EMSST thesis, Centre de Sociologie de la Défense nationale, 1974).

30. *See* François Cailleteau and Jean-Pierre Thomas, "La Réforme des sous-officiers de l'Armée de Terre," *Défense nationale* 32 (March 1976): 99–113.

31. Garcette, "Les Conséquences de la spécialisation du sous-officier," p. 64. Yet there are limits to such trends; *see* Etienne Schweisguth, "Les Attitudes envers le métier militaire chez les sous-officiers de l'Armée de l'Air," *Revue française de Sociologie* 16 (1975): 485–516.

32. Jean-Pierre Thomas, "Hypothèses pour une étude de mobilité sociale auprès des sous-officiers," *Revue française de Science politique* 22 (1972): 58 (also published in English as "The Mobility of Non-Commissioned Officers," in *The Perceived Role of the Military*, edited by M. R. Van Gils, p. 154).

33. Garcette, "Les Conséquences de la spécialisation du sous-officier," p. 64.

34. Moskos, "The All-Volunteer Military: Calling, Profession, or Occupation?" p. 3.

35. Gemili (Groupe d'études militaires), "La Tentation syndicale," *Armées d'aujourd'hui* 1 (1975): 54–55. For a general treatment of this question of the protection of military interests and unionization in France, *see* Joseph-L. Herry, *La Fonction militaire:* *évolution statutaire* (Paris: Berger-Levrault, 1976), pp. 208–35; Jean Lafitte, "La Défense des intérêts des militaires par leurs chefs: un nouveau service publique?" *Revue administrative* 166 (1975): 357–65; Lucien Mandeville, "Syndicalism in the French Military System," *Armed Forces and Society* 2 (1976): 539–52.

36. Paul M. Bouju and Jean-Pierre Thomas, "Problèmes de structure et de genre de vie," in *La Crise militaire française, 1945–1962*, edited by Raoul Girardet, p. 108–28.

37. *L'Express*, 25–31 March 1976, p. 66.

38. Allan R. Millett, *The General: Robert L. Bullard and Officership in the United States Army, 1881–1925* (Westview, Colo.: Greenwood Press, 1975), p. 3.

39. Garcette, "Les Consequences de la spécialisation du sous-officier," p. 65.

40. *See* Chapter 5.

41. Gwyn Harries-Jenkins, "The British Experience with the All-Volunteer Force," in *The All-Volunteer Force and American Society*, edited by John B. Keeley (Charlottesville: University Press of Virginia, 1978), p. 123.

42. E. Walter, "Notre enthousiasme," *Revue de Défense nationale* 26 (1970): 763.

43. Alain Bouchet, "Ne pas se renier," *Revue de Défense nationale* 24 (1968): 1889.

44. Proudhom, "Anthropos," p. 40.

45. *Le Monde*, 1 December 1973.

46. Pierre Sergent, *Lettre aux officiers* (Paris: Fayard, 1975), p. 36.

CHAPTER SEVEN ●
DISCIPLINE AND AUTHORITY

Discipline and authority in an institution are forms of organizational control that are determinant in its maintenance and functioning, as well as in its attainment of the goals that legitimate its role in the social system. The constraining degree of such control varies with the complexity of the organization, on the one hand, and with the nature of the goals to be attained by the organization, on the other. First, in a situation of increasing complexity, the organization's actors, caught in an expanding role diversification, become unable to evaluate properly, hence to maintain, the compatibility between one another's work, as well as between their efforts and the general organizational objectives. So, in order to insure efficiency in the coordination of all actions and reliability of the members' responses, or, as Robert Merton phrased it, "the ready calculability of others' behavior,"[1] and finally to insure adequate allocation of resources needed to fulfill all functions, a complex and pervasive system of control has been evolved. The nature of the goals of the organization is the second fundamental element in the definition of the type and nature of the control. The more crucially relevant the organizational goals are to the institution's own survival, and more importantly, to the survival of the larger parent social system, to which the institution is related by virtue of the social division of labor, the more compelling the level of control is expected to be.

For these reasons, discipline and authority have been paramount features of military institutions. The first forms of institutionalized discipline appeared in the military toward the middle of the sixteenth century. Several factors contributed to this development, particularly political factors with the centralization of political power and organizational factors with the separation of the warrior from the means of warfare. Cultural factors also played an important role: the impact of the Protestant ethic on the shaping of discipline in the military institutions of northern European countries is illustrative in this regard.

Of primary importance here is not so much the causes of the birth and development of military discipline as the nature and evolution of its content throughout time. Students of organizational control in the military have noted that under the effects of social change and of technological modernization military discipline was transformed considerably, shifting from an authoritarian pattern to a more liberal one.

For a long time, the extreme rigidity of discipline in the military organization was the result of the forms of warfare practiced, as well as of the attempt to maximize the efficacy and destroying power of existing weaponry. Recourse to impressed troops—the dregs of towns shanghaied out of taverns, impoverished laborers dragged from their rural hamlets, and the like—and the use of mercenary soldiers were supplementary reasons for maintaining harsh discipline and tight organizational control. Indeed, these elements of discipline were considered imperative to the functioning of preindustrial armies.[2] In this perspective, discipline entailed a strict obedience to orders issued by the higher echelons of the hierarchy. The goals of the military institution could be realized only if decisions thought to be relevant to the achievement of these goals were rigidly carried out from the top to the bottom of the rank order. Strategic, as well as tactical, aspects and the means of their execution were defined from the top in their minutest details. Discipline and authority were based upon domination in the sense that a person's behavior is influenced by "explicit instruction as to desired behavior without reference to the goals sought. Domination involves threats and negative sanctions rather than positive incentives."[3] Or, using Max Weber's definition, "The content of discipline is nothing but the consistently rationalized, methodically trained and exact execution of the received order, in which all personal criticism is unconditionally suspended and the actor is unswervingly and exclusively set for carrying out the command."[4]

Under specific circumstances, such a pattern of discipline became dysfunctional, especially during times in which methods of conducting warfare and technological improvements in weaponry were changing rapidly and when social and cultural contexts were being greatly modified. After the close of the nineteenth century, the increasing range and accuracy of weaponry meant that combat, which had formerly taken place according to a close-order design, in parade style, under the direct supervision of a strategist, now required a dispersion of men and a more open battle deployment. Consequently, the line officer and his men were no longer as closely united as they had been previously; the logistic units and the fighting units tended to be separated from one another by new elements of communication, and the individual soldier now fought on his own and was tied to the rest of his unit by frail links. As one young Saint-Cyr instructor at the beginning of the century said: "When a company deploys a rank, on a 290-meter front, many will not need orders. The men will no longer see their leaders. They have no one in front to lead them, no one behind to push them. . . . Nothing is left to keep them moving forward but the individual will to conquer. . . . The more armaments developed the more dispersal becomes necessary." Colonel Ardant du Picq in his celebrated *Etudes sur le combat* had foreseen this evolution and its consequences on future warfare. It is difficult to avoid quoting him at length, so insightful was his analysis.

> The leadership tends to slip out of the hands of the supreme and junior commanders. The inevitable disorder that a troop in action faces increases every day with the moral effect of the armament to the point that, in the middle of the hubbub and the fluctuations of the combat lines, the soldiers lose their commanders, the commanders their soldiers. . . . Now that combat is conducted scatteredly, the soldier no longer belongs to you, often he can no longer be directed. Hence, it becomes necessary . . . to make clear to immediate subordinates what one wants, where one wants to go, etc.

The tremendous transformation that war-making underwent with the expansion of heavy artillery during World War I and the increasing reliance on gasoline-propelled vehicles during World War II worsened this situation. Front lines now stretched out over more than ten kilometers, increasing the autonomy and the strategic responsibilities of the units and of the line soldiers participating in military operations. "The increased firepower of modern weapons causes military forces—land, sea, and air—to be more dispersed, in order to reduce exposure to danger. Each unit becomes increasingly dependent on its own organizational impetus once the battle has started."[5] Success in the front lines depended not so much upon the fact that the individual unit or man carried out his orders, for he might not have been given any, but upon the way he anticipated the development of the operation whether or not he took the appropriate measures. Because the achievement of the goals of the institution now depended to a certain extent on the responsible actions of everyone, initiative became a part of military training and an integral element of the functioning of the military institution.

In addition to such strategic considerations, technical considerations came into play and impinged upon the rigidity of military discipline and organizational control. The growing complexity of the weaponry, communication systems, and overall combat operations entailed a multiplication of, and a heavier reliance on, technical and managerial specialists whose role in the decision-making process was significantly increased. Therefore, before any decision was made, there were numerous informal interactions and collegial cooperations in which authoritarian domination had lost its significance. Given such complexity, all decisions became probabilistic and pluralistic. Each decision was one among many. The decision was no longer an end in itself—it remained flexible, open to change. As commands moved down through the hierarchy, enough initiative to allow for last-minute corrections in cases of modifications of the context in which the decision had been made was now required. As summarized by Janowitz and Little: "Military authority now more often relates to lateral coordination and cooperation than to a vertical exercise of authority between the lower and higher echelons. The task of the highest echelons is increasingly to maintain a suitable environment within which the middle strata of specialists can coordinate their efforts."[6]

Finally, social and cultural changes in the parent civil community, from which the military establishment drew its manpower, were such that they undermined dominative styles of authority. Accustomed to greater social permissiveness and more democratic forms of decision making, the civilian inducted into the military became, after World War II, increasingly less able to accommodate himself to unremitting discipline. In addition, the heightened level of education gave the young individual a more vivid awareness of his rights and capabilities. Thus, soon after the first decade following the war, the military was confronted with a new type of man whose personality had grown more sensitive, if not rebellious, to too strict forms of tutelage. The military, then, was led to deemphasize domination in favor of what has been labeled manipulation,[7] and to instill a greater degree of personal attention within the hierarchical relationships. This explains why, for example, an effort was undertaken seeking the subordinate's acquiescence to the order given or the decision made, an order or decision whose rationale is described, at least implicitly, in terms of its relevance not only to the functioning of the organization, but also to the interest of the recipient himself.

Aside from the variables just discussed, there existed various factors, also linked to the general process of "civilianization," that must be accounted for in this shift from domination to manipulation, from strict obedience to collaboration. The narrowing of the status differences between ranks was one such factor. For example, because of his experience and training, a senior NCO in the air force or the navy held as much professional status as any lieutenant or ensign freshly graduated from an academy; often the NCO's salary was even higher than that of the young junior officer. As a result of this decreasing social distance between ranks, authority and discipline took inevitably more liberalized forms. Increasingly frequent lateral cooperation, as that taking place in technical briefings and conferences, at the level of the chiefs of staff as well as that of the lowest units, was another reason for the transformation of the nature of organizational control in the military.

It is in the light of this generic pattern of evolution affecting military discipline and authority that we shall now examine the theory and practice of discipline and authority in the French military before discussing the various factors that have played a part in their transformation.

Discipline and Authority in Theory and Practice

Until 1 October 1966, the time at which a new military disciplinary regulation was decreed, discipline and authority in the French military were absolute.[8] It is not our purpose here to review these older regulations in detail; it will suffice to note that despite semantic variations generally attached to the term *discipline* in the texts, there was a striking continuity from 1815 to 1966. As pointed out by one student of military discipline, "To absolute obedience and execution of orders to the letter, demanded by the disciplinary regulation of 1818, the new regulation of 1833 added a request for a *soumission de tous les instants.*"[9] Later, in 1910, "punctual" obedience was demanded, a qualificative that was replaced by "strict" obedience in 1913. From World War I to 1966 disciplinary regulations reflected the same bent. The decree of 1 April 1933, defining the new principle of discipline and authority for the army and the air force, and the decree of 26 November 1937, for the navy, continued to refer to the authoritarian tradition that governed military disciplinary practices in the past; it continued to refer to the old tradition of rigid, paternalistic, and all-encompassing forms of control. Article 1 of the 1933 regulation is in this regard enlightening: "Discipline being the main strength of the armies, it is necessary that any superior obtain from his subordinates a total obedience as well as an unremitting submission. . . . Even outside the service, subordinates owe deference and respect to their superiors."[10] In addition, the sanctions attached to violations of the code and to failure to obey were essentially negative and severely repressive, giving further evidence of the dominant and absolute nature of military authority in the French services.

The decree of 1 October 1966, the "Règlement de discipline générale dans les armées,"[11] which rules and defines the principles of authority, obedience, and discipline in the French armed forces hierarchies, marked a change from past tradition, though it was not totally liberated from the grip of authoritative tradition. The 1966 regulation referred to two patterns of authority and discipline: the dominant pattern and a liberal pattern.

On the one hand, traces of dominant authority were still conspicuous: "The superior had the right and the duty to request obedience. Obedience remains the first duty of the subordinate. The latter must execute faithfully all the orders he is given." Furthermore, if a written, hence exhaustive, list of specified sanctions in cases of violations of disciplinary rules and of disobediences was instituted for NCOs and privates (limiting random and disproportionate arbitrary punishment), officers were still entirely submitted to the arbitrariness of the hierarchy. Thus, even though the soldier found himself better protected than ever before by a system of guarantees against repression, the discretion and authority of the hierarchy, less absolute than before, remained important. For example, the right to contest an obviously abusive order (except when an illegality was ordered) or the right to demand deferment of a sanction technically unjust was not institutionalized; these areas continued to be ruled through hierarchical superior discretion. The system of sanctions was still highly repressive, as these measures, as before, affected mainly the serviceman's individual freedom and basic rights. The 1966 disciplinary regulation did not cover every situation, leaving, consequently, room for personal arbitrariness, and continued to tolerate recourse to negative sanction and the enforcement of obedience by more or less suspect practices, such as the traditional "furlough blackmail" by which an officer could induce subordinates to perform a certain way by using the threat of denying requests for leave time.

On the other hand, elements of the modern style of organizational control could also be found. Most of those who have closely analyzed the 1966 regulation attest to the importance of the change it brought about. The key words are *participation* and *initiative* with an emphasis on adherence. "The cohesion relies upon the adherence of everyone to his duty, upon the quality of the bonds which link the members of the armed forces and upon the mutual trust which required solidarity in action." In theory the emphasis on initiative is unambiguous. The text of the regulation stipulates, "It is the duty of the superior to look for voluntary and active participation by his subordinates . . . he informs his subordinates about his intentions and the goal to be performed, he orients their initiative and obtains their active participation in the mission." In Article 22, no. 1, there is another clear reference to initiative, it states that the subordinate will have to interpret the intention of his superior. From reading, one gets the impression that an order should be seen as a directive that fixes a goal. As such, an order constituted a frame of action and participation for the subordinate. Another innovation was the reference to the idea of "professional competence" or "search for efficiency" as the guiding dynamic of military behavior. The attempt undertaken here is noteworthy because it abandoned the automatic response concept of discipline in favor of a new concept that made discipline part of a professional sense of duty. The *conscience professionnelle* (professional scrupulousness) became crucial.

Sometimes, however, this concurrent reference to both traditional and modern patterns of authority and discipline was extremely ambiguous. One even gets the impression that in certain instances references to modern forms of military discipline were given mere lip service, serving to make the implementation of the old forms of discipline more acceptable. Leafing through the text, one finds several odd juxtapositions of quasi-irreconcilable concepts that make the reader wonder about their usefulness in the everyday life of military personnel. For example: "The superior attempts to *convince* at the same time he *imposes*. . . . Obedience is the *active participation* brought *without failure* by the subordination to his superior" and "discipline *does not only* prescribe the *strict execution of an order*, but also requests *an initiative*" (emphasis added). The paradoxes are obvious—one may not but wonder how the subordinate who is asked for strict obedience or upon whom an order is imposed could also be requested to add his active participation or initiative in obeying.

But in the end these are only words, and ambiguity is a good thing, so to speak, because it leaves a margin for interpretation and allows for diversity in practice. Compared with the previous model of disciplinary regulation, the 1966 document is innovative. However, continuities with the past are recognizable. As recalled by William Coulet: "Indeed a considerable mutation has been realized. The conception of blind obedience is rejected without any ambiguity . . . but it [the regulation] still reaffirms clearly and frequently the perenniality and the strength of the principle of [strict] military discipline."[12] Though a new regulation was introduced in July 1975 (to be applied after 1 September 1975), one cannot say that it brought any significant change to the theory of military discipline.[13] With regard to the model set up in 1966, very little was modified. It is true that with the new regulation, the distinction between the discipline that rules the service and that which rules activities outside the service was introduced. Liberties and rights—a chapter of the new regulation was entitled "the rights of the military"—were more clearly stated and reliance on initiative was clearly reasserted as one of the most important principles of modern military discipline. But, on the whole, one should not lose sight of the fact that the 1975 regulation was not an *aggiornamento*. In actuality, the continuity with the preceding system was surprising. If new forms of liberalism were introduced, they concerned only those activities outside the service. Within the service, very little changed, and the necessity for strict discipline was reaffirmed. There is no doubt that in its modern terms, the theory of military discipline in the French armed forces remained ambivalent.

From this brief overview, one notes that until 1966 the normative pattern of military discipline and control was clearly based on domination and authoritarianism. After 1966, it evolved in a new direction, giving a greater emphasis to initiative, manipulation, and "fraternal" kinds of relations. But the new model of military discipline was not, for all that, disencumbered from the stigmas that had characterized the traditional pattern of rigid discipline. In many ways, the new French military model of discipline was a dualistic model in which old and new features coexisted.

It is interesting, therefore, that in its ambivalence the French pattern of military discipline mirrored the basic institutional dualism of the French armed forces that brought conventional, or preindustrial, types of military organizations together with technologically advanced types of organizations, an ambivalence, as we have seen, due mainly to a disparity in the level of exposure to technological modernization.

But this dualism, which characterizes the letter of the rule governing discipline in the French military institution, will appear with still more force in its practical application.

The respective examples of the army and the navy are particularly enlightening in this respect as they distinctly represent the traditional and the modern models of military authority and discipline. For advanced patterns of discipline and organizational control, the case of the navy is especially interesting. In effect, some of the innovations that were officially introduced by the 1966 regulation—in particular, the idea of initiative—were already in existence in the navy by virtue of the decree of 26 November 1937.[14] If the reading of this document showed that a dominative authority was still pervasive, it also showed a concern for the participation and initiative of subordinates, especially those of the middle ranks. If Article 1 stipulated that "[discipline] is materialized by a constant submission to the laws, decrees, and regulations in force and immediate obedience to orders," Article 2 stated that: "Any superior ought to attempt to inculcate in officers and other ranks under his command an exact notion of their duties and responsibilities. He should undertake to develop their qualities of initiative and authority, and to place each of them in an adequate position, to assign each a well-defined role under the orders of a specific chief. Thus, the whole functions harmoniously under the impulse of the authority which commands all the cog-wheels." Moreover, another official document, entitled *The Conferences on the Moral Forces of the Officer*, framed in 1937 for young naval academy graduates, emphasized the fact that discipline among officers should never be passive and mechanical; rather, it was to be an act in which the recipients put their intelligence to work understanding the motives of their superiors.

Despite reliance upon domination, the 1937 navy regulations, valid until 1966, were far more advanced than those of the army. In fact, the text of October 1966 seems to have borrowed many of its modern conceptions from these 1937 naval regulations.[15] The conviction regarding the functionality of flexible and manipulative forms of organizational control was actually developed as early as the beginning of the 1930s. Opinions of men such as Rear Admiral Frochot come to mind. In 1933, for instance, he defended the idea that orders should not be obeyed literally and that subordinates should not hesitate to alter their instructions if by doing so they could better achieve the objectives of such instructions.

In areas of discipline and military authority, the navy continued to be innovative and its practice of discipline and authority was extremely forward looking when compared to the rules set out by the 1966 regulation. *The Profile of the Navy Officer for the Years 1975–1980*, a 1968 document, approved by ministerial decision, providing additional guidelines to instructor officers at the naval academy, went quite a bit further than the official decree of 1966. This decree focused upon the necessity of obtaining the adhesion of groups through constant dialogue. Such a dialogue was needed to illuminate the decisions made by superior officers. The decision-making process became a group strategy, leaving subordinates with a large margin of initiative when applying an order. As explained by Frigate Captain Amet, the superior was no longer the unique owner of thoughts and energies, but a "federator" of several thoughts and energies.[16] In a pure managerial form, the subordinate was entrusted with a mission in a global sense. He was free to choose the means for the execution of the mission, and his superior was enjoined not to interfere in the process of this execution. In other words, there was a sort of subcontract between two individuals occupying different places within the hierarchy. The role of the superior was limited to creating an appropriate environment for the coordination of efforts and actions undertaken by his subordinates.

The navy demonstrated an interesting evolution in the procedures of initiative and manipulation. In 1937, such initiative existed, but it was an initiative of interpretation or imitation; in 1968, it became an initiative of innovation. This preoccupation for modern managerial forms of authority and control, not only in the navy, but also in the air force, was shown by the proliferation of articles in the technical service's periodicals, even the most prominent ones. Illustrating the importance of the concern for such modern styles of discipline in the navy, Amet commented on the frequent publication of articles dealing with this theme in the leading naval journal: "When one knows how the *Revue maritime* [Navy Journal] avoids publishing any articles which entail adventurous ideas, one measures the vigor of present expectations regarding initiative."[17]

An analysis of the practice of discipline and authority in the air force would have revealed a pattern similar to that of the navy. An observation of the styles of command on air force bases at the level of flying and combat units as well as of ground technical groups shows to what extent initiative and collective coordination displaced domination and rigidity. In this regard, authority and discipline in the navy and in the air force were no longer different from authority and discipline in any large-scale civilian organization.

In the army, however, things seemed to be quite different. In contrast to the navy there was no real effort to change the dominative and repressive pattern of organizational control; and over time, especially between 1945 and 1975, there was a striking continuity in the practice of military discipline. Although opinions like those of Frochot were currently voiced and practiced in the navy, those same opinions—like those of General Revault d'Allones, who tried to initiate reform of the harshest negative aspects of military discipline— appeared very exceptional in the army. Paradoxically, the experiences of two colonial wars, which should have been conducive to personal initiative and a liberal style of leadership, did not facilitate the modification of the old pattern of military authority. Despite the new 1966 regulation, which, as shown, was not as radical in the changes it proposed as might be supposed, the basic tendency in the practice of discipline and control was the same as that previously in force. Students and observers of the practice of discipline in the army have pointed out the frequency with which the reforms of 1966 were resisted or ignored and have suggested that the army was not a propitious ground for a full-fledged application of even mild reforms of authority or for original forms of discipline. The Army-Youth Commission, which praised the coming of the 1966 regulation, was soon obliged to admit that the new law changed very little if anything at all in the command patterns of the army. In an interesting case study dealing with an army unit—a marine regiment—Captain Lhoste described at length the extent of the rigidity of the organizational control and the practice of military discipline to which many internal dysfunctions were attributable.[18] The findings of the Lhoste study could probably have been applied to other branches of the army as well. In addition, all officers who, inspired by the reform, tried to introduce and apply more modern methods of leadership, relying, for example, on persuasion and initiative, complained about the difficulties they encountered in this task. Two surveys concerning innovative styles of military leadership among army colonels and captains focused on these difficulties.[19] Interviews with officers who sought to liberalize their command techniques and an examination of the difficulties they faced in applying these changes revealed how pervasive was the army's propensity "for seeking refuge behind the security of authoritarianism," or how "the hierarchy, at least a part of it, looks unfavorably upon all those who seek to transform or to modify," to quote two of the interviewees.[20]

Besides, when analyzing the more "advanced" styles of leadership, such as those that were the subject matter for the aforementioned surveys, one cannot say that they represented a great change. If they parted from the "spit and polish" tradition, they merely conformed to the 1966 regulation. After all, in their attenuation of the "negativeness" of military authority, they never went further than attempting to apply principles that had already been dictated. It is in such attitudes that one measures the degree of backwardness of military discipline in the army. As pointed out in a report on the style of command among captains: "The modes of action they [the interviewees] utilized, do not, in general, present any original character, and their style of command seems simply to be in sheer conformity with the spirit of the regulations and texts already in force. One may therefore wonder whether the fact of intelligently applying existing regulations does not constitute a factor of deviance for the average cadre who seems to ignore the new texts or who applies them only literally."[21] With respect to these attempts at dealing more liberally with military discipline, one observer severely, yet correctly, noted: "The deception is even greater when one analyzes the methods of command. To welcome kindly the draftee, to make every man responsible, to mobilize him for coordinated actions, to animate the whole system, to enter into dialogue with every echelon . . . are techniques that one would have thought would have become natural and current to the point of simply having to recall them to the officers in contact with the troops. The risk here is that such formulas appear as simple kitchen recipes, mechanically applied, or as mere demagogic expedients."[22]

Causes of Change and Resistance to Change in Discipline and Authority

What clearly emerges from the observations concerning the theory and practice of discipline in the French military institution, is an ambivalence noticeable across time and services. The fact that the traditional model based on domination and negative sanctions was preponderant in the army, whereas the modern model based on persuasion and manipulation dominated in the navy and in the air force, was certainly related to the existence of the dualistic format of the whole establishment, a duality of traditional and modernized services. This duality, as we saw earlier, was born from an unequal exposure to technological modernization. The army, the service least exposed to modern technology, saw little change in its basic structures. For example, a study of army organization through its rank structure suggests the continuing persistence of centralization. As one officer stated, "More and more, one has the impression of belonging to an army which bureaucratizes itself and tends to hypercentralization and which only acts through extraordinarily complex structures."[23] Such a pattern favored rigidity and domination-oriented vertical relations. Moreover, still as a consequence of its low exposure to technological modernization, the role of the army in the French national defense system decreased in importance. It is a well-known fact that it is in the services that have lost organizational dominance that tendencies to rely on older forms of authority are likely to persist. Janowitz observed, in this regard, "Often leaders who see their particular weapons becoming obsolete, and who see no approach to regaining their organizational dominance, are the most ritualistic and compulsive about older forms of military command."[24] Hence, as the French army appeared as the service least associated with those forces that were crucial to national defense, it was not surprising that traditional forms of authority and discipline continued to be of paramount importance.

Such an argument would be incomplete if it were not accompanied by additional explanations specifically related to French society. Though we shall insist on those factors that hampered a more liberal evolution of military discipline, a few remarks about several variables accounting for existing change, in the army particularly, are in order.

First it is interesting to note that, contrary to the traditional image of the French military establishment, in particular before World War II, there was a latent, or rather a hidden, stream of reformism that, if it was never dominant, could not be ignored. Since the end of the Second Empire, there was a tendency among a few officers to advocate a system of authority avoiding excessive reliance on domination and repression that ran parallel to the tendency that searched for and maintained the model of absolute discipline. The reforms attempted by General André, one of the most controversial war ministers of the Third Republic, deserve to be mentioned in this context. Embedded in André's new design for "republicanizing" the military and renovating the army were reforms that helped introduce greater initiative, decentralize leadership, and deemphasize punctilious, outmoded disciplinary rituals.[25] Also, before World War I, the widely shared attachment to the strategic concept of the *offensive* inevitably led to diffusion of the idea that initiative and decentralization were necessary ingredients for the success of such a doctrine. The work of young officers such as Grandmaison, Simon, and Altamayer furthered these new concepts.[26] Later, men like Generals Gallieni, Pétain, and Weygand, and Rear Admiral Frochot became the advocates of a more flexible concept of discipline, so persuaded they were that blind obedience could turn out to be detrimental not only to the morale of the personnel, but also to the functioning of the institution. During World War I, in 1917, Marshal Pétain introduced various changes in the disciplinary system setting up a climate of comradeship between officers and their men, organizing meetings during which subordinates could freely state their opinions and present various points to their superiors' attention.[27]

The existence of such a progressive tradition, although it did not always result in tangible modifications of the current pattern of military discipline and authority, did contribute to change when the organizational context was propitious, as it was in the more technical services. In the navy, particularly innovative ideas, such as those of Rear Admiral Frochot, were positively echoed.

The liberal trend that materialized in the promulgation of the decree of 1966 was also favored by other factors, external factors especially. In a world of increasing communication and standardization, the influence of international law and the echoes of change in foreign military regulations were certainly crucial factors leading to the undertaking of new reforms. Direct or even remote participation in a multinational defense system often had a unifying effect upon national participants' own military regulations. The constitution of a common military agency, such as the NATO alliance or the United Nations Emergency Force (UNEF), permitted a sort of uniformization of the different military regulations among closely and indirectly participating members. UNEF, by laying out its own system of regulations (for example, the rule of 2 February 1957) favored the creation of a sort of international norm in the area of military discipline.

Moreover, contiguity with military systems practicing liberalized regulations was another factor favoring change. As pointed out by students of comparative public laws, it seems that the influence of the German experience in military discipline was very strong on the French military. The concept of *Innere Führung*, destined to favor interhierarchical participation and collaboration, and advocating a discipline and an authority freely agreed upon by everyone, marked an obvious shift from domination to manipulation, from negative repression to positive incentive. The German soldier, according to these principles, benefited from a series of guaranties (for example, the institution of the *Jungend Offiziere* and the right to call for a parliamentary delegate to the defense against the arbitrariness of the hierarchy and against abuse of authority).[28]

Without going as far as their German counterparts, the authors of the new regulations of 1966 were nevertheless strongly influenced by them, especially as concerned the protection of private and individual liberties through the establishment of an exhaustive listing of faults and their sanctions. The fact that the Center of Military Studies and Sociology, which participated in the elaboration of the project for the new disciplinary code, had prepared various dossiers discussing historical as well as contemporary material about the state of military discipline in foreign countries is an implicit illustration of the influence that foreign forms of discipline might have had on the French regulation.[29]

Second as for factors other than those related to the army's low exposure to technological modernization that can be considered as having held back, if not obstructed, the liberalization of discipline and authority in the army, several remarks can be made. Let us note before going further that contrary to what could be argued, the existence of conscription, and therefore the keeping under arms of a large mass of draftees, was not actually a serious cause for the perennial reliance on traditional styles of authority and discipline observed in the army. Indeed, because the conscript soldier, drawn from the civilian world, was unaccustomed to operating in an unfamiliar large scale organization, because he could not envisage clearly the mission to be performed, nor the functional significance of an order, and because he did not possess the appropriate skills to be entrusted with initiative that must be relevant to the missions of the organization, it is at least logical to expect that strict obedience and tight organizational control were the only appropriate techniques to make optimal use of this manpower.

However, such an argument is only partially true: one, because it does not explain why the traditional pattern was also followed among professionals; and two, because many attempts at liberalizing the style of command by creating direct relationships between the highest echelons and the lowest ones were implemented precisely to match the expectations of the conscripts, whose awareness about initiative, the relevance of their skills, and their backgrounds regarding performance was quite high. One could therefore assume that if there was a source for the impetus to modify the pattern of authority, it was to be found at the level of the conscripted personnel. It is worth noting that among the grievances raised by conscripted personnel, termination of the most negative sanctions and demands for a larger margin of personal action (initiative) were recurrent themes of *corporatiste* demonstrations.

In the end, recourse to conscription had only a tangential impact on the continuing reliance on the army's dominating and rigid code of discipline. The most basic causes had to be sought elsewhere. Two causes appear especially relevant: the first is historical; the second is related to military professionalist styles in the army.

A preoccupation of the various political regimes that emerged from the Revolution and its Napoleonic aftermath and notably of the leaders of the Third Republic was the establishment of an appropriate means for assuring the loyalty of the military, or at least its political neutrality. After the fall of the First Empire, French political life became so volatile that not only could none of the governments rely on the army to maintain internal order, but also the morale and the behavior of the military itself was drastically affected—a predicament seen as the main cause of what one author referred to as "the moral crisis of the French Army."[30] For example, must officers who had sworn loyalty to one emperor or king leave the army if that ruler is repudiated? Must he swear a new oath of fidelity to the next ruler, or must he persist in defending his former liege? Moreover, could an officer's faithfulness possibly be counted on by the new regime despite, as was often the case, his having served with the same equanimity, if not devotion, a republic, a consulate, an empire, and one or two kings? And indeed as there were no real professional guidelines, political preferences, pragmatism, and opportunism that tended to shape military behavior, particularly after 1815, led to a crisis that reached its zenith in 1830. Royalist emigrés, Bonapartists, Republican officers, and junior, senior, and general officers denounced each other's former fidelities, attachments, and political preferences.[31] With the accession of Louis-Philippe to the throne, a semblance of order was restored in the military world, but it was only momentary, as the events of 1848, 1852, and 1871 were to show. Despite the fact that officers had to take a new oath under the bourgeois king, the malaise persisted because of the absence of a device for linking military service to the nation independent of the person of the ruler.[32] For this reason and in view of the innumerable problems created by the rapid and erratic turnover of regimes due to the confluence of heterogeneous ideological currents such as revolutionary tradition, monarchism, Bonapartism, republicanism, and Boulangism, a new and more stable pattern of civil-military relationships had to be set up. This model, established during the Third Republic, was governed by the famous theory of the *cantonnement juridique*. Its function was to prevent soldiers, through a system of juridical restrictions, from being drawn into ideological or political situations in which they could be forced to judge the legitimacy of the regime they served, hence the legitimacy of their service to this regime; it spared servicemen, in other words, from dilemmas created by conflicts between their personal convictions and their professional duties.

In their concern for enforcing both the isolation and the subordination of the military, those who elaborated this theory of the *cantonnement* were led to impose rules restricting political rights and other democratic liberties as well as to establish a system of strict discipline. And, meeting the secret expectations of most officers, it was decided that military behavior in the future would be governed by only one principle: orders from above were to be obeyed blindly, regardless of personal doubts and convictions.

Thus, in an attempt to establish an appropriate and stable pattern of civil-military relationships, a dominating model of military discipline and authority in which the military had no initiative and no responsibility was established. "If the *cantonnement* supposes subordination to civilian rule, this implies also the adoption of a rigorous discipline which leaves very little room for initiative. From this it follows that in the execution of an order, the military would not have to judge its legality. The order given constitutes a sufficient justification and the problem of the responsibility of the military in the execution of an illegal order is not at stake."[33]

Other factors related to the particularism of military professionalism help to explain this continuous reference to traditional forms of discipline and authority in the army. Among army officers, and especially among those coming from military academies, it can be said that failure to adopt a manipulative or fraternal style of authority was due to their early training and indoctrination, which seemed crucial to the development of future professional traits. In the navy, as demonstrated, the existence of a modern style of discipline was related to the cadets' early exposure to modern methods during their years at the naval school. A comparative investigation reveals that at Saint-Cyr the type and nature of cadet training was very different. A key element of differentiation was that during training at Saint-Cyr emphasis was put on traditional objectives of the military profession —combat in its most classic form. As emphasized by Colonel Fauchois: "[Preparation for combat] dominates the idea officers have of their role: an image of virility, self-assurance, but of drama and exacting demands too. They see themselves as the men who one day may have to lead others into battle (envisaged, furthermore, in the most violent terms as hand-to-hand fighting, as skirmishes) and they will have to give orders on which the life and the death of their subordinates depend."[34]

Therefore, the basic conception of the career was such that it created an atmosphere favorable to domination and absolutism, leaving no room for manipulation. The military career was seen as one in which quickness in execution and spontaneous and immediate obedience were critical. Thus in the socialization of the cadet, the dominating and absolute type of command, from which an authoritative model of discipline was derived, was functionally justified. The fact that the instructors were, in general, officers helped to secure a stricter obedience. Even in the area of intellectual and academic education, which could have been an occasion for developing discussion and initiative, it is noticed that the relationships between cadets and their instructors, often their hierarchical superiors, operated according to rather authoritarian patterns. All cadet education, military and academic, was based upon a unilateral diffusion with little or no room for discussion and dialogue. The instructor was the master who held the knowledge that was fed into empty brains. His charisma and authority did not depend on the depth of his knowledge or his pedagogic skills but upon such things as his military achievements and prestige. For a long time Saint-Cyr instructors were chosen from among those with the most prestigious service records in order, as indicated by Fauchois, "to back up their advancement and their authority as instructors with impeccable experience."[35]

In a way, such a conception of military training, especially the view that readiness for combat was the paramount objective of the military profession, created among the cadets a system of expectations that prevented any change in the model. The instructor had to perform his role in conformity with the absolute, heroic model. Recourse to civilian teachers for nonmilitary matters, the introduction of new pedagogic methods based on discussion and dialogue, group encounter, and student freedom did not have the effects that might logically be expected. This explains why young officers, after assuming troop duty, often seemed so reluctant to accept innovations, even those introduced from above, that tended to deviate from their conception of military activity. As noted by officers who tried to experiment with new command techniques, the introduction of manipulation and an increase of initiative, frequently considered "unhealthy and demagogic"[36] by young officers, proved unsuccessful. It was no coincidence that a survey of Saint-Cyriens, questioned on their views of military discipline, revealed that 61 percent of the respondents thought that discipline should not be liberalized and 58 percent thought that a more liberalized style of military life would jeopardize combat readiness. Students at the Interarms Military School apparently held the same conceptions: 65 percent of the answers indicated an opposition to the liberalization of military discipline, and 55 percent agreed that a liberal style of military life could affect combat readiness.[37] It is important to note that, asked about the incentives that led them to modernize or liberalize their attitudes and conceptions of discipline, none of the officers who were interviewed for having attempted to promote modern forms of leadership and discipline mentioned their early training at Saint-Cyr or special courses, not even at the War College; these schools were viewed as instilling prepatterned models of behavior rather than facilitating the development of individual skills. Reading these surveys, one sees that among captains, for example, there was agreement that the "captains course," at least with regard to preparation for command, was not useful. "This course does not particularly prepare one to assume the command of a unit; there is too much emphasis on tactics and staff techniques at the expense of a general military and political education and a good knowledge of human sciences."[38] One sees also that motivations for applying modern forms of leadership were often linked to unusual training, particularly to contacts during visits or tours of duty at foreign military establishments: among the colonels singled out for originality in their command methods, many had served with the United States Army.[39]

As a result, the number of innovators remained small, and they were always looked upon as exceptions by the rest of the hierarchy; sometimes they were even treated as deviant cases. At worst, innovation was opposed at one point or another upon the hierarchical range; at best, it was seen as too unimportant an issue to be given any priority. And given the high rate of turnover, especially at the regimental level, the chances for one innovator to fall under the command of another for a sufficiently long period of time were limited. The lack of appropriate structures for discussion and adjustment of views across the hierarchy in addition to the continuous lack of ready financial means hindered the task of the innovators; this explains why such efforts had marginal results at best.

In the lower echelons, notably among the junior ranks, the innovator's situation was even more difficult: in fear of jeopardizing his career, he was less inclined to challenge the hierarchy. Moreover, innovative styles of leadership among captains remained less consequential than those undertaken by colonels, and captains also found it more difficult to implement change. The survey conducted among innovative captains clearly shows that they felt strongly bound by professional solidarity and, as a consequence, rarely acted to antagonize their superiors on the question of the proper exercise of authority whenever tensions could occur.[40]

Another zone of resistance to modern forms of military discipline in the army can be identified among NCOs. This tendency was not so much due to the NCO's predilection for authority, but a result of the ambiguity of the NCO's standing in the hierarchy and of the nature of the functions he had to perform. One is even tempted to say that as far as military authority was concerned, the NCO did not match the stereotype of the "barking sergeant," or *adjutant Flick*, stubbornly enforcing orders, as he was too often described. A few surveys undertaken among NCOs revealed that there was great variety in their conception of career and the ways to approach and fulfill it. Not many NCOs resembled the brutal drillmaster in charge of instructing an apathetic mass of conscripts. In a 1968 study among army NCO candidates, only 19.5 percent of those interviewed saw themselves as the "perfect executive." But 34.3 percent thought of the role of the NCO as one of instructor, 17.7 percent saw it as an intermediary between the management and execution levels, 12.2 percent as a technical specialist, and 9.2 percent as a future officer.[41] Another survey of NCOs and their careers, undertaken by the Center of Military Studies and Sociology in 1970, revealed that they considered themselves as collaborators and assistants to officers (69 percent), technical specialists (44 percent), instructors (27 percent), and intermediaries between the management and execution levels (21 percent). As far as the NCOs' perception of the role of a military leader was concerned, competence, human feelings and care, and intelligence were the qualities most frequently cited (competence by 50 percent, human feelings and care by 47 percent, intelligence by 33 percent). Discipline ranked fourth (28 percent) and was referred to mostly by older NCOs.[42] These figures, consequently, make it clear that the NCO's conception of the military profession, which influenced his organizational behavior, was far from the public's stereotyped image. Furthermore, the above mentioned survey indicated that if NCOs were given a chance to command, they would prefer posts that permitted personal action and would tend to neglect those reminding them of or linking them to their hierarchical superior. Those entrusted with instruction and officering focused on the necessity of carrying out their responsibilities and taking initiative. They required support from their superior, autonomy, and confidence. "Command is a source of satisfaction only if it can be exercised in an autonomous manner and without sharing, yet without being on one's own, but within the frame of limits drawn by a competent superior."[43] These remarks show clearly that the idea of initiative, among others, was familiar to army NCOs. Yet the nature of the tasks they were most likely to perform forced them to rely on traditional styles of leadership. Most NCOs, as illustrated by several interviews and surveys, found themselves in a position of carrying the burden of all the tasks inherent to a traditional large-size army, that is, the "general service," "garrison service," and "internal service." These tasks, which in the navy and the air force were reduced to a minimum given their organization along functional specialties, still had great importance in the army. For example, the rather dull tasks of the general service considered as useless corvées were always numerous. Because of their uninteresting nature, these jobs inevitably suscitated among those responsible for their execution a strong resentment, and as a result all orders related to their fulfillment had to be enforced through authoritarian discipline. It was indeed difficult for an NCO to ask his men to take the initiative in or to discuss with them the daily cleaning of latrines. As for the tasks related to the garrison service, internal service, or even campaign service, that is, the training, officering, and so on, that also occupied a central place on the daily agenda of military life, they imply a similar logic. The sheer magnitude of the volume of manpower to be trained and officered, the high periodical rate of personnel turnover, and the length of allocated time, interacted in such a way that instructors had no other choice than that to rely primarily on styles of discipline and authority that proceed from domination rather than from collaboration or manipulation. This trend was reinforced by the fact that these activities were placed under the incumbency of older NCOs, who, by training, had a tendency to rely upon traditional dominant forms of authority; often, young NCOs, trained in the job by older NCOs, were compelled to follow the same methods.

Somewhat paradoxically, the decline of military vocation among NCOs, as we observed earlier, did add to such inclinations. In studying the career motivations of French military personnel, one noticed that a growing proportion of NCOs, even in the army, embraced the profession of arms not by vocation, not even for militaristic reasons, but simply to learn or perfect a trade, generally with the view of later pursuing this career as a civilian. From this one would have expected that, as they were basically motivated by secularized and civilian-oriented concerns, they would, during their time in the military, conform to a model of behavior closer—more liberalized—to that of the civil world than of the military. But interestingly, if most surveys show a rejection of military traditional norms among these men,[44] no common pattern of organizational behavior correlated to such rejection could be observed, for both liberalized and authoritarian styles coexisted. And one gets the impression that adoption of one or the other was guided by pragmatic considerations, that is, the easiest way of getting things done. This attitude was not in itself unusual, particularly since the mid-1960s. With changing career conceptions from vocational to professional and occupational approaches, NCOs, increasingly concerned with status and material rewards, sought in the army either a way to acquire, as rapidly as possible, skills negotiable on the civilian labor market or promotion to higher ranks in the hierarchy in order to maximize their salaries and future retirement benefits. Then, somewhat self-estranged from the military institution, which became a transient stage of their professional life, they lacked incentive for evolving, or at least pursuing, innovative forms of relationships and preferred to rely on existing traditional patterns of interaction. In addition, the poor integration between army NCOs and officers, accentuated by differences in social status, isolated NCOs from the upper part of the military organization and compelled them to assert their position in relation to the privates with whom they interacted constantly. But the fact that the majority of privates were draftees, who tended to identify NCOs with the repressive aspect of the institution, and interestingly, expected them to act as such, forced the NCOs to rely on domination.

It is also true that, in some circumstances, domination gave way to manipulation; it has been observed for example that many NCOs tried to relate with privates on a "buddy-buddy" basis. But in such cases, this was essentially the result of some sort of bargaining process by which NCOs could win the docility of the troops.[45] This situation, it should be noted in passing, had certain negative consequences. Given the difference in the reference environments of the two groups—the draftee was a civilian, a status of which the NCO tended to be jealous—and given the precariousness of the NCOs own situation and his isolation in the institution, it happened frequently that the NCO was led to espouse the disdain, or reluctance, of the draftee for the military and thereby increased his own estrangement.[46]

This situation occurred more infrequently in the other services, where privates were less numerous and at the same time more integrated in a functional and technical division of labor in which collaboration with NCOs was greater. The isolation of the NCO from the officer corps was also less pronounced in these services. An NCO combat pilot, for example, saw his salary swollen by substantial bonuses; this meant that in some cases his income was higher than that of a young air force lieutenant just out of the academy. In addition, social distance between officers and NCOs was, especially in the air force, reduced. A division of labor based on specialties brought together officers and NCOs with similar skills, concerned about the same questions; professional scrupulousness and collective responsibility further united the hierarchy.

It is probable that only a reform of the NCO's status, and a rationalization of the NCO tasks, oriented toward a technical division of labor based on the naval or air force model could have changed the organizational climate and internal mechanism of social interactions in the army. Such changes might have led to a reliance upon mild techniques of discipline and organizational control, but they would not have created this reliance automatically. It would have been necessary, before all else, to socialize career personnel to such methods; early training and indoctrination would have been the crucial moments for infusing a new approach toward authority and discipline. Introducing group strategy, breaking down the vertical hierarchical relation between instructor and students, establishing team tasks—these seem the most obvious solutions.

A short summary will help recapitulate the situation. Until 1966, the formal pattern of discipline in the French armed forces remained based mostly on rigidity and domination. Afterwards, it was governed by the old traditional values and a new rationale based on initiative and manipulation at the same time. Interestingly, modern styles of military authority characterized the discipline practiced by the air force and navy, whereas traditional styles continued to pervade the army model of discipline. Such an ambivalence was certainly a correlate of the dualism of the entire French military establishment, itself the result of an uneven exposure to technological modernization. But, in its most rigid and dominant version, military discipline was also the result of specific characteristics, historical as well as professional. Among historical factors, the search for a viable and consistent model of civil-military relations was a determinant one. Among professional factors, the nature of the early indoctrination of officers and the ambiguity of the role of NCOs constituted two important variables with regard to a continuing reliance on traditional forms of military discipline and authority in the army.

Notes

1. Robert K. Merton, "Bureaucratic Structure and Personality," *Social Forces* 18 (1940): 561–68.

2. An interesting discussion on the development and genesis of military discipline and its early historical forms can be found in Maury D. Feld, *The Structure of Violence: Armed Forces as Social Systems* (Beverly Hills, Ca.: Sage Publications, 1977); G. Teitler, *The Genesis of the Professional Officers' Corps* (Beverly Hills, Ca.: Sage Publications, 1977); and Jacques Van Doorn, *The Soldier and Social Change* (Beverly Hills, Ca.: Sage Publications, 1975).

3. Morris Janowitz, "Changing Patterns of Organizational Authority: The Military Establishment," *Administrative Science Quarterly* 3 (1959): 482.

4. Hans H. Gerth and C. Wright Mills, eds., *From Max Weber: Essays in Sociology* (New York: Oxford University Press, 1958), p. 253.

5. Morris Janowitz and Roger Little, *Sociology and the Military Establishment* (New York: Russell Sage Foundation, 1965), p. 42. *See also*

General J. Colin, *Les Transformations de la guerre* (Paris: Flammarion, 1937).

6. Janowitz and Little, *Sociology and the Military Establishment*, p. 37.

7. Janowitz, "Changing Patterns of Organizational Authority," p. 475.

8. In this chapter, we shall deal only with the evolution of the basic rationale for military discipline and, in particular, with the nature of vertical relationships within the organization. Questions concerning the legal and juridical conditions and liberties of military personnel will not be discussed; on these points, *see* Jean-Pierre Marichy, "Liberté d'expression des militaires de carrière en France" and Jacques Robert, "Ethique militaire, condition juridique et libertés publiques," both in *Le Système militaire français*, edited by Jean-Pierre Marichy (Toulouse: Université des Sciences sociales, 1977), pp. 57–84; Jacques Robert, "Libertés publiques et défense," *Revue du Droit public et de la Science politique* 93 (1977); Joseph-L. Herry, *La Fonction militaire* (Paris: Berger-Levrault, 1976), pp. 183–207; and M. Sénéchal, *Droits politiques et liberté d'expression des officiers des forces armées* (Paris: Librairie générale de Droit et de Jurisprudence, 1966).

9. William Coulet, "Le Nouveau Règlement de discipline générale dans les armées," *Revue du Droit public et de la Science politique* 84 (1968): 25.

10. The complete text of the Decree of 1933 can be found in Ministère de la Guerre, *Règlement du service dans l'armée* (Paris: Charles-Lavauzelle, 1957 edition), first part "Discipline générale," pp. 6–74.

11. "Décret n° 66-749 du 1er octobre 1966 portant règlement de discipline générale dans les armées," *Journal officiel, lois et décrets*, 8 October 1966, pp. 8853–74.

12. Coulet, "Le Nouveau Règlement de discipline générale dans les armées," p. 8.

13. "Décret n° 75-675 du 28 juillet 1975 portant règlement de discipline générale dans les armées," *Journal officiel, lois et décrets*, 30 July 1975, pp. 7732–38.

14. "Décret du 26 novembre 1937, discipline générale dans l'Armée de Mer," *Journal officiel, lois et décrets*, 20 January 1938, pp. 911–24.

15. *See* Capitaine de frégate Amet, "Evolution de la notion d'initiative dans le cadre de la discipline militaire," in *Les Militaires et leur formation dans un monde en évolution* (Paris: SPEI, 1972), pp. 134–35 (article also published in *Revue maritime* 281 [1970]: 1182–94).

16. Ibid., pp. 136–38.

17. Ibid., p. 138. *See also* Amet, "Essai sur le commandement des hommes," *Revue maritime* 268 (1969); Capitaine de frégate Frappat, "Plaidoyer pour l'initiative," *Revue maritime* 270 (1969); R. Dequet, "Reflexions sur l'initiative et la responsabilité," *Revue maritime* 270 (1970): 448–58.

18. Michel Lhoste, in "L'Institution militaire, une organisation en crise" (Ph.D. dissertation, Université Descartes, 1973).

19. Hommes et Stratégies, "Chefs de corps et styles de commandement," mimeographed (Neuilly, 1973); Hommes et Stratégies, "Commandants d'unités élémentaires et styles de commandement," mimeographed (Paris, 1975).

20. "Chefs de corps et styles de commandement," p. 85.

21. "Commandants d'unités

élémentaires et styles de commandement," p. 29.

22. Jacques Isnard, "Les Colonels
et la stratégie de commandement,"
Le Monde, 29 June 1973, p. 10.

23. "Chefs de corps et styles de
commandement."

24. Janowitz and Little, *Sociology
and the Military Establishment*, p. 105.

25. David B. Ralston, *The Army of
the Republic: The Place of the Military in
the Political Evolution of France, 1871–
1914* (Cambridge, Mass.: MIT Press,
1967).

26. Altamayer, *Initiative et discipline*
(Paris: Berger-Levrault, 1913); Major
de Grandmaison, *Le Dressage de l'infanterie en vue du combat offensif* (Paris,
1913).

27. Guy Pédroncini, *Pétain, général
en chef, 1917–1918* (Paris: Presses
Universitaires de France, 1974).

28. It is interesting to note that in
1973 the French Army Youth Committee prepared a project proposing
the nomination of an ombudsman
to whom defendants could appeal
outside of the usual hierarchical
channels.

29. Coulet, "Le Nouveau Règlement de discipline générale dans les
armées," p. 11.

30. Pierre Chalmin, "Les Crises
morales de l'armée française au XIXe
siècle," *Revue de Défense nationale* 6
(1950): 554–70; *see also* Raoul Girardet, *La Société militaire dans la France
contemporaine, 1816–1939* (Paris:
Plon, 1953), Chapter 7, "Crise de
conscience."

31. Regarding this point, *see* Doug-
las Porch, *Army and Revolution: France
1815–1848* (London: Routledge and
Kegan Paul, 1974).

32. Pierre Chalmin, *L'Officier français de 1815 à 1870* (Paris: M. Rivière,

1957), Part 3, Chapter 1.

33. Coulet, "Le Nouveau Règlement de discipline générale dans les
armées," p. 17.

34. B. Fauchois, "The Adaptation
of the Professional Soldier to New
Training Methods," in *The Perceived
Role of the Military*, edited by M. R.
Van Gils (Rotterdam: Rotterdam
University Press, 1971), p. 75.

35. Ibid., p. 76.

36. "Chefs de corps et styles de
commandement," p. 88 ff.

37. Francois Helluy, "Les Jeunes
Officiers de l'armée de terre"
(EMSST thesis, Centre de Sociologie
de la Défense nationale, 1974), pp.
80–82 and *in fine*.

38. "Commandants d'unités
élémentaires et styles de commandement," p. 28.

39. "Chefs de corps et styles de
commandements," p. 96.

40. "Commandants d'unités
élémentaires et styles de commandement," p. 30.

41. Henri Pillot, "L'Elève sous-
officier d'active" (EMSST thesis,
Paris, 1968).

42. CESM, "Le Sous-officier; son
métier, sa carrière, 1970," mimeographed (Paris, 1972). This survey,
conducted under the auspices of the
army staff, was an attempt to update
an earlier study, "Le Sous-officier et
sa profession, 1967."

43. Ibid.

44. Jean-Pierre Thomas, "The
Mobility of Non-Commissioned
Officers," in *The Perceived Role of the
Military*, edited by M. R. Van Gils,
pp. 153–54.

45. CESM, "Le Sous-officier, son
métier, sa carrière, 1970."

46. Because it was not our purpose
to consider the consequences of the

inadequacies of the traditional model of military discipline on the functioning of the military institution, we need not delve further into this matter. To date, this question has not been the object of an in depth study, except for Captain Lhoste's survey, "*L'Institution militaire, une organisation en crise.*"

PART FOUR ● THE SOCIAL DIMENSION OF THE FRENCH MILITARY ESTABLISHMENT

INTRODUCTION

The social recruitment of the career military is a traditional and much favored theme of intellectual reflection in the fields of military history and sociology. The list of works directly or obliquely related to this question is endless and the number of students involved in this type of research, who count among their illustrious predecessors Alexis de Tocqueville and Gaetano Mosca, is large. The logic for such a scholarly concern developed mainly from the intellectual preoccupation with uncovering the functioning of civil-military relations and, more precisely, with explaining the dynamics of the military's political role throughout the history of modern society. A commonly held opinion is that the social recruitment of the military was a significant variable with regard to its political behavior and ideological stands. Gaetano Mosca, by emphasizing the correlation between, on the one hand, the similarities in the social composition of the European officer corps and ruling elites and on the other hand, the noninterference of the former in politics—a phenomenon that he found to be one of the most distinctive and enduring features of European states—implicitly stated a causal relationship between these two parameters.[1]

Contemporary students of military societies continue to draw attention to the relationship between the political behavior of the military and its social recruitment. But they do so with a more healthy skepticism and with subtlety; they no longer give an explanatory priority to the latter variable. Moreover, the center of focus has moved toward new concerns: recent studies in military sociology tend to focus upon the nature and evolution of the social composition of the military rather than upon its political effects. The "democratization" of officers' origins, for example, is one of the more interesting phenomena on which these researches have shed light. Comparative inquiries have demonstrated that one of the most distinctive trends of the evolution of Western military institutions of the late nineteenth and early twentieth centuries was the progressive broadening of the social base upon which the recruitment of officers operated. Thus, throughout the West, the social structure of the officer corps is said to have democratized, in the sense that access to them, for a long time the almost exclusive reserve of the upper social stratum, was granted to new and less privileged groups beginning with an infusion from the middle-class. Albeit this trend did not develop at the same pace everywhere, on the whole it had a long-range uniformity that, in Western polities, resulted essentially in the increasing isomorphism of military elites with regard to the parent national socio-cultural organization.[2]

Yet, as shown by recent analyses, this process seemed to slow down and even reverse itself in a number of cases as the weight of elements coming from the periphery of the social fabric (peripheral from either a cultural, racial, regional, or occupational standpoint) tended increasingly to ballast the military establishment. Interestingly enough, such a shift in the pattern of the social structure of some military establishments occurred in situations where the development of the armed forces along the mass army model had come to an end. In this regard, the change in the social structure of the British and American all-volunteer forces is extremely significant.[3] Thus democratization is not an endless, self-perpetuating process; it is a process correlative with the evolution of the military format along the mass armed forces line.

The purpose of the considerations that follow consists simply of examining the nature and evolution of the social structure of the French military establishment following World War II in the light of these trends and to seek further explanations for some of the more noticeable particularities; of these, occupational inheritance, endorecruitment in other words, will be given special attention.

Though from time to time the present study limits itself to one particular sector of the military establishment, such as the officer corps, either because such sectors offer special interest or because poor availability of data imposes such a focus, in general, it addresses itself to the military establishment in its entirety and attempts to deal with the main segments of the officer corps as well as the NCO and enlistee populations. A study ignoring NCOs, for example, would be somewhat unrealistic given the key functions performed by this stratum in the main articulations and role-conflict zones of the military organization.

From a methodological viewpoint, this type of sociological investigation requires careful analysis of a series of specific variables including geographic, religious, familial, educational, and occupational origins. But, because the data available rarely covered such an array of items, we were led to focus on the occupational background (father's occupation) of French soldiers. It appears, however, that a significantly relevant amount of knowledge about the military can be derived from these data, as the occupational origin variable appeared not only as a fairly relevant proxy for social origins but also as a heuristic index for measuring both quantitative and qualitative changes over time with respect to such questions as democratization or elitism that have been the conceptual landmark in assessing the direction of the transformation of the social morphology of the military.

Notes

1. Gaetano Mosca, *Elementi de scienza politica* (Turin: Fratelli Bocca, 1923); for more details on this matter, *see also* Bengt Abrahamsson, *Military Professionalization and Political Power* (Beverly Hills, Ca.: Sage Publications, 1972), Chapter 2.

2. Morris Janowitz, "The Armed Forces and Society in Western Europe," *European Journal of Sociology* 6 (1965): 225–37.

3. On this question, in general, *see* George Kourvetaris and Betty Dobratz, *Social Origins and Political Orientations of Officer Corps in a World Perspective* (Denver: University of Denver Press, 1973); Morris Janowitz, "The Emergent Military," in *Public Opinion and the Military Establishment*, edited by Charles C. Moskos, Jr. (Beverly Hills, Ca.: Sage Publications, 1971), pp. 255–70. About the United States, *see* Charles C. Moskos, Jr., "The Emergent Military: Civil, Traditional or Plural," in *National Security and American Society*, edited by Frank Trager and Philip Kronenberg (Lawrence: University of Kansas Press, 1973); Morris Janowitz and Charles C. Moskos, Jr., "Racial Composition in the All-Volunteer Force: Policy Alternatives," *Armed Forces and Society* 1 (1974): 109–23. About Great Britain, *see* Peter J. Dietz and James F. Stone, "The British All-Volunteer Force," *Armed Forces and Society* 1 (1975): 159–90; Maurice Garnier, "Changing Recruitment Patterns and Organizational Ideology: The Case of a British Academy," *Administrative Science Quarterly* 17 (1972) 499–507.

CHAPTER EIGHT ● SOCIAL STRUCTURE

At this particular level of the analysis, the fact of having to operate at the same time with the diachronic and the interservice dimensions on the one hand and with the vertical dimension, the interrank dimension, on the other hand, raises a number of difficulties, particularly for defining trends. So in order to simplify the exposé, we shall be dealing first with the NCO and enlistee population and then with the officer corps. Only then shall we attempt, in the light of a summary of our findings, to determine and explain the nature of the evolution in this particular area of the French military establishment.

Social Origins of NCOs and Enlistees

For a long time, NCOs and enlistees were of little concern to students of the military. On the whole this was due to the fact that there was little information available about them, but there was also an element of elitist intellectual bias, as these strata of the military were not considered as relevant to the understanding of the military institution as the officer corps obviously was. Only recently have systematic surveys and mappings of NCO and enlistee populations been undertaken. Yet, given the particularism of these enterprises (most of them are conducted by the military or by a civilian research team under contract to the military), the data and findings made available for public use remain relatively poor.

The knowledge of the social structure of the NCO and enlistee populations is indeed crucial to an understanding of the social structure of the entire military establishment; this is true for several reasons. Most important, NCOs and enlistees constituted the major demographic bulk of the military; in the 1970s, NCOs alone—140,000 strong —made up 43 percent of the air force's manpower, 37 percent of the navy's, and 17 percent of the army's. This group also formed an important resource for the recruitment of officers. For example, between 1967 and 1973, 30 percent of the officers in the army, 25 percent of the officers in the air force, and 31.5 percent of those in the navy were former NCOs who had attended the special officer schools; and 45 percent of the officers in the army, 53.3 percent in the air force, and 32.3 percent in the navy were former NCOs who had been promoted up from the ranks.[1] Therefore, changes in the officers' social recruitment is also a function of changes in that of NCOs and enlistees.

Geographical Origins and Personal Vitae

Historically, the mainstay of the enlistee/NCO populations was the "demographic surplus" from rural areas. And until the end of the 1960s this tradition seemed to prevail, men from rural villages and regions being more favorably disposed toward a military career than their urban compatriots. After that time, however, sweeping changes took place as industrialized and urbanized areas became important sources of recruitment of enlistees and NCOs into all the services. A survey concerning long-term navy enlistees illustrated this evolution. Before 1960, nearly 55 percent of all navy enlistees came from the rural areas of western France, namely the five departments of the Brittany region. After that time there was an increasing recruitment from the urban and industrialized areas, not only from those situated in the west, but also in other parts of the country. There was a gradual, but noticeable, shift toward the Parisian region, the north (the Pas-de-Calais in particular), and the east (Lorraine and the Rhone Valley). The survey reveals that almost 60 percent of the enlistees came from urban areas of more than 10,000 inhabitants.[2] The same trend was also observed in the army. For example, among army enlistees eligible to prepare for NCO training (*élèves sous-officiers d'active*), 27.8 percent originally came from large towns (more than 50,000 inhabitants), 28.3 percent from middle-sized and small towns (from 5,000 to 50,000 inhabitants), 16 percent from villages (1,500 to 5,000 inhabitants), and 27.6 percent from rural or semirural areas (villages of less than 1,500 inhabitants).[3] In general, fewer enlistees and NCOs came from the poorer rural regions such as Corsica, the central part of France (the Cantal and the Lozère), and the upper Loire Valley. In regard to the parent community, the regional origin of NCOs and enlistees was even more urban, as nearly 57 percent came from urbanized areas, against an average of 54.4 percent of the civil community. Therefore, by the late 1960s it was the urban areas that provided the demographic surplus for the enlistee/NCO population.

An analysis of the familial and personal background of enlistees and NCOs sheds further light on the social structure of noncommissioned personnel. From the observations of familial background, two interesting characteristics emerge. First, it seems that the average size

of the NCO or enlistee family is smaller than that of the typical officer's family. For example, in 1968, among enlistees preparing for
NCO commission, 30 percent had three brothers and/or sisters while
41 percent of these enlistees came from families with only one or two
children. These figures continued to change afterward. According to
a more recent survey, in 1971 only 20.8 percent of army enlistees came
from families with three children. Second, as shown by several surveys a significant proportion of NCOs and enlistees came from a "disturbed" or unstable family background. Twenty percent of navy enlistees, 21 percent of all army enlistees, and 22 percent of the army enlistees eligible for promotion to NCO were orphans, sons of unknown
fathers, or sons of divorced parents.[4] These proportions were higher
than were those for the parent civil community. For example, in 1965
13 percent of all long-term navy enlistees were fatherless orphans as
compared to 9 percent of the civil community; 12 percent were sons
of divorced parents, compared to 7 percent of the civil community.

Age structure and the educational background also show the transformation of the NCO/enlistee population. Between 1945 and 1959,
the average age of NCOs was higher than it was after 1960. The same
trend was true for enlistees. For example, in 1972, among army enlistees, 40 percent were between seventeen and eighteen years of age,
33 percent between eighteen and nineteen, 17 percent between nineteen and twenty; only 10 percent were older than twenty. In the air
force and navy, the average population of enlistees was even younger: 54.3 percent in the navy and 67 percent in the air force were between seventeen and eighteen years of age.[5] This helps to explain
why more than 80 percent of the enlistees (90 percent in the navy)
were bachelors.

When discussing the educational background, a distinction has to be
made between army enlistees on the one hand and air force and navy
enlistees on the other. Though it had slowly improved over time, the
level of education of army enlistees was generally much lower than
that of navy and air force enlistees. Moreover, the educational background of navy and air force enlistees was considerably better than
that of the drafted population, particularly at the upper level of the
hierarchy. However, it must be said that in the army, although enlistees with high school education, baccalaureate, and above were unmistakably underrepresented with regard to draftees, categories with
basic primary education were better represented (table 8.1). As far as
the NCOs were concerned, the general level of education was slightly
higher; the proportion of men with a high school education, with a
baccalaureate, was always greater than among enlistees. However,

the same dichotomy observed in enlistees can be observed between the respective levels of army NCOs and air force and navy NCOs.

It should be noted in passing that this improvement in the educational level of noncommissioned personnel was a major factor in the transformation of career motivations and conceptions, notably in the increasing demand for professional and technical activities, and the correlative disinterest in military tasks. It was precisely because of such a shift in career expectations that the military institutions began increasing the number of training programs in the area of general education as well as in technical fields.

Useful as this information about the geographical and the educational background of enlistees and NCOs is, it has only a limited validity and ought to be complemented by additional studies. With regard to the evolution of the military's social structure, perhaps the best tool of measurement is the occupational origins of the population under observation. The two following sections will deal with this variable, first at the level of the enlistees, then at the level of the NCOs.

Occupational Origins of Enlistees

As pointed out, although a considerable effort has been made to systematically study the enlistee population of the French armed forces, empirical data available to the private researcher remain limited in scope; yet there is enough evidence to permit the drawing of a number of valid and relevant inferences, if not concluding assessments, about enlistees' social background. Table 8.2 dealing with the occupational origins of the men who joined the armed forces in 1975 provides a clear picture of recent trends in enlistee social origins across services.

Table 8.1. Education of Enlistees by Service, 1972–75 (percentages)

	1975			1972
	Army	Navy	Air Force	Draftees (All Services)
Baccalaureate and complete high school education	9.4	10.4	20	13
Partial high school education [a]	30.1	47.9	70	35
Primary school education [a]	43.1	41.7	10	35
Below primary school	17.4	—		17

Source: The data for enlistees was adapted from Marchand, "Ceux qui s'engagent," pp. 50–51.
[a] With or without degree.

In view of these data, it can be said that, in general, the social structure of the enlistee was fairly democratic, and, with regard to past trends, there was a tendency toward democratization. In this respect, the case of the army enlistees was particularly apropos as individuals from the lower occupations were increasingly better represented at the same time that there seemed to be a decline in the representation of the higher occupational sectors (see Table 8.3).

At closer examination, however, another picture emerges. First of all, an interservice inspection illustrated that the occupational background of navy and air force enlistees was somewhat less socially representative: for example, the proportion of individuals from the working class was lower than in the army. Moreover, the proportion of men from the upper occupational strata remained important, and in some cases, as among enlistees of the flying personnel in the air force (7.8 percent of all air force enlistees) constituted the largest group. This means that in the navy and in the air force, the process of democratization never developed into what could be called a "blueing" of the enlistees' social composition, as the lowest strata of the parent social structure were not represented. Microanalytical study of the army enlisted personnel shows that the democratization process was not complete, for similar tendencies seemed to occur, but at a lower level of the occupational structure. The following figure, borrowed from a survey covering the army enlistees population of 1970–71, illustrates this phenomenon by showing the underrepresentation of individuals from the lowest segments—sons of miners, rural and industrial unskilled workers—against an overrepresentation of those from a higher level—sons of foremen and skilled workers. Thus, if there was a greater tendency in the blueing of enlistee social origin in the army, it was nonetheless a limited one (see Figure 8.1).

Occupational Origins of NCOs

Given the significant tendency toward the democratization of the occupational background of French enlisted personnel, one would logically have expected to find a similar phenomenon at the NCO level, as NCOs were being recruited from among enlistees. This was not the case, as the data in Table 8.4 indicate. However, one cannot draw the conclusion that the social origins of French NCOs were elitist or even that the social structure was nondemocratic. This would be an exaggeration. Yet, compared to the male labor force occupational structure, the NCOs' occupational origins were far from mirroring the diversity of the civilian structure; particularly noticeable was the underrepre-

Table 8.2. Sociooccupational Origins of Enlistees by Service, 1975 (percentages)

Father's Occupation [a]	Army	Navy
1. Farm owner, farm laborer	5.5	1.7
2. Artisan, small or large business owner	6.8	9.5
3. Professional, executive (public and private sectors)	11.2	5.8
4. Managerial or technical employee	[b]	19.1
5. Sales or clerical employee	7.4	16.9
6. Worker, household employee	50.9	26.2
7. Military	5.9	7.7
8. Other	12.3	13.1

Sources: Marchand, "Ceux qui s'engagent," pp. 50–51 and 65; Laurent Thévenot, "Les Catégories sociales en 1975: l'extension du salariat," *Economie et Statistique* 91 (1977): 5.
[a] The categories of social occupations used here and on most tables throughout this chapter are the standard typology established by the National Institute of Statistics and Economic Studies. For details of the internal occupational components of each category, see Tables D.1 and D.2 in Appendix D.
[b] Included in category 3.
[c] Included in categories 3 and 8.
[d] Police included.

sentation of the lower segments of the occupational structure—the rural and industrial working class.

Furthermore, seen in a diachronic perspective, the data, which for the purpose of a longitudinal analysis refer to four different NCO populations (divided according to four categories of length of service used here as a surrogate variable for time) bring ample evidence about a decrease in the level of democratic representation. The proportion of sons of farmers decreased (sharply in the navy); but this followed the trend of the parent community. It is striking that the proportion of sons of workers remained stable in the army, declined in the air force, and increased slightly in the navy, over time, whereas the proportion of workers in the civilian labor force grew significantly. Closer inspection reveals that the elitist trend in the occupational background of the NCO population was marked not only by a declining representation of members from the working class and a concomitant increase of members from a white collar background (*employé*), but also by a

| Air Force | | National Labor |
Ground Personnel	Flying Personnel	Force, 1975
4.1	3.8	9.3
8.2	4.1	7.8
6.0	27.7	6.7
13.1	24.0	12.7
11.1	18.7	17.7
40.5	11.3	43.4
c	c	1.6[d]
17.0	10.4	0.8

sharp increase in the representation of the upper echelons of the social fabric. In effect, whereas among NCOs with more than eleven years of service, that is, among those who had been recruited in the late 1950s and at the beginning of the 1960s, the proportion of men from the higher occupational strata was lower than in the civil community, among NCOs with from one to ten years of service this proportion had grown and was higher than in the parent community.

Further, it is interesting to note that there was a great deal of homogeneity in the NCO occupational origins across services (notwithstanding the groups of NCOs in the navy who came from families working at sea, whose importance was declining over time). It almost seems as if there had been a convergence toward a common social structure for all armed forces NCOs.

Also, in the three services, the number of NCOs who were sons of military professionals represented 11 percent to 15 percent of the NCO population, a figure that, without being abnormally high as it was among officers, was far from being negligible. This is especially true when it is compared with the figures concerning NCOs with relatives (grandfather, brother, uncle) in the armed forces, figures that were surprisingly high.

To conclude this section on the NCO/enlistee social structure, it can be said that, despite a reversal of the "democratization" trend among NCOs and despite the fact that the occupational structure of NCOs did not mirror that of enlistees, the structure was, on the whole, fairly diversified.

Table 8.3. Sociooccupational Origins of Army Enlistees, 1963–75 (percentages)

Father's Occupation	1963	1967–68	1970	1972	1975
Farm owner, farm laborer	13	17	7	6	6
Professional, small or large business owner	32	26	19	19	18
Managerial or technical personnel, sales or clerical employee	15	5	8	9	7
Worker, household employee	27	44	48	49	51
Military	13	8	8	8	6
Other	—	—	10	9	12

Source: Data collected at the Centre d'Etudes et de Sociologie militaire.

Table 8.4. Sociooccupational Origins of NCOs by Service and Length of Enlistment (percentages)

	Army		
	Years of Service		
Father's Occupation	16+	11–15	6–10 1
Farm owner, farm laborer	14	16	13
Artisan, small business owner	11	9	8
Professional, executive (public and private sectors), large sales or industrial business owner	5	2	7
Managerial or technical personnel, sales or clerical employee	12	11	13
Fisherman, seaman in merchant navy	1	1	0
Worker or foreman	26	24	26
Military	13	19	16
Household employee	0	1	1
Other[a]	4	3	4
Occupation unknown, no answer	14	14	12
(Relatives in the military)	(54)	(57)	(60)

Sources: Centre d'Etudes et de Sociologie militaire, "Origines socio-professionnell des sous-officiers," mimeographed (Paris, 1973). INSEE, *Données sociales* (Paris, 197 1st edition, p. 24; Thévenot, "Les Catégories sociales en 1975," p. 5.
    [a] Policemen included.

Social Origins of Officers

In a way, the term "officer corps" is a misleading one, because it tends to suggest an impression of homogeneity, monolithism, or even unity. It is not so much the interservice discrepancies that lead to such an assertion as it is another kind of discrepancy, one linked to recruitment procedures. In the light of these recruitment procedures, the career development they generated, and the professional status they dictated, any sensation of unity across the officer corps that might have existed, evaporated.

It is not our purpose to study either the historical legacy of French officer recruitment or to detail the functioning of the different procedures for recruitment, yet let us state simply, as a matter of clarification, that three main avenues of access to the officer corps existed. Some had several distinct subroutes. First, there was direct recruitment, by which is meant admittance to the corps through the military academies. This avenue was open to baccalaureate holders who pre-

	Navy				Air Force			Total Labor Force			
	Years of Service				Years of Service						
6+	11–15	6–10	1–5	16+	11–15	6–10	1–5	1954	1958	1962	1975
14	12	7	6	13	11	10	8	26.7	20.1	14.9	9.3
9	8	6	11	12	11	10	7	10.5	9.2	8.1	6.7
2	4	9	9	3	4	7	11	4.3	5.3	6.3	7.8
2	13	14	19	18	17	18	22	16.6	20.3	24.5	30.4
3	6	6	4	1	1	1	1	0.4	0.3	0.3	0.2
2	23	28	29	28	25	21	25	33.5	36.5	37.6	37.5
3	19	13	11	9	17	16	12	1.6	1.9	1.7	1.6[a]
1	1	1	0	1	0	1	0	5.3	5.4	5.7	5.7
2	4	5	4	3	3	6	5	1.1	1.0	0.9	0.8
2	10	12	7	14	11	10	9	—	—	—	—
4)	(65)	(61)	(54)	(54)	(61)	(56)	(55)	—	—	—	—

Figure 8.1. Social Representativeness among Army
Enlisted Personnel, 1970–71

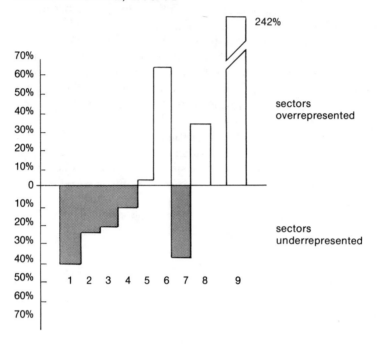

1 - Farm owners, farm laborers
2 - Small and large business
   owners
3 - Executives (public and
   private sectors, professionals
4 - Managerial and technical
   personnel

5 - Clerical and sales
   employees
6 - Foremen, skilled workers
7 - Workers, miners, seamen
   and fishermen
8 - Household employees
9 - Military (enlistees) and
   policemen

Source: Francois Vieillescazes, "Les Engagements volontaires dans l'Armée de
Terre," *Défense nationale* 33 (July 1977): 86.

pared for two years in special preparatory classes, either in public (lycées) and private institutions or in military schools of general learning, for the academy entrance examination. After two years of training at the academy, they received their commissions. There were three military academies, one for each service: Saint-Cyr (located in Coëtquidan) for the army, L'Ecole navale (Brest) for the navy, and L'Ecole de l'Air (Salon de Provence) for the air force. After World War II, L'Ecole Polytechnique, which in 1913 had provided around 12 percent of the newly recruited army officers, no longer provided more than a negligible proportion of officers. In addition to these academies, the main sources for direct recruitment, there were four specialized officer schools: two medical schools—one for the army (in Lyon) and one for the navy (in Bordeaux)—the Ecole du Commissariat (in Toulon), and the Ecole d'Administration de l'Inscription maritime (in Bordeaux). In August 1977, a new officer's school was opened, the Ecole militaire du Corps technique et administratif (in Coëtquidan), which recruits on the basis of a competitive examination. A second avenue into the officer corps was through semidirect recruitment, a particular procedure for young NCOs eligible to take a special examination enabling them to enter NCO officer schools, where they spent one year before being commissioned. There were five schools of this type. The Ecole militaire interarmes (EMIA) for the army (located at Coëtquidan), the Ecole militaire de la Flotte, and the Ecole militaire de l'Air constituted the main sources for semidirect recruitment. There were also the Ecole de formation des services (army) and the Ecole des officiers d'administration (navy). Third, there was indirect recruitment; this refers to promotion from the ranks and, to a very small extent, to recruitment from the reserves.[6] After 1964 (that is, the law of 26 December 1964) in the army and the air force, and after 1969 (that is, the law of 20 December 1969) in the navy, a new avenue for the indirect recruitment of officers was created, mainly to improve the level of this category of officers and to keep qualified men who had no other access to the officer corps in the active service. These men, called "technician-officers," were selected from among NCOs either through choice or competitive examination, and could not remain in active service for more than twenty-seven years, nor could they be promoted to a rank higher than captain. In practice, this reform failed for very few qualified NCOs could be selected; as a result this channel of promotion was abandoned in 1976.

After World War II, the proportion of each category of officers slightly varied. In the army, for example, that from direct recruitment decreased during the 1950s, and that from semidirect recruitment stabilized, and the proportion of officers from indirect recruitment and from the reserves increased. For the entire 1950–57 period, the respective proportions in each category were 28.5 percent for direct recruitment (35.9 percent in 1939), 35 percent for semidirect recruitment, 25 percent for recruitment from the ranks, and 8 percent for recruitment from the reserves. A similar trend can be observed in the air force: in the early 1950s, 24 percent of the officers came from a military academy (36 percent in 1939), 21 percent from semidirect recruitment (24 percent in 1939), 49.8 percent from the ranks (35.5 percent in 1939), and 5.1 percent from the reserves (4.4 percent in 1939).[7] These tendencies were maintained into the 1960s. Table 8.5 indicates the contribution of each procedure to the recruitment of the French officer corps between 1967 and 1972.

Given such a diversity in officer recruitment, any valid analysis of the social morphology of the officer corps ought to take into consideration these various categories. For this reason, we shall not only deal with the officer corps as a whole, but also with its various components, insofar as the existing evidence permits. Although most of the information will be derived from the analysis of the occupational origins of the officers, we shall begin with a brief discussion of other elements of their background.

Regional, Educational, and Personal Background

Historically and traditionally, officers were recruited chiefly from the least industrial, least urbanized regions of the country. Diachronic data about the geographic background of Western European officer corps show that most officers were recruited from rural areas and small town regions. There is no need for lengthy theorizing to com-

Table 8.5. Contribution of the Main Officer Recruitment Procedures, 1967–72 (percentages)

Recruitment	Army	Navy	Air Force
Direct	21.7	36.1	18.1
Semidirect	29.5	31.5	25.6
Indirect	45.0	32.3	56.3
Reserve	3.8	—	—

Source: Maquet, "Le Recrutement des officiers et des cadres civils supérieurs," Table 4 in fine.

prehend this phenomenon. First, in the context of pretechnological military warfare, rural ecology and culture appeared to be in structural congruence with military life and military functions. As pointed out by Morris Janowitz, "outdoors existence, the concern with nature, sport, and weapons, which is a part of rural culture, have a direct carry-over to the requirements of the pretechnological military establishment."[8] But with the advent and the development of industrialization and its subsequent effect on war-making, military technology, professionalization of the military career, and evolution of mass armed forces, the ascribed bases for the recruitment of officers narrowed. As in many other national institutions and public services, recruitment became less geographically contained. More and more officers came from urban centers. This tendency was all the more pronounced in the technical services, especially in the navy, as naval activities could hardly take place independent of complex and urbanized structures along the seacoast.

Looking at the data in Table 8.6 one notes that the regional disparity in the recruitment of French officers was such that it appears difficult to make any inferences regarding a shift from a nonindustrial milieu to a more industrialized and urbanized one. If the high proportion of officers born in the Parisian region leads one to believe that such an evolution was under way, the low percentage of officers coming from the north, a very industrialized urban region, could lead one to suppose the contrary. The latter supposition would be further corroborated by the fact that a large proportion of officers were born in those regions of France least affected by industrialization and urbanization, that is the southwest, southeast, and the center. From the perspective of a breakdown by service, it is to be noted that almost one-fourth (22 percent) of the navy officers were born in the Parisian area, and a similar proportion (26 percent) in the western regions. A more detailed observation reveals also that most of these navy officers came from fairly important coastal urban centers. The same would certainly be true for the 15 percent of navy officers that came from the southeast, for Toulon, one of the biggest French naval installations, was probably the most important area of origin.

The army and the air force followed a different pattern, one in contrast to that of the navy. In effect, putting aside the northern and the Parisian regions, which do not produce many army or air force officers, all the other regions provided a fairly equal proportion of military personnel. The geographic discrepancies between the east, west, southwest, southeast, overseas, and the center were, in effect, less pronounced than they were in the navy. The percentage of army

Table 8.6. Regional Origins of the Officer Corps by Service, 1971 (percentages)

	Army	Navy	Air Force
North	7.5	4.0	6.0
East	17.0	6.0	14.0
West	17.0	26.0	18.5
Southeast	12.5	15.0	14.5
Southwest	15.0	10.0	16.0
Center	10.0	10.0	10.5
Paris area	9.0	22.0	8.5
Overseas (former and present French territories)	11.0	6.0	11.0
Foreign countries	1.0	1.0	1.0
Total	100.0	100.0	100.0

and air force officers born overseas was almost twice that for naval officers. This can be explained by the fact that French military presence and, therefore, occupation of military installations, were assumed mostly by ground and air forces.

Furthermore, it should be noted that the central region, one of the least developed areas from an economic standpoint, provided 10 percent of the officers in each service. This offers an interesting indication of the fact that in poor rural areas a military career was still considered a channel of social mobility.

Unfortunately, it was not possible to obtain a breakdown of this information for officers who graduated from military academies and those who did not, in order to examine whether there were any significant differences in their respective regional origins. According to our own observations, if there were any differences, they were not very significant. A 1960 survey, conducted among military academy candidates, showed the same geographical distribution just observed for the entire officer corps in 1971.[9] The results of the 1960 survey also corroborate those of the analysis conducted by Raoul Girardet and his associates among officer-candidates at the Ecole spéciale militaire (Saint-Cyr and Interarms Military School) between 1948 and 1958 (see Figure 8.2).[10]

Preliminary conclusions drawn from these various observations will be, at best, vague. One could simply say that between 1945 and 1970 the regional background of the French officers, without regard

Figure 8.2. Geographical Origins of ESMIA Cadets, 1945–58 (density per 100,000 inhabitants)

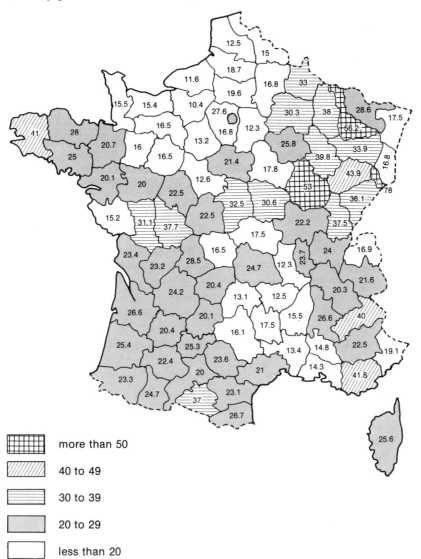

more than 50	
40 to 49	
30 to 39	
20 to 29	
less than 20	

to recruitment procedures, remained relatively stable. At the most, one could point out that for the more technical services the geographic point of origin seemed to have shifted slightly from the most rural and poorest sectors to more urbanized regions of the country. However, this shift never took place in the direction of the most industrialized sectors. The poorest regions, in terms of "military productivity," remained the north, the northwest (especially the extreme west: the Finistère), the east (with Belfort, the Meurthe-et-Moselle, and the Côte d'Or), and the southeast (Haute-Savoie, Hautes-Alpes, and the Var).

However, one should not exaggerate the import of these findings. The most critical element in these observations is not so much the industrial, urban, or rural character of the region of origin; rather, as underlined by close analysis, it is that sectors of high manpower "production" coincided with the geographical distribution of the principal military installations (naval in the west with the installations around Brest and southwest with Toulon; aerial in the southeast with Salon de Provence, in the southwest at Biscarosse and Mont-de-Marsan) and the principal garrisons (southwest in Tarbes and Pau, west in Poitiers, center in Limoges). Therefore, the apparent disparity in officers' regional origins corresponded, in reality, with the geographic distribution of military sites and installations.

The fact that the regional origin of a significant segment of the French officer corps coincided with areas where the concentration of military sites was the densest constituted a first indication of the existence of a propensity toward self-perpetuation. A more precise evaluation of the exact location of birth would prove irrelevant, because the frequency of geographic turnover of the military community around these military sites remained relatively high. And, because a significant proportion of officers seemed to come from military families, as will be confirmed in the course of this study, the regional origin of the entire officer corps was not a very useful index, unless used for a sample of officers born into the civilian community.

However, it is worth noting that the conspicuousness of recruitment from military sites indicates more than a self-perpetuation tendency in the military establishment. In effect, given the physical location of these sites, it can be concluded that an important proportion of the officer corps were geographically isolated, particularly with respect to large industrial and urban centers. Despite new styles in the defense deployment, this situation was likely to continue. In effect, this situation was the result of a set of historical events related to the industrial revolution of the nineteenth century. As aptly observed by Joseph Schumpeter, most military installations were built in regions generally unsuited to industrialization. The military installations, therefore, served important economic functions in the survival of these areas; they became principal sources of revenue, either because they supplied consumers for local markets or because they became a source of employment and economic change. And, unless industrialization was introduced, local authorities continued to put pressure on the state to maintain these installations and to continue allocating subsidies to them. A glance at a map of military installations and military-related industries confirms this thesis. In 1963, for example, the National Defense offered 44,740 jobs in the less industrialized regions of the country; this accounted for almost 70 percent of all national defense personnel.[11] Thus, paradoxically, the military regional tradition did not come from definite strategic situations as is often thought, but from the nature of industrial development during the nineteenth century.

The educational establishment frequented before entrance into the military is generally used as an additional indicator of the social origins of the officer personnel of the armed forces. Students of military affairs have shown that, during the last fifty years, in many countries of the Western world the proportion of officers coming from private educational institutions steadily decreased, which can be interpreted as indicating a more democratic social recruitment. Though the available data are not very accurate, France appears to exhibit a similar evolution. The figures presented in Table 8.7 show that in 1971 more than 75 percent of the officer corps had been educated in state schools. In the army and the air force nearly 90 percent of the officer corps had attended state schools. In the navy, however, the proportion of officers from private schools was twice as high as in the other two services.

Table 8.7. Educational Institutions Attended by Officers prior to Joining the Military, 1971 (percentages)

	Army	Navy	Air Force
Private schools	12	24	12
State schools	88	76	88
(Civil schools—national education)	(52)	(58)	(64.5)
(Military preparatory schools—national defence)	(36)	(18)	(23.5)
Total	100	100	100

Source: Centre d'Etudes et de Sociologie militaire, 1971.

As for officers from direct recruitment, one first notes that their educational background did not change significantly throughout the last thirty years following World War II; only inasmuch as the respective proportions of public and private school students are concerned was there a change, for, as we shall see, there had been an important increase in the number of students from the public military secondary schools. Data on all military academies candidates in 1960, for example, reveal that 35 percent of all candidates attended private schools during the major portion of their primary and secondary education; 50 percent attended civil public schools and 15 percent attended military secondary schools. Of particular interest when studying such figures is that the proportions of those from public schools and those from private schools regarding military academy candidates were very much the same as those for the civilian *grandes écoles* candidates.[12] A number of studies undertaken on the social recruitment of students at civilian *grandes écoles* showed that such recruitment was very far from faithfully reflecting the diversity of the French social structure. These surveys underlined, in effect, that a great proportion of *grandes écoles* students came from a very narrow section of the population: the section most favored on the economic level and highest in the social hierarchy.[13] This element of observation could constitute an indirect but nevertheless valid indication that the same conclusion could be inferred for the social structure of military academy officers. Later in the chapter, we shall have the opportunity to pursue this comparison and to confirm this preliminary conclusion.

Of greater interest, at least in the French context, when considering the officer's educational background, is that the key factor lies not in a comparison between the public and private aspects of a high school education (as stated, the ratio of public to private educational backgrounds did not vary much over time), but, rather, in the change in the proportion of officers who received their education in civil secondary schools, public or private, on the one hand, and those who received their education in military preparatory schools (colleges placed under the tutelage of the Ministry of National Defense), on the other.[14] Whereas before World War II, hardly 10 percent of all French officers attended military preparatory schools, in 1971 almost 25.9 percent of the officer corps received all or most of their education in military secondary colleges. This proportion was much higher among army officers (36 percent) than among air force (23.5 percent) or naval officers (18 percent).

The scope of change in the educational background was much more pronounced among officers who graduated from the military academies. Until World War II, the proportion of military academy graduates never surpassed 11 percent.[15] In 1960, a survey among military academy candidates undertaken by the Air Force Center for Psychological Studies (CEIPAA) showed that 15 percent of the candidates had attended military preparatory colleges.[16] After 1960 this proportion noticeably increased. In 1972, 77.3 percent of those who passed the entrance examinations for the military academies and subsequently attended Saint-Cyr or the navy and air force academies came from military schools.[17] As shown in Table 8.8, the contribution of military preparatory schools to the number of candidates and students at the military academies was the highest at Saint-Cyr and lowest at the naval academy. The contribution of these military schools was such that they actually seemed to have a monopoly on the inflow of manpower into the military academies.

Table 8.8. Military Academy Candidates Having Attended a Military Preparatory School or College, 1967–72 (percentages)

	1967	1968	1969	1970	1971	1972
Saint-Cyr						
Candidates applying	47.3	56.2	61.9	62.2	60.5	76.4
	(431)	(466)	(628)	(719)	(681)	(634)
Candidates admitted[b]	62.1	68.4	77.4	78.5	80.8	83.3
	(198)	(190)	(190)	(186)	(198)	(210)
Air force academy, Salon de Provence						
Candidates applying	31.7	30.0	39.8	39.0	44.6	51.0
	(385)	(429)	(490)	(615)	(446)	(306)
Candidates admitted[b]	49.3	50.7	50.5	53.4	59.6	61.2
	(73)	(69)	(91)	(58)	(52)	(67)
Naval Academy of Brest						
Candidates applying	77.6	n.a.	n.a.	n.a.	n.a.	n.a.
	(261)					
Candidates admitted[b]	34.2	30.9	58.6	47.1	62.5	74.2
	(76)	(68)	(58)	(70)	(72)	(62)
All military academies						
Candidates applying	39.9	43.7[a]	52.3[a]	51.1[a]	54.2[a]	62.0[a]
	(1,077)	(885)	(1,118)	(1,134)	(1,127)	(940)
Candidates admitted[b]	53.0	56.9	67.0	66.9	73.3	77.3
	(347)	(327)	(339)	(314)	(322)	(339)

Source: These calculations were computed from data collected by Maquet, "Le Recrutement des officiers et des cadres civils supérieurs."

[a] Includes only Saint-Cyr and Salon de Provence candidates.

[b] With the exception of Saint-Cyr, where the percentage indicates the proportion of candidates who passed the entrance examination, these percentages refer to candidates who not only passed the entrance examinations but also entered the academies.

From these observations about educational background, one idiosyncratic feature emerges conspicuously and deserves to be kept in mind: the increasing participation of military preparatory colleges in the education of officers, a contribution that represented an extremely high proportion as the military secondary schools supplied nearly 75 percent of the total military academy graduates. This was important, as these military secondary schools were attended mostly by sons of officers and NCOs; this is another indication of the process of intergenerational succession which was taking place in the French military.

The religious background of officers, their family size, and their social and athletic activities, for example, are also commonly used to discuss the nature of their social recruitment and to evaluate changes in this domain. But in the case of France, such indicators are rather deceptive. One can already eliminate the religious variable, first, because of the denominational homogeneity of the nation, and second, because of the absence of data relative to the level of church attendance among officers, which would be the only relevant data pertaining to that problem.

As for the family background, one could certainly say that in the least technical services, or in the most traditional branches, family size was relatively important in showing correlation between traditionalism and fecundity. Guy Michelat and Jean-Pierre Thomas reported that between 1945 and 1960, 46 percent of the 1,706 officer candidates to naval schools came from large families, that is, families with more than three children (30 percent came from families with five or more children).[18] Raoul Girardet and his associates demonstrated that during the same period of time, a major proportion of candidates who entered the former Ecole spéciale militaire interarmes came from large families. Twenty-eight percent of the students at Saint-Cyr, for example, were from families with at least five children. Thus, it would appear that between 1945 and 1960, traditional families occupied an important place in military society.[19] Whether any change occurred in the family structure of the French officer after 1960 is difficult to evaluate with accuracy. Some data, however, seem to show that if there was a change, it was a very small one. In 1973, among students at Saint-Cyr, 27.7 percent were from large families of four or more children, among students at the EMIA the proportion was slightly lower (22.4 percent).[20] Considering that in the parent community the average number of children dropped from 2.83 in 1962 to 2.59 in 1968, then to 2.1 in 1974 and to 1.9 in 1975,[21] the average size of the family in the military community remained exceptionally high.

The recreational and athletic backgrounds of officer candidates do not appear very informative. For example, it has been hypothesized that officer candidates most given to athletic activities tended to congregate in the more traditional branches of the service, and in 1960 almost all of these candidates who indicated that they were parachutists (36 percent of all aspirants) were candidates to Saint-Cyr. On the other hand, 60 percent of those adept at gliding and flying were candidates to the air force academy. In fact, all one can say is that youths applying to the military academies were, in general, slightly more sport oriented than their civilian counterparts: 50 percent as opposed to 30 percent.[22]

Social activities refer to all recreational activities in which the officers engaged during their early years. Membership in the Boy Scouts is the most classic example. Life in the open air, physical games, closeness to nature, and the like, are characteristics of activities that naturally coincide with a traditional background. Michelat and Thomas demonstrated this correlation in the case of naval officer candidates;[23] such a correlation was also to be found among army officers. Yet with such scanty indications, it is difficult to make any relevant observations.

Although these first series of variables do not have great usefulness, primarily because they lack precision, two things emerge from their examination: the extent of change within the officers' social structure appeared somewhat limited, especially in the army, and, more importantly, the participation of the military in the recruitment of officers seemed to be conspicuous.[24]

The following analysis of the occupational origins of French officers will shed more light on these points and permit us to assess with greater accuracy the nature and the evolution of officers' social origins.

Occupational Origins of Officers

The figures in Table 8.9, extracted from an official study on the military condition in France released in 1974 and known as the *Rapport Mourot*,[25] will serve as a point of departure for our discussion. Besides covering the three services, the data also dichotomize between two age-sets, thus permitting the identification of eventual change in social origins over time as well as of the direction of these trends. Yet given their imprecision they will serve only to identify the most conspicuous modifications.

In the light of these data, particularly when contrasted with the occupational structure of the parent society, the first noticeable feature is the somewhat elitist character of French officers' occupational

Table 8.9. Sociooccupational Origins of the Officer Corps by Service and Age-Group (percentages)

Father's Occupation	Officers older than 35		
	Army	Navy	Air Force
Farm owner, farm laborer	8	4	8
Artisan, small business owner	10	7	14
Professional, executive (public and private sectors) large sales or industrial business owner	10	27	11
Managerial and technical personnel, sales or clerical employee	13	11	16
Worker, foreman	11	7	14
Military officer	21	20	13
Military enlistee	16	7	10
(Military in the family)	(56)	(58)	(43)
Other [a]	12	17	14
Total	100	100	100

Sources: Mourot, *Rapport d'information fait au nom de la commission de défense nationale des forces armées sur la condition militaire en 1974*, p. 26; Thévenot, "Les Catégories sociales en 1975," p. 5.
[a] Policemen included.

origins. They are elitist in the sense that the upper sectors of the parent occupational structure were overrepresented while the lower sectors were underrepresented. In actuality, the imbalance in the representation of the lower-class segments was higher than it first appeared. A closer inspection reveals that the lowest sector of the industrial working class—unskilled or semiskilled workers—was much more underrepresented than the upper sector—skilled workers, foremen. The fact that the upper sector of the rural class, landowners, for example, was less underrepresented than the lower sectors, which included rural laborers, farmers, and *métayers*, who actually belonged to the working class, tended to further the inequality in social representativeness.

The second relevant difference between the officer corps' occupational structure and that of professionally equivalent occupations in the parent civil society was the importance of intergenerational succession: between 25 and 35 percent of the officers were the sons of military professionals. These figures were even higher if, instead of

Officers younger than 35			Total Labor Force			
Army	Navy	Air Force	1954	1962	1968	1975
5	3	8	26.7	20.1	14.9	9.3
8	6	11	10.5	9.2	8.1	6.7
16	40	13	4.3	5.3	6.3	7.8
12	10	14	16.6	20.3	24.5	30.4
10	6	11	33.8	36.7	37.8	37.7
19	20	15	1.6	1.9	1.7	1.6[a]
17	4	13				
(63)	(58)	(52)				
12	10	15	6.4	6.4	6.6	6.5
100	100	100				

considering only the father's occupation, one also takes into account the profession of grandfathers, uncles, and brothers since between 50 and 65 percent of the officers had a close relative in the armed forces.

These are characteristics that were common to all three services, though a great deal of variation in degree was remarkable between them. Evidently, of all officer corps of the French armed forces, the naval officer corps was the least democratic, given the extremely low representation of sons of workers and shopkeepers and the concomitantly high overrepresentation of officers of upper occupational origins. Over time there was a sharp increase of the latter, which would seem to indicate that the undemocratic trend tended to grow.

Opposed to the naval officer corps stood the air force officer corps, which was the most democratic, for the proportion of officers coming from lower and middle occupational strata was the highest and that of officers from higher sectors the lowest.

On a continuum of democratic representation, the army officer corps stood between these two extremes. In some respects it resembled the naval officer corps in that the proportion of men of higher occupational origins increased sharply over time though the overall proportion remained smaller than in the navy. The army officer corps exhibited some of the social characteristics of the air force, notably that the proportion of officers from the lower sections of the occupational organization was similar to that of the air force. However, one could say that, from a diachronic perspective, this similarity was only momentary. Between 1965 and 1976, the number of sons of workers continued to increase in the army officer corps (the decrease indicated in Table 8.9 is too small to be significant) whereas it seemed to stabilize, if not drop, in the air force. But finally, the army officer corps deviated from the other two services' officer corps in that the level of endorecruitment appeared to be much higher and, over time, the proportion of sons of NCOs and gendarmes tended to increase more rapidly than did the proportion of sons of officers.

At this point it would be somewhat premature to draw any conclusion from these preliminary observations. As stated earlier, the French officer corps was essentially a composite organization in which three large groups of men emerged. Consequently, an inquiry into the social background of the various categories of officers would be extremely useful to determine some of the more idiosyncratic features of the social structure of the officer corps.

Occupational Origins by Type of Recruitment

As illustrated by the data in Table 8.10 (taking the army officer corps as an example) there was a great deal of heterogeneity in the sociooccupational origins of each group of officers coming from each particular type of recruitment.

Though not very accurate, these figures clearly show that the social origins of the officers from semidirect and indirect recruitment were less elitist than were the officers from direct recruitment. Putting aside the case of reserve officers in a situation of active duty, one can distinguish between the technician-officer (actually indirect recruitment), whose social origins were fairly democratic though the lower segments of the occupational structure were still underrepresented, and the officers coming from semidirect recruitment, whose origins were somewhat less so. These two groups, moreover, presented a marked endogamous propensity, but in contrast to the case of officers from direct recruitment, the proportion of sons of NCOs and gendarmes was larger than was the proportion of sons of officers. The occupational origins of navy officers from semidirect recruitment were, compared with that of air force or army officers, less democratic. In part this seems attributable to the fact that many former petty officers who graduated from the Ecole militaire de la Flotte (the naval avenue for semidirect recruitment) were actually former candidates at the naval academy who had failed the entrance examinations, hence coming from the more elitist stock of those who composed the population of future navy officers from direct recruitment. This, together with the fact that in the navy officer corps the proportion of indirectly and semidirectly recruited officers was lower than in the army and in the air force, probably accounted for the less democratic character of the social structure of the navy officer corps. From a diachronic point of view, a difference seemed to emerge between the army officers from nondirect recruitment and naval and air force officers recruited in the same way. Among the latter, the proportion of officers from the lower occupational strata tended to decrease for the five years before 1976, following a long period of democratization (more intense among air force officers). In the army, on the contrary, the process of democratization seemed to continue, though it was accompanied by increasing endorecruitment. This is illustrated in Table 8.11, referring to the occupational origins of the students at the EMIA, the semidirect route for the recruitment of army officers.

Before ending these remarks, a last but important point must be discussed. Whatever its extent, the level of democratization in the social structure of the officers from semidirect or indirect recruitment was always lower than that in the parent population (the NCOs) from which these officers actually came. Table 8.12 highlights the differences between the sociooccupational origins of these officers, former NCOs, and that of the parent NCO population. The population of officers from semidirect recruitment was the least representative of the social structure of the NCOs, as there was, on the one hand, an overrepresentation of the higher occupational sectors and, on the other, an underrepresentation of the lower sectors. Among officers from indirect recruitment, only an underrepresentation of the lower occupational sectors was evident. In both cases, however, the level of occupational inheritance was significantly more important than among NCOs.

To a certain extent such a tendency helps explain why the officer corps' social structure was less democratized than might have been expected in view of the significant proportion of officers from indirect and semidirect recruitment, who were former NCOs. However, this

Table 8.10. Sociooccupational Origins of Army Officers by Channel of Commission, 1971 (percentages)

Father's Occupation	Saint-Cyr	Arts and Métiers[a]
Farm owner, farm laborer	3	10
Artisan, small business owner	6	—
Professional, executive (public and private sectors), large sales or industrial business owner	22	2
Managerial and technical personnel, sales or clerical employee	11	10
Worker, foreman	6	17
Military officer	26	12
Military enlistee	15	44
Other	10	5

Source: Centre d'Etudes et de Sociologie militaire, "Recrutement des Officiers, 1971," mimeographed (Paris: 1971).
[a]This procedure has been abandoned. Formerly, students who received a fellowship to study at the Ecole des Arts et Métiers had to spend several years in the military as officers.

elitist characteristic was essentially due to the social origins of the officers from direct recruitment, that is, those coming from the military academies.

Occupational Origins of Officers from Military Academies

The relevance of the study of this category of officers is not only linked to the fact that it accounted for a significant proportion of the entire officer corps (between one-fourth and one-third), but it also related to two other important factors. The first is that these officers constituted the main source for the recruitment of the elite nucleus of the French military establishment. Despite repeated attempts toward status and career homogenization between this group and officers recruited through other channels, differences relevant to patterns of career mobility were never eliminated. If in the lower ranks of the hierarchy, officers recruited from the military academies were in the minority, in the upper ranks, made up of senior and general officers, they tended to hold a monopoly. In the decades following World War II, it was calculated that 16 percent of the Saint-Cyr graduates would

ЭIIA [b]	OR [c]	OT [d]	ORSA [e]
6	9	10	7
9	10	8	14
12	15	5	14
12	14	10	21
12	9	16	13
16	14	11	9
19	10	25	13
14	19	14	9

[b] Those commissioned after graduation at the officers schools for NCOs.
[c] Reserve officers.
[d] Technical officers, see note 4 at end of chapter.
[e] Reserve officers on active duty.

Table 8.11. Sociooccupational Origins of EMIA Students, 1953–75 (percentages) [a]

Father's Occupation	1953–58	1958–64	1964–70	1970–75
Professional, executive, industrial business owner, engineer	9.3	4.3	11.5	15.7
Civil service personnel	12.8	12.9	9.0	4.4
Artisan, sales business owner	12.8	10.6	8.5	7.9
Farm owner, farm laborer	6.6	8.2	4.8	8.5
Sales or clerical employee, worker	15.9	16.2	18.1	25.4
Military and other	42.6	47.3	47.2	38.0

Source: See data on the social structure of the French military establishment in Table D.4, Appendix D.
[a] Percentages may not total one hundred percent due to rounding.

Table 8.12. Sociooccupational Origins of Army Officers from Nondirect Recruitment, 1971 (percentages)

Father's Occupation	Semidirect Recruitment	Indirect Recruitment	Active Reserve	NCO
Farm owner, farm laborer	6	10	7	14
Artisan, small business owner	9	8	14	11
Professional, executive (public and private sectors), large sales or industrial business owner	12	5	14	5
Managerial or clerical personnel, sales or clerical employee	12	10	21	12
Worker, foreman	12	16	13	26
Military officer	16	11	9	13
Military enlistee	19	25	13	
Other	14	14	9	19

Source: Centre d'Etudes et de Sociologie militaire.

become generals and 43 percent colonels, whereas only 3 percent of the former NCOs, graduates from the EMIA, would be generals and 14 percent colonels. In 1958, 75 percent of all army colonels, 56 percent of lieutenant colonels, and 43 percent of majors were former Saint-Cyriens. In the early 1970s, despite a slight decline, the trend remained the same; 66 percent of the colonels and 50 percent of the lieutenant colonels graduated from Saint-Cyr. Furthermore, the great majority of officers attending the Ecole supérieure de Guerre (the highest level of military education, equivalent to the U.S. War College), which constituted the main source of high-ranking staff officers, was composed of graduates from the military academies. In 1975, of the fifty-six officers enrolled at the army War College, fifty-three had come from Saint-Cyr.[26] Consequently, an analysis of the social origins of the graduates of the military academies constitutes a useful tool for delineating the social structure of the professional elite nucleus of the armed forces.

The second factor is that, simply stated, the military academy–recruited officer constituted an important model of reference within the officer corps and enjoyed high visibility in both the civil and military communities. As Maquet stated: "The officer of direct recruitment is the prototype of the officer corps. The military institution exercises pressures in that direction. . . . Such an action has two consequences: public opinion tends to identify every officer with the officers from direct recruitment; and, in the military community, these officers make up the reference group for the opinions and the behavior of other officers."[27]

Data related to the candidates and students at the military academies will be used for the purpose of this analysis. Table 8.13 seeks to contrast information concerning the social background of cadets at the three military academies with data available for earlier periods; this will also permit a kind of diachronic examination.

Clearly, the social recruitment of military academy students was highly elitist as both the level of overrepresentation of students from privileged occupational milieus and the level of underrepresentation of those from the lower ones were more pronounced than has been observed previously. The elitist feature was also fostered by the importance of the proportion of students who were sons of military professionals, especially sons of officers. In general, the navy officer corps was more elitist than were the army and air force officer corps; the latter shared similar characteristics.

Although diachronic change is more difficult to assess, three tendencies can be identified. First, in the three services there was an increase in the representation of the higher occupational sectors notably at the level of liberal professions and upper cadres. Second, among air force and naval cadets, the proportion of individuals from the lower occupational strata did not increase—indeed, it might even have declined. Upon closer inspection, what seems to have occurred is that there was an increase in this group until the early 1960s, followed by a reversal of the trend. But, at the same time and in both groups, the number of cadets coming from the middle or lower-middle rungs of the occupational structure rose. Table 8.14 illustrates this tendency among students at the air force academy: between 1969–74, the proportion of students who came from technical and engineering background and, at a lower level, from clerical background increased noticeably.

The Saint-Cyr population presented a different, yet more classic, pattern of evolution: there was a continuous growth in the representation of the lower occupational sector—workers, foremen, clerical employees—though the process tended to occur at the "less blue collar—more white collar" (employee-foreman) level of that sector. Table 8.15 (which uses a slightly different typology of occupations) gives ample evidence about this process at Saint-Cyr and confirms the increasing overrepresentation of the higher professional sector; it also indicates the decline in the proportion of sons of functionaries and the stability of the proportion of sons of shopkeepers and craftsmen.

Third, as we shall see in the next chapter in more detail, there was a significant increase of endorecruitment over time, but the number of sons of officers appeared to expand more slowly than did the number of sons of NCOs and gendarmes.

Table 8.13. Sociooccupational Origins of Military Academy Students by Service 1960–72

Father's Occupation	1945–58		1960
	Army	Navy	All Services
	Saint-Cyr 1945–58	Naval School	All Military Academies 1960
Farm owner, farm laborer	5.0	4.0	6.0
Artisan, small or large business owner	9.0	15.0	7.0
Professional, executive (public and private sectors)	21.5	33.0	26.0
Managerial or clerical personnel, Sales or clerical employees	9.0	8.0	7.0
Worker, foreman	6.5	8.0	5.0
Military officer	29.0	31.0	30.0
Military enlistee, gendarme	11.0	1.0	14.0
Other	9.0	—	5.0

Sources: CEIPAA, "Attitudes et motivation des candidats aux grandes écoles militaires," p. 137; Girardet, ed., *La Crise militaire française*, p. 41; Maquet, "Le Recrutement des officiers et des cadres civils supérieurs," in fine; Michelat and Thomas, "Contribution à l'étude du recrutement des écoles d'officiers de la Marine," pp. 64–65; Thévenot, "Les Catégories sociales en 1975," p. 5.
[a]Policemen included.

Finally, the agricultural sector of the occupational structure was, on the whole, underrepresented, a tendency that has accentuated over time. Yet one must take into account that the parent rural population was also slowly shrinking.

Before ending this section, it might be useful, in order to assess more precisely the nature of the social composition of the armed forces academies' population, to contrast it with that of university students and students at the other *grandes écoles*, the institutions of higher learning in France. Table 8.16 demonstrates that, in general, the social origins of the students at the military academies were less democratic than were those of university students, but more democratic than those at the top *grandes écoles*—Polytechnique, Ecole nationale d'Administration, Ecole normale supérieure. The social origins of the air force academy students were more democratic than that of most students at the *grandes écoles*, whereas the social background of naval cadets ranked among the least democratic. In a distribution ranking the institutions of higher learning according to the degree of

| 1967–73 | | | 1962–68 | | | |
| Army | Navy | Air Force | Total Labor Force | | | |
Saint-Cyr 1967–72	Naval School 1973	Air Force Schools 1973	1954	1962	1968	1975
2.7	2.0	4.0	26.7	20.1	14.9	9.3
6.5	5.7	11.0	12.0	10.6	9.6	7.8
25.3	39.0	23.5	2.9	4.0	4.9	6.7
6.5	12.0	19.5	16.6	20.3	24.5	30.4
11.0	6.0	12.5	33.8	36.7	37.8	37.7
28.2	23.0	18.5	1.6	1.9	1.7	1.6[a]
16.1	—	9.0				
3.4	12.3	2.0	6.4	6.4	6.6	6.5

Table 8.14. Sociooccupational Origins of Air Force Academy Students (percentages)

Father's Occupation	1969	1970	1971	1972	1973	1974
Officer	14.3	14.0	21.0	31.8	22.5	13.0
NCO	8.8	10.8	8.8	1.5	6.0	8.0
Gendarme	3.3	3.4	5.3	4.6	4.0	8.0
Civil servant	13.0	5.2	10.5	9.2	5.0	9.0
Teacher	10.0	1.7	5.3	7.7	9.5	3.5
Engineer, technical or managerial personnel	6.6	19.0	14.0	12.5	12.0	15.5
High civil servant	6.6	5.2	3.5	6.2	6.5	3.5
Business owner	—	10.3	3.5	1.5	2.5	2.0
Artisan	—	5.2	—	6.2	1.5	1.0
Professional	4.4	4.7	3.7	4.6	4.0	4.5
Clerical or sales employee	12.0	1.7	10.5	12.5	16.0	14.5
Farm owner, farm laborer	3.3	8.6	5.3	1.5	2.5	6.5
Foreman	—	1.7	1.7	1.5	1.5	1.0
Worker	5.5	1.7	1.7	6.2	5.0	6.5
No profession	—	—	—	—	2.5	3.5

Source: Service du personnel de l'Armée de l'Air, "Origine sociale des élèves entrés à l'Ecole de l'Air," mimeographed (n.d.).

Table 8.15. Sociooccupational Origins of Saint-Cyriens, 1953–76 (percentages) [a]

Father's Occupation	1953–59	1958–65	1964–71	1970–76
Professional, engineer, large sales or industrial business owner, executive	16.9	14.0	14.2	20.7
Civil servant	15.8	14.7	11.1	5.8
Artisan, small business owner	7.9	5.7	6.5	5.3
Farm owner, farm laborer	3.4	3.5	3.0	2.9
Sales or clerical employee, worker, foreman	6.3	9.9	13.2	12.3
Military and other	49.7	52.5	52.0	53.0

Source: See data on the social structure of the military establishment in Table D.4, Appendix D.
[a] Percentages may not total one hundred percent due to rounding.

Table 8.16. Sociooccupational Origins of Students with Higher Education, 1967–72 (percentages)

		Military Schools (1967–71)		
Father's Occupation	Saint-Cyr	Ecole Navale	Ecole de l'Air	Ecole Polytechnique 1965–71
Farm owner, farm laborer	2.7	2.0	4.0	2.3
Artisan, small or large business owner	6.5	5.7	11.0	15.0
Professional, executive (public and private sectors)	53.5	62.0	42.0	57.5
Managerial or technical personnel	6.5	12.0	19.5	16.5
Clerical or sales employee Worker, foreman	11.0	6.0	12.5	6.0
Other (enlistees included)	19.5	12.3	11.0	1.5

Sources: Maquet, "Le Recrutement des officiers et des cadres civils supérieurs"; see also *Journal officiel, Sénat* (5 March 1975) for ENA; Gérard Grunberg, "L'Ecole polytechnique et 'ses grands corps,'" *Annuaire international de la Fonction publique* (1973–74): 383–407, for Ecole Polytechnique; Ministère de l'Education nationale, "Origines socio-professionnelles des étudiants: situations des universités en 1974–1975," *Informations statistiques de l'Education nationale* 76-15 (30 April 1976), for the other schools and universities.
[a] Ecoles supérieures are technical schools that train future civil servants for technical ministries or the private industrial sector.
[b] Ecole nationale d'Administration; there are two competitive examinations at entrance, one for students (*recrutement externe*) and one for civil servants (*recrutement interne*).

overrepresentation of the higher occupational segments, the naval academy population ranked third, the Saint-Cyr population eighth, and the air force academy population tenth (see Table 8.17).

*Social Structure of the Officer Corps
in a Comparative View*

In order to minimize the risks of error in the conduct of this comparative analysis, we shall avoid reliance upon the detailed taxonomy of occupations that have been used up to this point. Each nation, in effect, follows different classification patterns; thus, when it comes to details, a certain amount of confusion that might impinge upon the relevance of the comparison tends to occur. To provide a minimum, but heuristic, level of comparability, we shall arrange the socioccupational structure into three levels: high, medium, and low. In addition, as our goal is mainly to contrast the nature of the social structure of the French officer corps with as much accuracy as possible, we shall use data that deal with the entire officer corps, regardless of recruit-

			Civil Schools		
oles	ENA		Ecole Normal	Grandes	
up.	1967–72[b]		Sup.	Ecoles	University
'71[a]	ext.	int.	1967–71	1972	1973–74
7.7	3.0	7.0	2.0	4.2	6.7
5.6	10.7	9.5	8.7	13.2	11.9
5.9	74.6	48.4	54.5	49.2	32.6
5.4	7.2	12.7	16.7	19.1	16.2
3.6	3.0	15.7	8.4	3.4	9.4
).4	0.7	5.7	4.0	3.8	13.3
.5	0.5	1.0	5.7	7.0	9.9

Table 8.17. Elitism in Institutions of Higher Learning (percentages of students from higher sociooccupational background)

National School of Administration (ENA)	80
Polytechnique	75
Naval academy	70
Superior business schools	65
Ecole normale supérieure	60
Engineering schools	60
Business schools	60
Saint-Cyr	60
Highschool teachers	55
Air force academy	50
University students (average)	40

Source: Maquet, "Le Recrutement direct des cadres dans les armées françaises," p. 10.

ment procedure, as these data offer a situation of maximum democratization of the French officer corps' social composition. Because of this methodology, any slight difference between France and other countries will have an even greater significance (see Table 8.18).[28]

Despite the fact that the figures for other Western officer corps are not very recent and that they sometimes refer only to officers or cadets who are graduates of military academies, that is to say, to the least democratic segment of the officer corps, it is evident that the social composition of the French officer corps was among the least socially heterogeneous. The social recruitment of Greek, Irish, Australian, Canadian, and Dutch officers presented a situation in which there existed only a slightly higher upper-class representation than in France (and yet this could be cited as sample selectivity). But, such an upper-class domination was tempered by a high representation of elements of lower sociooccupational extraction. On the contrary, in the French officer corps and in the Spanish officer corps, elements coming from a lower-class background were the most poorly represented, especially when one considers the high proportion of such social sectors in the parent community. It should be noted in passing that if in Holland the proportion of lower-class elements in the officers seemed extremely low, it was, however, closely representative of this sector of the Dutch civil community. On the whole, the social recruitment of the Dutch officer corps was among the most democratic in Western Europe, and, as pointed out, the officer profession had ceased to be the privilege of a social elite.[29]

Table 8.18. Sociooccupational Origins of Officers in Western Countries (percentages) [a]

	Level of Father's Occupation				
	High [b]	Medium [c]	Low [d]	Military	Other or n.a.
France 1971					
Army	16	23	12	36	12
Navy	40	18	7	24	10
Air Force	13	30	14	28	14
Australia 1956	36	30	22	8	2
Belgium 1965					
Military Academy Cadets	7	43	27	21	2
Canada 1966					
Army	25	25	37	11	2
Navy	25	30	35	7	3
Air Force	22	22	39	4	3
Greece 1968					
Total Officer Corps	40	8	34	18	
Total Army	29	11	49	11	
Holland 1951	38	38	2	13	
Ireland 1963					
Cadets	29	35	14	11	11
Norway	8	31	40	7	4
Spain 1964–68					
Army	8	8	2	80	2
Navy	16	9	5	66	4
Air Force	16	14	6	56	8
Sweden 1958					
Cadets	15	52	22	11	
U.S.A. 1960	40	13	19	25	3
West Germany					
Officers 1960–61	30	25	30	12	3
Cadets 1961	44	20	23	11	2

Sources: France: Mourot, *Rapport d'information sur la condition militaire en 1974*, p. 26. Australia: S. Encel, "The Study of Militarism in Australia," in *Armed Forces and Society: Sociological Essays*, edited by Jacques Van Doorn (The Hague: Mouton, 1968), p. 143. Belgium: Guy Van Gorp, "Le Recrutement et la formation des candidats officiers de carrière à l'armée belge" (Ph.D. dissertation, University of Louvain, 1969), p. 170. Canada: Pierre Coulombe, "Social and Cultural Composition of the Canadian Armed Forces," paper delivered to the Committee on Armed Forces and Society at the 7th World Congress of Sociology (Varna, 1970). Greece: J. Brown, "Military Intervention and the Politics of Greece," in *Soldiers in Politics*, edited by S. W. Schmidt and G. A. Dorfman (Los Altos: Geron-X, 1974), p. 234; George A. Kourvetaris, "The Contemporary Army Officer in Greece: An Inquiry into Its Professionalism and Interventionism" (Ph.D. dissertation, Northwestern University, 1969). Holland: Jacques Van Doorn, "The Officer Corps: A Fusion of Profession and Organization," *European Journal of Sociology* 6 (1965): 278. Ireland: J. A. Jackson, "The Irish Army and the Development of the Constabulary Concept," in *Armed Forces and Society*, edited by Jacques Van Doorn, p. 121. Norway: Francesco Kjellberg, "Some Cultural Aspects of the Military Profession," *European Journal of Sociology*, p. 286. Spain: Julio Busquets Bragula, "Social Origins, Prestige, Intellectual Level and Multiemployment of Spanish Army Officers," paper delivered at the Congress of Military Sociology (Bendor, September 1970). Sweden: Olof Frändén, "Notes on Mobility into and out of the Swedish Officer Corps," in *Military Profession and Military Regimes: Commitments and Conflicts*, edited by Jacques Van Doorn (The Hague: Mouton, 1969) pp. 111 ff. United States: Morris Janowitz, *The Professional Soldier*, pp. 91 and 96. West Germany: Eric Waldman, *The Goose Step Is Verboten: The German Army Today* (New York: The Free Press, 1964).

[a] Percentages may not total one hundred percent due to rounding.
[b] Includes: liberal professions, high civil servants, business managers.
[c] Includes: clerical workers, small merchants, artisans, professionals.
[d] Includes: workers, foremen, farmers and other rural workers.

It should be stressed that had figures relative to officers who were sons of officers been entered along with those concerning officers from upper civilian sociooccupational origins, as is usually done, France would have had one of the largest groups of officers with a privileged background.

In a discussion about ranking Western officers corps according to the democratic nature of their social composition, three allocative categories may be defined. The first category, which could be labeled "elite-dominated," borrowing a denomination from Bengt Abrahamsson's typology, includes the officer corps of France and Spain.[30] In both countries, the officer corps was characterized by a high level of occupational inheritance. In Spain, however, the proportion of officers coming from civilian privileged social strata was less conspicuous than in the French case. At the same time, officers from the middle and lower sociooccupational strata were more poorly represented in Spain. A final difference is that in France there seemed to be an increasing representation of officers coming from the higher occupational categories, whereas the reverse occurred in Spain, especially in the early 1970s.

The second category, "quasi-democratic," includes nations such as Greece, the United States, Germany, and Ireland, in which the social composition of the officer corps was still in a process of democratization. The proportion of officers from the middle-class remained quite high, but that of officers from the lower-class was slowly rising. Greece, obviously, stood apart. The large representation of upper-class officers would, at first glance, lead one to classify it with the elite-dominated; however, the representation of officers of lower sociooccupational origins was too preponderant to label the Greek officer corps in such a manner.

The third category, labeled as "democratic," includes Belgium, Holland, Norway, and Sweden. For these countries, the social recruitment of officers more closely mirrored the social organization of the parent community. Yet differences existed: for example, the Swedish officer corps was more middle-class dominated than was the Norwegian.

True, this summary and attempt to classify Western officer corps according to their social composition is somewhat caricatural. For a fuller picture, it would have been necessary to include other nations from the Western area, from the Eastern area (which had a working-class dominated officer corps) and from the Third World. But it was not our goal to conduct a worldwide sociological analysis of officer corps. More limited in scope, our goal has been to oppose the social structure

of the French officer corps to those of its Western European counterparts and to demonstrate that the latter, which had been less democratic than the French corps before 1945, were more democratic by
1976.

Social Structure of the
French Military in Perspective

At this point it is appropriate to summarize our findings as the picture emerging from the preceding observations may seem confusing.
In effect, having attempted to assess the evolution of the French
military's social structure at several levels—diachronic, interservice,
interrank—we discussed several facets of the problem simultaneously without projecting a simpler, coherent image; such a coherence
was also impaired by the rather disparate assemblage of empirical
evidence. In this section, our comments about the evolution of the
social structure of the French military establishment will be made in
reference to the process of democratization, that is to say, in relation
to the degree of representativeness that the various segments of the
parent social structure achieved. The concepts of overrepresentation
or underrepresentation used are relative estimates of the degree of
representation of each segment of the national social structure in the
military.

The first point to keep in mind is that it is difficult, if not impossible,
to speak of the social structure of the military as a whole, considering the importance of the internal discrepancies, across ranks in particular. The French military's social fabric is actually a composite formed
of three structures, each differing somewhat from the others. Interestingly enough, this seems to be a fundamental constant, one that can
be identified independent of time and service, though variations in
degree might emerge. At the lowest level of the military organization,
the enlistee level, the social structure was quasi-democratic as it was
characterized by a fair representation of the different sectors of the
parent community. Yet with regard to the representation of the lower
sectors of the parent community, the navy and the air force enlistee
populations were less democratic than was the army's. At the upper
level of the organization, the officer corps, the social structure was
elitist in that the highest segments of the social community were overrepresented and those at the lowest underrepresented. This elitist
proclivity was more pronounced in the navy than in the army, and, of
course, in the air force, the least elitist of the services. At the NCO

level, although the social structure cannot be said to have been highly democratized, it was not particularly elitist. This was true across the three services.

Such disparities were all the more unexpected as, from the viewpoint of the recruitment of their personnel, the three population subsystems were apparently closely related to one another: most NCOs were recruited from among the enlisted personnel, and an important proportion of the officer corps was recruited from among NCOs. But the basic patterns of social structure did not duplicate each other from one level to another. The social origins of the NCOs who became officers were significantly different, more elitist, than were the origins of the parent NCO population as a whole.

Across services the social distance separating each level varied. In the navy and the army, the social distance between officers and NCOs was more important than in the air force. Yet, at the same time, in the navy and the air force the social distance between enlistees and NCOs was much less than in the army; in the air force and navy the enlistee population was less representative of the parent social structure than it was in the army. Figure 8.3, visually summarizing these observations, helps give a better idea of the social structure of the French military establishment.

Figure 8.3. Social Representativeness across Services

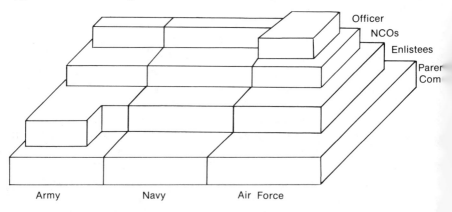

Diachronically it is more difficult to define the pattern of change, as the evolution looks, at first glance, erratic. Several dominant trends, however, can be identified, particularly if assessed in terms of the level of representation of the higher, middle, and lower segments of the parent social structure in each service and in each category of personnel of the military establishment.

At the enlistee level, the tendency in the army was toward a growing representation of the lower segments of the social structure, though the very lowest seemed to become more and more underrepresented. In the air force and navy, a similar form of democratization was observed initially, but, beginning with the early 1970s, the lower segments became more and more underrepresented, whereas the proportion from the middle sectors was increasing. The NCO social structure was fairly homogeneous across services and was modified only slightly over time. In the course of this transformation, there was a tendency toward a greater underrepresentation of the lower sectors and an increase in the representation of the middle sectors. The higher sectors were increasingly overrepresented.

Among officers, there seemed to be, until the early 1960s, a movement toward a broadening of the social composition in that the lower sectors were no longer as underrepresented. Afterwards, there seemed to be a reversal in the trend, except in the army, where it continued. In addition, the overrepresentation of the higher sectors of the social structure grew significantly for all three services. This elitist tendency was reinforced by the increasing proportion of sons of military professionals who entered the officer corps.

These trends corresponded to those that could have been predicted given the change that the French armed forces had undergone in response to the alteration of the environment after World War II. Some elements of dissonance were introduced by factors specific to the French social nature itself; these tended to affect the anticipated result of these environmental changes and, consequently, the expected social stratification that would have been generated by the changes. On the whole, however, there was little deviation.

The army social structure clearly evolved in conformity and in continuity with the pattern of change generally associated with the mass army format. The main characteristic of this evolution was, according to most observers, a broadening of the social base of recruitment in favor of the less privileged, more modest sectors of the community, which formerly had no access to the military profession. Because of the contrast with the earlier practices, this broadening was highly visible in the officer corps; though less obvious, this tendency also affected

NCO and enlistee populations, whose social recruitment had also become more urbanite and industrial. And many of the assessments made about the social morphology of the army for the period of the colonial wars had validity for the fifteen years that followed. Until 1960, no student of the French military establishment failed to point out the lower-middle-class character of the army social recruitment.[31] Later, with the growing number of officers and NCOs coming from this milieu, the previous trend continued to develop. Some authors have not even hesitated to reutilize in that regard the suggestive expression of proletarianization.[32] However this view appears somewhat incorrect as it conveys a distorted image of the social composition of the army, given the fact that there was also an increase in the proportion of men coming from the higher social milieus, a point to which we shall return presently. The fact that this evolution was continuous over the entire period under consideration, in other words, the fact that the army social structure followed closely the type of change observed in all military institutions conforming to the mass army model, can be explained by reference to the nature of the environment in which it operated between 1945 and 1975, which was characterized by a low level of technological modernization, and the type of activities it performed. In contrast to the army, the air force exhibited a social structure that evolved according to a different pattern. During the first period, it presented similarities in evolution with patterns associated with the development of the mass army format, as evinced by the democratization which lasted until the early 1960s. In the second period, however, this tendency reversed itself, a pattern found in association with a military organization more fully professionalized and exposed to swift technological change. Indeed, in light of environmental changes of the post-1960s air force, especially with regard to its significant role in nuclear strategy, this evolution was not surprising. The navy social structure evolved in a similar fashion, but the overall level of democratization remained far lower than in the air force.

Though large discrepancies in the classes represented, with a high degree of both overrepresentation and underrepresentation, are common features of the social composition of the all-volunteer and quasi–all-volunteer forces, in general, the middle and lower sectors of the social structure tend to be overrepresented and the upper ones underrepresented. In France, paradoxically, the reverse occurred: throughout our study we consistently noticed an overrepresentation of the upper sectors. Yet, this does not contradict the basic paradigm. With the increased level of technology, recruitment of highly skilled personnel became systematic, even after the armed forces instituted programs to ensure the training of personnel. This signifies that new personnel had to be recruited from those sectors of society that had access to education; in France these sectors were situated toward the middle and upper levels of society.

This factor alone, however, does not completely explain the overrepresentation of higher social sectors. Otherwise, the overrepresentation of the upper classes would not have been so important. Given that the army continued to operate as a mass army and to underutilize modern technology, such an explanation, while valid for the air force and the navy, both of which were immersed in a more technologically advanced environment, had little relevance to the army.

Therefore, to understand the increase in the overrepresentation of the higher social sectors and the elitization of the military, other explanatory elements must be advanced. Given the nature of the phenomenon at hand, these elements were perhaps not unrelated to the social and political context of French society as a whole. A few hypotheses of particular significance for the officer corps can be proposed to supplement the explanations derived from the basic paradigm.

The first proposition that comes to mind relates to the perceived prestige of all occupations, civil and military, associated with service to the state. In France, indeed, such functions have always been viewed as a source of prestige and status and as such were valued as appropriate occupations for the social elite. There is no need to elaborate on this. As with many cultural traits of modern France, one has to look back to the *ancien régime*, to a time when the very social essence of the regal ruler and the sacredness of his legitimacy, instilled prestige and importance in all functions linked with the service to the king. This legacy was preserved in postrevolutionary and modern Republican culture and institutions, which, as aptly shown by Tocqueville, have taken more than they have destroyed from the *ancien régime*. This is best illustrated by the enduring centrality and sanctity of the state, service to which, then, continues to be regarded as a suitable role for the society's elite.

An examination of the social origins of aspiring civil servants is, in this regard, enlightening. The background of students at the law schools of provincial universities preparing to enter the social security and health administrations or the nationalized banking system or the background of graduates of the Paris Institut d'études politiques cramming for entrance to the Ecole nationale d'Administration (ENA), the royal road to the famous *grands corps* of the state, clearly reveal the predominance of individuals of upper social origins.[33]

Elitism among French officers, then, stemmed perhaps from a similar logic, as the profession of arms is the military aspect of the service to the state with which the elite of the society had consistently concerned itself. As did their *ancien régime* cousins, Charles V's legists, Louis XIV's *grands commis*, and army officers who were recruited from the aristocracy or the mercantile bourgeoisie (which constituted itself as a new aristocracy during and after the Renaissance and then became a quasi-administrative class), the contemporary republic's civil servants and officers tended to come from a similar recruitment.

But this is only one side of the argument. In addition, it could be argued that if the elitist proclivity observed in the institutions dedicated to the service to the state in general and in the officer corps in particular developed to such an extent, it was a result of the recruiting procedures that favored the members of the elite to the disadvantage of those with a less privileged background. As stated, officers commissioned from the military academies or from the special officer schools for young NCOs were actually recruited after having taken a special competitive exam. The competitive exam (the *concours*) is the standard procedure of recruitment into the various echelons of the public service in France, from the prestigious *grands corps*, such as the *inspection des finances*, to lower administrative posts, such as town hall secretaries, and from tenured, full professorships at the university to public health administrators. The *concours*, combining meritocratic and egalitarian ideologies, is a legacy of Revolutionary social thought and of Napoleonic bureaucratization.[34] Viewed as the ne plus ultra of rational legal bureaucratic recruiting procedures, in the Weberian sense, the *concours* is also thought to be the most efficient and egalitarian device for recruiting the most qualified, in other words, it is the most democratic mechanism for recruiting the elite. It is the essence of the meritocratic thinking by which, to quote Raymond Aron, "the modern societies reconcile the inequalities of facts with the equality of rights."[35]

As shown by numerous studies dealing with *grandes écoles* recruitment, such a procedure is far from being the best means of impartial selection. Quite the contrary, for various reasons, the rationale of the *concours* is corrupted in such a way that it tended to accentuate the existing inequalities between classes in favor of candidates from the upper social sectors. As one student of recruiting procedures in the civil service stated, "This mechanism is not neutral but . . . constitutes a barrier to social mobility, increasing the handicaps borne by the lower sectors."[36]

Interestingly, the elitization effect created by the *concours* not only occurs at the level of the recruitment of high civil servants but also at lower levels and at the so-called "internal levels" (special *concours*: the *concours internes*, for civil servants seeking promotion to higher ranks). As shown by several surveys, these channels, the institutionalization of which was often justified on egalitarian grounds, does not correct inequalities; rather, they accentuated them, albeit to a lesser extent than did the "external" channels. In general, they have, for latent functions, to serve as the second chance platforms for unsuccessful candidates at the *concours externes*; sometimes they serve a compensatory function, as on occasions when the number of candidates from "external recruitment" was too low.[37]

Consequently, candidates coming from the upper class seem to be privileged by such a recruiting procedure. Recruitment at the ENA, for example, provided ample evidence of this. Between 1952 and 1969 it was observed that at both *concours externes* and *internes*, of an average 41.5 percent candidates from lower social backgrounds, only 34 percent passed, whereas of 58.4 percent from upper levels, 65.6 percent succeeded.[38] In the entire population of high civil servants, 49.5 percent came from upper sociooccupational sectors.

Thus, even if the *concours* favors a broader recruitment than before, in the sense that it prevents corrupt practices, such as favoritism, venality, co-optation, and nepotism, that formerly tended to profit the civil servant community, it does not contribute to a democratization of the recruitment, for it opens itself only to subgroups of the upper social strata.[39] This explains why social rigidity in the civil service is higher than in the parent upper sociooccupational stratum.

Because entrance into the officer corps, the military equivalent of the high-level civil service, followed an identical pattern (except for a small percentage promoted up from the ranks) one may wonder whether the logic that produces the elitism in the civil service would not be the same as that that produced elitism in the officer corps. Thus the fact that the army and navy officer corps were more elitist than the air force officer corps can be explained by the higher number of officers recruited by the *concours*: in the air force 48 percent were recruited in this way, in the navy 65 percent, and in the army 56 percent. Furthermore, the analogy to recruitment in the civil service, notably with "internal recruitment," helps to enlighten one as to why the background of young NCOs who took the examinations to enter the special officers school was more elitist than was the social structure of the parent NCO community. In effect, many young NCOs who chose this route to be commissioned were either failed candidates to the military academies who, probably because the age limit prevented their retaking the *concours*, enlisted in order to later apply for the special schools, or they were potential candidates to the academies who, fearing failure, decided to take the easier exam for the special officer schools for NCOs.

Now, since the tendency toward elitism increased over time as we have seen, it may be as a part of the larger phenomenon of elitism in the French high-level civil service, where an increase in the proportion of individuals from upper social backgrounds has been identified (for example, the case of the ENA recruitment); it may also be because, with the establishment of the technician-officer class (the grades usually given to officers recruited directly from the ranks), half of the officers commissioned were admitted by the *concours*, a procedure that, if one relies on the preceding observations, encouraged the recruitment of those with a higher status. On the whole, one could say that the disposition toward elitism in the military was simply one manifestation of general phenomenon referred to as social rigidity. Such an assertion seems relevant in the French case because in France not only was the overall level of social mobility fairly low (an INSEE survey revealed that of the generation born in the interwar period, nearly half stayed in the same social category as their fathers),[40] but social rigidity was also all the higher when it took place at the upper echelons of the occupational structure. Considering that the profession of officer belonged to the upper categories of occupations and that it was precisely at this level of the occupational structure that the rate of rigidity was the highest, it is not surprising that an important proportion of men from the upper strata entered the officer corps.

In addition to these various factors, one could raise the question of whether such an overrepresentation of the upper occupational sector of the community in the officer corps did not also have political reasons. And one could hypothesize—indeed there is not an empirical way to substantiate this supposition—that the increasing entry into the officer corps by members of the upper social sectors expressed a sort of political action of the conservative segment of the society's upper strata, manifesting an opposition to the rising social-democratic proclivities, if not the perceived liberal orientation of the post-1968 regimes. Thus, the elitization of the French officer corps was, to a certain extent, strengthened by conservative members of the upper class for whom entrance into the military constituted an act of political affirmation, if not of political protest. But, such a hypothesis should be handled with precaution, unless data on the political and ideological opinions of officers could be secured. Interestingly, the Left had implicitly questioned the common belief in the French officers' conservatism. According to the Socialist party, for example, nearly 40 percent of the officer corps would have voted for Mitterand in the 1974 presidential election, and in 1975, Mitterand himself declared that French officers had actually no particular allegiance to the capitalist society. But, if the Socialists were right to doubt the idea of military conservatism, their evidence, for obvious reasons, was hardly reliable. It is true that, reading the newspapers, one encountered editorials by officers sympathetic to the Left, but this was a fairly limited trend and one that actually had been historically recurrent in France. So even for recent periods, as illustrated by informal interviews and analyses of the military literature, conservatism—under its modern forms, indeed—was still a dominant trait of the French officer corps' political culture.[41]

If, as we have pointed out, these various interpretations are especially relevant with regard to the elitism of the French officer corps, this does not mean that they did not also apply to the NCO population in which the overrepresentation of members from the higher occupational strata was noticeable. Obviously the hypothesis placed on political grounds applies to NCOs as well as to officers. Moreover, considering that the NCO profession is classified as a middle occupational category, the presence therein of members of upper occupational origins would simply have been the result of the limited mobility taking place between the higher and middle occupations, but in this particular instance, flowing downward. One is even tempted to add that in the French military establishment this was an old tradition. In the nineteenth century and the pre–World War I period, the NCO corps, as pointed out by military historians, usually sheltered a large number of sons of the upper class who for various reasons, ranging from misbehavior (or indebtedness) to failure to acquire the appropriate education, joined the military and followed careers as NCOs.[42] Examples of well-to-do *fils de famille* who failed their baccalaureate or were about to be drafted and thus chose to enlist in the military irrespective of whether or not they wished to become officers continue to prevail.

Until now, we have not sought to deal with the noted phenomenon of intergeneration occupational succession, although our observations revealed its importance. To some extent, endorecruitment, as it is also referred to, could be interpreted as a manifestation of the reversal of the democratization trend that accompanied the transformation of mass armed forces into all-volunteer forces. However, in the case of France, as shown by closer inspection, endorecruitment appeared to have taken too anomalous a dimension to be viewed as a feature of the outgrowth of the rise of all-volunteer force tendencies alone; elsewhere, where all-volunteer forces have emerged, it was never as high. Therefore, it is likely that endorecruitment in France proceeded from a completely different logic, the study of which will be the subject of the next chapter.

Notes

1. André Maquet, "Le Recrutement des officiers et des cadres civils supérieurs: étude comparative, 1967–1973," mimeographed (Paris: Centre de Sociologie de la Défense nationale, 1974).

2. Service de Psychologie appliquée, "Enquête sociologique sur les engagés volontaires de longue durée dans la Marine," mimeographed (Saint-Mandrier: Direction des Personnels militaires de la Marine, 1973).

3. Henri Pillot, "L'Elève sous-officier d'active: motivation et personalité" (EMSST thesis, Paris, 1968).

4. See Service de Psychologie appliqué, "Enquête sociologique sur les engagés volontaires de longue durée dans la Marine"; Pillot, "L'Elève sous-officier d'active," Centre d'Etudes et de Sociologie militaire (CESM), "Evolution sociale et psychologique des engagés dans l'Armée de Terre," mimeographed (Paris, 1973).

5. Ibid; see also Philippe Marchand, "Ceux qui s'engagent," Armées d'aujourd'hui 17 (January–February 1977): 50–51 and 65.

6. The officers recruited directly from the ranks were promoted during campaigns and wars without having been trained in any special school. Today this channel of promotion has dried up. Active reserve officers (ORSA) serve under contract for five to eight years; the contract is renewable to twenty years.

7. Raoul Girardet and Jean-Pierre Thomas, "Problèmes de recrutement," in La Crise militaire française, 1945–1962, edited by Raoul Girardet (Paris: A. Colin, 1964), p. 27; D. Gaxie, "Morphologie de l'Armée de l'Air," in Recueil d'articles et d'études, edited by Service historique de l'Armée de l'Air (Vincennes, 1977), pp. 74–75.

8. Morris Janowitz, The Professional Soldier (Glencoe, Ill.: The Free Press, 1960), p. 85.

9. Centre d'Etudes et d'Instruction psychologiques de l'Armée de l'Air (CEIPAA), "Attitudes et motivation des candidats aux grandes écoles militaires," Revue française de sociologie 2 (1961): 136.

10. Girardet and Thomas, "Problèmes de recrutement," pp. 59–62.

11. Rapport fait au nom de la Commission des finances, de l'économie générale et du plan sur le projet de loi programme relative à certains équipements militaires, Doc. Assemblée nationale, n° 1195 (1st session ordinaire, 1964–1965).

12. In addition to the universities, the grandes écoles are an important component of French scientific institutions of higher education. By tradition, their prestige has been greater than that enjoyed by the universities. With the exception of the Ecole normale supérieure and the Ecole nationale d'Administration, the grandes écoles (approximately twenty of them) train students to become technical

specialists for the technical ministries. The main advantages of these scientific institutions are that they provide students with a fixed salary as soon as they matriculate and, after two years of training, offer them professional positions as high civil servants. The prestige attached to some of these establishments is such that many *grandes écoles* students are able to find highly paid positions in the private sector. For a detailed account, *see* Robert Gilpin, *France in the Age of the Scientific State* (Princeton: Princeton University Press, 1968); Michalina Vaughan, "The *Grandes Ecoles*," in *Governing Elites: Studies in Training and Selection*, edited by Rupert Wilkinson (New York: Oxford University Press, 1969), pp. 74–107.

13. In 1961, 65 percent of the students at the *grandes écoles* came from only 5 percent of the total population (81 percent from 18 percent of the population); *see* "Les Anciens Elèves de quatre écoles," in *La Réussite sociale en France: ses caractères, ses lois, ses effets*, edited by Alain Girard (Paris: Presses Universitaires de France, 1961), pp. 163–200. Although a slight degree of democratization was noticeable after 1960, the social recruitment of the *grandes écoles* remained undemocratic.

14. These institutions are the *prytanée militaire* of La Flèche, the military college of Saint-Cyr (near Versailles and not to be confused with the army academy of Saint-Cyr located at Coëtquidan), the preparatory military schools of Aix-en-Provence, Autun, and Le Mans, the naval college at Brest, and the School for Air Orphans at Grenoble. For details, *see* Chapter 9.

15. For example, in 1865, 9.2 percent of all Saint-Cyr graduates came from the *prytanée* of La Flèche, the only military college then preparing students for the Saint-Cyr entrance examinations in addition to offering a secondary school curriculum. In 1876, 5.8 percent and in 1887, 6.7 percent came from La Flèche.

16. CEIPAA, "Attitudes et motivation des candidats aux grandes écoles militaires," p. 136.

17. To explain this phenomenon, one could argue that in civil preparatory classes for the military academies the number of candidates preparing several examinations (both for civil and military *grandes écoles*) was higher than in the military preparatory schools where students concentrated upon military academy examinations (except at La Flèche, where they were also able to prepare for Polytechnique). Having passed two exams, say one civil and one military, students tended to choose the civil *grandes écoles*, where professional prospects seemed better. Another reason was that the quality of the curriculum in military secondary schools was adapted toward successful entrance to the military academies. This was especially true for the preparation for the naval and air force academies.

18. Guy Michelat and Jean-Pierre Thomas, "Contribution à l'étude du recrutement des écoles d'officiers de la Marine," *Revue française de sociologie* 9 (1968): 54.

19. Girardet and Thomas, "Problèmes de recrutement," p. 52.

20. François Helluy, "Les Jeunes Officiers de l'Armée de Terre" (EMSST thesis, Centre de Sociologie de la Défense nationale, 1974).

21. Daniel Noin, *Géographie démographique de la France* (Paris: Presses Universitaires de France, 1973), pp. 58–61; for a more recent French demographic survey, *see Le Monde*, 22 January 1976, pp. 1 and 30.

22. CEIPAA, "Attitudes et motivation des candidats aux grandes écoles militaires," p. 137.

23. Michelat and Thomas, "Contribution à l'étude du recrutement des écoles d'officiers de la Marine," pp. 64–65.

24. This question will be dealt with extensively in Chapter 9.

25. Jean-Paul Mourot, *Rapport d'information fait au nom de la Commission de Défense nationale et des forces armées sur la condition militaire en 1974*, n° 945, Doc. Assemblée nationale (2nd session ordinaire du 1973–74).

26. Paul Bouju and Jean-Pierre Thomas, "Problèmes de structure et de mode de vie," in *La Crise militaire française*, edited by Raoul Girardet, p. 85; Helluy, "Les Jeunes Officiers de l'Armée de Terre"; Bernard d'Astorg, "L'École supérieure de Guerre de l'Armée de Terre française," mimeographed (Toulouse, 1976).

27. André Maquet, "Le recrutement direct des cadres dans les armées françaises," mimeographed (Toulouse, 1976), p. 3.

28. As the data used for this section are secondhand, provided by various existing surveys and studies on Western military institutions, it is assumed that, in each case, methodological precautions for enhancing statistical validity were taken.

29. Jacques Van Doorn, "The Officer Corps: A Fusion of Profession and Organization," *European Journal of Sociology* 6 (1965): 277–79.

30. Bengt Abrahamsson, *Military Professionalization and Political Power* (Beverly Hills, Ca.: Sage Publications, 1971).

31. François Gromier, "Une Conception archaïque," *Les Cahiers de la République* 5 (November–December 1960): 15–30; Jean Planchais, "Crise de modernism dans l'armée," *Revue française de Sociologie* 2 (1961): 120–23; Raymond J. Tournoux, "A Proletarian Army," *The Reporter*, 18 February 1960, pp. 19–21; Paul-Marie de la Gorce, *The French Army: A Military-Political History* (London: Weidenfeld and Nicolson, 1963), p. 549. These views, which also stress the fact that these strata remained outside the economic transformation of the nation, led to an analysis of military behavior based on what could be called the "poujadist syndrome"; for a critique of such views *see* Michel L. Martin, "Un Cas d'endorecrutement: le corps des officiers français, 1945–1975," *European Journal of Sociology* 18 (1977): 37–41.

32. Rémy Baudoin, Michel Stack, and Serge Vignemont, *Armée-Nation: le rendez-vous manqué* (Paris: Presses Universitaires de France, 1975), pp. 233–51.

33. On this important point, *see* Thomas Bottomore, "La mobilité sociale dans la haute administration française," *Cahiers internationaux de sociologie* 13 (1952): 167–78; Alain Girard, *La Réussite sociale en France* (Paris: Presses Universitaires de France, 1971); Alain Darbel and Dominique Schnapper, *Morphologie de la haute administration française*, vol. 1, *Les Agents du système administratif* (The Hague: Mouton, 1969/1972); Ezra N. Suleiman, *Politics, Power and*

Bureaucracy in France (Princeton: Princeton University Press, 1974); Pierre Birnbaum, *Les Sommets de l'Etat: éssai sur l'élite du pouvoir en France* (Paris: Seuil, 1977).

34. Vaughan, "The *Grandes Ecoles*"; *see also* Pierre Sadran, "Recrutement et selection par concours dans l'administration française," *Revue française d'Administration publique* 1 (January–March 1977): 53–107.

35. From *La Révolution introuvable* (Paris: Calmann-Levy, 1969) as quoted by Sadran, "Recrutement et selection par concours," p. 85.

36. Sadran, "Recrutement et selection par concours," p. 79.

37. Ibid., p. 76; Catherine Lalumière, "Les Concours internes," *Revue du Droit public et de la Science politique* 3 (1968): 481–542.

38. Jean-Luc Bodiguel, "Sociologie des élèves de l'Ecole nationale d'Administration," *Revue internationale des Sciences administratives* 40 (1974): 231–44.

39. Alain Darbel and Dominique Schnapper, "Les Structures de l'administration française," *Revue internationale des Sciences administratives* 40 (1974): 339–40; for more details *see also* their *Morphologie de la haute administration française.*

40. Michel Pradrerie and Monique Passagez, "La Mobilité professionnelle en France entre 1959 et 1964," *Etudes et Conjoncture* 10 (1966): 1–166; for a more systematic treatment of this problem *see also* Chapter 9 of this work.

41. An IFOP poll conducted among a sample of 254 officers before the legislative elections of 1973 shows that only 6 percent would have voted Left (and yet only for the Socialists). *See Sondages* 1 (1973): 32.

42. *See* Pierre Chalmin, *L'Officier français de 1815 à 1870* (Paris: M. Rivière, 1957).

CHAPTER NINE ● OCCUPATIONAL INHERITANCE

Upon even superficial analysis of the data presented in the preceding chapter, one cannot fail to notice the existence of a major stumbling block to the democratization of the social structure of the French military institution, especially the officer corps—namely the tendency toward endorecruitment. Considering the extent and the consequences of this phenomenon, the issue of endorecruitment is too crucial to be overlooked as it seems to have been in the few extant studies dealing with the French military institution. The purpose of this chapter is, therefore, first to assess in detail the exact dimensions of the phenomenon as it developed in the French military and then to propose an explanation for its causes.

Empirical Findings

The figures in Table 9.1 indicate the proportion of sons of professional servicemen in the various categories of service and give a good idea of the import of the phenomenon throughout the armed forces. It is noticeable that occupational inheritance is most pronounced at the level of the officer corps, in general, and the army officer corps, in particular. For this reason we shall often focus on these particular areas of the military.

There is another reason for focusing on these segments of the military establishment. Looking at the data for the officer corps, one realizes that endorecruitment is a phenomenon that tends to increase over time. Systematic statistical evidence concerning the Saint-Cyrien population after 1945 perfectly illustrates this trend. Before World War II, the proportion of soldiers' sons in the army academy never exceeded one-fourth of the effective force; after the war, as shown by a statistical examination of Saint-Cyr cohorts between 1945 and 1976, it increased regularly from an average of 36 percent for 1945–53, to 41.2 percent between 1953 and 1959, then to 43 percent during 1958–71, and finally to 49.1 percent between 1970 and 1976. For several years after 1970, this percentage rose above the threshold of half of the entire Saint-Cyr population, reaching 52 percent in 1971, 53 percent in 1972, and 51 percent in 1973. In short, as shown by a curve of yearly values of the proportion of sons of soldiers at Saint-Cyr after 1953, together with its companion best-fitted regression line (see Figure 9.1), endorecruitment was a phenomenon whose growth could be traced in the years following World War II. Table 9.2 indicates that a similar growth occurred among cadets at the air force and naval academies.

Though the rate of endorecruitment was not as high and did not seem to increase as greatly as among military academy officers, it was, nonetheless, also significant among officers commissioned from indirect recruiting procedures. In this regard, the case of the Inter-arms school students is enlightening: the average proportion of sons of military men reached 32 percent between 1945 and 1958, 35 percent from 1967 to 1971, and 33 percent from 1970 to 1975. Moreover, if one particularizes the data, another interesting trend emerges. It becomes evident that although the proportion of sons of military professionals in general increased, the number of sons of officers remained fairly stable, at least when compared to the significant growth in the number of sons of NCOs and gendarmes. This trend was particularly apparent among officers who did not come from the military academies. The social composition of the students at the EMIA is a good example. The school, whose student body was made up of 18.5 percent sons of officers compared to 13.5 percent sons of NCOs between 1945 and 1958, saw an equalization of these proportions between 1958 and 1966 (21.6 percent of the students were sons of officers, 21.5 percent sons of NCOs), and then a reversal after 1967 (14.9 percent sons of officers against 19.3 percent sons of NCOs). Among officers coming from the ranks, the number of sons of NCOs was, in general, twice as high as that of sons of officers. Among technician-officers, in 1971, 25 percent were sons of enlistees and 10 percent were sons of officers.

But this peculiarity was not unique to officers from indirect recruitment; it also developed among the military academy officers. Before World War II there were five times as many cadets at Saint-Cyr with a father holding a commission as there were sons of NCOs.[1] Our own computations, corroborated by several recent studies,[2] reveal a steady continuity in the shifting pattern of endorecruitment in the officer corps. Since 1958, for an average proportion of officers' sons varying from 29 percent for 1945–58, to 26.6 percent for 1958–68, and 28 percent for 1968–76, corresponding averages for NCOs' sons ranged from 11 percent for 1945–58, to 16 percent for 1958–68, and then to 18

Table 9.1. Endorecruitment in the French Military Institution, 1945–72 (percentages)

	Sons of Officers	Sons of NCOs	Total
Officer corps			
Officers older than 35 years			
Army	21.0	16.0	37.0
Navy	20.0	7.0	27.0
Air force	13.0	10.0	23.0
Officers younger than 35 years			
Army	19.0	17.0	36.0
Navy	20.0	4.0	24.0
Air force	15.0	13.0	28.0
Military academies			
All academies (1960)	30.0	14.0	44.0
Saint-Cyr			
1945–1958	29.0	11.0	40.0
1967–1971	28.2	16.1	44.3
Naval Academy			
1945–1960	—	—	31.0
1967–1971	23.0	—	—
Air Force Academy (1967–1971)	18.5	9.0	27.5
Officers from semidirect and indirect recruitment (army)			
NCOs candidates at special officers schools			
1945–1958	18.5	13.5	32.0
1967–1971	13.9	21.4	35.3
Technician officers (1971)	11.0	25.0	36.0
	9.0	13.0	22.0

NCOs with more than 10 years of service		
Army	—	13.0
Navy	—	13.0
Air force	—	9.0
NCOs with 11–15 years of service		
Army	—	19.0
Navy	—	19.0
Air force	—	17.0
NCOs with 6–10 years of service		
Army	—	16.0
Navy	—	13.0
Air force	—	16.0
NCOs with 1–5 years of service		
Army	—	15.0
Navy	—	11.0
Air force	—	12.0
Enlistees (army)		
1963	—	13.0
1973	—	8.0
Total labor force		
1954	—	2.1[a]
1968	—	1.8[a]

Sources: Centre d'Etudes et de Sociologie militaire, "Origine socio-professionnelle des sous-officiers," mimeographed (Paris, 1973); Centre d'Etudes et d'Instruction psychologique de l'Armée de l'Air, "Attitudes et motivation des candidats aux grandes écoles militaires," *Revue française de Sociologie* 2 (April–June 1961): 26; Jean-Paul Mourot, *Rapport d'information fait au nom de la Commission de la Défense nationale et des forces armées sur la condition militaire en 1974*, n° 945, Doc. Assemblée nationale (2nd session ordinaire, 1973–74), p. 26; Raoul Girardet, ed., *La Crise militaire française* (Paris: A. Colin, 1964), p. 41; André Maquet, "Le Recrutement des officiers et des cadres civils supérieurs," mimeographed (Paris: Centre de Sociologie de la Défense nationale, 1974), p. 11-B; Guy Michelat and Jean-Pierre Thomas, "Contribution à l'étude du recrutement des écoles d'officiers de la Marine," *Revue française de Sociologie* 9 (1968): 54.
[a]Policemen included.

Figure 9.1. Endorecruitment among Saint-Cyriens, 1953–76 (percentages)

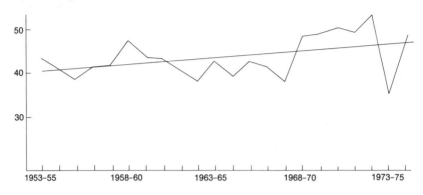

Source: See data on the social structure of the military establishment in table D.4, Appendix D.

Note: The data summarized by the regression line ($y = 40.51 + .29x$) reveals a steady and significant increase ($F = 4.046$) in the number of sons of military at Saint-Cyr.

Table 9.2. Endorecruitment among Military Academy Students, 1948–73 (percentages of sons of military)

	1948–60	1969	1970	1971	1972	1973
Saint-Cyr	40	—	42	52	53	51
Naval academy	31	—	54	36	40	—
Air force academy	—	26	28	35	20	33

Sources: Girardet, ed., *La Crise militaire française*, p. 41; Michelat and Thomas, "Contribution à l'étude du recrutement des écoles d'officiers de la Marine," p. 54; "Réponse du ministre de la défense nationale à une question écrite," Assemblée nationale (August 25, 1973); Service du personnel de l'Armée de l'Air, "Origine sociale des élèves entrées à l'Ecole de l'Air," mimeographed (n.d.).

percent for 1968–76. Figure 9.2 provides a detailed picture of yearly changes in these proportions; the differences in their variations over time are summarized by the two regression lines.

The same phenomenon developed among cadets at the air force academy. Between 1969 and 1974, the proportion of sons of NCOs and gendarmes rose from 12.1 percent to 16 percent, whereas that of officers' sons maintained itself at around 13 percent. As far as the naval academy officers were concerned, changes in the respective number of sons of officers and sons of petty officers was less rapid. The proportion of officers' sons seemed to remain higher than did that of petty officers' sons.

Such a trend actually was even sharper than appears evident from the comparison between the number of sons of officers and sons of enlistees, because many officers who were the sons of junior officers should ideally be classified as sons of former NCOs. Indeed, junior officers who had a son attending a military academy (a son between the ages of eighteen and twenty-two—from 1958 to 1972, 59.6 percent of the Saint-Cyriens were twenty-two or older) had probably been promoted from the ranks, because they were, at the most, captains between the ages of forty and fifty. Though hierarchical mobility in the French military was by tradition a rather slow process, it is almost certain that had these officers been recruited from a military academy they would have reached a senior officer rank by this age.

Although detailed, systematic surveys related to the number of sons of junior and senior officers are not available for an extended period of time, a cross-examination of the existing material indicates that a significant number of officers were sons of junior officers. This was particularly evident among Saint-Cyriens. Between 1945 and 1958, 10 percent out of 29 percent of these sons of officers were junior officers' sons,[3] and in 1973, this figure still measured 8 percent out of 31 percent of the officers' sons.[4] It is clear that over time an even larger number of officers were sons of NCOs and gendarmes, and when they were the sons of junior officers, it is probable that their fathers were former NCOs.

Finally, to complete this survey of self-perpetuation in the French military, three additional comments deserve to be made. One, the disposition toward self-recruitment not only characterized a situation by which an officer's, an NCO's, or a gendarme's son was inclined to embrace the profession of arms, but also indicated a situation in which he was led to choose the same service in which his father had served. For example, in 1973, of the sons of professional soldiers at Saint-Cyr 81 percent were sons of officers or NCOs with army ca-

Figure 9.2. Proportion of Officers' Sons and NCOs' Sons at Saint-Cyr, 1953–76 (percentages)

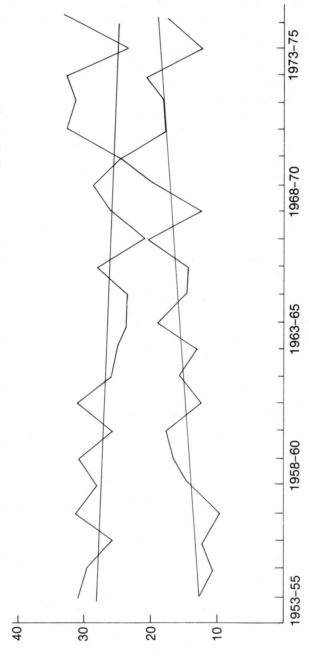

Source: See data on the social structure of the military establishment in table D.4, Appendix D.

Note: The very small F ($F = .014$) for the regression line ($y = 27.99 - .0142x$) summarizing the evolution in the number of Saint-Cyriens who were sons of officers is indicative of the lack of any significant increase or decline over the time period examined. As for the regression line concerning the change in number of Saint-Cyriens who were sons of NCOs and gendarmes ($y = 12.061 + .306x$), it shows a significant increase over time given the value of F ($F = 8.204$).

reers.[5] The same characteristic has been observed among navy officers with a father in that service.[6] Second, when considered not
solely in terms of intergenerational occupation succession (father-to-
son), but rather in terms of a professional similarity with close relatives—cousins, grandfathers, uncles, brothers—endorecruitment
took on an even more impressive dimension. In 1971, for example,
among young officers under thirty-five years of age, 63 percent in the
army, 58 percent in the navy, and 52 percent in the air force had a
close relative who had followed a military career. Except in the navy,
where they remained the same, these percentages were smaller
among older officers (56 percent in the army, and 43 percent in the air
force); this corroborates our observations about the accentuation of
endorecruitment tendencies. Among officers from the military academies, these figures were higher. In 1973, for instance, 75.4 percent
of the Saint-Cyriens had either a father or close relative in the service; 48.3 percent had more than one relative serving; a good third
had three or more relatives in the military service, and, interestingly,
8.4 percent had one or more brothers currently attending or matric-
ulated in one of the three military academies.[7] Third, as revealed by
further investigation, a relatively important fringe of officers whose
father's occupation was a civil one came, nevertheless, from social
clusters closely related to the military milieu. Accounts of social con-
nections, family relations, or personal associations before entry into
the military support this. It has been noticed, for example, that the
spouses of a fairly large number of married Saint-Cyriens having
civilian fathers were officers' daughters; in 1972, more than a fourth
of all married Saint-Cyriens had a military father-in-law.[8]

Although these last remarks have but a limited indicative value,
associated with the larger sum of information they add detail to the
picture. Based on this information, it appears that endorecruitment
was a phenomenon that was undoubtedly a conspicuous feature of
the French officer corps and in particular for graduates from military
academies. At the same time, one should keep in mind that this tendency, though much less developed, was also noticeable among other
sectors of the military establishment. Among NCOs and, to a lesser
extent, enlistees, the proportion of sons of military personnel was
never negligible—20 percent of all NCOs were sons of military and
more than half had a relative in the armed forces.

In view of the preceding evidence, there is no doubt that, compared
to any other occupational group in French society, those from a military background are clearly the most overrepresented in the armed
forces. We shall next deal with the search for an appropriate explanation for such a phenomenon.

Origins of Endorecruitment

As pointed out in the preceding chapter and by students of Western military institutions, the decline of class representativeness in military establishments tends to occur in association with a shift in the organizational format, notably the decline of the mass army model. Endorecruitment, a process obviously somewhat antithetical to social representativeness, would then be the result of such a change in the format of the French military establishment. As seen, the disengagement from colonial warfare and the adoption of a nuclear stance, with its modernizing effects on the military, contributed to the decline of the traditional form of military organization and to the emergence of a new organizational pattern, with all its attendant consequences for the social structure of the military.

But this factor alone only partially explains the endorecruitment syndrome in the French military. This is true for two reasons. First, as a comparative inquiry would show, one is forced to notice that even among military institutions more advanced in the all-volunteerization process than was the French military establishment, the level of occupational inheritance was never as high as it was in the French case. After 1973, the number of soldiers' sons in the U.S. officer corps, for example, never amounted to more than 25 percent of the effectives. In the Australian and Canadian military, it was even lower: in the 1970s, less than 8 percent of Australian army academy cadets were sons of military; among Canadian officers the levels were 11.4 percent in the army, 7.3 percent in the navy, and 3.9 percent in the air force. In the case of the British military, endorecruitment was more important. C. B. Otley pointed out that the military constituted the largest professional group providing recruitment for the British military elite.[9] According to Peter Dietz and James Stone, this trend declined after 1968. In 1967, 52 percent of the candidates attending the Regular Commissions Board had fathers who held commissions; in 1970, 39 percent of the candidates were in this category.[10] Second, one has to point out that it was in the army that the level of self-recruitment was highest, in other words, in the service that was least affected by the process of volunteerization.

Consequently, it appears that any explanation derived from the basic paradigm regarding the respective levels of change in the armed services with respect to the mass army/all-volunteer force continuum does not exhaust the complexity of the phenomenon. It deserves further inquiry.

When endorecruitment is viewed as a generic phenomenon in the

French military, two other factors rooted in the context of the French environment appear to account for its existence. First, it could be argued that occupational inheritance in the armed forces was simply the reflection in the military world of that perennial disposition toward social rigidity that characterizes the French social organization. In effect, as indicated by numerous studies, social inertia across generations constituted one of the most distinctive features of French society.[11] A survey undertaken in the 1960s by the French Institute of Statistics and Economic Studies (INSEE) reveals that of a generation of men and women born during the interwar period (5,309,000 people), nearly half (46 percent) stayed in the same occupational categories as their fathers and 28 percent changed occupations merely for reasons linked to changes in the parent occupational structure.[12] Another inquiry based on data from the early 1970s shows that this tendency was not really modified over time: apparent change—a slight decrease in the probability of a son's embracing his father's occupation—was solely the effect of structural mobility and not of social mobility (see Table D.3).[13] Moreover, social rigidity tended to be more developed at the level of the upper occupational strata. Recent computations estimated that the index of rigidity (the ratio of observed mobility to theoretical mobility) reached 6.2 in the upper end of the occupational structure, compared to 1.6 in the middle and 1.2 at the lower end (1 being the expected index should the occupational flow across generations be governed by randomness).[14] Measured in terms of coefficient of rigidity (actually a more accurate estimate), social inertia at the higher sectors of the occupational structure of the active population in 1970 reached 0.200 among high cadres, 0.175 in liberal professions, and 0.220 in industrial and trading businesses.[15] These figures were the highest of all groups except for the case of rural laborers among whom social rigidity was, for reasons easy to understand, also very high. Therefore, considering that the officer profession belonged to the upper occupational categories and that it was precisely at this level of the occupational structure that the rate of intergenerational succession was the highest, it is not surprising that an important proportion of the officer corps came from the military.

This is only one part of the argument, for the logic of endorecruitment in the military did not proceed only from that which governed social inheritance in the upper stratum. The military being an intimate component of the public service (the *fonction publique*), there is reason then to infer that its social structure exhibited many similarities with that of its civilian counterpart. Interesting in this respect is the fact that occupational inheritance was one of the most noticeable characteristics of the French civil service. Coefficients of rigidity were generally higher in the public service than among socially equivalent positions in the private sector. In the late 1960s, the coefficient of social rigidity among high-level civil servants averaged 0.385, whereas it reached 0.320 for the higher cadres in general; among petty functionaries, this coefficient was 0.205 in the public service and only 0.072 among all cadres in the same category.[16] This led two students of public administration in postwar France to hypothesize that the likelihood of access to public service was greater if the occupational background was linked with it. For instance, the probability of a daughter or a son of a high-level cadre, professional, or officer entering the public service varied from 24 to 57 percent if the father was a public functionary and from 6 to 9 percent if he was not.[17] Analysis of the social origins of candidates to the entrance examinations at various French administrative training schools or of members of the civil service highlights the preponderance of sons of civil servants. This propensity was all the greater at the higher echelons of public service: of a total of 253 members of the French administration *grands corps* and diplomatic service, the upper tip of the civil service, who graduated from the National School of Administration between 1953 and 1963, 103 had a father in the civil service (ninety of whom were in the high civil service).[18]

Occupational inheritance in the French officer corps, the military equivalent of the high-level civil service, was not, therefore, an unusual circumstance. As for the fact that a significant number of NCO's sons entered the officer corps, this was partly the result of the overall intergenerational succession in the public service, and partly the result of the upward mobility taking place from the middle to the upper sector of the occupational structure. In effect, rigidity in the French social structure was not total; upward mobility did exist. This, however, seemed to be limited between the middle and upper strata. For example, the coefficient of ascending mobility from the middle sector toward the upper sector was 2.8, whereas it was below 1.0 (0.3) for movement from the lower stratum toward the higher one.[19]

With regard to occupational inheritance in the civil service, the role of the competitive entrance exam (the *concours*) appeared to be, according to several in-depth studies, crucial. Not only did it, as seen in the preceding chapter, favor the upper strata, but one also gets the distinct impression that its function was to ensure the recruitment of "a proportion of agents already familiarized by the intermediary of their familial milieu with the [organization's] functioning norms and value system."[20]

In the light of these observations, occupational inheritance in the military did not appear as a particularly exceptional phenomena. Rather, it seemed simply to participate in the same logic that animated self-recruitment among medical doctors, lawyers, and *notaires* on the one hand, and high-level civil servants on the other (the two occupational groups comparable to the officer profession). This being said, however, such an interpretation based on the perenniality of social rigidity in the upper sectors of the occupational structure, in general, and in the liberal professions and the civil service, in particular, does not explain all aspects of the phenomenon as it developed in the military. The resemblance has its limits. An important difference, for instance, existed in the fact that in the liberal professions or the civil service the trend toward endorecruitment stabilized, when it did not decline, whereas it continuously increased in the military. A recent evaluation of the index of rigidity in liberal professions estimates it at 25.1,[21] whereas it reached 34 in 1964. On the whole it seems that there were fewer *notaires* or lawyers who were sons of *notaires* or lawyers than had been the case prior to World War II. In 1976, according to a simple computation we made among members of the interdepartmental Chamber of Paris *notaires*, a fairly representative sample of the entire *notaire* population, only 27.4 percent had a father in the profession.

Diachronic data about the social structure of the French civil service, furthermore, show that endorecruitment also stabilized for this sector. If, as we argued, the *concours* that ensures entrance into the civil service, especially at the higher levels, did not contribute to the democratization of the candidates' social composition, it did, when compared with the earlier recruitment procedures it replaced, have some attenuating effect on occupational inheritance by favoring a greater recruitment from outside the civil service community yet within the upper occupational sector.[22]

Moreover, despite their apparent resemblance, the military profession, the high-level civil service, and the liberal professions did not really belong to the same occupational universe and were not, therefore, governed by the same logic. In the liberal professions, for example, endorecruitment can be best understood in relation to the issue of the transfer of a practice. The existence of clienteles and the nature of the accumulated investments—technical and reputational—render any transfer an operation at one and the same time uncertain (for the future of the office) and costly (for the contracting parties). Therefore, it is almost inevitable that among prospective applicants, the son of the owner would be the best suited to step into the succession. By transferring the practice to a son, as opposed to selling it to an outsider, the name, hence, the perceived reputation, is protected and capital losses are avoided (this is especially true with modern medical and legal practices whose value can never be appraised accurately). Other accessory expenses are also eluded, especially the capital-gains tax, which is fairly high, and commissions charged by professional broker-age firms, whose assistance, either as a consultant for price expertise or as a broker, is often technically imperative.

As for the civil service, it also was not very analogous to the military profession. Without going into detail, it may be said that to talk of endorecruitment in the civil service actually makes very little sense (even limiting the rationale to the civil servants of the upper categories). The civil service constituted a vast and highly diversified array of dissimilar occupations, especially with the increasing complexity of the division of public labor; it was clearly more heterogeneous than the military profession. Thus, there is little validity to assimilate the situations of, say, the son of a *sous-préfet* becoming finance minister, the son of a *chargé de mission* in a department of social affairs, who ends up as an obscure clerk in the veterans' administration, a *conseiller d'Etat*'s son entering the municipal bureaucracy, or the son of a petty *chef de service* in a consulate, becoming the President's advisor with the more precise and homogeneous status of the son of an army sergeant or colonel attending the army academy. Besides, given the rapid growth of the public administration—it doubled between 1952 and 1975 and by 1975 there were 1,750,000 public civil servants; 8.3 percent of the active population, 10.3 percent of the salaried population—probabilities for an intergenerational succession in the civil service inevitably multiplied. In other words, when a profession such as the civil administration expands to the point of reaching a significant proportion of the active population, endorecruitment tends to occur by chance alone.

These observations lead to the conclusion that the logic of occupational reproduction in the civil society cannot serve as a completely valid explanation for similar propensities among the military establishment, especially with regard to officers. In France, the main logic of endorecruitment among officers developed from another source, one whose primary importance in the causal structure of the phenomenon is sufficient to warrant a somewhat more extended treatment. The hypothesis that we propose to explore in the next sections consists in showing that occupational inheritance in the military, particularly among officers from the military academies, was the result of institutional engineering practices undertaken in response to the declining prestige of the military career and its subsequent effects upon the recruitment of officers; such practices were made possible by the existence of a favorable institutional and historical context.

The Historical Context of Endorecruitment

As with many other critical features of the military, the circumstances which were to promote endorecruitment must be sought in the folds of history and, to be more precise, in the particularism of civil-military relations during the eighteenth and nineteenth centuries. Briefly, one would argue that they were the result of various administrative decisions and reforms taken throughout the *ancien régime* and the nineteenth century in favor of members of the military community, especially the sons of military men. A twofold tradition presided over the enactment of these measures: the Revolutionary legacy on the one hand, and what can be labeled the military "welfare" legacy on the other.

These decisions were inspired by the Revolutionary tradition, as they sought to reestablish equality among all citizens. Summoned to the service of the fatherland, the soldier was, thereby, barred from the benefits and enjoyment of a peaceful professional life in the civilian community by reason of his absence or by reason of the mutilations received during the completion of his service. Therefore, it seemed only just that he and his dependents should receive material compensation placing them on the same level of economic benefit as the civilian citizen. This view sheds some light on the reforms undoubtedly inspired by the revolutionary ideology: in 1793 the *Convention* declared that war-disabled soldiers would be promoted to the rank of honorary second lieutenant and would receive a yearly retirement pension of 600 livres; a 1794 decree established the first pension system for war widows (without any distinction as to the rank of the deceased husband); and in 1798 the sons of military personnel were given the right to register on the French army muster roll.[23] These policies, symbolizing the gratitude of the nation, were attempts to repay the debt of the state vis-à-vis those who had ensured its safety. They were, in other words, a sort of nonwritten obligation—a contract sealed between the nation-state and the military community.

But in such decisions there also appeared the influence of what we have called the military welfare legacy, actually somewhat older than the Revolutionary tradition. The *ancien régime* teemed with all sorts of striking evidence in this respect. The Maison de charité du faubourg Saint Marcel, created by Henri IV in 1604, the *commanderie* of Saint-

Louis, established by Richelieu in 1631, the Bicêtre hospital, and, above all, the famous Hôtel royal des Invalides, built under the instigation of Louvois,[24] were institutional milestones of what can be viewed as a genuine state-sponsored military welfare policy. To a great extent the military establishment itself latently functioned as a quasi-philanthropic agency. This was done, first, with regard to such segments of society as the impoverished rural aristocracy. There is little doubt that it was the very needs of the petty nobility that dictated the shaping of the format of the military toward the end of the *ancien régime*, for the granting of an officer's commission often constituted a way of subsidizing younger sons from poor noble families "driven by hunger from their cold castles," to use Alfred Vagts's imagery.[25] This explains the idiosyncratic pattern of the officer corps at that time and, particularly, why in 1775 for an army of less than 200,000 men, there was one officer for every fifteen soldiers, more than 1,100 colonels for only 200 regiments, and a total of almost 1,200 general officers.[26] But the military establishment also functioned as a charitable institution for nonserving members of the military community, notably the sons of military personnel. And it is at this juncture that the links with the question under study in this work lie. As clearly established by the works of Edgar Boutaric, Henri Guerlac, Léon Hennet, and Louis Tuetey to name but a few,[27] the newly created centers for military education were not actually outgrowths of professional necessity as is usually believed, but rather agencies of economic assistance for the sons of disabled soldiers, impoverished gentlemen, and wounded or dead officers. The celebrated Ecole militaire, created by Louis XV under the joint efforts of the banker Paris-Duverney and Jeanne de Pompadour, was one of the most conspicuous instances of such a tradition. From the 1751 edict and its subsequent applications notably regarding the conditions of admission, it appears that the five hundred places offered by the school were reserved for war orphans or sons of disabled soldiers, sons of men in service, and offspring of impoverished noble families in need of the king's help.[28] Financed by a lottery, the education offered by the school, though scanty, was entirely free. The Ecole des orphelins militaires, created by Paulet in 1773, the Ecole des enfants de l'Armée de Liancourt, established in 1780 by the duc de La Rochefoucauld-Liancourt, and several other similar institutions (the School for Military Orphans of Popincourt, the School of the Orphans of the *Patrie*) fulfilled exactly the same functions.

If, as was the case with the military *prytanée* of La Flèche, the Revolution contributed to restoring the professionalist function of military schools[29]—at the same time, the welfare role did not disappear as evinced by the establishment of the School of Mars or the School for the Wards of the Guard—it also continued the actions of the *ancien régime* by providing new privileges for the military community. It thus built the basis for a tradition of assistance that continued throughout the nineteenth century. An analysis of the ordinances of 14 April 1832, of July 1837, and 28 May 1858, defining the *enfant de troupe* status; of the law of 13 March 1875, establishing the first *enfants de troupe* school; or the law of 19 July 1884, eliminating the *enfants de troupe* corps from the regiments and creating instead six military preparatory schools, clearly shows that it was the intention of the state to subsidize the military families with the greatest need.[30]

Obviously the question comes to mind, how were these reforms, aimed at institutionalizing a program of military assistance, able to favor the formation of endorecruitment tendencies? The answer is quite simple: this phenomenon began for purely technical reasons. In other words, because of economic and bureaucratic rationality, the state, which provided the assistance, organized the distribution of this assistance in such a way as to reduce and to pay off its expenses. Thus, the regiments and public institutions such as state or communal schools offered the most appropriate locus for the provision of assistance to the military community. As at the beginning of the nineteenth century, the military educational institutions were largely state institutions, and because they were equipped with adequate domestic and educational accommodations, they became, for a while, the only institutions into which the state could channel its dependents. This explains, to a large extent, why the privileges and the assistance given to the sons of soldiers could materialize only in such teaching institutions. Moreover, being the administrative authority for these establishments, the state could channel its assistance-oriented expenditures back into the public treasury.

Thus were created structural conditions propitious to the formation of an endogamous recruitment. The sons of these military men, beneficiaries of such subsidies, became socialized to military values and as a result were induced to embrace the career of arms because of the impact of the place where assistance was made available to them, that is, the military preparatory schools. For many reasons, however, this endogamous tendency never developed out of proportion. Until World War I, with the welfare tradition prevailing, there was little concern with the intellectual achievements of the pupils; admission was based on the wealth, or lack of it, of an applicant's family rather than on scholastic ability.[31] As a result, very few pupils who successfully passed the admission criteria were also capable of passing the matriculation examination, such as the baccalaureate, or the competitive examination for entrance to the military academies. At the same time, even for those students capable of such considerable academic achievement, entrance to the superior military academies was far from easy, for the curriculum was patterned in such a way as to make it almost impossible for the majority of even the brightest students to take the entrance examination within the required age limits. Access to the courses of the *cycle primaire supérieur* (the first two years of high school education) offered by the so-called *écoles de base* (Les Andelys, Billom, Rambouillet, Saint-Hyppolyte du Fort) could not be applied for before the age of fourteen. Consequently, it was not until they were nineteen that the best students could pass their first baccalaureate, not before twenty that they could pass the second baccalaureate; they then had just one year to prepare for and pass at the *prytanée* of La Flèche, the military academy entrance examination. Of the 3,000 or so pupils[32] that the military preparatory schools could accommodate, only a minority were able to enter the military academies and be commissioned; these boys actually were *"brutions,"* the students schooled at La Flèche, and, until World War I, represented less than 10 percent of the Saint-Cyriens. The other pupils did not proceed further than the *cycle primaire supérieur* and elected, generally around the age of sixteen or seventeen, to join the service after one year of military training.

If the reforms introduced in 1919, 1927, and 1936 helped to improve the programs of the military preparatory schools and to increase the numbers of baccalaureate holders, they never had the effect of intensifying endorecruitment. On the average, students who entered the army through these channels made up only a small percentage of the total number of officers. Until World War II, the objectives of such schools, when not strictly confined to the fulfillment of the welfare tradition, consisted solely of the attempt to further the recruitment of the lower cadres of the military.

However, even if endorecruitment did not expand anomalously and remained contained at the level of the NCOs, the institutional conditions for its existence were created. And it was out of such provisions that its abnormal development occurred after World War II.

The Postwar Dynamic of Endorecruitment

The thesis which we propose is that the increasing rate of endorecruitment in the French officer corps after 1945 can be attributed to the rational, if not deliberate, use of the administrative policies originally established to subsidize the education of soldiers' sons with the view of increasing the number of those who would choose to become officers, a policy enacted to respond to the postwar crisis of military vocation.

In France, as in most advanced industrial nations, economic growth was, in effect, accompanied by a cortege of social problems, value upheaval, and the delegitimatization of traditional institutions and sources of social control. New styles of life, improvements in the standards of living, heightened hedonism, decreasing tolerance for traditional duties related to social citizenship, in brief, all conditions associated with the emerging ethos of affluence called into question the attractiveness of traditional professions such as the military career. Furthermore, the multiplicity of lucrative professional opportunities offered by an expanding and more technological economic marketplace, as well as the relative deterioration of the material conditions of life in the military, impaired the prestige attached to a career in the armed forces and made such a career a less obvious choice as a professional vocation.

Not unexpectedly, the army was the service most affected by these trends. First, because in an era of growing industrial sophistication, it had less appealing professional potential than the more secularized and technologically advanced air force and navy. Second, because of the centrality of its role in nearly fifteen uninterrupted years of colonial wars and the detrimental effect of these wars upon the welfare of officers, it was the service most in need of manpower.[33]

The shortfall in recruitment at Saint-Cyr illustrates these problems very well. Between 1946 and 1950, the number of candidates for the entrance examination dropped from 1,366 to a meager 563 (see table 9.3). If the number of candidates increased between 1951 and 1962 (during this period, the annual number of candidates averaged 870, mainly due to the introduction of a somewhat easier humanities examination in 1952), it fell to a somber 431 in 1967.[34] These numbers are extremely low, especially when compared to those of the 1930–47 period, a time when there was an average of 1,500 candidates per year. Even during the worst moments of prewar recruitment crises (1909–11 and 1925–30), the average number of candidates never dropped to this post–World War II level.[35] Correlatively, the decline in the number of applicants considerably affected the intellectual level of the army's officer corps at the same time that it so dramatically reduced the total number of military academy graduates in the army. In effect, to prevent the phasing out of direct recruitment, it became necessary to lower the admission requirements to the academies to the point of stripping the entrance examination of its essential function—the selection of the most intellectually qualified candidates. Usually such a function was considered fulfilled if the number of candidates passing the exam reached between 20 percent and 25 percent of the total number applying. Analysis of the results of the examinations taken after 1945 reveals that this proportion was usually surpassed: between 1949 and 1952, for example, it reached 50 percent.[36]

Therefore, it can be wondered whether the state, in order to give a new impetus to military vocation and to favor a normal growth of the officer corps, particularly to that portion of the corps coming from the academies, did not seek to introduce a new dimension to the old welfare program by transforming it into a genuine program of anticipatory recruitment and preparation for a professional career. By reforming the institutional environment established in the nineteenth century and by converting it into an appropriate system of solicitation and anticipatory socialization, the state, without, it must be noted, abandoning the welfare function of the education system,[37] appeared to want to ensure that the beneficiaries would be inclined to embrace a career of arms. This double function was explicitly stated in the White Book: "The taking over by the armed forces of such a type of

Table 9.3. Candidates Applying and Admitted to Saint-Cyr, 1945–68

Year	Candidates Applying	Candidates Admitted	Year	Candidates Applying	Candidates Admitted
1945	1,666	270	1957	n.a.	n.a.
1946	1,366	276	1958	n.a.	n.a.
1947	929	n.a.	1959	n.a.	n.a.
1948	675	n.a.	1960	838	350
1949	564	274	1961	972	335
1950	563	268	1962	1,004	251
1951	586	339	1963	988	247
1952	762	413	1964	844	250
1953	846	348	1965	782	221
1954	888	363	1966	443	194
1955	909	283	1967	431	198
1956	n.a.	n.a.	1968	466	190

Sources: Jeanblanc, "Etude sociologique du corps des officiers de l'Armée de Terre," in fine; Malgré, "Recrutement des officiers et structure sociale."

education responds to an eminently social goal and enables them to secure a regular source of recruitment."[38]

Thus the years following the Liberation witnessed the first series of modifications in the military preparatory school organization. The age of admission was progressively lowered by two years to increase the number of students who, at the end of their secondary studies, would be able to take the military academy examinations without being affected by the age requirements. The former system of the *école de base* was abandoned. The school of Autun was no longer the sole transitional station between these schools and La Flèche, and La Flèche was no longer the only institution equipped to prepare students for the baccalaureate and for entrance to the military academies. Most of the military preparatory schools began to offer a complete secondary curriculum in addition to special courses called *corniches* for the preparation for the army academy entrance examinations; the channels leading to the examinations were thus multiplied. Consequently the total number of officer candidates among the sons of military professionals increased.

In 1950, the Aix-en-Provence school offered three preparatory classes for the baccalaureate in the sciences and mathematics. Later, the school added special preparatory classes for the entrance examination in the sciences and the humanities at Saint-Cyr. In 1952, the Autun school began to accept students who wanted to prepare for the humanities entrance examination at Saint-Cyr. In October 1952 the school of Les Andelys and in October 1953 the Billom school began offering a complete secondary school curriculum.

In addition to these reforms, new military preparatory schools were created. The technical school of Le Mans, the military college of Saint-Cyr (located near Versailles), and the school of Tampon, for example, now prepared students to enter Saint-Cyr. The naval college, like the *prytanée* of La Flèche, provided training toward entrance at the three service academies. The school of Grenoble offered preparatory classes for entrance into the air force academy. All these institutions—the military preparatory schools and the military college and the *prytanée*, now called military schools of general learning (hereafter referred to as EMEG)—offered the full secondary curriculum (or if not, the four highest grades) and the entrance examinations to the military academies.

In short, whereas before World War II the sons of military personnel registered in the military schools and colleges had only one educational itinerary to follow for entrance to the officers' academies, postwar reforms contributed to the creation of six new paths. Such an arrangement allowed a greater number of soldiers' sons to benefit from the right to enroll in these military preparatory schools, to continue their education, to pass the baccalaureate, and eventually to take an academy entrance examination. Between 1931 and 1940, only 245 of the candidates who passed the entrance exam of the military academies came from the military secondary schools. This number reached 302 between 1941 and 1950 and 629 between 1951 and 1960. In the 1970s, as illustrated by Table 9.4 (and the more detailed Table 8.8), the proportion of cadets at the military academies coming from these military preparatory schools and military colleges grew more numerous.

It is quite clear that these observations would have little meaning if the existence as well as the efficiency of the socialization process that operated within these institutions and that induced pupils to enter a military career were not assumed. A few words about this subject might be useful at this point. It is understood that the beneficiaries of the education offered by these schools were by no means compelled to become military professionals, at least at La Flèche and the college of Saint-Cyr (in the military preparatory schools applicants were required to sign a five-year enlistment contract). Then, if these institutions constituted the main source for the recruitment of military academy officers, there must have existed a system of imperious psychological solicitations. In this respect, analysis of the environment of these schools is enlightening. The modern EMEG no longer resembled the old *enfants de troupe* schools from which they were descended. A formidable effort of modernization and sanitization had been accomplished since World War II; of the once lugubrious (some were former barracks), semipenitentiary establishments, very little remained. Behind the high stone walls and around austere courtyards à la française, the dining hall, the kitchens, the sleeping quarters, and the classrooms were no longer different from those of any civilian high school in France. However, the schools continued to exhibit most of the characteristics by which one defines a "total institution."[39] A board-

Table 9.4. Contribution of Military Preparatory Schools and Colleges to the Recruitment of Military Academy Students (percentages)

	1967	1968	1969	1970	1971	1972
All military academies						
Candidates applying	39.9	43.7	52.3	51.1	54.2	62.0
	(1,077)	(885)	(1,118)	(1,134)	(1,127)	(940)
Candidates admitted	53.0	56.9	67.0	66.9	73.3	77.3
	(347)	(327)	(339)	(314)	(322)	(339)

Source: See table 8.8.

er's life was still governed by a system of immutable rules, incomparably stricter than those of the most severe parochial school. As paradoxical as it may seem, the social control exerted by the modern EMEG was relatively tighter than it had been in the past. At the end of the nineteenth century or at the beginning of the twentieth, even students enrolled at the earliest permissible age (October of the year of the thirteenth birthday) never remained in the same establishment for more than two or three years; at that time, their secondary school instruction extended chronologically over three different schools, starting at the *écoles de base*, continuing at Autun, and ending at La Flèche (the only institution that offered preparation for the baccalaureates and the officers' academies). In addition, it often happened that, for purely practical reasons, some of the pupils' activities were beyond the authority of the military school. This occurred when courses were taken outside the institution itself, as was the case for the Autun school boarders, who had to attend their classes at the municipal college. To some extent then, the pupils exposed to a pluralistic, if not conflicting, system of authority and norms were somewhat insulated against the effects of the socializing values of the military environment.

In the modern schools, by contrast, all aspects of the boarder's life were placed under the control of the tutelary establishment. His intellectual, moral, and civil education, his physical and mental health, and his leisure—everything that contributed to the maturing of his personality and the development of his future—were under the domination of one institution only. The simple fact that these schools were open to the sons of military personnel beginning with the first year of the modern secondary program—accessible to students at a relatively young age, between ten and twelve—greatly facilitated their socializing influence.[40]

With the stabilization of the young pupil's mobility, in space as well as in time, the conditioning to the dominant value system was reinforced. Therefore, even though the nature of these values and norms was not in itself more militaristic than it had been previously, its influence was nonetheless more pervasive. Inevitably, the school's "emotional background" (museums, the iconography of illustrious alumni or battlefield heroes), the regularity of military rituals ("spit and polish" inspections, morning salutes to the flag, memorials, the exaltation of military bravery), the wearing of uniforms, a military organization into companies and sections, the physical and mental initiation into military life,[41] the service records of teachers,[42] and an early indoctrination of the intellect toward preparation for the military academy examinations were the principal parameters of the pupil's socialization to military culture and his career plans.

The effects of socialization were such that in general the candidates who failed to enter the academies did not return to civilian life; rather, they enlisted in the ranks and prepared, as NCOs, for the easier examinations of semidirect recruitment.

Let us also note that this process of socialization was all the more successful when it took place among young pupils from families with a deeply rooted conviction that a military career was a source of status gratification. This was precisely the case in the NCO community: for many NCO families, access to the rank of officer was an unquestioned form of upward social mobility. Perhaps this is a first explanatory element for the significant increase in the number of sons of NCOs, gendarmes, and lower-ranking officers (former NCOs in most cases) in the officer corps. In the officer community itself, however, one has the feeling that the relative deterioration of the military profession was felt with more bitterness and that, consequently, many officers seemed to renounce the idea of having their sons participate in the cult of a profession whose prestige had been seriously downgraded; this accounts for the lack of increase of the proportion of officers' sons in the military profession.

This being said, one could now question the hypothesis that French army officers tended to be recruited mainly from among the military sons educated in the EMEG, where they developed an interest for the trade. One could argue that most of the indicators we have used up to this point are related solely to the locus of the preparation for the entrance examination to the academy and do not, therefore, necessarily indicate that the students enrolled in the *corniches* at these special secondary schools completed their entire secondary school education at these institutions, nor does it indicate that the majority were sons of military personnel, for enrollment in these institutions was not exclusively reserved for members of the military community. This point deserves to be emphasized. In effect, preparation and training for the competitive examinations in lycées for entrance to the civilian *grandes écoles* as well as military academies deteriorated to such a degree (the success indices at the military academy entrance examinations in the civilian lycées' *corniches* barely reached 30%) that many candidates from regular lycées sought enrollment in the *corniches* at EMEG, where the chances for success were much higher.

Granted the validity of this observation, it remains that in these institutions the proportion of sons of military personnel always was important. First, because it was only recently that the military preparatory schools (Aix-en-Provence, Le Mans, Tampon, etc.) were opened to students from civilian origins. Second, even though the contingent of civilians' sons was not necessarily negligible, the number of candidates at the college of Saint-Cyr and the *prytanée* of La Flèche (both institutions that were not open to civilians except under certain conditions to sons of civil servants) who came from the military community, was considerable: in 1975, of the 800 students at the college of Saint-Cyr, 88 percent were soldiers' sons. But precisely, these are the two institutions that prepared the greatest number of candidates for Saint-Cyr: 56 percent of all the sons of soldiers at the army academy between 1968 and 1970, and more than 60 percent between 1970 and 1972, came from La Flèche and Versailles. On the other hand, if the number of officers who had attended the EMEG for their entire secondary education was relatively small, the number who attended these schools for a part of the time was more significant. For instance, in 1973, nearly 40 percent of the Saint-Cyriens had completed all or a goodly part of their secondary schooling in the EMEG. Since it was rare, except at Aix-en-Provence and Le Mans, for sons of civilians to attend these colleges, one can logically deduce that at least two-thirds of the soldiers' sons entering Saint-Cyr had gone through the EMEG.

As for the objection that students preparing for the entrance examinations to the military academies at the EMEG had not gone through the whole secondary curriculum therein, hence could not be said to have been socialized to take up a military career, it is not pertinent. First, as pointed out, in any case, between a third and two-fifths of the students at the military academies did attend the EMEG for their entire secondary education or at least a large part of it. Second, there is certainly a positive correlation between the duration of the socializing process and its impact, but it is a diminishing one; a few years, generally, being enough to suscitate a military vocation.

In the face of so many indications, it is difficult to avoid resorting to the idea of institutional engineering in order to grasp the significance of these reforms, and, consequently, the logic of "professional endogamy," in the postwar French officer corps. Even if the introduction of these reforms, and particularly those aimed at remodeling the military preparatory schools, was guided by the desire to coordinate the syllabi and to enhance the quality of education to a level comparable with civilian high schools, its coinciding with the recruitment crisis cannot be viewed as entirely fortuitous. There was a deliberate attempt to "open," as the White Book states, "their [students'] minds to the greatness of the military profession and in general to the service to the state"[43]—in other words, to safeguard a reservoir from which to recruit future army officers. And, it was not accidental that the number of candidates at the military academies increased slightly after 1967; for example, the total number of registrations for the entrance examinations at Saint-Cyr rose from 431 in 1967 to 791 in 1974. Undoubtedly, such an increase favored raising the level of the examination scores (now considered the equivalent of a second-year university diploma) and the intellectual level of the candidates admitted. The data in Table 9.5 clearly show the growth in the number of candidates for Saint-Cyr as well as the declining ratio of applicants over the admitted candidates, which can be considered indicators of the improvement of the competitive examination and of the scholastic level of the Saint-Cyr student.

In summation, the beginnings of endorecruitment were rooted in the military context itself. The increasing rate of occupational inheritance in the military over the thirty years following World War II seemed to be the result of the intentional displacement of the function of the old welfare tradition established during the nineteenth century to assist the military community. Such an operation, destined to preempt, by interposed generations, the services of the military community, was a way of compensating for the decline of military vocations. If such a policy contributed to maintaining somewhat normal sources of recruitment for the officer corps, it also tended to exacerbate the withdrawal of the military community into itself. By maintaining this isolation, it made the military institution risk irre-. mediable social alienation. As one defense *rapporteur* at the National Assembly said, "Endorecruitment is a pernicious tendency, which sooner or later cannot but render more difficult the integration of our officers into society."[44] In the context of the transformation of the military into a force-in-being format, the consequences could materi-

Table 9.5. Competitiveness of the Saint-Cyr Examination after 1968 (defined as the ratio of candidates admitted to candidates applying)

	1945–58	1960–68	1969	1970	1971	1972	1973	1974
Candidates applying	860	739	680	806	745	690	744	791
Candidates admitted	318	243	190	186	198	210	209	198
Percentage of candidates admitted	37	33	28	23	26	30	28	25

Sources: These figures were computed from data in Girardet and Thomas, "Problèmes de recrutement," in *La Crise militaire française*, edited by Raoul Girardet; Jeanblanc, "Etude sociologique des fficiers de l'Armée de Terre"; and in *Défense nationale* 31 (April 1975): 155–56.

alize through a rapid erosion of the links that bound the armed forces to the nation and through deterioration of citizen interest and participation in national defense.

Notes

1. Jacqueline Bernard, "L'Origine sociale des officiers," *Le Monde*, 28 December 1960, pp. 1ff.

2. André Maquet, "Le Recrutement des officiers et des cadres civils supérieurs," mimeographed (Paris: Centre de Sociologie de la Défense nationale, 1974).

3. Raoul Girardet and Jean-Pierre Thomas, "Problèmes de recrutement," in *La Crise militaire française*, edited by Raoul Girardet (Paris: A. Colin, 1964), p. 46, note 18.

4. François Helluy, "Les Jeunes Officiers de l'Armée de Terre" (EMSST thesis, Centre de Sociologie de la Défense nationale, 1974), p. 42.

5. Ibid., p. 4, *in fine*.

6. Guy Michelat and Jean-Pierre Thomas, "Contribution à l'étude du recrutement des écoles d'officiers de la Marine," *Revue française de Sociologie* 9 (1968): 61.

7. Helluy, "Les Jeunes Officiers de l'Armée de Terre," p. 6, *in fine*.

8. Maurice Bracoud, "Les Débuts du Saint-Cyrien en corps de troupe" (EMSST thesis, Paris, 1970).

9. C. B. Otley, "Militarism and the Social Affiliations of the British Military Elite," in *Armed Forces and Society: Sociological Essays*, edited by Jacques Van Doorn (The Hague: Mouton, 1968), pp. 84–108.

10. Peter J. Dietz and James F. Stone, "The British All-Volunteer Force," *Armed Forces and Society* 1 (1975): 181.

11. This theme has been a flourishing intellectual industry and has given birth to important writings: we will refer only to Daniel Bertaux, "L'Hérédité sociale en France," *Economie et Statistique* 9 (1970): 37–45; C. Levy-Leboyer, *L'Ambition personnelle et la mobilité sociale* (Paris: Presses Universitaires de France, 1971); Michel Praderie and Monique Passagez, "La Mobilité professionnelle en France entre 1959 et 1964," *Etudes et Conjoncture* 10 (1966): 1–166. Recently the idea of social rigidity in France has been questioned by Maurice Garnier and Lawrence Hazelrigg, "Father-to-Son Occupational Mobility in France: Some Evidences from the 1960s," *American Journal of Sociology* 80 (1974): 478–502; *see also*, Jane Marceau, *Class and Status in France: Economic Change and Social Immobility* (New York: Oxford University Press, 1977).

12. Praderie and Passagez, "La Mobilité professionnelle en France."

13. Claude Thélot, "Origine et position sociales: faits et interpretation," *Economie et Statistique* 81–82 (1976): 73–88.

14. Bertaux, "L'Hérédité sociale en France," p. 44.

15. Alain Darbel, "L'Evolution récente de la mobilité sociale," *Economie et Statistique* 71 (1975): 18.

16. Alain Darbel and Dominique Schnapper, "La Probabilité d'entrée dans la fonction publique," *Economie et Statistique* 4 (1969): 18.

17. Ibid.

18. Data from Archives de l'ENA, cited by Pierre Birnbaum, *Les Sommets de l'Etat: essai sur l'élite du pouvoir en France* (Paris: Seuil, 1977); for an excellent treatment of this question see Ezra N. Suleiman, *Politics, Power and Bureaucracy in France* (Princeton: Princeton University Press, 1974).

19. Bertaux, "L'Hérédité sociale en France," p. 44.

20. Darbel and Schnapper, "Les Structures de l'administration française," *Revue internationale des Sciences administratives* 40 (1974): 340.

21. Darbel, "L'Evolution récente de la mobilité sociale," p. 4.

22. *See* Laurent Blanc, *La Fonction publique* (Paris: Presses Universitaires de France, 1968); Marie-Christine Kessler, "Historique du système de formation et de recrutement des hauts fonctionnaires," *Revue française d'Administration publique* 1 (1977): 9–52.

23. *See* André Corvisier, *Armées et sociétés en Europe de 1494 à 1789* (Paris: Presses Universitaires de France, 1976); M. de Riencourt, *Les Militaires blessés et invalides: leur histoire, leur situation en France et à l'étranger* (Paris, 1875); Isser Woloch, "War Widows Pensions: Social Policy in Revolutionary and Napoleonic Periods," mimeographed (Princeton: Institute for Advanced Study, 1974).

24. For details on this interesting question, *see* Corvisier, *Armées et Sociétés en Europe de 1494 à 1789*, pp. 95–99 and 186–91; M. Prévost, "L'Assistance aux invalides de la guerre avant 1670," *Revue des questions historiques* (October 1914); August Solard, *Histoire de l'Hotel royal des Invalides depuis sa fondation jusqu'à nos jours* (Blois, 1845).

25. Alfred Vagts, *A History of Militarism* (New York: Meridian Books, 1959 edition), p. 52.

26. Corvisier, *Armées et sociétés en Europe de 1494–1789*, p. 115.

27. Edgar Boutaric, *Les Institutions militaires de la France* (Paris: Plon, 1863); Henri Guerlac, "Science and War in the Old Regime" (Ph.D. dissertation, Harvard University, 1941), mentioned by Samuel P. Huntington, *The Soldier and the State: The Theory and Practice of Civil-Military Relations* (New York: Random House, 1957), p. 470; Léon Hennet, *Les Compagnies de cadets-gentilshommes et les écoles militaires* (Paris, 1889); Louis Tuetey, *Les Officiers sous l'ancien régime: nobles et roturiers* (Paris: Plon-Nourrit, 1908).

28. Robert Laulan, "Pourquoi et comment on entrait à l'Ecole royale militaire de Paris," *Revue d'Histoire moderne et contemporaine* 4 (1957): 143.

29. Samuel F. Scott, "The French Revolution and the Professionalization of the French Officer Corps, 1789–1793," in *On Military Ideology*, edited by Morris Janowitz and Jacques Van Doorn (Rotterdam: Rotterdam University Press, 1971), pp. 3–56.

30. For a description of the nature and the functioning of the schools for *enfants de troupes*, *see L'Armée française en 1879* (Paris: Hetzel et Cie., n.d.), Chapter 3, second part.

31. Direction des personnels militaires de l'Armée de Terre (DPMAT), "Les Ecoles militaires préparatoires," *Revue historique de l'Armée* 10 (1954): 177.

32. The number of students at the military preparatory schools varied depending on the times. The figure

of 3,000 pupils is the maximum quota planned at the time of the creation of the first schools. The military preparatory schools established in 1884 were Rambouillet, Saint-Hippolyte-du-Fort (in 1946 they merged to become the school of Aix-en-Provence), Les Andelys, Montreuil-sur-Mer, Autun, and Billom.

33. The annual average of officer attrition between 1949 and 1953—the time of the Indochina War—reached 175 men. It decreased, afterwards, to 94 men between 1954 and 1961, at the time of the Algerian War. Besides this fairly high rate of attrition due to war casualties, losses due to the immediate postwar *dégagement des cadres* (between 1945 and 1948, 13,941 officers left the armed forces) and similar measures afterwards (a yearly average of 309 officers left the service until 1958; between 1958 and 1966 that average mounted to 1,289) imposed considerable strain on the French army officer corps.

34. P. Jeanblanc, "Etude sociologique du corps des officiers de l'Armée de Terre: 1815–1968," mimeographed (Paris: Centre des hautes études militaires, 1968), *in fine*; Jean Malgré, "Recrutement des officiers et structure sociale: la crise de Saint-Cyr et ses remèdes," *Revue politique et parlementaire* 8 (1956): 21–22.

35. The nadir in officer recruitment during the crisis of 1909–11 reached 871 (in 1911) and during the crisis of 1925–30 it reached 614 (in 1927).

36. Girardet and Thomas, "Problèmes de recrutement," in *La Crise militaire française*, edited by Girardet, pp. 34–38.

37. The welfare tradition of these schools was still tangible. One cannot overlook the fact that tuitions were either nonexistent or very low. At the colleges of Brest and Saint-Cyr and at the *prytanée* of La Flèche, fees amounted to 1,200 francs per year ($240). At the military preparatory schools there was no tuition at all. Moreover, students who could also apply for regular fellowships through national education could eventually receive special scholarships to study in these schools.

There were other remnants of the welfare mission of the military, exercised outside of any concern for manpower recruitment. This was notable in those schools that provided free primary and secondary education for the daughters of officers with the Légion d'honneur, such as the schools of the Légion d'honneur at Saint-Denis and of the Loges, or for daughters of large families and female orphans whose fathers were or ' .d been in the air force, such a   the Maison des Ailes d'Echoubouıains.

38. *Livre blanc sur la Défense nationale*, vol. 2, p. 63.

39. Erving Goffman defines a total institution in the following manner:

> The central feature of total institutions can be described as a breakdown of the kinds of barriers ordinarily separating those three spheres of life. First, all aspects of life are conducted in the same place and under the same single authority. Second, each phase of the member's daily activity will be carried out in the immediate company of a large batch of others, all of whom are treated

alike and required to do the same thing together. Third, all phases of the day's activities are tightly scheduled, with one activity leading at a prearranged time into the next, the whole circle of activities being imposed from above through a system of explicit formal rulings and a body of officials. Finally, the contents of the various enforced activities are brought together as parts of a single over-all rational plan purportedly designed to fulfill the official aims of the institution.

Erving Goffman, "Characteristics of Total Institutions," in *Symposium on Preventive and Social Psychiatry* (Washington, D.C.: Walter Reed Army Institute of Research, 1957), pp. 43–84; *see also* his *Asylums: Essays on the Social Situation of Mental Patients and Other Inmates* (New York: Doubleday, 1961).

40. Furthermore, one should not overlook that the stability as well as the quality of the education offered in these schools constituted supplementary seductive incentives for families in which the father's occupation was characterized by high geo-graphic mobility; the military professional life epitomized such mobility perfectly as, between 1946 and 1959, 47 percent of all French army officers moved between four and six times and 24 percent moved between seven and nine times in the course of their career. Though the number of moves decreased after the 1960s with the phasing out of overseas assignments, the level of mobility was still important.

41. Students had to attend physical training courses as well as military training instruction. Moreover, they could take the paratrooper military preparation course, and, at the College of Brest, they received an initiation to sea life on navy ships.

42. The schools and the colleges were commanded by senior officers; training and formation were in the hands of officers and NCOs. Only the academic aspects of the life in these schools were the responsibility of civilian teachers.

43. *Livre blanc sur la défense nationale*, vol. 2, p. 63.

44. Jean-Paul Mourot, *Rapport d'information fait au nom de la Commission de la Défense nationale et des forces armées sur la condition militaire en 1974*, n° 945, Doc. Assemblée nationale (2nd session ordinaire de 1973–74).

CONCLUSION ● FUTURE TRENDS

It is not without a feeling of frustration that one brings this study to an end. The contemporary French military establishment, much more than any other Western military institution, and perhaps much more than under its earlier forms, remains resistant to a systematic empirical investigation. Thus, having had to rely on rather fragmentary information and an ideal-type approach, we found it almost impossible to avoid being impressionistic and very difficult to convey a faithful image of the institution's reality and complexity. Recalling a theme dear to Virginia Woolf, that nothing could be grasped in its perfection, or remembering that the Weberian symptom of *entzauberung* also developed out of the scholar's powerlessness to describe the infinite complexity of the outside world offers a meager consolation. Furthermore, throughout our exploration, we have been led to leave some aspects of the institution in a shadowy background and to neglect some of its most relevant dimensions. This was all the more frustrating because often data and information concerning these aspects of the French military institution existed somewhere; but we did not have access to them.

This realism, however, should not lead to any complacent pessimism. After all, such a predicament is common to all researchers pursuing poorly explored fields. And if the present work, by offering a spur to constructive criticisms and refutation, furthers new avenues of research, it will have achieved something positive.

These remarks out of the way, let us return to the topic in order to summarize briefly our argument and to propose a number of reflections about the future development of the French military institution.

Viewed from its organizational, professional, and social dimensions, and conceived from a macroanalytical perspective, the modern French military establishment appears to have evolved in the three decades following World War II from a rather homogeneous model, in which internal pluralism remained well contained, to a sharply dualistic structure—dualistic in the sense that features perennial to the classic mass armed forces model, a model derived from the Revolutionary concept of the nation in arms, continued to coexist with newly developed features generally associated with the force-in-being format. Significant differences at the level of social composition or at that of the use of drafted manpower, for example, differences in the basic patterns of military authority and discipline, differences in the internal division of labor, and so on, clearly illustrate such a dualism. Yet, what is remarkable is that this dualism tended to coincide with an interservices dichotomy. The features associated with the traditional mass armed forces structure, indeed, tended to be dominant in the army, whereas the modern features derived from the force-in-being model were dominant in the navy and air force.

Although a unicausal form of explanation rarely does justice to reality, in the case of the French military establishment it seems that the main cause for this dualistic trend was to be found in the degree of exposure to technological modernization, itself the result of strategic and budgetary considerations. It has been argued that because of the preindustrial and rather archaic nature of all military activities entailed by the colonial conflicts into which French armed forces were drawn until the early 1960s, the level of technological modernization to which they were exposed remained minimal. Considering that exposure to technological change is one of the most relevant sources of organizational change, it can be deduced that the French military establishment remained patterned on the pre-World II model of military organization for the decade and a half after the Liberation; this model was derived from the mass army format. And, because it was the main protagonist of the colonial engagement, the army presented the characteristics of the traditional model with more distinctiveness than did the navy or the air force, which were intrinsically technical services and already presented some traits of the force-in-being model.

The ending of the colonial adventure in the early 1960s and, above all, the decision to adopt a nuclear defense posture suddenly threw the military establishment into a new environment characterized by intensive technological change. In practice, however, the diffusion of modernization within the institution continued to be very uneven. First, the basic principles guiding the organization of French strategy and the use of the defense devices (independence and insularization) led to an emphasis on the nuclear power and its supporting systems of forces. Second, as a consequence of, and also as a reinforcement of, this tendency, the budgetary flows within the military institution became rather discriminatory, particularly with regard to the systems of force not directly relevant to nuclear strategy, which, as a result, remained in an environment of minimal technological change. Because most of the branches of services that were supposed to operate below the nuclear level were concentrated in the army, thus it can be said that from 1960 to 1976 the army found itself in a technological situation reminiscent of the previous decade and a half. The navy and the air force though, because they were in command of almost all missions at the nuclear level, emerged as more technologically exposed services.

To a great extent, this dualistic technological environment explains the dualism in the organizational, professional, and social profile of the French military establishment after 1960: services such as the air force and the navy, closely patterned along the force-in-being format, coexist with a service like the army, organized along the old traits of a mass armed force system. It is obvious that the nature of the technological environment was, in reality, highly heterogeneous, and that, as a consequence, the level of exposure to technological modernization varied widely within the military establishment, not only from one service to another, but also within each service. Approached from a more microscopic perspective, each service was composed of branches and subbranches whose profiles borrowed from the two ideal models of organizational format. But in terms of dominant profile, a clear distinction emerged between the army, in which there was a large concentration of organizations patterned on the mass model, and the navy and the air force, in which organizations patterned on the mass model were in the minority. Since we have chosen to place ourselves at a general level of analysis rather than at a microscopic one, we have not sought to push this observation beyond the definition of these dominant types.

Naturally, from time to time during the course of our inquiry, deviations from the expected dualism derived from the logic of our basic paradigm were observed at one level or another of the military institution. In a few cases, for example, we noted that there was either a strong accentuation of the expected trends or features, or an attenuation of these traits, sometimes to the point that one had the impression to be confronted with the institutional characteristics opposite to those anticipated. Indeed, given the macroanalytical level of the analysis as well as the idealized version of the paradigm, such contradictions were inevitable. Yet, in most cases, it is not the validity of the basic hypothesis that should be questioned, for most deviations appeared to be the result of extraneous factors, related either to some historical oddity of the military establishment or to the cultural particularism of the parent society, which showed through here and there in the military institution.

In the remaining part of this conclusion, it is our purpose to discuss the future of such a model of military organization. This discussion could begin by raising the question of whether this dualistic form of military institution will perpetuate itself, or whether it will evolve toward what seems to be the agreed upon expected future format of the modern Western military establishment—the all- or quasi-volunteer force.

Although elements that could be collected toward a valid answer are far from being abundant, they are present in sufficient number to allow the formation of an idea about the direction of the evolution. New elements that one could expect to have a direct effect upon the nature of the technological environment—the assumed key source of institutional change—to which the French military establishment, particularly all systems of forces below the nuclear level, is exposed have appeared since 1976–77. There are elements that, in the light of what is and will be the political context of at least the next three years (the March 1978 legislative elections having reestablished the mandate of the conservative ruling coalition), can be regarded as reliable points of departure for discussion and prediction. Such elements can be found, first, in the change affecting the French strategic doctrine and, second, in the new pattern of budgetary allocation established by the 1977–82 six-year plan for French defense.

In Chapter 1, we alluded to the fact that until 1976, the strategic doctrine of France was largely modeled upon the Gaullist conception of national defense, and thus was founded upon a strictly independent use of atomic deterrence under the form of a swift, if not immediate, escalation to massive nuclear retaliations in case of an attack or an explicit threat of attack on French territory. In case of a major crisis menacing the sanctuary, the government and the military staff would use as an ultimate warning small nuclear armaments before unleashing strategic nuclear fire. This view had one important consequence for the armed forces; the conventional forces, that is all systems of forces operating below the nuclear level, did not need to be extensively developed.

After 1976, however, a change in French strategic thought seemed slowly to take shape. Among the manifestations of this modification, the most tangible one, at least from a doctrinal and formal standpoint, was the publication of "Une armée pour quoi faire et comment?" in the official *Défense nationale*, by General Méry, the armed forces chief of staff.[1] Though in practice, no radical break or turnaround was expected—such a change, understandably, could only be incremental—though the reference to the traditional Gaullist paradigm continued to be reaffirmed in appearance, it was certain that a new strategic direction was about to be followed, a direction by which France would seek to avoid relying on a premature use of nuclear fire, even at the tactical level, and would instead seek to rely on conventional fire to face any threat to, or any violation of, its territorial or maritime boundaries. Moreover, it seemed, and this appeared quite clearly in the concept of "forward strategy" developed by this new doctrine, a concept by which the French forces could be militarily engaged against the enemy on an ally's territory if necessary, that the French strategic doctrine was moving toward a less nationalistic conception of what could be the "military space" or the "military battlefield" in which France would eventually engage her troops, which would then fight in cooperation with other Western forces. As a document prepared by the defense ministry, based on declarations by the president, the prime minister, and the defense minister, reads: "Finally it is not in the interest of France to retire egoistically and passively into the sanctuary of her boundaries rendered inviolable by the possession of nuclear fire. As has been recalled . . . we want to be liable to our European partners and allies. In case their security should be compromised and, by way of consequence, ours, we should be able to make it clear, by appropriate decisions, that we feel involved, and if we think it necessary, to participate in the combat which might result."[2]

Necessarily, such a new orientation would have direct and important consequences on the French conventional forces, of which the army is the main component. As it would be playing a more decisive role than before, its modernization became a crucial factor. Already, the reorganization of the army, with its new model of division (lighter and more powerful), the modernization of its equipment, notably the extension of the heavy tanks pool, and the introduction of new weaponry such as the heavy self-propelled 155 millimeter gun and the antitank SAM-type devices constitutes the first sign of this evolution.[3]

Furthermore, the new six-year military plan for 1977–82[4] seems to give an unseen precedence to the conventional forces and to the army, whose part in a growing defense budget (in 1982, it should reach 20 percent of the public spending, against 17 percent in 1976) is being increased. Particularly relevant with regard to the modernization of the army is the increase not only of its global allocation (averaging 31 percent of the total), but also its equipment allocation as 25 percent (for the period running from 1977 to 1982) of the total expenditure for equipment (Title 5) which will increase from 41.2 percent in 1977 to 47.8 percent in 1982 (see Table C.1).[5]

Thus, it seems that the focus of attention has finally turned toward the conventional forces and, in particular, toward the army. As has

Table C.1. Defense Budget by Service and Category of Expenditure, 1977–82 (percentages)

	1977	1978	1979	1980	1981	1982
Common services	20.12	19.78	19.43	18.87	18.50	17.95
Army	31.72	31.72	31.55	31.26	30.98	30.70
Navy	16.86	17.08	17.33	17.70	17.98	18.29
Air force	21.08	21.29	21.65	22.24	22.67	23.46
Gendarmerie	10.22	10.13	10.04	9.92	9.87	9.60
Total allocation in millions of francs	58 000	66 460	76 155	87 260	99 990	114 575
Personnel/operation expenditures (Title 3)	58.8	58.2	57.1	55.5	54.0	52.2
Equipment expenditures (Title 5)	41.2	41.8	42.9	44.5	46.0	47.8

Source: Service d'Information et de Relations publiques des Armées, "Les Armées françaises de demain," *Dossier d'Information* 49 (October 1976): 8–9.

been pointed out, de Gaulle wanted a credible defense for France, but he knew that everything could not be undertaken and accomplished at one time; "Later," he is supposed to have said, "one will rebuild the classic force." The present government has undoubtedly judged that this moment has finally come.[6]

From the viewpoint of the nature and the evolution of the military institutional format, then, it is probable that, by reason of this greater exposure to modernization, new conditions will be created so that there will be an attenuation, if not a phasing out, of the most conspicuous mass army features in the ground forces. A decline of army personnel strength (a reduction of 20,000 men has been planned for the period between 1977 and 1982) and the introduction of a new formal division of labor based on industrial-type specialties such as exist in the navy and the air force, to replace the traditional dichotomy between "arms and services," constitute the most tangible indications of this forthcoming shift.

But because change in institutional format is not solely the result of exposure to technological modernization, it is necessary to examine all the other factors that account for the nature and, eventually, the evolution of the military organizational format. In general, the most visible institution that determines the place a military establishment occupies on the continuum between the mass armed forces and the all-volunteer force-in-being models is compulsory conscription, but conscription in its classic form: egalitarian and universal. In effect, conscription is not by simple virtue of its existence a sufficient condition to determine the mass army quality of a military institution. A short and highly selective form of military service indicates a quasi-volunteer force form of military institution, whereas an egalitarian and universal style of draft indicates the opposite model.

In France, we have seen that the maintenance of a universal and egalitarian form of conscription was the result of many factors; it was not solely related to the level of technological modernization. Among these were budgetary factors and factors linked to the professional soldier's attachment to such a type of recruitment, and, above all, factors related to the preferences of the public and the ideology of the political classes. Yet in the last few years, it has appeared more and more obvious that the draft, although not under out and out attack, has become the object of increasingly frequent questioning and discussion. In this regard, it can be said that with the coming of the second half of the 1970s, the process of the "detabooization" of the draft has begun. Browsing through books of military literature, hearing political speeches before parliament or other conventions, and reading proposals of reform dealing with defense matters, one readily becomes aware of this phenomenon. Though the institution of the draft has remained, and will probably continue to remain, untouched for a while yet, the fact that its existence is now regularly reaffirmed means that it is no longer taken entirely for granted.

Although it would be unrealistic to predict the suppression of this institution in the near future, important modifications, notably in the sense of a lesser emphasis on the forms that conscription has adopted until now, can be expected. Such a change would be the result of several variables, often reinforcing one another.

Paradoxically, as far as the major variable is concerned, the main problem is not a problem of legitimacy, as one might have expected in the cultural context of an advanced industrial welfare state. In France, the legitimacy of the draft appears relatively stable. Between 70 and 75 percent of French public opinion still favors an armed force recruited through universal draft; only a small percentage supports the idea of an all-volunteer force or of a selective draft. These proportions tend to modify somewhat as one moves toward the younger generations. But, here too, whatever their level, the proportions have stabilized. Anyway, as we have tried to show, the significance of the results of such polls are not as clear as would at first appear. It is often difficult to determine to exactly what extent opposition to military service expresses a rejection of the institution itself rather than a kind of a ritual opposition that is socially acceptable and that takes place in the anonymity of public polls. But let us not push the argument too far and thereby convey a false impression that there is no opposition to the draft in France. As in most other Western democracies, military service, the legitimacy of which fed on the role it had played with regard to the process of political enfranchisement (and beyond to the access to citizenship, with regard to democratic development), gradually stopped fulfilling such functions in proportion to the enlargement of the definition of citizenship.[7] We simply want to suggest that the development of opposition to the draft was not such as could have been inferred either from the amplitude of past draft-related demonstrations or from what happened in other Western nations.

If there is a problem in this domain, it is situated at another level. By tradition, conscription has been legitimized in reference to the revolutionary philosophy of which equality and universalism are the two most important pillars. This factor, as well as other more recent historical ones (the defeat of 1870, the preparation for revenge, and so forth), have contributed to creating a strong and rather enduring cultural intolerance toward lapses from the universalism of the draft. Today, leafing through parliamentary debates, draft reform proposals, political declarations, and so on, one notes that although the legitimacy of the draft is not being questioned, its universalism and egalitarianism are being contested. And, though the level of service exemptions remains relatively inconspicuous, particularly when compared to the situation in neighboring nations or to past practices— only a third of the contingent does not serve—it seems that this level constitutes a limit beyond which the credibility of the draft as an egalitarian and universal institution is jeopardized. And in the light of the forthcoming declining need for drafted personnel by the armed forces (growing technology requires well-trained rather than a great number of personnel), and in light of the increasing size of the coming age-classes, (see Figure C.1), to which ought to be added an increasing number of naturalized sons of migrant laborers (who account for 7.5 percent of the French population) for whom military service is a means of social integration, and women (since 1972 they have had the right to serve in the armed forces), it is certain that the proportion of those who will be exempted from serving in the years to come will probably increase significantly.

One could argue that the level of exemptions could be controlled so as not to exceed 35 percent of the contingent (after all the growth of the size of the coming age-classes is not that dramatic; it will in any case stabilize after 1985) so that the credible fiction of an egalitarian and universal military service could be maintained.[8] But, even admit-

Figure C.1. Changing Size of the Age-Classes between 1971 and 1990

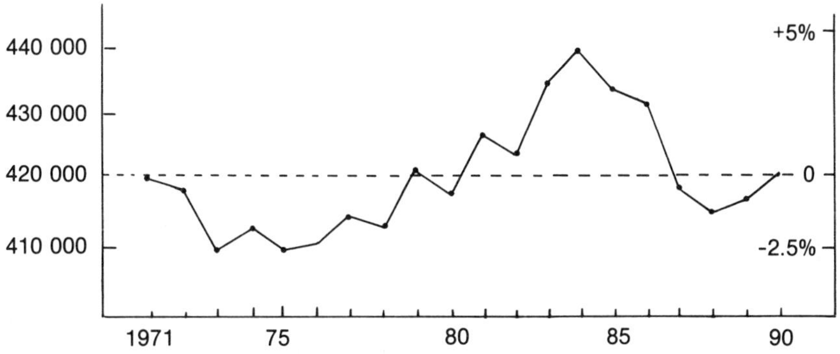

Source: "Démographie et conscription," *Armées d'aujourd'hui* 8 (1976): 24.

ting this possibility, the problem of equality will not be solved, for the egalitarian perception is changing significantly. For the last few years, mainly because there has been a ubiquitous emphasis in France on issues generally referred to as "social inequalities" in the forefront of all electoral programs and political declarations (for example, the president's *La Démocratie française*), there has been a growing awareness of such questions in the national collective consciousness. Inevitably, sensibility toward the principles of equality and universalism of conscription has gone beyond sheer numerical aspects to address itself to the qualitative dimensions of these principles. And what gives particular acuteness to the problem is that the social composition of the drafted population tends to be increasingly perceived as being at variance with the parent community. Sons of workers, of sales and clerical personnel, of artisans and small business owners, in other words, people coming from the lower and lower-middle social categories, now seem to be carrying the brunt of the military service; to a great extent young men from the upper social strata (the majority of them being university students) avoid their military service, and if not, at least avoid serving in combat or combat-related units. "The only chap we ever had from the *seizième* [an upper bourgeois and residential district of Paris] was the son of a Portuguese maid," once bantered the commanding officer of the 20th airborne brigade, depicting quite accurately the present situation. (Let us remark in passing that the overrepresentation of the less privileged classes is all the more impressive because individuals from these categories are more likely to be found mentally, physically, or morally unfit for service.)

Thus it is not a coincidence that proposals for suspending the draft or phasing it out, which have flourished in the second half of the 1970s, have articulated their arguments and legitimized their propositions of reform mainly in relation to this issue of equality and universalism. The following declaration by Pierre Messmer, a former premier and defense minister under de Gaulle and Pompidou and the author of a proposition for modifying the present code of the national service, before the National Assembly in 1976 is symptomatic in this regard: "All declarations, as sincere as they may be, which praise the civic virtues [of the military service] will not always be able to hide the fact that the universal service, that is to say, obligatory for everyone, is only a memory because exemptions and dispensations are more and more numerous. . . . If the law of national service entails so many exceptions, it is because the service has become inapplicable for reasons about which nothing can be done; it is therefore necessary to change the law."[9]

The same reaction can be observed on the Left, too. Commenting on the present state of the military service, a member of the directorial committee of the Radical party wrote:

> But the essential reasons for the Radicals' disavowal of the draft at the creation of which they had taken part, relate to the flagrant injustice of this institution. . . . The fact that the so-called universalism of the military service has been reduced to two-thirds of the age-class is already a scandal; all the worse considering who escapes through the mesh of this service. Out of the 140,000 men who arrive each year at the baccalaureate level, nearly half will not serve. . . . The truth is that the sons of the bourgeoisie evade their military duties in an unacceptable proportion.[10]

To some extent, therefore, one is tempted to say that in the case of France, if an assault on the legitimacy of the draft is to be launched, it will be not so much on the ground of its very essence, but rather on the ground of its corruptness as a democratic institution.

But this is not the only element that might, in the long run, oppose the maintenance of the draft in its present form. The second element is of a more economic nature. As pointed out in Chapter 5, it appears clearer every day that the classic economic argument praising the cheapness of conscription as a source of military manpower is losing its relevance before new realities. In the early 1970s, it became obvious that the economies realized through the use of the draft tended to be less and less significant, even supposing the cost of drafted manpower remained lower than that of manpower recruited through voluntary enlistments. Today, at the end of this decade, the argument appears to have lost even more ground as the computations found in all reform proposals argue that a smaller, yet equally efficient, all-volunteer or quasi-volunteer force would cost no more than a military force recruited through universal draft. It is indubitable that with the continuing relative deterioration of the draftees' material conditions of life, all the more acute given the draftees' rising expectations, a point will soon be reached when a drastic reform will have to be undertaken if conscription is to be maintained. This is explicitly acknowledged in all official papers and declarations. Such measures will, however, be costly ones, given the present situation, and will inevitably contribute to a considerable increase in the cost of conscription. It is certain that, despite the increases in the last ten years, draftees' pay, which remains among the lowest in Europe, will have to rise further. And one can safely assume that the recent pay raise of June 1978 will be followed by others.[11] It is planned that by 1982 the allocation for draftees' pay will amount to 480 million francs. The refurbishing of barracks, to mention another rather urgent issue, will also entail a fairly large investment; in France more than 44 percent of all barracks date back to the nineteenth century (only 14 percent were built after 1945).[12] Compared to such an unavoidable escalation in the cost of the draft, many of the quasi-volunteer forms of service, notably those entailing short enlistments (from eighteen to twenty-four months), appear relatively inexpensive even if the number of volunteers would have to be increased given the declining quality of the recruits that such a system implies.

In this review of the various elements that do or will contribute to the growing inadequacies of compulsory and universal military service as presently practiced in France, a third factor deserves to be examined. Compared to the two just analyzed, this third factor is strictly military. Its importance has come into full view in the light of recent events, namely those of spring 1978. In effect, France's willingness and readiness to fulfill her international engagements, especially those she has contracted with the countries formerly under her colonial tutelage and those she has contracted as a participant in peacekeeping missions, poses serious problems in the context of a conscript armed force. The simultaneous intervention in Africa (in Chad and Mauritania, to help local governments curb subversive activities of the FroLiNat and the Polisario; and in May 1978 in Zaire) and in Lebanon (as a member of the UNIFIL) revealed the fragility and the limits of a system of forces (Forces of Intervention) relying on conscripted manpower. Indeed, since the 1964 intervention in Gabon draftees cannot be sent overseas or into foreign countries without the preliminary authorization of the National Assembly; thus the entire intervention capability of the French forces is actually in the hands of the enlisted personnel. Inevitably, this means that in the event of the need for simultaneous action, as has lately been the case, a rather unbalanced force mostly of draftees must be left behind on French territory, a force that could be poorly operational should another conflictual eventuality occur. Even without reasoning in the framework of an extreme situation, severe problems, if not an impasse, could occur. In the situation of prolonged interventions, for example, one wonders whether the fighting capacities of the forces might not be weakened because, since it would be impossible to call for draftees, it would be necessary to lengthen the tour of combat duty on exposed fronts. Under such a system, France would have no capacity for "one war and a half." And this is only one problem of many.[13]

By reason of their very tangible effects on military readiness and capability, such problems, it can be assumed, will influence the perennial attachment that, as seen in Chapter 5, the majority of professional servicemen have traditionally felt toward conscription—an attachment, let us note in passing, which, at least among the youngest generation of officers, seems to have declined somewhat as revealed through informal interviews and by the literature produced by young military intellectuals.

All this being said, there is a last, but crucial, factor without which an eventual phasing out of universal conscription would not occur: this is the attitude of the political Left. In our exploration of the variables accounting for the perennial utilization of the compulsory universal draft in France, we saw how important the Left's attachment to this institution has been and we examined the reasons explaining this situation.

In this domain, indeed, changes do not seem as tangibly appreciable as they do in the case of the Right (to use an awkward but useful oversimplified dichotomy), whose interest in the draft has recently withered away as shown by the proposal by Messmer or the Rassemblement pour la République (the RPR succeeded the Gaullist UDR).[14] However, lately there has been a leftist political formation, the Radical party, that proposes to abandon the draft.[15] In light of this development it seems reasonable to suggest that the Left's attachment to the draft, at least as far as the large political formations are concerned, will not last very long and will not be as unanimous as it has been in the past. Two distinct arguments can be brought forth to support this view. We have seen that the Left's adhesion to the traditional style of military organization essentially based on universal citizen mobilization was rooted in the fear that an all-volunteer force would be used as an instrument of internal policing, or that it would offer too fertile a ground for the emergence of praetorian proclivities. In the light of recent events, such an attitude appears more and more groundless, and the Left is conscious of this. This is not to say that domestic disorders could no longer occur. Quite the contrary, the great upheaval in values, together with latent pluralism bordering in some cases on disintegration, that has affected Western democracies has multiplied the instances of hostility between citizens and the forces of order. But precisely because dissension has become somewhat pervasive and civil unrest frequent, there has been an increasing concern for the establishment, in well-defined roles and functions relative to social control, and strengthening of specific forces of law and order, particularly the special branches of the gendarmerie (the Gendarmerie mobile) and the Compagnies républicaines de sécurité that are now technically capable of meeting and quelling any disturbance. This makes obsolete the use of the regular armed forces for internal police purposes, and the issue of maintaining conscription, so long as it is related to the question of an eventual resort to the regular military for the operations of domestic order, tends no longer to be a critical one.[16] Next, in the relation of conscription to the question of preventing military adventurism, the Left's second important axiom for its traditional adherence to universal conscription, recent historical experiences have shown that conscription is an ambivalent institution in this respect; or, to put it otherwise, it is not a very reliable tool in the service of civilian control over the military; in fact, it is barely adequate to prevent praetorianism on the part of the active career soldier. Neither in Greece nor in Chile were conscripts able to prevent putschist officers from dismantling civil governments. Then too, the red versus white vision of the Left with respect to military attitudes is slowly changing. Fewer people believe that operations of the type that took place in Algiers in April 1961 could be repeated. In a recent interview, Charles Hernu, a former Socialist party defense expert, went as far as to say, "[Should we be in power,] I do not see why the army that we would have, if it were an all-volunteer force, would be praetorian."[17] Furthermore, events such as the Portuguese military revolution have significantly aided in changing some of the leftist prejudices about the military's so-called conservatism and have contributed to eroding previous convictions and biases regarding career personnel, their professional role and their ideological attitudes.

Finally, the theme of the internal enemy is rapidly losing its significance. There is less and less reason for the Left to feel, even if it remains an opposition political formation, that it is one of the targets at which the national defense network would eventually be directed. The ideological cleansing of leftist programs, and here the case of the Communist party is more than symptomatic, the respect for the democratic rules of the political games, and the increasing distance from former external mentors have contributed greatly to favor the legitimatization of the Left in the country. And even if the Left were still seeking external affiliation, this would have far less importance than it did twenty years ago, because the source of inspiration has diversified. Socialism or Communism is no longer the ideological appanage of the Soviet Union. It is also found in Cuba, China, and Southeast Asia, in other words, in countries not necessarily viewed as potential enemies, sometimes quite the contrary. Also, many communist and socialist regimes have changed their objectives with regard to the international scene, and rather than seeking to propagate internal disruption in capitalistic systems (an aim not entirely abandoned, however), they tend to seek a modicum of peace, at least enough to maintain the world balance and the international status quo.

This is one side of the argument. The other is certainly of a more speculative nature without being purely academic. It might be said that the Left's view with regard to conscription and of an all-volunteer force might change simply because it appears that the Left has, over the years, shown a great deal of versatility as far as defense matters are concerned. Consequently, there seems to be no reason to reject the hypothesis of a turn-about with respect to the Left's position regarding conscription. One cannot avoid referring to a practical instance of such a possibility, namely the change in the leftist attitude toward nuclear force. It is hardly necessary to recall that for a long time the Left was adamantly opposed to the Strategic Nuclear Force, mocked as a powerless though expensive *"bombinette"* and pictured as a reason for the deteriorating conditions of the conventional armament and the weakness of the French national defense and as an obstacle to any disarmament policy. For example, in the Communist program for a democratic government adopted by the central committee in October 1971, it was explicitly stated: "The renunciation of the Strategic Nuclear Force is a peremptory requisite for an authentic national defense. [It is essential] that a democratic government renounce a striking nuclear force and tactical atomic weaponry."[18] A similar stand was taken by the three leftist parties, cosignatories of the June 1972 program of government; Chapter 2, Part 4 of this program stipulates: "(a) the renouncement of a nuclear strategic force under whatever forms; immediate transforming of the military nuclear industry into a pacific atomic industry. . . . In no case, will the problems raised by such a reconversion be used to maintain the military nuclear industry; (b) immediate stopping of nuclear tests and adhesion to nuclear test-ban and nuclear armament non-proliferation treaties."[19]

Indeed, it can be argued that between 1971 and 1972 there were already signs of change, for no mention of tactical armament was made in the 1972 document. In the next five years, both Socialist and Communist parties radically changed their positions. The Socialist party opened the way, starting with a series of *petites phrases* by François Mitterand, its secretary general; as early as May 1974 Mitterand admitted that the strategic nuclear force was a given and could not be "drowned like puppies." The shift in attitude (we are referring to the average attitude of the majority as, given the fact of internal pluralism, not to say absence of any consensus, there was a variety of contradictory currents in this domain) materialized in November 1976 with an official statement by the party's managing committee and with the decision voted (after lively discussion) by the party convention in January 1978, during which Mitterand declared that "the striking force is a heritage that a leftist government has no other choice than to preserve. . . . The nuclear force is the condition of the defense of our country and by way of consequence of national independence."[20]

By the time the Socialist party's convention met, seven months had passed since the Communist party's spectacular decision regarding the nuclear force. On 11 May 1977, Jean Kanapa, a key member of the central committee, declared that the nuclear force "represents the only real deterrent that the country has at its disposal for the time being to face a threat of aggression."[21] And in the concluding part of the exposé that followed, the party's general secretary, Georges Marchais, stated explicitly: "Today this [nuclear] armament not only exists but, given the priority that has been accorded it, has also become the only efficient means of defense that the country has and will have for some time. Today, under such conditions, a decision to renounce it would amount to renouncing any genuine defense for the country."[22]

In many ways, this aggiornamento, far more radical than that of the Socialist party which questioned the maintenance of the Mirage fleet and the SSBM,[23] which not only assumed the maintenance of the strategic nuclear force but also implied, if not the development, at least the adjunct of qualitative technological improvement to keep up its deterrent function, was not surprising. Important, though unofficial, statements had been made even earlier. In 1973, when phasing out of nuclear equipment was discussed, only the Mirage fleet and the SSB S-2 missile were explicitly designated, leaving out the three SLBM systems. Then, between 1974 and 1976, new positions in foreign policy and strategy, plus changing attitudes with respect to Soviet diplomacy, were voiced by important members of the Communist party political bureau showing that the nuclear force was being taken into account in one way or another. Statements made by Louis Baillot, a leading party defense expert and vice-chairman of the Communist group at the National Assembly on 8 April 1976 before the scientific committee of the Foundation for Defense Studies and, later in 1976, by Jean Elleinstein, who was in charge of negotiations with the Socialist party on defense matters, paved the way for the official declaration of May 1977.[24]

That there is no complete convergence between the two leftist parties' views is undeniable. The Communist party leans toward a Gaullist-like "all-azimuths" strategy, whereas the Socialist party favors a neo-Atlanticist approach (that, at least, is how the Communists view the developing Socialist stance), though a good deal of dissension between pronuclear and antinuclear elements, Atlanticists, nationalists, and even pacifists tends to leave one with an impression of confusion rather than of a basic agreed upon policy. Moreover, the breakdown in the relations between the partners of the Common Program of Government that occurred in September 1977, a few months before the elections, further served to break apart the position of the Left regarding the question of national defense. But for the purpose at hand, this is not what is important. Rather, what counts is that in this domain nothing is finalized: if the attitude of the Left toward the nuclear force has evolved quite radically, there is no reason to not anticipate that the same might happen to its attitudes regarding the military organizational format.

Such possibility for a modification of the Left's attachment to a traditional format of military organization cannot be based only upon the observation of a changing view in other domains of national defense.

Obviously, such a likelihood also exists because of the very consequences implied by the transformation of the leftist attitude with regard to these other domains, and particularly the consequences that would be conjunctive with the adoption of a nuclearized system of defense. In effect, the correlation between the shift from a conscript to an all-volunteer force and the establishment of the nuclear paradigm of defense is hardly refutable; this is a fact that no one in the Left ignores. After all, it is not a complete coincidence that the armed forces of the two other Western members of the atomic club became all-volunteer forces. Therefore, how could the Left realistically continue to oppose a tendency that is a quasi-direct result of the existence of a nuclearized defense?

The Radical party has already crossed the Rubicon, and observing the other parties of the Left, one notes that more and more convinced leftists no longer adamantly oppose the quasi-volunteer forms of military organization as they once did, even if they continue to subscribe to the official rhetoric scorning such examples of military institutions and to praise a return to a militia-styled military. More than one member of the Socialist party now believes that the time of a compulsory universal draft is over. Charles Hernu, who once stated that his position on the draft and the volunteer force was not, on the whole, very different from that of Jacques Chirac, is one such member. In December 1976, during an interview with the weekly *Politique-Hebdo*, he revealed his views; they not only encapsulate a reconciliation with the idea of phasing out the draft, but also reveal an awareness of the ineluctable effect of voluntarization sequential to the exposure to technological change: "I think that with a modern armed force, equipped with sophisticated armament and with nuclear weapons, there is no need for a troop of five hundred thousand men. . . . We could have either a short-term active service, with reserve periods and voluntary enlistments, or voluntary enlistments only. I am among those who believe that it is necessary to have an armed force of technicians with a reduced draft."[25]

Furthermore, one could say that the reduction of the length of the military service to six months, as has been proposed by both the Socialist and the Communist parties, which, should it be institutionalized, would constitute a step toward modification of the organizational format into a quasi-volunteer system, indicates a departure from the traditional view. This is true even if many continue to think in an Engelsian fashion that "the length of service is a secondary issue . . . the main point being the realization of the principle of obligatory service for all," to quote Marx's alter ego's *Der Deutsch-*

Französische Krieg 1870/71. In effect, with a six-month service period, the number of volunteers for a long-term enlistment would have to be increased in order to occupy the positions that could no longer be manned by draftees whose level of training would not be sufficient given the reduction of the draft. Even if everyone were to be called up, the training received would be too elementary to have great relevance to the normal military activities of an increasingly technical armed force. Thus military service, under this form or under any other form—short-term or periods-based service such as various groups of the Left have proposed—would lose all military essence for it would no longer serve to procure the manpower necessary to fulfill the functions related to the institution's military role, as was the case with conscription in the context of the traditional mass armed forces model. Arming the people with pikes, clubs, and eventually rifles had some functionality in 1793 considering the level of technology at which the Revolutionary infantry operated. But this is no longer congruent with the level at which modern infantries operate. In reductio ad absurdum the kind of training that can be offered in these modern versions of radical militias is barely more elaborate than that received by the soldiers of the Revolutionary *levées en masse*. Fueled more with enthusiasm than with know-how and equipment, such training would be so much at variance with modern military activities that it would contribute to, rather than prevent, the formation of a professional volunteer force with a highly skilled manpower capable of manning a technologically advanced military organization. In sum these alternatives of military organization would continue to deepen the gap that has already opened between an army of professionals essentially oriented toward manipulating the instruments of warfare and the accomplishing of military tasks and an army of nonprofessionals functioning mainly on a nonmilitary level.

Undoubtedly, no one on the Left ignores this possibility. These alternatives to classic conscription are actually symbolic fictions of the nation in arms (which could as well be labeled nation under uniform). Perhaps these shams of citizen mobilization constitute only the price that the Left is requesting of contemporary times for putting an end to an institution with which its existence has been closely associated.

The question that still remains, before putting an end to these remarks, is when and how will a volunteer-oriented type of military organization emerge? The response, it is obvious, can only be tentative. It is clear that given the historical and cultural significance of universal compulsory military service, given its deep imprint on the

French collective mind, it will not be terminated at a moment's notice; the process of phasing out will necessarily be gradual.

First, should a change become institutionalized, it would not be before the 1980s. In effect, as the March 1978 legislative elections renewed the mandate of the so-called *majorité* in the government, it is likely that as far as the organization of the national defense, and in particular that of the military service, is concerned, all decisions taken in the military programming for 1977–82 will be carried out. Thus, one-year conscription in the format of a compulsory and universal military service will continue in operation for a while.

Second, because of the enormous cultural importance of the draft in the French psyche and because of the technical and financial difficulties that the establishment of an all-volunteer force would entail, a full-fledged termination of conscription will probably never materialize. What will probably emerge is rather a quasi-volunteer force composed of 60 to 70 percent volunteers (who amount to only 50 percent presently) and 30 to 40 percent draftees recruited through a selective system (probably a volunteer service such as the present military service for women). It is noteworthy that even the staunchest partisans of the all-volunteer force feel it necessary in the elaboration of their proposal to compromise and include a modicum of citizen participation in the military. The proposals of Alexandre Sanguinetti, Jacques Chirac, and Pierre Messmer, for example, are unambiguous in this regard. They all favor a system essentially based on voluntarism, but also suggest that military service, which should be a right for the citizen rather than a duty, as Messmer puts it, be organized for those who wish to serve (this with a system of appropriate rewards such as privileged access to positions in the civil service).[26]

Finally, in addition to the ideological and political factors, there are various, more objective, factors that will intervene and impose limitations on the process of evolution toward a full all-volunteer force. They cannot all be mentioned and discussed in detail; however, two of these factors, which appear particularly relevant, deserve to be mentioned briefly.

First, and here we come back to the basic paradigm that has served as the framework of our arguments in this study, it is without doubt that the process of modernization (the key element with respect to the modification of the institutional format) that has been undertaken in the army will be limited in scope. Given the fact that highly sophisticated systems of forces tend to become inappropriate for a number of low-key military operations and that these are precisely the type of

operations pertaining to the French conventional forces, the technological modernization of these forces will always remain relatively
self-contained. Second, despite a slight increase, which would stabilize after 1982, the defense budget will not in general be very ex-
pandable. As the French defense organization and its credibility ultimately depend on the nuclear force, the demands imposed by the
various components of this force are necessarily priority holders; this
priority operates at the expense of the demands emanating from the
systems of forces operating below the nuclear level, forces such as the
army, for example. And the demands from the nuclear force will likely
increase, maybe in the early months of 1982, as a result of its extension (the undertaking of the postponed construction of the sixth nuclear submarine, the burying of a new battery of silo SSBMs, the extension of part of Pluton TNW devices, the eventual adoption of cruise
missiles, and so on), or as the result of the refurbishing of existing
equipment including replacement of present warheads by new and
"harder" MIRV-type warheads and of the Mirage IV strategic bomber
fleet.[27]

Thus, the modernization process that the conventional forces are
presently undergoing will certainly slow down, if not stop entirely,
in the not too distant future. And, if one admits the relationship between the level of technological modernization to which an institution
is exposed and the nature of its organizational format, it can be assumed that if the process of modernization in the French armed forces
remains somewhat limited, so will the process of modifying the organizational format into an all-volunteer force.

Among these factors, there is one that seems to be particularly
relevant: this is the negative effects of the perceived semifailure of the
all-volunteer force experiences in the West, notably in Great Britain
and in the United States. The recent difficulties with which these two
military establishments have been confronted in their manpower recruitment policies constitute strong deterrents against the development of an all-volunteer force policy: French defense officials have
been quick to seize on this: "To suppress it [conscription] for fashionable reasons, or a so-called sense of history at a time when those
who have engaged themselves in this direction think to come back to
it, would be a grave error and a condemnable one."[28] The dualism,
then, that has characterized the French military establishment over the
last decade and a half, will probably persist in the future but under
less conspicuous forms. In a sense, the French military establishment
will lose its originality and become more like the quasi-volunteer military systems in other parts of Europe.

In conclusion, let us point out that in this domain, all predictions remain fragile, even those that have been based on objective factors. The *rebus sic stantibus* clause, in this context, is a theoretical state that has a very narrow validity in reality, given the complexity of the causal network and its sensitivity to imponderables or to any change occurring within its confines. There is, for example, a condition under which the scope, the extent, and the speed of the aforementioned evolution could be greatly affected—namely, if the question of the organizational format of the military institution, or, to be more precise, the abandonment of the compulsory draft, were to become an electoral stake during the next presidential election. This is not mere political fiction, as it would not be the first time that French elections have turned out to be powerful catalysts for change. Important reforms, such as those concerning the domain of birth control, were precipitated by electoral confrontations in 1974: the issue of abortion legislation was so affected. This phenomenon, due, among other things, to the fact that today elections tend to be won with smaller majorities, made up of fleeting votes that, because of a lack of ideological or partisan identification, have to be attracted on specific grounds, could be repeated in 1981. One could thus realistically imagine that in order to attract, for instance, the young votes (a key group in the electorate as the voting age was lowered to eighteen), a conservative presidential candidate might make the abandonment of the draft part of a campaign program; an important part of the young electorate would probably approve of such a stand because, according to opinion polls, opposition to the draft tends to increase proportionally as age decreases. And as opposition to the draft does not vary greatly across political affiliations, it might even be said that, to a great extent, even the young who are sensitive to the leftist appeal might be detracted from their ideological preferences.

Notes

1. *Défense nationale* 32 (June 1976): 11–34.

2. Service d'Information et des Relations publiques des Armées (SIRPA). "Les Armées françaises de demain," *Dossier d'information* 49 (October 1976): 16.

3. For additional details, *see* Appendix A.

4. "Loi no. 76-531 du juin 1976 portant approbation de la programmation militaire pour les années 1977–1982," *Journal officiel, lois et décrets*, 20 June 1976, pp. 3699–707.

5. Equipment (or capital) allocations for the period considered were distributed between the services as follows:

Nuclear armament	27.5%
Ground forces	25.0%
Air force	24.0%
Navy	16.0%
Common services	5.0%
Gendarmerie	2.0%

6. "Que vaut l'armée française?" *L'Express*, 21–27 November 1977, p. 100.

7. This refers to the classic treatment of the evolution of the notion of citizenship in the West, by T. H. Marshall, *Citizenship and Social Class* (Cambridge, Mass.: University Press, 1950). *See also* Introduction and Chapter 5.

8. "Conscription et démographie," *Armées d'aujourd'hui* 8 (March 1976): 24.

9. Assemblée nationale, 8 November 1976.

10. Alain Bloch, "Le Service national: un tabou," *Le Monde*, 26 January 1978.

11. The private's daily salary (*le prêt du soldat*) rose to 8.5 F., that of a corporal to 9.5 F., that of a corporal-chief to 10.5 F., that of a sergeant to 12 F., and that of an aspirant to 18 F., *see Journal officiel*, 23 February 1978.

12. *Avis présenté au nom de la Commission de Défense nationale et des forces armées sur le projet de loi de finance pour 1975*, Doc. Assemblée nationale, no. 1233 (1st session ordinaire, 1974–75), pp. 49–50.

13. Beside this question, these interventions and, in particular, the Lebanese operation threw a crude light on the chinks in the conventional French armor and brought forth the proof of some of the inadequacies in France's conventional armament. (In an interview given on 8 June 1978 to radio network Europe I, French Armed Forces Chief of Staff General Méry admitted the weakness of the French capacity for faraway intervention, the lack of reserve cadres, and the inappropriateness of individual weaponry.) Though tangential, this remark is not without relevance, particularly in respect to our comments on the reorganization of the French army. It is indubitable that this situation will help to reinforce the process of modernization of the army. Moreover, the effect of the modernization of the army's active forces, which tend because of their increasing technological sophistication to be manned by professional soldiers, combined with the effects of the doctrine of utilization of these forces, which, as evidenced by the events of the first half of 1978, entrust the professional soldiers with the most combat-oriented activities, tend to breach a deep gap between what could be an army of professionals in charge of all military activities and an army of nonprofessionals, mostly draftees, involved in nonmilitary tasks, such as all interventions of a public interest nature (struggle against pollution, for example). On this point *see* Jacques Isnard, "Janus ou les deux visages de l'armée," *Le Monde*, 12 May 1978, p. 12.

14. Pierre Messmer, *Proposition de loi portant modification du code du Service national pour ce qui concerne le service militaire*, Doc. Assemblée nationale, no. 3186 (1st session ordinaire, 1977–78); Rassemblement pour la République, *Une Politique de défense pour la France, 1978–1990* (Paris, 1977).

15. *L'Autre Défense* (Chaumont: France-Editions, 1977).

16. This conception of the use of military forces has not yet disappeared. During a recent meeting organized by Information of the Soldier's Rights (IDS), leftist sympathizer Admiral Sanguinetti declared that the reorganization of the army undertaken in 1975 had actually been planned in order to face an eventual crisis in March 1978; see Le Monde, 2 March 1978.

17. La Dépêche du Midi, 31 December 1976.

18. Changer de cap (Paris: Editions sociales, 1971), p. 220.

19. Programme commun de gouvernement du Parti Communiste français et du Parti Socialiste: 27 juin 1972 (Paris: Editions Sociales, 1972), p. 171.

20. Le Figaro, 1 January 1978.

21. Le Monde, 13 May 1977, p. 13.

22. Ibid.

23. Actually, the position of the Socialist party in this domain was not as clearcut as that of the Communist party. During the last Socialist convention, January 1978, the authority of François Mitterand, a partisan of the nuclear force, was needed to impose some coherence on an extraordinarily complex imbroglio of ideas and tendencies. Reading the various Socialist proposals, one gets the impression that, to quote one defense expert, "the Socialists want it [the nuclear force] and at the same time deny it." On this point see Le Monde, 8 and 9 January 1978.

24. Michel L. Martin, "Conscription and the Decline of the Mass Army in France," Armed Forces and Society 3 (1977): 396.

25. La Dépêche du Midi, 31 December 1976.

26. Pierre Messmer and Jean-Pierre Chevènement, Le Service militaire (Paris: Ballard, 1977).

27. See President Giscard d'Estaing's declaration to the NBC network about the preparation of a long-term plan for the nuclear armament of France. This question was also the object of discussions at the Defense Council at the end of 1977.

28. SIRPA, "Les Armées françaises de demain," p. 29.

APPENDIX A

The Organization, Equipment, and Deployment of the French Armed Forces

For a description of the organization and equipment of the French armed forces, we shall simply follow the pattern of presentation by "systems of forces" (referred to as "major programs" before 1977) utilized in all official documents, especially in the new budgetary presentation. There are nine levels:

1. Strategic nuclear force
2. Tactical nuclear armament
3. Conventional forces
4. Overseas forces
5. Research and development
6. Formation and training
7. Personnel maintenance
8. Equipment maintenance
9. General administration

We shall focus essentially on the first four systems as they are the ones involved in the performance of military missions.

We shall also briefly examine how these various forces fit into the composition and structure of the French defense deployment.

Organization and Equipment

A. Strategic Nuclear Force (FNS)

    1. Strategic Air Force (FAS)

        a. Two squadrons of 58 Mirage IV A (actually, only 48 are available and only 36 operational). The Mirage IV A, equipped with atomic bombs of 50 or 75 kilotons, are based at six airfields (Cazaux, Mont-de-Marsan, Orange, Avord, Saint-Dizier, and Luxeuil); 18 are ready to take off on thirty minutes notice. The flight range of the Mirage is 3,000 kilometers at mach 2.2 with in-flight refueling. There are 11 flying tankers (KC 135 C).

        b. Two units of 9×2 intermediate range SSBM, silo-buried on the Albion Height. They have a range of 3,000 kilometers and are armed with S2-type warheads (150 kilotons). In the next five years, thermo-nuclear S3 warheads will replace the S2s.

2. Oceanic Strategic Force (FOST)

Based at l'Ile Longue, near Brest, the FOST is composed of five nuclear submarines, each equipped with 16 missiles. Four of the submarines are operational at present, the *Redoutable, Terrible, Foudroyant* and *Indomptable*. The *Tonnant*, launched in 1975, should be operational by 1979. The *Terrible, Redoutable,* and *Foudroyant,* armed with M1 or M2 missiles (2,500 to 3,000 kilometer range, 450 kilotons power), have been, since 1976–77, equipped with M20 missiles (4,000 kilometer range). The *Indomptable* will also be armed in this way in the near future. A program of renewal of equipment should be undertaken soon to place new M3 and M4 missiles with "hard" and multiple reentry warheads on board.

3. In 1977, 17,670 military (5,719 draftees) and 213 civilians served in the FNS. The budget amounted to 1,595 million francs for ordinary expenditures, and 7,306 million francs for capital (or equipment) expenditures.

B. Tactical Nuclear Armament (ANT) [1]

1. Tactical Air Force (FATAC)

The FATAC is composed of two squadrons of Jaguar A/E fighter-bombers and two squadrons of Mirage III E with AN 52 bombs (25 kilotons).

2. Naval Forces

The navy provides aircraft carriers with Jaguar and Super-Etendard fighters.

3. Ground Forces

The army TNW is the Pluton armed with MR50 warheads of 10 or 25 kilotons capacity. The 3rd regiment of artillery (of Mailly) received the first two Pluton units in 1974; the other units became operational in 1975 and 1976. In 1977 there were four Pluton regiments.

4. In 1977, 6,117 men (4,485 draftees) served under these systems; the budget amounted to 782 million francs (165 million francs for ordinary expenditures and 617 million francs for capital expenditures).

C. Conventional Forces

1. Ground Forces
   a. Large Units and General Reserves

   These are made up of (1) The First Army, composed of two army corps: the 1st Corps is stationed in France (the 4th Division in

Nancy, the 6th Division in Strasbourg, the 7th Division in Besançon, and the 10th Division in Chalons-sur-Marne); the 2nd Corps is based in Germany (the 1st Division in Trier, the 3rd Division in Freiburg, and the 5th Division in Landau); and (2) five other divisions, two of infantry (the 14th and the 15th, based in Lyon and Limoges), one of marines (the 9th, in Saint-Malo), one of paratroopers (the 11th, in Pau) and one alpine (the 27th, in Grenoble). The divisions of the First Army follow the 67 model; each has approximately 15,000 men divided into three brigades (two motorized, one mechanized). Each brigade is made up of four regiments (one motorized, two mechanized, one artillery).

b. The territorial commands and "non-divisioned" combat and support units.

c. Total effectives reached 417,394 (with 175,112 draftees) military and 9,147 civilian personnel. The budget amounted to 6,903 million francs for ordinary expenditures and 3,835 million francs for capital (equipment) expenditures.

d. In 1977 equipment for the ground forces included:
  961 AMX-30 tanks, with 97 AMX-30 repair tanks
  105 self-propelled 155 millimeter howitzers with high firing frequency
  5 Roland SAM systems
  433 Milan systems (antitank guided weapons)
  400 AMX-10 P and PC tanks
  80 front-armored vehicles
  258 Puma SA 330 and Gazelle SA 341 helicopters

2. Air Force

a. Tactical Air Force (FATAC)

The FATAC had seven squadrons of Jaguar, Mirage III E, R, RD and V, and a few F-100s. Four squadrons have a nuclear capability; this is used for support, attack and reconnaissance.

b. Air Defense Command (CAFDA)

The CAFDA is used to protect French territory against enemy attacks and to protect French nuclear sites. There are two centers of operation with sophisticated detection and control devices for high and middle altitudes. The CAFDA is equipped with four squadrons of Mirage F1 and IIIC interceptors.

c. Air Transport Command (COTAM)

The COTAM has five squadrons of DC 8, Noratlas 2501, Transall 160 aircraft and helicopters.

d. Training Command (CEAA)

e. In 1977, effectives numbered 53,491 (22,108 draftees) military and 1,763 civilian personnel. The budget was 3,422 million francs for ordinary expenditures and 3,236 million francs for capital expenditures.

f. In 1977 Air Force equipment included:

FATAC
    90 Mirage IIIE ⎫
    30 Mirage VF   ⎬ fighter-bombers
    10 F-100D
   105 Jaguar A/E ⎭
    16 Vautour IIB/N   light bombers (to be withdrawn)
    58 Mirage IIIR/RD   reconnaissance
    30 Mirage IIIB/BE/C ⎫
    15 Jaguar A/E   ⎬ operational conversion units

CAFDA
    75 Mirage F1   ⎫
    20 Mirage IIIC   ⎬ interceptors
    15 Super Mystère B2 ⎭
      Crotale and STRIDA II air defense system

COTAM
     5 DC-8F   ⎫
   37 Tansall C-160
   70 Noratlas 2501   ⎬ transport
   18 Frégate
    8 Mystère 10/20
    1 Caravelle   ⎭

COTAM
   24 Paris   ⎫
   12 Broussard ⎬ liaison
    1 Rallye   ⎭

CEAA
   700 Magister, T-33, Mystère IV, Flamant, Noratlas

3. Maritime Forces

a. The maritime forces participate in the surveillance of the coasts, in the defense of continental territory, in the security of naval traffic, and in the defense of the nation's interests overseas and on the seas. They are divided into two subsystems. The multi-purpose maritime forces with two centers of operation (Brest and Toulon) are deployed on seven bases; they operate in the eastern Atlantic Ocean, the Mediterranean Sea, and the western Indian Ocean. The forces of

Defense and Public Service serve to protect harbors, to patrol the seas, and to assist the merchant and the fishing fleets.

b. The marine forces are made up of 33,922 (9,004 draftees) military and 1,285 civilian personnel. In 1977 the budget was 3,025 million francs for the ordinary expenditures and 2,882 million francs for capital expenditures.

c. In 1977 major equipment of the maritime forces included:

Multipurpose Maritime Forces
3 light attack aircraft carriers
40 surface ships of over 1,200 tons: 20 destroyers (two with Masurca SAM and Malafon, four with Tartar SAM, five for general purpose) and two cruisers (with Exocet, Masurca and antisubmarine helicopters)
18 frigates and mine destroyer ships
21 attack submarines
75,000 tons for logistic ships

127 embarked combat aircraft (24 Etendard IVM, 20 Crusader, 24 Alizé, 30 Atlantic, 10 SP-2H Neptune, 8 Etendard IVP)
40 assault helicopters, (14 Super-Frelon, 12 Alouette III/II, 24 HSS-1)
30 communication aircraft (DC-6, C-47, HSS-1, Alouette, Super-Frelon)
20 search and rescue helicopters (Alouette II/III)
3 training squadrons of Nord 262, C-47, Fouga CM-175, Etendard, Alizé, Rallye

Forces of Defense and Public Service
54 surface ships (of under 1,200 tons) with mine destroyer ships, and fast patrol boats
13,000 tons for logistic ships

4. Gendarmerie

The gendarmerie insures the protection of individuals and the collective safety of the nation. It is dispersed throughout the territory and composed of multipurpose units, many highly specialized. The gendarmerie is organized into:

a. Territorial Gendarmerie (38,897 gendarmes, with 2,224 draftees) with 3,600 territorial brigades (300 specialized brigades, 21 detachments of intervention and 21 mountain units).

b. Mobile Gendarmerie (16,309 men, no draftees) with 130 squadrons.

c. Traffic Police (6,960 gendarmes, with 547 draftees) with 93 motorized squadrons, and 58 highway patrols.

d. Republican Guard (4,009 men).

e. Air Traffic Gendarmerie (of the French forces in Germany and of the armament).

In 1977 the gendarmerie equipment included:

> 33 land vehicles
> 121 AML
> 133 armored vehicles on wheels
> 37 tanks
> 9 helicopters Alouette II
> 6 helicopters Alouette III
> 6 light aircraft

5. Overseas Forces

Missions of the overseas forces include safeguarding the security and integrity of overseas departments and territories, participating in assisting (technically or militarily) friendly nations, and guaranteeing French influence and the safety of French citizens overseas.

The overseas forces are deployed into six interservice commands: Antilles-Guyanne, Cap Vert (West Africa), Djibouti, South Indian Ocean, New Caledonia, and Polynesia. In addition there are two independent commands, Port Bouet (Ivory Coast) and Libreville (Gabon). (See Fig. A.1.)

There are a total of 16,933 men (2,828 draftees).

The equipment includes:

Army
> 130 light armored vehicles
> 11 helicopters
> 15 Milan SAM

Air Force
> 12 combat aircraft
> 16 transport aircraft
> 18 helicopters

Navy
> 13 fast patrol boats, frigates, and light transport ships

Gendarmerie
> 32 light armored vehicles
> 7 helicopters

Figure A.1. French Military Overseas Deployment

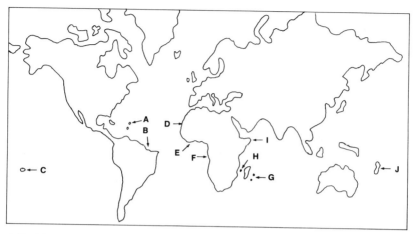

A *Martinique and Guadeloupe*	**E** *Ivory Coast*	**J** *New Caledonia*
33rd RIMa	4th BIMa	Pacific RIMa
SMA regt.	**F** *Gabon*	7th BCS
2 comps. BCS	6th BIMa	
B *Guyane*	**G** *Reunion*	
3rd REI	2nd RIMa	
9th BIMa	15th BCS	
SMA regt.	SMA regt.	
C *Polynesia*	MPE	
BIMa Tahiti	**H** *Mayotte*	
5th mixed Pacific regiment	Foreign Legion	
502nd BCS	**I** *Djibouti*	
815 GTT	13th DBLE	
D *Senegal*	5th RIAOM	
10th BIMa	6th RAMa	
	6th BCS	
	ALAT	

ALAT	Army Aviation
BIMa	Marines Infantry Battalion
BCS	Command and Support Battalion
DBLE	Foreign Legion Armored Division
GTT	Transit Group of Tahiti
MPE	Military Preparatory School
RAMa	Marines Artillery Regiment
REI	Foreign Infantry Regiment
RIAOM	Interarms Overseas Regiment
RIMa	Marines Infantry Regiment
SMA	Adapted Military Service

D. Other Systems of Forces
  1. Research and Development
  With laboratories, research centers and test fields

Effectives	Budget	
military: 6,611 (2,313 draftees)	ordinary expenditures:	1,072 million francs
civilian: 7,622	capital expenditures:	1,479 million francs

  2. Organisms of Formation and Training
  This category includes the military academies of the three services, the school of the gendarmerie, the medical schools, interservices higher education, the Polytechnique school, the school of the armament, and military preparatory schools.

Effectives	Budget	
military: 83,281 (37,247 draftees)	ordinary expenditures:	3,674 million francs
civilian:　5,367	capital expenditures:	2,838 million francs

Equipment includes:

Army
  100 heavy tanks AMX-30
  11 AMX-30 tow tanks
  20 front-armored vehicles
  26 Milan
  13 SA-30 helicopters
  42 light tanks AMX-10 P and PC

Air Force
  198 Fouga Magister
  83 T-33
  42 Mystére IV
  12 Nord 2501
  45 Flamant

  3. Personnel Maintenance
  This includes the supply, commissariat, health and medical service, social security, recruitment, and personnel perquisites.

Effectives	Budget	
military: 32,593 (10,132 draftees)	ordinary expenditures:	3,697 million francs
civilian: 19,926	capital expenditures:	302 million francs

4. Equipment Maintenance

Effectives	Budget	
military: 19,703 (7,157 draftees)	ordinary expenditures:	2,296 million francs
civilian: 19,225	capital expenditures:	1,315 million francs

5. General Administration

Effectives	Budget	
military: 17,430 (4,621 draftees)	ordinary expenditures:	2,367 million francs
civilian: 13,375	capital expenditures:	313 million francs

Defense Deployment of the French Armed Forces

With regard to the principles established by the French national defense policy, the French armed forces have been invested with a fourfold military mission. They are required to have the capacity of massive nuclear retaliation, to defend the national territory, intervene outside the nation's borders in Europe, and to intervene in other parts of the world.

Four systems of forces have been established to execute these various missions: the Strategic Nuclear Force (already discussed), the Forces of Security, the Forces of Maneuver, and the Forces of "Presence" and Intervention.

A. Forces of Security

It is the role of the Forces of Security to protect strategic devices and other vital installations from enemy penetration and to pursue the struggle in case of defeat after the first battles. Ground defense devolves upon the army, which furnishes the Forces of the Territory (formerly the DOT) composed of two alpine brigades, twenty infantry regiments, three light cavalry regiments, and one artillery regiment. This makes up a total of about 26,000 men plus 6,000 men from the Foreign Legion. In case of conflict, these units are to be reinforced by the mobilization of reserves.

Airspace defense is mainly the role of the air force, although the navy, with its detection system, also participates in this. The role of the air force is to detect as soon as possible the enemy activities and to intercept and destroy them. To achieve this Mirage III and F-1 interceptors, as well as a surface-to-air Crotale system are employed. The navy's role is to protect the nuclear submarine installations and infrastructure. The gendarmerie plays an important role as a security force. In case of crisis, the gendarmerie is to organize the mobilization, to intervene against parachuted enemy personnel, and to stay in close contact with the populace.

B. Forces of Maneuver

The main role of the Forces of Maneuver is to contain any enemy that might attack France or one of her allies. The Forces of Maneuver are composed of the First Army (140,000 men), the FATAC, the Pluton regiments (see above), and various units of the navy and the naval air force.

The army is the main element of the Forces of Maneuver. The composition of the First Army, as it was before the reorganization, follows:

Headquarters: Strasbourg
Forces of Maneuver in Germany: 2nd Army Corps, headquarters: Baden-Oos

1st Division (Trier)
1st Mechanized Brigade (Sarrebourg)
3rd Mechanized Brigade (Wittlich)
11th Motorized Brigade (Landau)
3rd Division (Freiburg)
5th Mechanized Brigade (Tübingen)
12th Mechanized Brigade (Offenburg)
13th Motorized Brigade (Konstanz)

Forces in Berlin

Forces of Maneuver in France: 1st Army Corps, headquarters: Nancy

14th Division (Verdun)
10th Mechanized Brigade (Reims)
15th Mechanized Brigade (Verdun)
16th Mechanized Brigade (Metz)
7th Division (Mulhouse)
6th Mechanized Brigade (Strasbourg)
8th Motorized Brigade (Luneville)
8th Division (Compiègne)
2nd Mechanized Brigade (Saint-Germain)
4th Motorized Brigade (Beauvais)
14th Mechanized Brigade (Laon)

C. Forces of "Presence" and Intervention

These forces defend France's strategic position and her communications; they also contribute to the security of the nations linked to France by treaties. In addition to the units permanently assigned overseas, the Forces of Intervention are essentially made up of elements from the army. The air force and the navy provide transportation and, if needed, support fire. The Forces of Intervention are composed of the two paratroop brigades from the 11th Paratroops Division (Pau), the 20th Brigade (Toulouse), and the 25th Brigade (Pau). Until very recently, the 9th Marines Brigade (Saint-Malo) was integrated with the Forces of Intervention.

The Reorganization of the French Ground Forces

In 1976 the principles for the reorganization of the army were decided upon. Reorganization was to be spread over a period of six years and was to be completed in the early 1980s. This reorganization seeks to achieve six objectives. It is hoped that it will give the French ground forces greater diversity, greater mobility, better homogeneity in command structure, alleviation of most overhead charges, and better geographical deployment.[2]

According to plan, the size of the army will be reduced to 310,000 men between 1976 and 1982; in 1977 there were 330,000 men. The active forces, rather than being made up of five divisions with three brigades each and several territorial defense units, is to be composed of sixteen divisions (eight armored divisions, six infantry divisions, one division of paratroopers, and one alpine division), one logistic brigade (regrouping of the health, equipment, and supply services that were formerly spread throughout the division), and a number of organic units (heavy artillery, combat helicopters, TNW regiments, etc.).

The internal organization of the active forces is to follow the outline below:

Armored division
2 mechanized regiments
2 tank regiments (with AMX 30/10 and front-armored vehicles)
1 or 2 artillery regiments (with SAM and 155 millimeter self-propelled guns)
1 scouting company
1 antitank company
1 engineering regiment
1 command and support regiment

Infantry division
3 motorized infantry regiments
1 regiment of light armored vehicles
1 artillery regiment
1 engineering company
1 command and support regiment

Alpine division
6 alpine battalions
1 regiment of light armored vehicles
1 artillery regiment
1 command and support regiment
1 engineering company

Division of paratroopers
6 regiments of paratroopers
1 regiment of light armored vehicles
1 artillery regiment
1 engineering company
command and support units

"Organic" units
2 or 3 regiments of TNW (Pluton)
1 regiment of motorized infantry
2 reconnaissance regiments
2 regiments of surface-to-surface artillery
4 regiments of surface-to-air artillery
2 engineering regiments
2 army light air force (ALAT) regiments
1 *acquisition d'objectif* regiment
command and support units

Figure A.2. Territorial Military Organization of France

Note: The number of military regions has varied over time. In 1873, there were eighteen regions. In 1934, there were sixteen; in 1946, nine; in 1966, seven; and in 1976, when the Fifth and Seventh regions were consolidated, six.

These active forces are to be regrouped in army corps or deployed autonomously. There will be three army corps. The 1st Army Corps (Headquarters Metz) will be composed of four armored divisions (the 4th, 6th, 7th, and 10th) in the territory of the Sixth Military Region; the 2nd Army Corps (Headquarters Baden-Baden) will be made up of three armored divisions (the 1st, 3rd, and 5th) in Germany. The 3rd Army Corps, to be created in 1979, will be composed of four divisions (the 2nd and 8th armored divisions and the 12th and 16th infantry divisions) in the area of the First and Second Military Regions. In addition to the three army corps, the 9th Division of Marines (Saint-Malo) in the Third Military Region, the 15th Infantry Division (Limoges) in the Fourth Military Region, the 11th Division of Paratroopers (Pau) in the Fifth Military Region, and the 14th and the 27th divisions (Lyon and Grenoble) in the Fifth Military Region are to be organized into independent units. The geographic deployment of these forces is illustrated in Figure A.3.

The classic distinction between the Forces of Maneuver and the territorial units (DOT) is to be abandoned. The division that will become the basic unit of the ground forces is a newly designed division model (type 77), smaller in size (8,200 men in an armored division and 6,500 in an infantry division), more powerful, and endowed with greater autonomy than the old model. As for the army corps, they are to be the leading group when the division enters an engagement. The classic intermediary command echelons between the divisional level and the army corps are to be eliminated. The army corps will be responsible for the employment of tactical nuclear fire, air and ground maneuvers, and logistical support.

The modernization of the active forces will progress noticeably with the mechanization of the infantry regiments; their being equipped with Milan system and other antitank devices is part of the program. Armored regiments are to be equipped with AMX-30 tanks; the transformation of the classic artillery regiment into a tactical nuclear regiment armed with the Pluton, the construction of new stations for landing assistance for combat helicopters (Spartiate system), a new generation of communication systems, and a new command organization (Rita system) are all integral parts of the program.[3]

In addition to the reorganization of the active forces, the reform will also deal with the reserve forces. During the second half of 1978 a new program concerning the reserves and mobilization principles was undertaken. Prior to that, in September 1976, the inspection of reserve personnel, now the inspection of reserve and mobilization, was reformed. Reserve advisors (reserve officers in active service)

Figure A.3. Deployment of the Reorganized Ground Forces

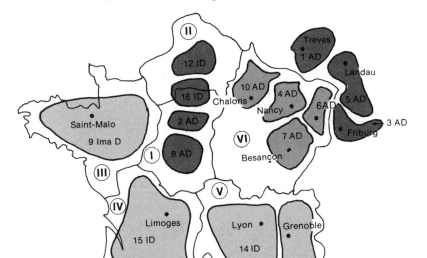

Reorganized in 1976

Reorganized in 1977

Reorganized in 1978

Military region

ID	Infantry Division
AD	Armored Division
ImaD	Marines Division
PD	Airborne Division
AlpD	Alpine Division

have been named to advise the military authorities in this particular area. A key principle in the reorganization of the reserve forces is the duplicating of the existing active units. Each division and each regiment forms and trains a new division or regiment—command structure, personnel, and equipment. The combat training of these units is to take place during field maneuvers. Thus, ten reserve divisions have been or will be derived from existing forces; to these divisions four more, made up of personnel from the military schools, could be added in case of war. In time of conflict, the fully mobilized army would thus consist of thirty divisions.

Notes

1. To have a complete account of the forces operating at the tactical nuclear level, one should add the forces currently being integrated with the conventional forces.

2. *See* Lagarde, "La Réorganisation de l'Armée de Terre," *Terre-Information*, June 1975.

3. For futher details about this reorganization, *see Terre-Information*.

APPENDIX B
The National Defense Budget

It should be pointed out that there is some degree of discrepancy between the figures presented in Tables B.1 and B.2 on the one hand and in B.3 on the other. These discrepancies are the inevitable result of the plurality of sources used; it was not possible to find one source that covered the entire period under consideration. Though the sources used had a common governmental origin, the figures varied from one subagency to another, mostly because of differences in techniques of computation and methods of presentation. Within each table, however, we have sought to arrange the data so as to maintain a diachronic as well as synchronic statistical consistency; thus the relative values that can be derived from these figures remain valid.

Table B.1. National Income Accounts and Military Expenditures, 1946–76

| | | | | Military Expenditures[c] | |
Year	GNP[a]	National Income	Public Expenditures[c]	Army, Navy Air Force	Overseas Military
1946	—	315	521.2	142.7	8.3
1947	—	341	689.5	181.9	21.1
1948	—	366	992.2	252.4	30.7
1949	206.9	414	1,204.8	273.5	39.3
1950	221.9	448	2,356.8	310.6	105.5
1951	234.7	477	2,913.8	509.7	297.7
1952	242.8	490	3,656.4	849.8	406.2
1953	249.0	505	3,801.1	918.7	371.0
1954	259.4	531	3,702.4	907.6	289.9
1955	271.6	564	3,945.1	946.4	138.6
1956	287.8	593	4,647.7	1,311.5	83.0
1957	304.8	629	5,640.3	1,399.9	66.7
1958	313.5	636	5,490.4	1,394.7	84.2
1959[b]	323.1	648	5,946.3	1,540.7	91.9
1960	346.1	680	60.0	15.8	0.9
1961	364.7	—	66.5	16.9	1.0
1962	367.2	—	76.9	17.6	0.9
1963	412.0	—	90.8	17.8	0.8
1964	439.2	—	90.6	19.2	—
1965	459.8	—	98.2	19.5	—
1966	485.5	—	106.5	20.5	—
1967	509.7	—	122.0	21.9	—
1968	535.0	—	133.6	24.3	—

1970	610.9	—	162.2	—	28.7
1971	644.2	—	175.6	—	31.4
1972	679.0	—	194.0	—	33.7
1973	—	—	220.0	—	36.3
1974	—	—	—	—	—
1975	—	—	—	—	—
1976	—	—	—	—	—

Sources: For GNP, INSEE, *Annuaire statistique de la France, 1975* (Paris, 1975), p. 595. For national income, Alfred Sauvy, "Rapport sur le revenu national présenté au nom du Conseil économique le 23 mars 1954," *Journal officiel, avis et rapport du Conseil économique* (7 April 1954); Colin Clark, *The Conditions of Economic Progress* (New York: St. Martin Press, 1957); INSEE, *Annuaire statistique de la France, 1961: résumé rétrospectif* (Paris, 1961). For public and military expenditures prior to 1964, INSEE, *Annuaire statistique de la France, 1966: résumé rétrospectif* (Paris, 1966), pp. 492–93; for later data, "Finances de l'Etat," in the *Annuaire statistique de la France* (Paris, published annually).

[a] The value of the GNP is expressed in billions of francs at the 1963 market price. The table below gives another estimate of the GNP at 1970 market price for 1959–73.

1959	434.7	1964	588.3	1969	763.9
1960	464.9	1965	614.5	1970	808.4
1961	490.9	1966	648.8	1971	851.1
1962	524.0	1967	680.5	1972	899.4
1963	552.5	1968	711.8	1973	953.6

For the last few years, the GNP as a measure of the nation's wealth has been replaced by gross internal product (P.I.B.).

[b] Until 1959 the figures are in billions of old francs; from 1960 on they are in billions of new francs. In 1958 an important monetary reform took place in France. At that time the French government adopted the Pinay-Rueff reform, devaluing the franc by 17.55 percent and creating a new currency. The new franc amounted to 100 former francs; one new franc was equal to 18 milligrams of gold or 20.3 U.S. cents.

[c] The data concerning public and military expenditures came from the Direction de la comptabilité publique. Although these figures are slightly different from those that were entered in the budget, they have been used here because they are statistically coherent with all data relative to the other items in this table; they are all part of the INSEE statistical series.

Table B.2. Defense Budget by Service, 1946–77

Year	Common Services	Army	Navy	Air Force	Overseas	Total
1946[a]	52.8	65.8	12.2	11.9	8.3	151.0
1947	15.5	86.9	36.6	42.8	21.1	203.5
1948	41.0	106.4	50.0	55.0	30.7	283.1
1949	42.7	113.6	56.7	60.5	39.3	312.8
1950	51.5	116.0	64.2	78.9	105.5	416.1
1951	69.5	193.1	100.0	147.1	297.7	807.4
1952	97.8	318.0	149.8	284.2	406.2	1,256.0
1953	91.3	353.3	167.7	306.4	371.0	1,289.7
1954	119.9	328.8	178.4	280.5	289.9	1,197.5
1955	111.4	377.2	172.8	285.0	138.6	1,085.0
1956	129.6	605.8	189.3	386.8	83.0	1,394.5
1957	146.2	640.2	200.7	412.8	66.7	1,466.6
1958	170.9	638.9	194.4	390.5	84.2	1,478.9
1959	202.4	697.8	218.1	422.4	91.9	1,632.0
1960[b]	2,150	7,106	2,224	4,317	923	16,720
1961	2,184	7,576	2,403	4,728	956	17,847
1962	2,661	7,384	2,601	4,934	930	18,510
1963	3,203	6,650	2,667	5,295	795	18,610
1964	3,873	6,631	2,638	6,044	—	19,186
1965	4,346	6,225	2,788	6,177		19,536
1966	4,731	6,418	3,623	5,702		20,474
1967	4,951	6,718	4,060	6,200		21,929
1968	5,582	7,302	5,038	6,372		24,294

				23,910
1970	7,828	8,378	5,165	7,296	28,667
1971	8,511	9,068	5,441	8,369	31,389
1972	10,935	8,652	5,685	8,444	33,716
1973	11,663	9,875	5,695	9,040	36,273
1974	13,491	10,272	6,424	8,033	38,221
1975	16,098	11,690	7,107	8,891	43,786
1976	18,244	13,761	7,936	10,055	50,000
1977	21,267	15,863	9,693	11,589	58,412

Sources: For 1946–65, the figures are those of the Direction de la comptabilité publique, in INSEE, *Annuaire statistique de la France, 1966: résumé rétrospectif*, pp. 492–93, and the annual volumes of the *Annuaire statistique* afterward. For 1965–77, see also "Budget voté—dépenses des services militaires." In *Projet de loi de finance* (Paris: Imprimerie nationale, published annually).

[a] 1946–59 in billions of francs (old currency).

[b] 1960–76 in millions of francs (new currency; see note b on Table B.1).

Table B.3. Defense Budget by Service and Type of Expenditure, 1948–77

	Common Services			Army			Air Force	
Year	Personnel[c]	Operation[c]	Equipment[c]	Personnel[c]	Operation[c]	Equipment[c]	Personnel[c]	Operation
1948[a]	35.2	2.7	1.3	26.2	49.1	10.8	8.7	18.9
1949	39.4	11.8	2.1	51.4	51.5	12.7	18.3	23.3
1950	14.2	5.4	2.7	47.3	47.6	16.6	19.1	19.2
1951	17.3	9.3	6.0	61.0	75.3	84.0	25.3	32.4
1952	13.7	20.1	14.7	131.7	45.9	127.7	62.3	30.7
1953	17.8	16.0	13.3	136.1	42.4	134.9	65.2	34.6
1954	17.8	12.8	37.1	139.5	40.00	100.2	73.7	37.3
1955	n.a.	n.a.	n.a.	n.a.	n.a.	n.a.	n.a.	n.a.
1956	n.a.	n.a.	n.a.	n.a.	n.a.	n.a.	n.a.	n.a.
1957	54.3	32.4	20.7	171.0	48.3	88.6	77.2	42.1
1958	184.8	35.0	54.2	305.0	87.9	150.3	94.6	44.2
1959	33.7	36.8	76.4	330.9	102.7	193.1	115.4	60.8
1960[b]	392.3	364.7	873.1	3,602.8	1,336.9	1,823.7	1,214.6	613.0
1961	407.5	373.9	1,227.1	3,737.4	1,400.4	1,765.0	1,287.3	637.8
1962	535.6	489.3	1,985.3	3,841.5	1,440.6	1,728.1	1,970.8	49.3
1963	479.1	512.8	1,967.9	3,102.2	1,351.5	1,893.2	1,402.5	649.2
1964	913.0	554.1	3,768.6	3,345.1	1,073.0	1,732.5	1,444.3	625.4
1965	589.8	550.6	4,559.6	3,131.5	1,003.9	1,701.0	1,471.8	684.2
1966	482.7	582.8	4,912.0	3,189.7	933.3	1,755.4	1,546.6	703.5
1967	1,990.6	846.2	1,616.9	3,302.9	992.8	1,719.4	1,613.8	762.5
1968	743.8	789.3	5,375.1	3,419.7	1,034.4	2,120.7	2,014.9	830.3
1969	1,021.5	776.0	4,519.3	3,829.7	1,030.5	2,589.9	1,689.7	807.
1970	1,361.1	898.2	4,200.0	3,956.1	1,075.1	2,839.3	1,750.7	880.
1971	1,331.6	991.5	4,394.1	4,415.7	1,113.6	2,774.3	1,960.5	937.
1972	2,779.2	1,097.1	4,333.0	3,769.6	1,178.3	3,053.0	1,941.1	1,032.
1973	2,923.9	1,158.8	5,092.9	4,204.4	1,314.9	3,683.7	2,140.9	1,195.
1974	3,329.3	1,097.1	5,582.0	3,802.0	2,409.6	4,060.0	2,094.9	1,603.
1975	4,778.1	1,303.7	6,027.0	4,425.9	2,813.5	4,451.0	2,418.9	1,960.
1976	6,797.0		6,708.0	8,852.0		4,909.0	5,063.0	
1977	7,799.3		7,773.6	10,437.7		5,425.1	6,015.2	

Source: "Budget voté—dépenses des services militaires." In *Projet de loi de finance* (Paris: Imprimerie nationale, published annually).

[a] 1958–59 in billions of francs.
[b] 1960–76 in millions of francs.

[c] Personnel and operation spendings group all ordinary expenditures of Title III (and Title IV when it existed). Equipment expenditures group the capital expenditures of Title V. The trichotomization between these expenditures has been established as follows:

Title III:
personnel: salaries
maintenance of personnel } Personnel
social assistance of personnel
equipment and operation of services
maintenance
subvention for operation } Operation
other expenses
Title IV:
assistance to families of military personnel deceased } Personnel
during wars and to war or resistance prisoners

Equipment[c]		Navy			Gendarmerie		
		Personnel[c]	Operation[c]	Equipment[c]	Personnel[c]	Operation[c]	Equipment[c]
24.5	1948[a]	9.2	21.9	12.6	4.1	2.1	0.2
30.0	1949	16.5	25.3	16.8	10.6	2.5	0.6
37.6	1950	17.5	24.6	15.1	10.5	2.3	2.5
73.8	1951	25.6	35.7	37.6	21.7	7.7	1.8
184.7	1952	64.6	24.5	63.8	38.0	4.6	2.0
175.7	1953	63.7	27.0	79.8	35.9	5.0	2.0
157.1	1954	65.5	26.0	78.3	35.2	5.1	0.7
n.a.	1955	n.a.	n.a.	n.a.	n.a.	n.a.	n.a.
n.a.	1956	n.a.	n.a.	n.a.	n.a.	n.a.	n.a.
166.9	1957	64.0	27.8	96.9	41.4	6.5	1.7
200.8	1958	76.8	28.1	84.0	52.1	6.9	6.8
207.0	1959	92.8	33.8	102.5	80.7	9.2	7.7
1,901.0	1960[b]	997.1	342.4	1,153.4	812.1	100.3	74.1
1,585.2	1961	1,067.8	377.5	1,027.5	800.7	111.7	67.9
1,385.5	1962	1,107.1	409.0	1,049.1	933.0	126.3	6.0
2,065.4	1963	1,274.9	295.7	1,128.7	906.8	72.5	137.7
2,238.3	1964	1,246.3	396.3	1,274.5	993.4	134.3	86.4
2,499.8	1965	1,307.1	472.8	1,528.2	1,081.1	134.1	89.0
2,910.4	1966	1,435.4	480.5	1,613.0	1,264.5	137.1	78.0
3,108.5	1967	1,498.7	540.5	1,871.6	1,312.2	146.4	101.5
3,139.5	1968	1,182.4	829.3	2,233.6	1,358.0	166.4	113.3
3,150.1	1969	1,325.8	810.5	2,404.3	1,689.7	189.0	129.5
3,410.0	1970	1,390.0	864.7	2,467.0	1,732.6	203.2	159.0
3,375.0	1971	1,548.1	912.6	2,759.3	1,893.4	229.5	219.0
3,737.0	1972	1,444.9	1,037.7	3,061.0	2,081.6	242.0	331.0
3,938.0	1973	1,589.3	1,117.1	3,389.9	2,379.2	275.7	395.6
4,335.0	1974	1,560.2	1,465.1	3,399.0	2,521.3	513.8	488.0
4,511.9	1975	1,814.6	1,699.7	3,592.7	2,926.0	592.6	469.4
,992.0	1976	4,125.0		3,810.0	4,209.0		530.0
,574.1	1977	5,127.7		4,564.8	5,519.6		549.9

APPENDIX C
The French Military Manpower

Table C.1. Army Manpower, 1639–1870

Year	Personnel Strength	Year	Personnel Strength
1639	100,000 (148,630)	1844	348,901
1672	100,000	1845	356,626
1674	185,000 (278,500)	1846	372,059
		1847	380,078
1708	108,000	1848	441,526
1710	200,000 (360,000)	1849	450,840
1720	110,000	1850	416,691
1735	152,000	1851	406,432
1738	115,000	1852	389,560
1746	164,571	1853	361,468
1751	130,000	1854	472,734
1760	168,600	1855	588,857
1763	135,000	1856	539,506
1792	120,000	1857	384,043
1793	300,000	1859	540,035
1800	350,000	1860	473,095
1805	400,000	1861	467,579
1806	600,000	1862	432,352
1812	600,000	1863	420,850
1818	240,000	1864	414,716
1830	270,000	1865	402,824
1839	310,802	1866	391,397
1840	481,638	1867	410,102
1841	429,490	1868	422,946
1842	396,122	1869	444,191
1843	361,784		
		1870	600,000

Sources: For the seventeenth and eighteenth centuries, André Corvisier, *L' Armée française de la fin du XVII* siècle au ministère Choiseul: le soldat* (Paris: Presses Universitaires de France, 1964) and H. Methivier, *Le Siècle de Louis XIII* (Paris: Presses Universitaires de France, 1966). For the nineteenth century, A. Gervais, "La Question des effectifs," *Revue politique et parlementaire* (December 1902), pp. 454–81.

Table C.2. Army and Navy Manpower, 1871–1936

Year	Army	Navy	Year	Army	Navy
1871	—	36,268	1905	575,179	51,264
1872	—	29,999	1906	582,676	52,335
1873	461,043	32,222	1907	567,484	52,392
1874	426,198	31,579	1908	564,676	54,105
1875	432,218	32,103	1909	585,704	55,496
1876	449,950	33,893	1910	595,551	56,977
1877	568,859	36,629	1911	—	56,226
1878	486,655	38,705	1912	—	57,773
1879	470,493	37,529	1913	—	62,347
1880	490,949	36,489	1914	4,246,000	68,518
1881	529,269	38,174	1915	5,130,000	117,398
1882	466,420	39,133	1916	5,289,000	122,552
1883	455,608	40,914	1917	5,692,000	127,832
1884	456,172	40,413	1918	5,663,000	138,101
1885	451,941	45,708	1919	—	144,151
1886	471,517	44,015	1920	—	65,788
1887	457,677	39,423	1921	568,000	58,792
1888	507,360	39,960	1922	—	54,526
1889	520,700	39,392	1923	571,000	54,386
1890	523,235	38,291	1924	—	—
1891	522,172	39,876	1925	—	—
1892	524,719	42,491	1926	547,000	54,500
1893	525,697	44,509	1927	—	—
1894	536,125	44,135	1928	460,000	57,900
1895	544,459	44,294	1929	—	—
1896	564,643	47,592	1930	426,000	58,800
1897	585,037	41,111	1931	—	—
1898	610,722	46,498	1932	—	—
1899	605,857	48,076	1933	—	52,700
1900	572,029	48,509	1934	—	57,300
1901	554,219	49,190	1935	—	57,400
1902	562,392	48,207	1936	486,526	68,767
1903	564,099	50,126			
1904	545,503	50,149			

Source: INSEE, *Annuaire statistique de la France, 1946: résumé rétrospectif* (Paris: Imprimerie nationale, 1947).

Table C.3. Military Manpower by Service, 1938–76 (I)

Year	Army	Air Force	Navy	Gendarmerie	Total[a]
1938	665,000	77,000	56,000	49,000	847,000
1946	370,000	52,000	75,000	49,000	546,000
1947	316,000	53,000	67,000	54,000	490,000
1948	—	—	—	—	612,000
1949	455,000	55,000	66,000	58,000	634,000
1950	479,595	53,602	66,890	56,049	656,136
1951	566,901	60,388	91,107	61,568	779,964
1952	664,449	68,050	111,000	61,996	905,495
1953	632,252	68,135	117,757	65,777	888,921
1954	639,366	71,696	133,058	64,269	908,389
1955	642,000	68,000	140,000	63,000	913,000
1956	734,000	81,000	152,000	63,000	1,030,000
1957	829,000	86,000	175,000	63,000	1,153,000
1958	774,467	125,451	78,221	67,387	1,045,526
1959	731,489	140,292	78,234	69,429	1,019,444
1960	764,378	143,283	78,759	70,034	1,056,454
1961	745,043	138,337	78,730	70,519	1,032,629
1962	721,100	139,875	78,506	69,325	1,008,806
1963	497,500	128,000	75,500	—	765,000
1964	409,213	123,945	75,000	67,281	675,439
1965	344,727	112,952	71,139	66,985	595,803
1966	333,262	111,228	69,438	67,027	580,955
1967	331,867	110,306	69,511	67,441	579,125
1968	330,421	107,584	68,998	68,215	575,218
1969	323,727	104,380	68,320	62,921	571,260
1970	323,653	104,332	68,440	62,902	571,013
1971	322,169	102,213	67,969	65,490	569,256
1972	326,982	101,175	67,833	66,533	573,809
1973	331,617	100,966	68,382	70,317	582,415
1974	338,459	104,983	70,267	72,569	594,909
1975	331,522	102,078	68,315	73,647	584,405
1976	331,495	101,606	68,273	75,152	585,403

Sources: For 1938–68: the Defense Ministry. For 1969–76: "Décret portant répartition des effectifs budgétaires des personnels militaires des armées." In *Journal officiel, lois et décrets* (Paris, published daily).
[a] All military personnel included.

Table C.4. Military Manpower by Service, 1948–76 (II)[a]

Year	Army	Air Force	Navy	Total[b]
1948	368,905	76,010	57,680	502,595
1949	301,000	67,433	53,583	422,016
1950	306,428	64,611	53,169	424,208
1951	368,208	88,868	60,393	517,469
1952	396,323	116,050	67,208	579,581
1953	416,329	115,991	67,218	599,538
1954	410,167	131,283	71,110	612,560
1955				
1956				
1957	440,223	144,656	70,800	655,679
1958	653,234	124,569	73,962	851,765
1959	635,151	138,073	77,281	850,505
1960	672,230	141,267	74,583	888,080
1961	666,882	135,493	74,581	876,956
1962	665,512	139,873	75,621	881,006
1963	457,118	127,755	74,086	658,959
1964	405,644	123,945	72,113	601,702
1965	333,407	112,323	68,252	513,982
1966	333,262	111,728	69,438	514,428
1967	331,867	110,806	69,511	512,184
1968	328,504	108,600	68,876	505,980
1969	324,987	105,937	68,945	499,869
1970	324,859	105,926	69,070	499,855
1971	323,344	103,709	68,586	495,639
1972	327,722	102,423	68,308	498,453
1973	332,357	102,226	68,915	493,498
1974	331,547	102,167	68,330	502,044
1975	331,522	102,078	68,315	501,915
1976	331,495	101,606	68,273	501,374

Sources: "Effectifs budgétaires moyens," in the *budget voté* of the annual appendix on the national defense budget of the *Projet de loi de finance* (formerly entitled *Projet de loi présenté à l'Assemblée nationale relatif au développement des crédits affectés aux dépenses de fonctionnement des services militaire*) (Paris: Imprimerie nationale, published annually).

[a]For technical reasons related to the absence of coherence in the presentation of the data in the official documents and to maintain a modicum of statistical consistency diachronically, we have reported only the personnel actually paid out of the defense budget under chapters 31-11 and 31-12, "arms and services." Consequently, active personnel on leave and serving in other organizations and paid out of their budgets have been excluded; this includes such people as military attachés. This table is included here because it served as the basis for the analysis of rank structures in Chapter 4.

[b]The personnel of the common section (the health service, military justice, and central administration), of the gendarmerie (which were computed with the common section until 1973), and of the Ministerial Delegation of the Armament (DMA) have not been entered in the above computations, because the content of the common section has changed too frequently.

APPENDIX D

The Social Structure of French Society and Its Military Institution

Table D.1. Sociooccupational Categories of the National Institute of Statistics and Economic Studies, INSEE (French Ministry of Economy and Finance) and Their Breakdown into Three Subcategories

0 Farm owners

1 Farm laborers

2 Sales and industrial business owners
   21 Industrial business owners   ← a
   22 Artisans   ← b
   23 Fishermen (owners)   ← b
   26 Large sales business owners   ← a
   27 Small sales business owners   ← b

3 Professionals and Executives
   30 Liberal Professions
   32 Teachers (high schools, universities), scientific and literary professions
   33 Engineers   ← a
   34 Executives (public and private sectors)

4 Technical and managerial personnel
   41 Schoolteachers
   42 Social and medical services   ← b
   43 Technical personnel
   44 Managerial personnel

5 Employees
  51 Clerical employees ⎫
  53 Sales employees   ⎬   ← c

6 Workers
  60 Foremen
  61 Qualified workers
  63 Skilled workers
  65 Miners   ← c
  66 Seamen and fishermen
  67 Apprentices
  68 Unskilled workers

7 Service personnel
  70 Household employees
  71 Cleaning employees   ← c
  72 Other service employees

8 Other categories
  80 Artists   ← b
  81 Clergy
  82 Military and police   ← a

a. Upper sociooccupational origins.

b. Middle sociooccupational origins.

c. Lower sociooccupational origins.

Table D.2. Sociooccupational Categories in the Censuses of 1954, 1962, 1968, and 1975

Sociooccupational Categories	Total			
	1954	1962	1968	1975
Farm owners	3,966,015	3,044,670	2,464,156	1,650,865
Farm laborers	1,161,356	826,090	584,212	375,480
Sales and industrial business owners	2,301,416	2,044,667	1,955,468	1,708,925
Industrial business owners	91,067	80,660	80,720	59,845
Artisans	757,380	637,897	619,080	533,635
Fishermen (owners)	18,747	19,312	18,380	15,835
Large sales business owners	181,717	172,833	210,344	186,915
Small sales business owners	1,252,505	1,333,965	1,026,216	912,695
Professionals and executives	553,719	765,938	994,716	1,459,285
Liberal professions	120,341	125,057	140,572	172,025
Teachers, scientific and literary professionals	80,380	125,126	213,420	377,215
Engineers	75,808	138,061	186,184	256,290
Executives (public and private sectors)	277,190	377,694	454,540	653,755
Technical and managerial personnel	1,112,543	1,501,287	2,005,732	2,764,95
Schoolteachers	384,984	421,189	562,096	737,42
Social and medical services		110,101	172,748	298,45
Technical personnel	193,206	343,986	530,716	758,89
Managerial personnel	534,353	626,011	740,172	970,18
Employees	2,068,118	2,396,418	2,995,828	3,840,70
Clerical employees	1,627,548	1,885,508	2,371,128	3,104,10
Sales employees	440,570	510,910	624,700	736,59
Workers	6,489,871	7,060,790	7,705,752	8,207,10
Foremen	3,052,953	306,142	363,216	443,30
Qualified workers		2,286,459	2,630,040	2,985,80
Skilled workers	1,816,265	2,394,102	2,670,328	2,946,80
Miners	239,155	191,588	144,696	73,4
Seamen and fishermen	54,865	48,061	43,344	38,2
Apprentices	201,310	251,044	256,208	106,6
Unskilled workers	1,125,323	1,583,394	1,597,920	1,612,7
Service personnel	1,017,789	1,047,312	1,166,252	1,243,4
Household employees	320,758	306,602	280,876	234,3
Cleaning employees	239,408	222,467	227,328	154,1
Other service employees	457,623	518,243	658,048	855,0
Other categories	513,937	564,023	525,860	524,0
Artists	45,089	42,184	50,196	59,0
Clergy	171,394	165,634	137,124	116,9
Military and police	297,454	356,205	338,540	347,9
Total	19,184,764	19,251,195	20,397,976	21,774,8

Source: Thévenot, "Les Catégories sociales en 1975: l'extension du salariat," Laurent *Economie et statistique* 91 (1977): 4–5.

Annual Rate of Variation (%)			Structure (%)				Female Strength (%)			
1954–62	1962–68	1968–75	1954	1962	1968	1975	1954	1962	1968	1975
−3.3	−3.5	−5.6	20.7	15.8	12.1	7.6	41.5	39.2	38.1	34.3
−4.2	−5.6	−6.1	6.0	4.3	2.8	1.7	15.0	11.5	10.3	11.6
−1.5	−0.7	−1.9	12.0	10.6	9.6	7.8	37.2	36.7	35.2	33.4
−1.5	0.0	−4.2	0.5	0.4	0.4	0.2	14.9	14.2	13.7	13.5
−2.1	−0.5	−2.1	4.0	3.3	3.0	2.5	18.3	16.0	14.7	11.9
+0.4	−0.8	−2.1	0.1	0.1	0.1	—	14.9	11.1	11.1	10.2
−0.6	+3.3	−1.7	0.9	0.9	1.0	0.9	29.2	30.2	32.9	30.8
−1.2	−1.7	−1.7	6.5	5.9	5.1	4.2	51.7	51.3	50.2	48.2
+4.1	+4.5	+5.6	2.9	4.0	4.9	6.7	13.8	15.9	19.1	23.2
+0.5	+2.0	+2.9	0.6	0.6	0.7	0.8	15.6	17.3	19.3	22.2
+5.7	+9.3	+8.5	0.4	0.7	1.1	1.7	39.9	43.0	44.7	47.0
+7.8	+5.1	+4.7	0.4	0.7	0.9	1.2	2.1	3.2	3.4	4.4
+3.9	+3.1	+5.3	1.5	2.0	2.2	3.0	8.6	11.1	13.4	17.1
+3.8	+4.9	+4.7	5.8	7.8	9.8	12.7	36.7	39.6	40.6	45.2
	+4.9	+4.0	2.0	2.2	2.8	3.4	68.3	65.1	62.7	63.5
	+7.8	+8.4		0.6	0.8	1.4		84.8	83.2	79.0
+7.5	+7.5	+5.2	1.0	1.8	2.6	3.5	7.1	7.9	11.3	14.4
+2.0	+2.8	+3.9	2.8	3.2	3.6	4.4	24.6	31.9	34.9	44.9
+1.9	+3.8	+3.6	10.8	12.5	14.7	17.7	52.8	58.8	61.0	63.9
+1.9	+3.9	+3.9	8.5	9.8	11.6	14.3	53.0	59.4	61.9	65.0
+1.9	+3.4	+2.4	2.3	2.7	3.1	3.4	52.0	57.0	57.7	59.4
+1.1	+1.5	+0.9	33.8	36.7	37.8	37.7	22.7	21.6	20.4	22.4
(1)	+2.9	+2.9	15.9	1.6	1.8	2.0	20.0	5.9	7.1	5.9
(1)	+2.4	+1.8		11.9	12.9	13.7		17.3	16.3	13.5
(1)	+1.8	+1.4	9.5	12.5	13.1	13.6	31.8	26.3	23.0	26.8
−2.7	−4.6	−9.2	1.2	1.0	0.7	0.3	0.8	0.4	0.3	0.3
−1.6	−1.7	−1.8	0.3	0.2	0.2	0.2	1.7	3.1	3.8	4.6
+2.8	+0.3	−11.8	1.0	1.3	1.3	0.5	20.3	14.0	9.3	4.9
(1)	+0.2	+0.1	5.9	8.2	7.8	7.4	21.6	27.9	30.1	38.1
+0.4	+1.8	+0.9	5.3	5.4	5.7	5.7	80.7	80.9	79.1	77.9
−0.6	−1.5	−2.6	1.7	1.6	1.4	1.1	96.7	96.0	95.6	96.5
−0.9	+0.4	−5.4	1.2	1.1	1.1	0.7	100.0	100.0	99.2	98.4
+1.6	+4.1	+3.8	2.4	2.7	3.2	3.9	59.3	63.7	65.1	69.1
+1.2	−1.2	−0.1	2.7	2.9	2.6	2.4	26.1	23.4	20.7	19.1
−0.8	+2.9	+2.4	0.2	0.2	0.2	0.3	36.4	34.8	32.9	30.4
−0.4	−3.1	−2.2	0.9	0.8	0.7	0.5	65.5	65.4	61.8	60.2
+2.3	−0.8	+0.4	1.6	1.9	1.7	1.6	1.8	2.5	2.3	3.5
+0.04	+0.97	+0.94	100.0	100.0	100.0	100.0	34.8	34.6	34.9	37.3

Table D.3. Sociooccupational Mobility in France, 1970

Father's occupation	Son's occupation 1	2	3	4
1 Farm owner	38.8	6.3	1.3	5.4
2 Farm laborer	6.6	15.6	0.7	7.2
3 Industrial business owner, large sales business owner, liberal profession	1.0	0.2	20.1	10.7
4 Artisan, fisherman (owner), small sales business owner	2.2	1.4	5.3	24.6
5 Executive	1.9	0.5	7.2	3.6
6 Technical and managerial personnel	0.5	0.3	3.5	4.2
7 Clerical or sales employee, artist, police and military	0.9	1.2	2.3	7.0
8 Worker	1.0	1.4	0.9	5.2
9 Household personnel	1.0	1.6	1.2	6.
Total	11.2	3.4	2.7	8.

Source: Claude Thélot, "Origine et position sociales: faits et interprétation." In *Economie et Statistique* 81–82 (1976): 76.

5	6	7	8	9	Total
1.7	3.8	6.8	34.9	1.0	100.0 (25.6)
1.2	3.6	8.1	55.3	1.7	100.0 (6.5)
19.7	18.2	12.2	16.1	1.8	100.0 (3.7)
7.1	11.4	10.4	35.6	2.0	100.0 (12.0)
35.2	25.0	10.3	15.6	0.7	100.0 (3.6)
18.3	31.7	15.2	25.1	1.2	100.0 (4.3)
9.3	18.8	18.6	39.8	2.1	100.0 (9.5)
3.2	10.6	11.8	63.9	2.0	100.0 (33.2)
4.0	17.6	15.0	50.2	2.8	100.0 (1.6)
6.1	11.1	10.9	44.9	1.7	100.0 (100.0)

Table D.4. Sociooccupational Origins of Saint-Cyr Cadets, 1953–76

Year	Total	Military Origins					
		Officer		Enlistee		Total Military	
		Number	%[a]	Number	%[a]	Number	%[a]
1953–55	341	105	30.8	43	12.6	148	43.4
1954–56	361	108	29.9	39	10.8	147	40.7
1955–57	277	71	25.6	35	12.6	106	38.3
1956–58	309	98	31.7	30	9.7	128	41.4
1957–59	307	86	28.0	42	13.7	128	41.7
1958–60	351	109	31.0	57	16.2	166	47.0
1959–61	327	85	25.9	58	17.7	143	43.7
1960–62	344	106	30.8	42	12.2	148	43.0
1961–63	329	85	25.8	51	15.5	136	41.3
1962–64	240	60	25.0	31	12.9	91	37.9
1963–65	246	59	24.0	46	18.7	105	42.7
1964–66	246	59	24.0	37	15.0	96	39.
1965–67	220	62	28.2	32	14.5	94	42.
1966–68	195	41	21.0	40	20.5	81	41.
1967–69	198	51	25.7	24	12.1	75	37.
1968–70	201	58	28.8	37	18.4	95	47.
1969–71	192	47	24.5	47	24.5	94	49.
1970–72	187	61	32.6	31	16.6	92	49.
1971–73	199	59	29.6	33	16.6	92	46.
1972–74	209	68	32.5	42	20.1	110	52.
1973–75	216	51	23.6	26	12.0	77	35.
1974–76	197	62	31.5	33	16.8	95	48.

Civilian Origins							
Functionary		Business, Cadre, Engineer		Liberal Profession		Trade, Artisan	
Number	%[a]	Number	%[a]	Number	%[a]	Number	%[a]
70	20.5	24	7.0	31	9.1	24	7.0
41	11.4	41	11.4	27	7.5	34	9.4
44	15.9	12	4.3	32	11.6	16	5.8
44	14.2	24	7.8	38	12.3	27	8.7
52	16.9	9	2.9	32	10.4	26	8.5
50	14.2	28	7.9	31	8.8	31	8.8
34	10.4	6	1.8	36	11.0	23	7.0
49	14.2	18	5.2	47	13.7	16	4.7
35	10.6	9	2.7	35	10.6	14	4.3
35	14.6	6	2.5	21	8.8	12	5.0
25	10.2	4	1.6	17	6.9	10	4.1
15	6.1	6	2.4	28	11.4	28	11.4
37	16.8	20	9.1	21	9.5	8	3.6
17	8.7	22	11.3	13	6.7	12	6.2
23	11.6	12	6.0	18	9.1	11	5.5
22	10.9	19	9.4	8	4.0	11	5.4
25	13.0	4	2.1	7	3.6	12	6.2
21	11.2	8	4.2	10	5.3	14	7.5
12	6.0	20	10.0	6	3.0	12	6.0
6	2.9	47	22.5	3	1.4	8	3.8
11	5.1	67	31.0	7	3.2	8	3.7
8	4.1	37	18.8	4	2.0	12	6.1

[a]Percentages may not total one hundred percent due to rounding.

Table D.4 *continued*

Year	Civilian Origins					
	Farmer		Employee, Worker		Other	
	Number	%[a]	Number	%[a]	Number	%[a]
1953–55	13	3.8	14	4.1	17	5.0
1954–56	15	4.2	23	6.4	33	9.1
1955–57	6	2.2	21	7.6	40	14.1
1956–58	16	5.2	15	4.9	17	5.5
1957–59	9	2.9	27	8.8	24	9.8
1958–60	13	3.7	23	6.0	9	
1959–61	14	4.3	40	12.2	30	
1960–62	13	3.8	33	9.6	20	5.8
1961–63	8	2.4	55	16.7	37	11.2
1962–64	6	2.5	27	11.3	42	17.5
1963–65	11	4.5	24	9.8	50	20.3
1964–66	5	2.0	27	11.0	41	16.7
1965–67	7	3.2	23	10.5	10	4.5
1966–68	7	3.6	42	21.5	1	0.5
1967–69	4	2.0	45	22.7	10	
1968–70	3	1.5	19	9.4	23	
1969–71	12	6.2	12	6.2	26	
1970–72	4	2.1	10	5.3	28	
1971–73	4	2.0	19	9.5	34	
1972–74	6	2.9	28	13.4	1	0.5
1973–75	10	4.6	34	15.7	2	0.9
1974–76	6	3.0	33	16.8	2	1.0

Table D.5. Sociooccupational Origins of EMIA Students, 1953–76

		Military Origins					
		Officer		Enlistee		Total Military	
Year	Total	Number	%[a]	Number	%[a]	Number	%[a]
1953–54	338	73	21.6	78	23.1	151	44.7
1954–55	276	51	18.5	59	21.4	110	39.9
1955–56	201	32	15.9	34	16.9	66	32.8
1956–57	178	28	15.7	27	15.2	55	30.9
1957–58	181	36	19.9	40	22.1	76	42.0
1958–59	191	39	20.4	32	16.8	71	37.2
1959–60	197	37	18.8	46	23.4	83	42.1
1960–61	182	23	12.6	35	19.2	58	31.8
1961–62	156	37	23.7	41	26.3	78	50.0
1962–63	126	21	16.7	29	23.0	50	39.7
1963–64	107	24	22.4	21	19.6	45	42.0
1964–65	163	59	36.2	28	17.2	87	53.4
1965–66	184	42	22.8	49	26.6	91	49.5
1966–67	202	43	21.3	53	26.2	96	47.5
1967–68	221	35	16.0	46	21.1	81	37.1
1968–69	214	32	14.9	30	14.0	62	28.9
1969–70	189	20	10.5	35	18.5	55	29.0
1970–71	208	30	14.2	36	17.3	66	31.5
1971–72	209	29	13.8	45	21.5	74	35.4
1972–73	228	31	13.6	46	20.2	77	33.8
1973–74	214	37	17.3	44	20.6	81	37.9
1974–75	218	27	12.4	32	14.7	59	27.1

Table D.5 *continued*

	Civilian Origins					
	Functionary		Business, Cadre, Engineer		Liberal Profession	
Year	Number	%[a]	Number	%[a]	Number	%[a]
1953–54	42	12.4	10	2.9	48	14.
1954–55	32	11.6	6	2.2	9	3.
1955–56	33	16.4	5	2.5	12	5.
1956–57	22	12.4	5	2.8	9	5.
1957–58	22	12.2	2	1.1	8	4.
1958–59	36	18.8	4	2.1	9	4.
1959–60	36	18.3	2	1.0	—	—
1960–61	26	14.2	2	11.0	3	1.
1961–62	13	8.3	3	1.9	—	—
1962–63	12	9.5	7	5.6	—	—
1963–64	1	9.3	4	3.7	—	—
1964–65	14	8.6	9	5.5	—	—
1965–66	14	7.6	21	11.4	—	—
1966–67	16	7.9	13	6.4	13	6.
1967–68	29	13.3	18	8.2	15	6.
1968–69	19	8.8	19	8.8	7	3
1969–70	14	7.4	10	5.2	10	5
1970–71	9	4.3	12	5.7	5	2
1971–72	7	3.3	9	4.3	5	2
1972–73	10	4.4	38	16.7	7	3
1973–74	11	5.1	38	17.8	7	3
1974–75	10	4.6	42	19.3	6	2

[a] Percentages may not total one hundred percent due to rounding.

Civilian Origins							
Trade, Artisan		Farmer		Employee, Worker		Other	
Number	%[a]	Number	%[a]	Number	%[a]	Number	%[a]
45	13.3	20	5.9	18	5.3	4	1.2
34	12.3	20	7.2	63	22.8	2	0.7
30	14.9	12	6.0	34	16.9	9	4.5
26	14.6	13	7.3	40	22.5	8	4.5
15	8.3	13	7.2	32	17.7	13	7.2
20	10.5	16	8.4	22	11.5	13	6.8
17	8.6	19	9.6	33	16.8	7	3.6
20	10.9	13	7.1	50	27.4	8	
19	12.2	13	8.3	18	11.5	12	7.7
10	7.9	11	8.7	25	19.8	11	8.7
7	6.5	7	6.5	12	11.2	22	
8	4.9	6	3.7	24	14.7	15	9.2
13	7.1	9	4.9	27	14.5	9	4.9
24	11.9	14	6.9	18	8.9	8	4.0
33	15.1	7	3.2	31	14.2	4	
29	13.5	7	3.2	57	26.6	14	
28	12.1	14	7.4	55	29.1	8	
19	9.1	20	9.6	63	30.2	14	
10	4.7	13	6.2	68	32.5	23	
15	6.6	23	10.1	54	23.7	4	1.8
17	7.9	19	8.9	35	16.4	6	2.8
17	7.8	17	7.8	54	24.8	13	6.0

BIBLIOGRAPHY

Notes on Sources

The evocation of seemingly insurmountable obstacles scattered in the path of scientific investigation, obstacles that materialize with, for instance, a Kafkaesque inaccessibility to information, a pervading obsession with the cult for secrecy or a deep-seated archival chastity, is, in the domain of research in military studies, a ritual to which the researcher is legitimately tempted to sacrifice. Sometimes it can be an easy device to force a credible alibi to justify lacunae, ideological biases, or simply one's indifference toward this kind of topic, and though research conducted in civilian administrative milieus faces the same difficulties, the problem, when it comes to the French military institution, is not without tangible foundation.

While in the United States and in many other Western countries, researchers are able to find a decent amount of basic material in copious, regularly published official documents and can easily get authorization to undertake wide-ranging interviews in the military establishment, in France the researcher has very little factual material to deal with. Too often, he has only parsimoniously distributed brochures in which neatly glazed photographs and lulling descriptions of the military world replace columns and rows of hard data. As for interviews and field research, unless he is highly recommended and careful to address himself solely to ordinary topics, systematic inquiries are difficult to undertake.

But as always there are variations in degree as well as in the nature of the difficulties met; much depends upon the particular aspects of the military institution one wants to investigate. In many areas dealing with the organizational dimension of the establishment, first- and second-hand data are, in theory, rather easy to collect, and the military is not unwilling to cooperate. In such cases the researcher has to overcome only the classic problems faced in all research: the data are scattered across various services, some in Vincennes, some in the boulevard Saint-Germain or boulevard Victor, and they are difficult to gather unless the military provides the personnel or unless the researcher has a score of assistants; the data may simply not exist (though a venerable and complex bureaucracy, the military institution has often just begun collecting data that one would have expected to exist for centuries); finally, the data exist but no one is aware of them or knows where to find them.

There are other areas where the military researcher is bound to stumble over endless hindrances, and, in this regard, the professional and the sociological dimensions of the military establishment offer a rather stubborn resistance to inquiry. In this domain, the military legitimizes its reluctance to open its files or to allow systematic field research with the fear that an abusive usage of the information could be detrimental to the institution. Therefore, although it remains possible to glean an ill-matched assortment of information from various sources, it is rare to be able to find reliable and systematic data covering a significant as well as representative segment of the entire establishment. Moreover, the feeling of deprivation experienced by the researcher in these particular areas is all the stronger for the need for an elaborate and precise set of data has become more and more pressing because of an increasing reliance on complex statistical methodologies and a desire to test or build more sophisticated theories.

On the whole, however, one must be fair and point out that it is undeniable that the military is becoming less distrustful of civilian interest in its world and has begun to half open the door of the military establishment to civilian researchers. Today many a unit commander would allow the student of the military to distribute a questionnaire dealing with all kinds of preoccupations to his NCOs or officers. And, taken individually, members of the military institution are no longer automatically opposed to the development of serious research dealing with their organization. When it does occur, the old reflex of secrecy and rejection is often a manifestation of the military collective consciousness, so to speak, which seems essentially an appendage of the central bureaucracy.

One is also tempted to point out that the difficulties encountered in gathering substantial documentation are not uniquely attributable to the military. Many civil research organizations, university or para-university, that have succeeded in obtaining information from the military hesitate to diffuse this information to researchers who are not part of their system. This attitude is somewhat justified. Yet one would easily concede that this attitude is not at all propitious to the accumulation of knowledge in a field that clearly suffers from the absence of identifiable sources of information. Moreover, it contributes to feeding an atmosphere of concurrence and distrust somewhat incompatible with the principles of the academic ethos and spirit of research; however, it is true that one touches upon the larger and seemingly insurmountable issue of the traditional distrustful individualism still in vogue in French academic milieus. Despite all these difficulties, the importance of which should not be exaggerated, there exists, in the public domain beyond the reach of military or other "censorship," a solid mass of information on the military establishment that seems insufficiently explored.

These remarks being made, let us comment briefly on the sources of information used in the present work in addition to the material listed in the bibliography that follows. This discussion will be arranged in such a way as to provide those interested in writing on the French military establishment with a brief yet comprehensive guideline to the main sources of information that can be consulted.

MILITARY SOURCES

Military Information Services

A great deal of first-hand information, both hard and soft, has been collected by the intermediary of a few services attached to the military institution, mostly central or interarmies services. The most well-known of these services is the Service d'Information et de Relations publiques des Armées (SIRPA). It is through SIRPA that key information about the national service, its organization and various components, as well as information about the organization of the French national defense and the strategic deployment of armed forces has been collected. Yet, however useful, these data are of too general a nature or, on the contrary, too fragmentary in nature to be self-sufficient. Most of the sociological (social origins, for instance) and professional (career motivations) material has been obtained through the efforts of the former Centre d'Etudes et de Sociologie militaire (CESM), now the Centre des Relations humaines, as through the psychosociological department of the Direction des Recherches et Moyens d'essais (DRME), which was able to provide additional information about the draftee population. These two organisms constitute the two most important sources for adequate and competent assistance to the researcher. The Directions des personnels, the personnel bureaus, of the various services constitute another category of organisms from which the researcher could obtain useful sets of data, particularly concerning the social and organizational structure of armed forces personnel.

Periodicals

The documentation periodically published by the military institution constitutes an important complementary source of information in which the researcher is able to find useful data and commentaries on a wide range of topics.

There are two levels of periodicals. At the first level, one finds various regularly published periodicals, which are not widely distributed, that have as their objective keeping the members of the military establishment informed. There are three sorts of documents: 1) all the periodicals published by the central services of the military institution, such as the *Notes*, the *Dossiers*, and the *Bulletin d'information* of SIRPA, and all interservice journals such as *Terre Air Mer*, *Forces armées françaises*, which has become *Armées d'aujourd'hui*; 2) journals relative, on the one hand, to each service, such as *L'Armée*, which has become *Terre-Information* for the ground forces, *Air actualitiés* for the Air Force, the *Bulletin d'Information de la Marine* and *Cols bleus* for the navy, and, on the other hand, to each branch of service like *Médecine-Armées* for the armed forces medical corps, *Saumur* for the cavalry, and *Képi blanc* for the Foreign Legion; and 3) journals for the military establishment, such as those published by associations of former students at the military academies (*Le Casoar* for Saint-Cyr, *La Jaune et la rouge* for Polytechnique, *Piège* for the air force academy) and associations of members of the career personnel, retired or on active duty, officers or enlistees (*Epaulette*, *Bulletin trimestriel des officiers en retraite*, *Bulletin de l'Association des amis de l'Ecole supérieure de Guerre*, and so on).[1]

If these publications have no particular goals—they simply serve as organs of liaison and information—they do present the researcher with an advantage by offering a wide-open panorama on military public opinion. In addition, they are a source of statistical information about a wide range of topics, such as military service, the organization of the armed forces, and, sometimes, the social and professional aspects of one or another category of career personnel.

Perhaps before proceeding to the second level of analysis, one should mention that aside from the aforementioned periodicals there exists a very interesting document, *L'Annuaire des officiers*, a directory of all French officers, which is published every year for each service (a directory for the officers of the common services has been appearing for a few years and the directory for the army has been divided into two sections, one for the *officiers des armes* and the other for the *officiers des services*); the directory has been published for a long time; the oldest directory goes back to 1854. The usefulness of this document, which simply lists all French officers in active service, is invaluable, even though its handling is somewhat cumbersome, often requiring a respectable amount of time or manpower, should, for instance, the *Annuaire* be used for diachronic purposes. It allows one, among other things, to assess with precision the size of the officer corps of any service or branch of service and its evolution over time, as well as the age, the type of recruitment, the position, the rank, the branch of service of each officer; by way of consequence, not only can the evolution of the rank structure be accurately estimated, but also that of the age structure, that of the length of time spent in each rank, and so forth. Unfortunately, since the Algerian War the *Annuaire*, now published by the Ministry of Defense, has become a document of restricted access (for fear that the organization of the French armed forces might become known), thereby raising some problems for the civilian researcher.

On the second level, one finds a small number of periodicals with academic pretensions (a small number indeed, especially when compared with the number of journals published in the United States or in the United Kingdom). The *Revue historique des armées* will be mentioned here *pour mémoire*; because our study dealt with the contemporary period, this interesting journal was not of great direct utility, though useful information was picked up for our analysis of the military preparatory schools. The *Revue militaire générale* (which has not appeared since 1972) and the *Revue de défense nationale* (which has been retitled *Défense nationale*) are the two other most important journals emanating from the military. All key elements about the official defense and foreign policies, the defense organization and deployment, strategic considerations, and military doctrine can be collected through an analysis of the articles in these reviews.[2]

Moreover, *Défense nationale* published, in addition to these analyses, a series of chronicles about the French national defense, about each of the armed forces, and about the positions taken by the newspapers on military and defense questions. These chronicles provide the reader with extremely useful and up-to-date information, in particular on the budgetary and legal aspects of the military institution and on its equipment, armament, and manpower.

Unpublished Monographs

Under this heading, we are actually referring to a substantial body of literature made up of theses written by young officers in the course of their higher military education. In general, these theses were prepared to obtain the Technical Certificate of Superior Military Studies (BTEMS), which validates the second phase in one of the two curricula of the higher military education in France, the Scientific and Technical Superior Studies (EMSST).[3]

When undertaken in the field of social sciences, these monographs, often book-length works, deal with the military establishment itself. As such they constitute extremely valuable sources of information particularly with regard to the sociological and professional dimensions of the institution.

As many of them were fieldwork undertakings, they offer a mine of first-hand data that could never have been obtained in any other way by the civilian student. Prepared under the guidance of competent advisors, they not only present a good deal of theoretical sophistication, but also provide the researcher with a highly valid and reliable statistical tool.

Unfortunately, access to such studies is not always easy. However, when they constitute an element of an academic pursuit in a university (M.A.s or doctoral degrees) they can also be found in the library of the department or the university where they were prepared. In general, copies of these works may be available at the library of the War College in the buildings of the Ecole militaire.

NONMILITARY SOURCES

If the researcher continues to suffer from a feeling of frustration because the military sources, despite their relative importance, are perceived as still too unsystematic, especially in the context of a macrosociological analysis covering all services over a relatively long period of time, or because access to them is severely limited, will nonmilitary sources rescue him from such a predicament? One is tempted to answer yes and no at the same time. No, because, on the whole, nonmilitary sources about the contemporary military establishment are rather scant. Yes, because these sources are less negligible than one would think at first and, if they are far from being sufficient to undertake a good study of the military institution, they adequately complement the existing military sources.

Official Publications

The most convenient and accessible sources of hard data, legal, budgetary, and organizational, are furnished by the publications of the *Journal officiel*. First, the *Comptes-rendus des débats à l'Assemblée nationale* and *au Sénat* and the *Journal officiel, lois et décrets* are the best known instruments, containing first-rate political and legislative data. All the *Avis* and *Rapports* made or presented at the National Assembly or the Senate in the name of the National Defense Commissions and sometimes of the Economic and Finance Commissions each time a reform, a project of law, or a budget concerning the military institution is being discussed in Parliament are exceedingly useful. These form a second key source of information with first-hand data on various problems ranging from the armament and equipment of the military to the budgets, the social and professional problems, the military service, and the status of personnel. A third category of documents is the annual *Loi de finance* with its appendix on the national defense. Besides the details of budgetary allocations, it contains information on the effectives in each rank for all services and is an extremely useful document for the study of rank structure.

Periodicals

A distinction ought to be made between two categories of periodicals. From the first category, which encompasses all scientific journals, only a modest amount of information has been collected. Moreover, the data gathered tended to center essentially on strategic and defense questions, on the one hand, and on historical matters, on the other. Very little was found that dealt with the sociological or the professional aspects of the military establishment. As pointed out elsewhere, the study of the military institution as a social system has not yet attracted the sociologist, the political scientist, or even the student of law.[4] For example, less than a half dozen articles on this topic have appeared in the *Revue française de Science politique* since its creation. The same can be said for the *Revue française de Sociologie*, though perhaps the number of articles is somewhat higher.

The second category of periodicals is made up of a mass of journals that are of neither a military origin nor an academic origin. They are either parauniversity publications, such as *Esprit*, *Projet*, and *Les Temps modernes*, or political journals, such as the *Nouvelle revue socioliste*, *Les Cahiers du communisme*, and *Nouvelle critique*.[5] If we allude to these reviews, it is because for the last five or six years, they have opened their pages to a significant number of articles dealing with the French military institution.[6] Some of these sources, in particular those emanating from political or parapolitical organizations, have even been created for this specific purpose. This is the case, for instance, of the conservative journal *Nation armée*, of *Armée nouvelle*, the journal of the Socialist party's defense study group; and of *Armée nation*, edited by the Communist party. This is also the case for all publications prepared under the auspices of various political groups of the nonparliamentary Left, such as *Crosse en l'air*, *Lutte antimilitariste*, and *Objection*, or by local committees of soldiers, such as *Soldats en Lutte*, *Pleins les guêtres*, and *Radio-Bidasse* (the latter are irregularly published).[7] These journals constitute an interesting material for, because of their ideological biases, they contain much fruitful information about the position of the various political groups on military affairs.

To complete the review of documents used in the present study, one must mention the leading daily and weekly newspapers, and in particular *Le Monde*, *L'Express*, and *Le Point*, whose articles concerning the military institutions and the French defense are regularly published by competent specialists. These articles are of a remarkable quality as they not only offer the reader an important mass of firsthand information but also contribute, by the soundness of their analyses, to a better understanding of this field.

Centers for Military Studies

The recent interest in military and defense studies in France has materialized with the development, in universities and research institutions, of numerous centers dealing with the historical, political, and sociological aspects of military affairs. Though still in their infancy, these centers, the listing of which is annually published by the General Secretariat of the National Defense (SGDN), have already assembled a fairly large amount of material, not only reviews, journals, and papers, but also firsthand data collected during various field researches that were undertaken in the military. Yet, it should be pointed out that all data are not always available for consultation as many of them were collected in the course of surveys undertaken under contract to the military establishment, and consequently are under restricted use by outsiders who lack the institution's clearance.

Added to this note on the sources, a succinct survey of the existing bibliographical corpus is in order. The following list of references does not pretend to be an exhaustive one.[8] First, all references used in this book, especially those related to detailed, and, second, to general works not immediately related to the subject matter of this study, such as classic sociological studies to which we have often referred, have been omitted in order to avoid weighing down this bibliography with items that could impinge upon its usefulness as an instrument of reference.

The bibliography is organized into four categories of references. The first part deals with material concerning French society and immediately related topics. Various works on French Foreign policy and defense strategy are listed in the second part. This is followed in a third part by a series of references on the French military institution. The fourth and last part is a collection of general studies on the military and military sociology.

Except in the third part, we have been content in our presentation to separate books and book-length monographs from articles and papers. In effect, because it focuses upon the French military institution per se, the main concern of analysis of this book, we have thought it useful to organize the material relevant to the third part around four different themes, sometimes divided into subthemes: the first one deals with the military establishment in society; the second concerns the military service, the drafted personnel, and all related problems; the third is related to career military personnel; and the last one covers various questions on the military condition, such as perception of the profession, and authority and discipline.

Notes

1. For a detailed inventory of the periodical documentation published by the military, *see* Brigitte Grandchamp, "La Presse militaire dans la France contemporaine" (master's thesis, Université des Sciences sociales, Toulouse, 1976) and Monique Michaux, *Iconographie militaire française: bibliographie 1570–1970* (Vincennes: Service historique de l'Armée de Terre, 1971).

2. In the last few years, *Défense nationale* seems more and more to mirror the position and opinion of the technocratic central administra-

tion rather than, as before, the whole range of opinions throughout the military institution.

3. The first curriculum is the classic avenue of higher military training, marked by the Military Study Diploma (DEM), the Superior Military Studies Certificate (BEMS), prepared in the academy of each service. It was in order to train highly qualified technicians and to undertake the technical "recycling" of career officers, rendered imperative in an environment of swiftly developing technology, that the second curric-

ulum, the EMSST, was created in January 1947. Also composed of various steps, it addresses itself to a wide range of fields, among them the social sciences. Interestingly, a large part of the teaching and research is done in the civilian academic system, institutes, *grandes écoles*, and universities (in addition to their military degrees, the officers may also receive the regular academic degrees, such as master's degrees, doctoral degrees, and so forth).

In 1976 and 1977 a reform seeking to fuse the two curricula was undertaken (it should be achieved in 1980). The third levels of both curricula had already been unified.

For further details about the French higher military education, *see* "L'EMSST," *Terre Air Mer*, 10 May 1969, p. 21; "L'Enseignement militaire supérieur," *Forces armées françaises* 4 (1972): 9–14; Lieutenant Colonel Colard et al., "L'Evolution de l'enseignement et de la pédagogie à l'Ecole supérieure de Guerre," *Bulletin de l'Association des amis de l'Ecole supérieure de Guerre* 60 (1973): 35–48.

4. See the introduction of this book and Michel L. Martin, "Le Développement de la sociologie militaire aux Etats-Unis et en France: étude comparative," in *Le Système militaire des Etats-Unis*, edited by Lucien Mandeville (Paris: Delarge, 1976), pp. 311–42.

5. For an exhaustive list of the French periodicals *see Répertoire de la presse et des publications périodiques françaises*, répertoire H. F. Raux (Paris: Bibliothèque Nationale, 1973).

6. *See* for instance "L'Armée française," *La Nef* 18 (July–September 1961): 5–127; "La Force de frappe," *Esprit* 12 (December 1963): 753–88; "Une Armée pour quelle défense," *Projet* 79 (November 1973): 1007–34; "La Défense en question," *Paradoxes* (January 1975): 8–41; "L'Armée dans la crise," *Economie et humanisme* 222 (March–April 1975): 9–65; "L'Armée: autopsie d'une crise," *Autrement* (Spring 1975): 103–27; "L'Armée," *La Nouvelle critique* (May 1975): 8–22; "L'Armée et la défense," *Esprit* (October 1975): 365–434; "L'Armée dans la nation," *Projet* 104 (April 1976): 428–58.

7. For a more exhaustive list, *see* Grandchamp, "La Presse militaire dans la France contemporaine."

8. For a more complete listing of works concerning the contemporary French military establishment, *see* Michel L. Martin, *L'Institution militaire et la défense nationale en France, 1945–1978: recension des travaux* (forthcoming).

French Society: Political, Administrative and Cultural Aspects

BOOKS

Ardagh, John. *The New French Revolution: A Social and Economic Study of France, 1945–1968*. New York: Harper and Row, 1969.
Aron, Raymond. *L'Algérie et la République*. Paris: Plon, 1958.

————. *Immuable et changeante: de la IVe à la Ve République*. Paris: Calmann-Lévy, 1959.

Beaujeu-Garnier, Jacqueline. *La Population française après le recensement de 1975*. Paris: Gallimard, 1976.

Birnbaum, Pierre. *Les Sommets de l'Etat: essai sur l'élite du pouvoir en France*. Paris: Seuil, 1977.

Birnbaum, Pierre; Barucq, Charles; Bellaïche, Michel; and Marié, Alain. *La Classe dirigeante française: dissociation, interpénétration, intégration*. Paris: Presses Universitaires de France, 1978.

Blanc, Laurent. *La Fonction publique*. Paris: Presses Universitaires de France, 1968.

Bodiguel, Jean-Luc. *Les Anciens Elèves de l'E.N.A.* Paris: Presses de la Fondation nationale des Sciences politiques, 1978.

Boudon, Raymond. *Effets pervers et ordre social*. Paris: Presses Universitaires de France, 1977.

Brown, Bernard E. *Protest in Paris: Anatomy of a Revolt*. Morristown: General Learning Press, 1976.

Crozier, Michel. *Le Phénomène bureaucratique*. Paris: Seuil, 1963.

————. *La Société bloquée*. Paris: Seuil, 1970.

Darbel, Alain, and Schnapper, Dominique. *Morphologie de la haute administration française*. 2 vols. The Hague: Mouton, 1969–72.

Duverger, Maurice. *La Cinquième République*. Paris: Presses Universitaires de France, 1976.

Flower, J. E., ed. *France Today: Introductory Studies*. London: Methuen, 1971.

Gilpin, Robert. *France in the Age of the Scientific State*. Princeton: Princeton University Press, 1968.

Girard, Alain. *La Réussite sociale en France*. Paris: Presses Universitaires de France, 1971.

Hamilton, Richard F. *Affluence and the French Worker in the Fourth Republic*. Princeton: Princeton University Press, 1967.

Hoffmann, Stanley. *Decline or Renewal: France since the 1930's*. New York: Viking Press, 1974.

Hoffmann, Stanley; Kindleberger, Charles P.; Wylie, Laurence; Pitts, Jesse R.; Duroselle, Jean-Baptiste; and Goguel, François. *In Search of France: The Economy, Society and Political System in the Twentieth Century*. Cambridge, Mass.: Harvard University Press, 1963.

Kessler, Marie-Christine. *La Politique de la haute fonction publique*. Paris: Presses de la Fondation nationale des Sciences politiques, 1978.

Kosciusko-Morizet, Jacques. *La Mafia polytechnicienne*. Paris: Seuil, 1973.

Lavroff, Dmitri-Georges. *Le Système politique français: la Ve République*. Paris: Dalloz, 1975.

Leites, Nathan. *The Rules of the Game in Paris*. Chicago: University of Chicago Press, 1969.

Levy-Leboyer, Claude. *L'Ambition personnelle et la mobilité sociale*. Paris: Presses Universitaires de France, 1971.

Lord, Guy. *The French Budgetary Process*. Berkeley: University of California Press, 1973.

Lüthy, Herbert. *France against Herself*. New York: Praeger, 1955.

Marceau, Jane. *Class and Status in France: Economic Change and Social Immobility 1945–1975*. New York: Oxford University Press, 1977.

Quin, Claude. *Classes sociales et union du peuple de France*. Paris: Editions Sociales, 1976.

Stillman, Edmund; Bellini, James; Pfaff, William; Schloessing, Laurence; and Story, Jonathan. *L'Envol de la France dans les années 80*. Paris: Hachette, 1973.

Suleiman, Ezra N. *Politics, Power and Bureaucracy in France*. Princeton: Princeton University Press, 1974.

Vincent, Gérard, and Aubert, Véronique. *Les Français 1945–1975: chronologie et structures d'une société*. Paris: Masson, 1977.

Waterman, Harvey. *Political Change in Contemporary France: The Politics of an Industrial Democracy*. Columbus: Charles E. Merril Publishing Co., 1969.

Williams, Philip M., and Harrison, Martin. *Politics and Society in De Gaulle's Republique*. London: Longman, 1971.

Wright, Vincent. *Government and Politics of France*. New York: Holmes and Meier Publishers, 1978.

Zeldin, Theodore. *France, 1848–1945*. 2 vols. Oxford: Clarendon Press, 1973–77.

ARTICLES

Badeyan, Gérard; Durvy, Jean-Noël; and Quarré, Dominique. "Les Agents de l'Etat en 1975," *Economie et Statistique* 86 (1977): 11–28.

Bertaux, Daniel. "L'Hérédité sociale en France." *Economie et Statistique* 9 (1970): 37–48.

Bodiguel, Jean-Luc. "Sociologie des élèves de l'Ecole nationale d'Administration." *Revue internationale des Sciences administratives* 40 (1974): 231–44.

Bottomore, Thomas. "La Mobilité sociale dans la haute administration française." *Cahiers internationaux de Sociologie* 13 (1952): 167–78.

Darbel, Alain. "L'Evolution récente de la mobilité sociale." *Economie et Statistique* 71 (1975): 3–22.

Darbel, Alain, and Schnapper, Dominique. "La Probabilité d'entrée dans la fonction publique." *Economie et Statistique* 4 (1969): 43–50.

Garnier, Maurice, and Hazelrigg, Lawrence. "Father-to-Son Occupational Mobility in France: Some Evidences from the 1960's." *American Journal of Sociology* 80 (1974): 478–502.

Hoffmann, Stanley. "Protest in Modern France." In *The Revolution in World Politics*, edited by Morton A. Kaplan, pp. 69–91. New York: John Wiley, 1962.

Kessler, Marie-Christine. "Historique du système de formation et de recrutement des hauts fonctionnaires." *Revue française d'Administration publique* 1 (1977): 9–52.

Pitts, Jesse R. "Continuity and Change in Bourgeois France." In *In Search of France*, edited by Stanley Hoffmann et al., pp. 235–304. Cambridge, Mass.: Harvard University Press, 1963.

———. "La communauté délinquante." *Esprit* 38 (1970): 69–81.

Praderie, Michel, and Passagez, Monique. "La Mobilité professionnelle en France entre 1959 et 1964." *Etudes et Conjoncture* 10 (1966): 1–166.

Sadran, Pierre. "Recrutement et sélection par concours dans l'administration française." *Revue française d'Administration publique* 1 (1977): 53–107.

Seys, B., and Laulhé, P. "Enquête sur l'emploi de 1975." *INSEE* 42 (December 1975) series D.

Shils, Edward. "Plenitude and Scarcity: The Anatomy of an International Cultural Crisis." In *The Intellectuals and the Powers and Other Essays*, edited by Edward Shils, pp. 265–97. Chicago: University of Chicago Press, 1972.

Thélot, Claude. "Origine et position sociales: faits et interprétation." *Economie et Statistique* 81–82 (1976): 73–88.

Thévenot, Laurent. "Les Catégories sociales en 1975: l'extension du salariat." *Economie et Statistique* 91 (1977): 3–30.

Vaughan, Michalina. "The Grandes Ecoles." In *Governing Elites: Studies in Training and Selection*, edited by Rupert Wilkinson, pp. 74–107. New York: Oxford University Press, 1969.

French Foreign Policy and Defense Strategy: Organizational, Doctrinal, and Economic Aspects

BOOKS

Ailleret, Charles. *L'Aventure atomique française: souvenirs et réflexions.* Paris: Grasset, 1968.

Albord, Tony, ed. *La Défense nationale.* Paris: Presses Universitaires de France, 1958.

Arrivé, Dominique; Laffranque, Marie; and Vanderville, Bernard. *L'Etat de défense: économie, société et répression.* Paris: Maspéro, 1970.

Brachet, Olivier; Pons, Christian; and Tachon, Michel. *La France militarisée.* Paris: Cerf, 1976.

Brossolet, Guy. *Essai sur la non-bataille.* Paris: Ed. Belin, 1975.

Carmoy, Guy de. *Les Politiques étrangères de la France, 1944–1966.* Paris: La Table Ronde, 1967.

Carrias, Eugène. *La Pensée militaire française.* Paris: Presses Universitaires de France, 1960.

Catroux, Georges. *Deux actes du drame indochinois.* Paris: Plon, 1959.

Chantebout, Bernard. *La Défense nationale.* Paris: Presses Universitaires de France, 1972.

―――. *L'Organisation générale de la défense nationale en France depuis la fin de la seconde guerre mondiale.* Paris: Librairie générale de Droit et de Jurisprudence, 1967.

Debas, Philippe. *L'Armée de l'atome.* Paris: Copernic, 1976.

Delmas, Claude. *Histoire politique de la bombe atomique.* Paris: Albin Michel, 1967.

―――. *L'O.T.A.N.* Paris: Presses Universitaires de France, 1960.

Doly, Guy. *Stratégie France-Europe: sécurité de la France et Union européenne.* Paris: Ed. Media, 1977.

Furniss, Edgar S., Jr. *France, Troubled Ally: De Gaulle's Heritage and Prospects.* New York: Harper and Brothers, 1960.

Gallois, Pierre-M. *L'Adieu aux armées.* Paris: Albin Michel, 1976.

―――. *Le Renoncement: de la France défendue à l'Europe protégée.* Paris: Plon, 1977.

Girardet, Raoul. *Les Problèmes contemporains de défense nationale.* Paris: Dalloz, 1971.

―――. *L'Idée coloniale en France de 1871 à 1962.* Paris: La Table Ronde, 1972.

Goldschmidt, Bertrand. *L'Aventure atomique.* Paris: A. Fayard, 1962.

Grosser, Alfred. *La Politique extérieure de la Ve République*. Paris: Seuil, 1965.

―――. *La IVe République et sa politique extérieure*. Paris: A. Colin, 1961.

Harrison, Michael M. "France and the Atlantic Alliance: The Process of Political and Military Dealignment." Ph.D. dissertation, Columbia University, 1976.

Hernu, Charles. *Le Soldat-citoyen: essai sur la sécurité de la France*. Paris: Flammarion, 1975.

Horne, Alistair. *A Savage War of Peace: Algeria 1954–1962*. New York: Viking Press, 1977.

Kohl, Wilfred. *French Nuclear Diplomacy*. Princeton: Princeton University Press, 1971.

Kolodziej, Edward A. *French International Policy under de Gaulle and Pompidou*. Ithaca: Cornell University Press, 1974.

Livre blanc de la défense nationale. 2 vols. Paris: CEDOCAR, 1972.

Mendel, Wolf. *Deterrence and Persuasion: The French Nuclear Armament in the Context of National Policy, 1945–1969*. New York: Praeger, 1970.

Morse, Edward L. *Foreign Policy and Interdependence in Gaullist France*. Princeton: Princeton University Press, 1973.

Organisation générale de la défense: Ordonnance n° 59-167 du 7 janvier 1959 modifiée et textes d'application. Paris: Journaux officiels, 1976.

Osgood, Robert E. *NATO: The Entangling Alliance*. Chicago: University of Chicago Press, 1962.

Paret, Peter. *French Revolutionary Warfare from Indochina to Algeria: The Analysis of a Political Military Doctrine*. New York: Praeger, 1964.

Pinatel, Jean-Bernard. "Les Effets de la politique et des dépenses militaires sur la croissance: le cas français 1965–1972." Ph.D. dissertation, Ecole pratique des hautes études, VIe section, 1974.

―――, ed. *L'Economie des forces*. Paris: Fondation pour les études de Défense nationale, 1976.

Radoux, L. *La France et l'O.T.A.N.* Paris: UEO, 1967.

Rose, François de. *La France et la défense de l'Europe*. Paris: Seuil, 1976.

Ruehl, Lothar. *La Politique militaire de la Ve République*. Paris: Presses de la Fondation nationale des Sciences politiques, 1976.

Sanguinetti, Alexandre. *La France et l'arme atomique*. Paris: R. Juillard, 1964.

Sanguinetti, Antoine. *Le Fracas des armes*. Paris: Hachette, 1975.

Scheinman, Lawrence. *Atomic Energy Policy in France under the Fourth Republic*. Princeton: Princeton University Press, 1965.

Serfaty, Simon. *France, De Gaulle and Europe: The Policy of the Fourth and the Fifth Republic Toward the Continent.* Baltimore: Johns Hopkins Press, 1968.

ARTICLES

Ailleret, Charles. "Défense dirigée ou défense 'tous azimuts.'" *Revue de Défense nationale* 23 (1967): 1923–32.
———. "Evolution nécessaire de nos structures militaires." *Revue de Défense nationale* 21 (1965): 947–55.
———. "La France et la puissance atomique." *Tendances* (March 1960).
———. "L'Arme atomique, arme à bon marché." *Revue de Défense nationale* 10 (1954): 315–24.
———. "Opinion sur la théorie stratégique de la 'Flexible Response.'" *Revue de Défense nationale* 20 (1964): 323–40.
Arnaud de Foïard, Paul. "Armament nucléaire tactique et dissuasion." *Défense nationale* 29 (October 1973): 55–68.
Aujac, Henri. "L'Efficacité militaire et les structures économiques, sociales et politiques." *Revue économique* 22 (1971): 561–84.
Barbery, Jean. "L'Impact industriel du IIIe plan militaire." *Revue de Défense nationale* 27 (1971): 1755–72.
Beaufre, André. "French Defence Policy." *RUSI Journal*, March 1970, pp. 3–6 and 9–12.
Beauvallet, Jacques. "Cybernétique de défense et secrétariat général de la défense nationale." *Défense nationale* 29 (August–September 1973): 3–28.
Brenner, M. J. "France's New Defense Strategy and the Atlantic Puzzle." *Bulletin of the Atomic Scientists*, November 1969, pp. 4–7.
Buis, Georges. "La Politique militaire de la France," and "Débat sur la politique militaire de la France." *Projet*, November 1973, pp. 1041–74.
Cabanier, [Admiral]. "Le Sous-marin nucléaire français." *Revue de Défense nationale* 22 (1966): 595–605.
Chassin, L. M. "Vers un encerclement de l'Occident." *Revue de Défense nationale* 12 (1956): 531–53.
Chirac, Jacques. "Au sujet des armes nucléaires tactiques françaises." *Défense nationale* 31 (May 1975): 11–16.
Combeaux, Edmond. "Défense tous azimuts? oui mais. . . ." *Revue de Défense nationale* 24 (1968): 1600–18.
Debré, Michel. "La France et sa défense." *Revue de Défense nationale* 28 (1972): 6–21.

Delmas, Claude. "Vers une nouvelle politique militaire française." *Revue politique et parlementaire* 71 (June 1969): 75–84.

Duroselle, Jean-Baptiste. "Changes in French Foreign Policy since 1945." In *In Search of France: The Economy, Society, and Political System in the Twentieth Century*, edited by Stanley Hoffmann et al, pp. 305–58. Cambridge, Mass.: Harvard University Press, 1963.

Ely, Paul. "Notre politique militaire." *Revue de Défense nationale* 13 (1957): 1033–51.

Enthoven, Alain C. "US Forces in Europe, How Many? Doing What?" *Foreign Affairs* 53 (1975): 513–32.

Fourquet, Michel. "Emploi des différents systèmes de forces dans le cadre de la stratégie de dissuasion." *Revue de Défense nationale* 25 (1969): 757–67.

Friedrich, Paul J. "Defense and the French Political Left." *Survival* 16 (1974): 165–71.

———. "L'Union de la gauche et la défense nationale." *Esprit* 43 (1975): 426–34.

Georges-Picot, [General]. "Pour une défense nationale." *Le Monde*, 25, 26, 28, and 29 September 1970.

Girardet, Raoul. "Réflexions critiques sur la doctrine militaire française de la guerre subversive." *Revue des travaux de l'Académie des Sciences morales et politiques et comptes rendus de séances* 113 (1960): 233–45.

Godard, Jean. "La Contribution alliée aux charges militaires de la France." *Revue de Défense nationale* 12 (1956): 436–45.

Goldsborough, James O. "The Franco-German Entente." *Foreign Affairs* 54 (1976): 496–510.

Greenwood, David. "The Defence Efforts of France, West Germany and the United Kingdom." *ASIDES* 1 (October 1973).

Hamon, Léo. "Puissance nucléaire et dissuasion: alliance et neutralité." *Revue de Défense nationale* 22 (1966): 234–57.

Juin, Alphonse. "Que devons-nous penser de la sécurité française." *Revue de Défense nationale* 13 (1957): 5–16.

Keens-Soper, Maurice. "Foreign Policy." In *France Today: Introductory Studies*, edited by J. E. Flower, pp. 99–126. London: Methuen, 1971.

Kolodziej, Edward A. "France Ensnared: French Strategic Policy and Bloc Politics after 1968." *Orbis* 15 (1972): 1085–108.

Lachaux, Claude. "Economie et défense." *Défense nationale* 32 (April 1976): 29–46.

Lacheroy, Charles. "La Guerre révolutionnaire." In *La Défense na-*

tionale, edited by Tony Albord et al., pp. 307–30. Paris: Presses Universitaires de France, 1958.

Lamson, A. "L'Organisation de la défense nationale et des forces armées." *Revue politique et parlementaire* 58 (June 1956): 240–55.

Lepotier, [Rear Admiral]. "La Force de 'dissuasion' sous-marine." *Revue de Défense nationale* 18 (1962): 1666–82.

———. "La Stratégie sous-glacière." *Revue de Défense nationale* 16 (1960): 1931–48.

LePuloch, [Général]. "Avenir de l'Armée de Terre." *Revue de Défense nationale* 20 (1964): 947–60.

Long, Marceau. "L'Incidence des dépenses des armées sur l'économie." *Revue de Défense nationale* 24 (1968): 987–1000.

Lüthy, Herbert. "De Gaulle: Pose and Policy." *Foreign Affairs* 43 (1965): 561–73.

Macridis, Roy C. "The New French Maginot Line: A Note on French Strategy." *Journal of Political and Military Sociology* 2 (1976): 105–12.

Martin, André. "L'Armée de l'Air dans le contexte nucléaire." *Revue de Défense nationale* 20 (1964): 1499–1517.

Maurin, François. "Pérennité et nécessité de la défense." *Défense nationale* 29 (July 1973): 21–34.

Méry, Guy. "Une Armée pourquoi faire et comment?" *Défense nationale* 32 (June 1976): 11–34.

Mesnard, André. "National Security and France." *The Annals of the American Academy of Political and Social Sciences* 241 (1945): 160–66.

Messmer, Pierre. "L'Armée de demain." *Revue des deux mondes*, 15 February 1962, pp. 481–93.

———. "L'Atome, cause et moyen d'une politique militaire autonome." *Revue de Défense nationale* 24 (1968): 395–402.

———. "Notre politique militaire." *Revue de Défense nationale* 19 (1963): 745–61.

Nemo, [Colonel]. "La Guerre dans le milieu social." *Revue de Défense nationale* 12 (1956): 605–23.

Pinatel, Jean-Bernard. "Politique militaire et croissance économique: le cas français 1945–1973." *Défense nationale* 30 (October 1974): 115–28.

Routside, Pierre. "Budgets militaires et équilibre national." *Revue de Défense nationale* 19 (1963): 951–65.

Salzedo, [Capitaine de Corvette]. "Les Moyens d'une force de dissuasion." *Revue de Défense nationale* 18 (1962): 82–90.

Serfaty, Simon. "The Vth Republic under Giscard d'Estaing: Steadfast or Changing." *World Today*, March 1976, pp. 95–103.

Service d'Information et de Relations publiques des Armées. "Les

Armées françaises de demain: programmation 1977–1982." *Dossier d'information* 49 (October 1976), special issue.

Smith, Tony. "The French Colonial Consensus and People's War, 1946–1958." *Journal of Contemporary History* 9 (1974): 217–47.

Usureau, Bernard. "Défense civile et stratégie de dissuasion." *Défense nationale* 29 (August–September 1973): 41–52.

Ximénes et al. "La Guerre révolutionnaire: données et aspects, méthodes de raisonnement, parade et riposte." *Revue militaire d'information* (February–March 1957), special issue.

The French Military Establishment

THE MILITARY ESTABLISHMENT IN THE FRENCH SOCIETY: HISTORICAL AND CONTEMPORARY ASPECTS

Ambler, John S. *The French Army in Politics 1945–1962*. Columbus: Ohio State University Press, 1966.

Bankwitz, Philip C. F. *Maxime Weygand and Civil-Military Relations in Modern France*. Cambridge, Mass.: Harvard University Press, 1967.

Boulègue, Jean. "Société militaire et crise de société." *Esprit* 43 (1975): 365–90.

Boutaric, Edgar. *Les Institutions militaires de la France*. Paris: Plon, 1863.

Corvisier, André. *L'Armée française de la fin du XVIIᵉ siècle au ministère Choiseul: le soldat*. 2 vols. Paris: Presses Universitaires de France, 1964.

de Gaulle, Charles. *La France et son armée*. Paris: Plon, 1938.

———. *Vers l'armée de métier*. Paris: Berger-Levrault, 1934.

Doughty, Robert A. "De Gaulle's Concept of a Mobile, Professional Army: Genesis of the French Defeat." *Parameters* 4 (1974): 23–34.

Ely, Paul. *L'Armée dans la nation*. Paris: A. Fayard, 1961.

Feller, Jean. *Le Dossier de l'Armée française: la guerre de "cinquante ans," 1914–1962*. Paris: Librairie académique Perrin, 1966.

Furniss, Edgar S., Jr. *De Gaulle and the French Army: A Crisis in the Civil-Military Relations*. New York: Twentieth Century Fund, 1964.

Girardet, Raoul. *La Société militaire dans la France contemporaine, 1816–1939*. Paris: Plon, 1953.

Jaurès, Jean. *L'Armée nouvelle*. Paris: Jules Rouff, 1911.

La Gorce, Paul-Marie de. *The French Army: A Military-Political History*. London: Weidenfeld and Nicolson, 1963.

Lech, Jean-Marc. "L'Evolution de l'opinion des Français sur la défense à travers les sondages de 1972 à 1976." *Défense nationale* 33 (August–September 1977): 47–56.

Léonard, Emile. *L'Armée et ses problèmes au XVIIIᵉ siècle.* Paris: Plon, 1958.

Loubère, Leo. "Left-Wing Radicals, Strikes, and the Military, 1880–1907." *French Historical Studies* 3 (1963): 93–105.

Loubet del Bayle, Jean-Louis; Mandeville, Lucien; and Picard, Alain. "Les Forces de maintien de l'ordre en France." *Défense nationale* 33 (July 1977): 59–76.

Malbosc, François. *Civils si vous saviez.* Paris: Maspéro, 1977.

Marichy, Jean-Pierre, ed. *Le Système militaire français: bilans, problèmes et perspectives.* Toulouse: Université des Sciences sociales, 1977.

Marrane, Jean. *L'Armée de la France démocratique.* Paris: Ed. Sociales, 1977.

Maurin, [Général]. *L'Armée moderne.* Paris: Flammarion, 1938.

Menard, Orville D. *The Army and the Fifth Republic.* Lincoln: University of Nebraska Press, 1967.

Monteilhet, Joseph. *Les Institutions militaires de la France, 1814–1924.* Paris: Félix Alcan, 1926.

Paxton, Robert O. *Parades and Politics at Vichy: The French Officer Corps under Marshal Pétain.* Princeton: Princeton University Press, 1966.

Pognon, Edmond. *De Gaulle et l'armée.* Paris: Plon, 1976.

Rabaut, Jean. *L'Antimilitarisme en France 1810–1975, faits et documents.* Paris: Hachette, 1975.

Ralston, David B. *The Army of the Republic: The Place of the Military in the Political Evolution of France, 1871–1914.* Cambridge, Mass.: MIT Press, 1967.

Soucy, Robert. "France—Veterans' Politics Between the Wars." In *The War Generation: Veterans of the First World War,* edited by Stephen A. Ward, pp. 59–103. Port Washington, N.Y.: Kennikat, 1975.

Stupak, Ronald J. "The Military's Ideological Challenge to Civilian Authority in Post–World War II France." *Orbis* 12 (1968): 582–604.

Valluy, Jean. "L'Armée française en 1961." *Revue des deux mondes,* 15 June 1961, pp. 577–94.

Villefosse, Louis de. "Armée nationale ou armée de guerre civile." *Esprit* 18 (1950): 732–48.

CONSCRIPTION AND ITS PROBLEMS

Baudoin, Rémy; Stack, Michel; and Vignemont, Serge. *Armée-Nation: le rendez-vous manqué*. Paris: Presses Universitaires de France, 1975.

Cain, E. R. "Conscientious Objection in France, Britain and the United States." *Comparative Politics* 2 (1970): 275–307.

Cattelain, Jean-Pierre. *L'Objection de conscience*. Paris: Presses Universitaires de France, 1973.

Challener, Richard D. *The French Theory of the Nation in Arms, 1866–1939*. New York: Russell and Russell, 1965.

Code du service national. Paris: Journal officiel, 1976.

Dabezies, Pierre. "Milices, conscription, armée de métier." *Projet*, November 1973, pp. 1076–86.

Genevey, P. "Le Service national." *Revue de Défense nationale* 15 (1959): 395–401.

Isambert-Jamati, Viviane. "Remarques sur le service militaire." *Revue française de Sociologie* 2 (1961): 100–105.

Koenig, Gilbert. "Affectation des ressources et systèmes de conscription en France." *Revue économique* 24 (1973): 66–108.

Kovacs, Arpad. "French Military Institutions before the Franco-Prussian War." *American Historical Review* 51 (1946): 217–35.

———. "French Military Legislation in the Third Republic: 1871–1940." *Military Affairs* 13 (1949): 1–13.

"Le service militaire pourquoi faire?" *France-Soir*, 6–9 June 1973.

Loyer, André. "Les Mécanismes d'application de la conscription en France en 1976." *Défense nationale* 32 (October 1976): 35–64.

MacCearney, James. "Les lois de recrutement de 1905, 1928 et 1970: analyse thématique des débats à la Chambre des députés et à l'Assemblée nationale." Mimeographed. Paris: Centre de Sociologie de la Défense nationale, 1976.

Marey, Georges. "Le Service national et le code du service national." *Revue militaire générale* 10 (1971): 655–76, and 1 (1972): 31–48.

Martin, Michel L. "Conscription and the Decline of the Mass Army in France, 1960–1975." *Armed Forces and Society* 3 (1977): 355–406.

Messmer, Pierre, and Chevènement, Jean-Pierre. *Le Service militaire*. Paris: Balland, 1977.

Métayer, Pierre. "La Réforme du service militaire: une loi anti-démocratique." *La Revue socialiste*, October 1965, pp. 89–94.

Mitrani, Daniel. *Où va le service militaire*. Paris: Tema-Editions, 1976.

Montmollin, Maurice de. "Le Niveau intellectuel des recrues du contingent." *Population* 13 (1958): 259–68, and *Population* 14 (1959): 233–52.

Pelletier, Robert, and Ravet, Serge. *Le Mouvement des soldats: les comités de soldats et l'antimilitarisme révolutionnaire.* Paris: Maspéro, 1976.

Pennac, Daniel. *Le Service militaire au service de qui?* Paris: Seuil, 1973.

Pinto, Louis. "L'Armée, le contingent et les classes sociales." *Actes de la recherche en Sciences sociales* 1 (May 1975): 18–41.

Richard, Denis, and Carrière, Elisabeth. *Le Procès de Draguignan.* Paris: Edition du Rocher, 1975.

Sablières, Pierre. "Le Statut légal de l'objection de conscience en France." Ph.D. dissertation, Paris, 1971.

Sallentin, Xavier. *L'Epreuve de force.* Paris: Fondation pour les études de Défense nationale, 1976.

Tricot, Bernard. "Dossier pour la réforme de recrutement." *Revue de Défense nationale* 21 (1965): 956–84.

Vimont, Claude, and Baudot, Jacques. "Etudes des caractéristiques sanitaires et sociales des jeunes du contingent." *Population* 18 (1963): 499–530.

———. "Les Causes d'inaptitude au service militaire." *Population* 19 (1964): 55–78.

Zaniewicki, W. "Un Centenaire: le service militaire obligatoire." *Revue de Défense nationale* 28 (1972): 1127–37.

THE CAREER SOLDIER

The Enlisted Personnel

Cailleteau, François, and Thomas, Jean-Pierre. "La Réforme des sous-officiers de l'Armée de Terre." *Défense nationale* 32 (March 1976): 99–113.

Garcette, Jack. "Les Conséquences de la spécialisation du sous-officier sur le recrutement et la conception du metier." In *Les Militaires et leur formation.* Paris: SPEI éditeur, 1972.

Lejeune, Bernard. "Les sous-officiers: exemple de schéma directeur relatif aux carrières des sous-officiers dans les trois armées." EMSST thesis, Centre de Sociologie de la Défense nationale, 1974.

Marchand, Philippe. "Ceux qui s'engagent." *Armées d'aujourd'hui,* January–February 1977, pp. 50–52 and 65.

Pillot, Henri. "L'Elève sous-officier d'active: motivation et personalité." EMSST thesis, Paris, 1968.

Schweisguth, Etienne. "Les Attitudes envers le métier militaire chez les sous-officiers de l'Armée de l'Air." *Revue française de Sociologie* 16 (1975): 485–516.

Service de psychologie appliquée. "Enquête sociologique sur les engagés volontaires de longue durée dans la Marine." Mimeographed. Saint Mandrier: Direction des personnels militaires de la Marine, 1973.

Thomas, Jean-Pierre. "Etude psychosociologique du personnel sous-officier des trois armées." Mimeographed. Paris: Centre de Sociologie de la Défense nationale, 1973.

———. "Hypothèses pour une étude de mobilité sociale auprès des sous-officiers." *Revue française de Science politique* 22 (1972): 55–76.

Vieillescazes, François. "Les Engagements volontaires dans l'Armée de Terre: un engagé ou des engagés?" *Défense nationale* 33 (July 1977): 77–88.

The Officer Corps

Beaufre, André. "Officier, pour quel office? la vocation militaire et la tradition." *Le Casoar* 43 (1971).

Bernard, Jacqueline. "L'Origine sociale des officiers." *Le Monde*, 28 and 29 December 1960.

Bonneville de Marsangy, Bernard. "Contribution à l'étude de la fonction militaire: les officers techniciens des armes dans l'armée de terre." Ph.D. dissertation, University of Paris II, 1976.

Bracoud, Maurice. "Les Débuts de Saint-Cyrien en corps de troupe." EMSST thesis, Paris, 1970.

Cailleteau, François. "Les Officiers des troupes de marine: contribution à l'étude de mobilité professionnelle." EMSST thesis, Centre de Sociologie de la Défense nationale, 1972.

Centre d'Etudes et d'Instruction psychologiques de l'Armée de l'Air. "Attitudes et motivation des candidats aux grandes écoles militaires." *Revue française de Sociologie* 2 (1961): 133–51.

Chalmin, Pierre. *L'Officier français de 1815 à 1870*. Paris: M. Rivière, 1957.

"Essai sur la structure sociale de l'armée française." *Nouvelle Critique*, June 1957.

Gaxie, D. "Morphologie de l'armée de l'Air: les officiers (1924–1976)." In *Recueil d'articles et d'études*, edited by Service historique de l'Armée de l'Air, pp. 37–86. Vincennes, 1977.

Girardet, Raoul, ed. *La Crise militaire française, 1945–1962: aspects sociologiques et idéologiques*. Paris: A. Colin, 1964.

Guilleminot, M. "Essai sur un problème de sociologie militaire: le corps des officiers, origine et structure." EMSST thesis, Paris, 1960.

Helluy, François. "Les Jeunes Officiers de l'Armée de Terre: une étude psycho-sociologique." EMSST thesis, Centre de Sociologie de la Défense nationale, 1974.

Hilbert, L. "L'Officier français à notre époque." *Revue libérale* 37 (1962): 69–76.

Jeanblanc, P. "Etude sociologique du corps des officiers de l'Armée de Terre: 1815–1968. Mimeographed. Paris: Centre des hautes études militaires, 1968.

Lejeune, Bernard. "Les officiers techniciens." EMSST thesis, Centre de Sociologie de la Défense nationale, 1976.

Malgré, Jean. "Recrutement des officiers et structure sociale: la crise de Saint-Cyr et ses remèdes." *Revue politique et parlementaire* 58 (April 1956): 21–29.

Maquet, André. "Le Recrutement des officiers et des cadres civils supérieurs: étude comparative, 1967–1973." Mimeographed. Paris: Centre de Sociologie de la Défense nationale, 1974.

Martin, Michel L. "Un Cas d'endorecrutement: le corps des officiers français, 1945–1975." *European Journal of Sociology* 18 (1977): 27–54.

Michelat, Guy, and Thomas, Jean-Pierre. "Contribution à l'étude de recrutement des écoles d'officiers de la Marine, 1945–1960." *Revue française de Sociologie* 9 (1968): 51–70.

Monteil, Vincent. *Les Officiers.* Paris: Seuil, 1968.

Moreigne, Jean-Paul. "Officiers pour quel office?" *Revue de Défense nationale* 27 (1971): 718–27.

Ponton, Remy. "Le Thème de la vocation dans le système de valeurs des Saint-Cyriens d'après les éditoriaux et les chroniques du Casoar, 1962–73." *Le Casoar* 58 (1975): 72–73.

Scott, Samuel F. "The French Revolution and the Professionalization of the French Officer Corps, 1789–1793." In *On Military Ideology,* edited by Morris Janowitz and Jacques Van Doorn, pp. 3–56. Rotterdam: Rotterdam University Press, 1971.

T. and A., [Captains]. "Capitaines ou bas-officiers? Essai sur la structure sociale de l'armée française." *Nouvelle Critique,* June 1959, pp. 43–86.

Talbott, John E. "The Myth and Reality of the Paratrooper in the Algerian War." *Armed Forces and Society* 3 (1976): 69–86.

Thiéblemont, André. "Les Fines et le Grand Carré: étude d'une élite réputationnelle à Saint-Cyr." EMSST thesis, Centre de Sociologie de la Défense nationale, 1975.

Tournoux, Raymond. "A Proletarian Army." *The Reporter,* 18 February 1960, pp. 19–21.

Tuetey, Louis. *Les Officiers sous l'ancien régime: nobles et roturiers.* Paris: Plon-Nourrit, 1908.

THE MILITARY CONDITION: TRAINING, ORGANIZATION, AND DISCIPLINE

Amet, [Capitaine de frégate]. "Essai sur le commandement des hommes." *Revue maritime* 268 (1969).

————. "Evolution de la notion d'initiative dans le cadre de la discipline militaire." In *Les Militaires et leur formation dans un monde en évolution*, pp. 131–42. Paris: SPEI, 1972.

Ardoino, J. "Evolution de la notion d'autorité et de la pratique du commandement." In *Les Militaires et leur formation dans un monde en évolution*, pp. 39–48. Paris: SPEI, 1972.

Bosmelet, Pierre de. *L'Armée éducatrice.* Paris: Comporapid, 1969.

Carbonneaux, [Major]. "L'Ecole d'état-major: 1946–1973." *Bulletin de l'Association des amis de l'Ecole supérieure de Guerre* 56 (1972): 33–50.

Colard, [Lieutenant Colonel], et al. "L'Evolution de l'enseignement et de la pédagogie à l'Ecole supérieure de guerre." *Bulletin de l'Association des amis de l'Ecole supérieure de guerre* 60 (1973): 35–68.

Coulet, William. "Le Nouveau Règlement de discipline générale dans les armées." *Revue du Droit public et de la Science politique* 84 (1968): 5–82.

Direction des Personnels militaires de l'Armée de Terre. "Les Ecoles militaires préparatoires." *Revue historique de l'Armée* 10 (1954): 171–88.

Dournel, Jean-Pierre. "L'Armée de l'Air en 1946." In *Recueil d'articles et d'études*, edited by Service historique de l'Armée de l'Air, pp. 251–303. Vincennes, 1977.

Fauchois, B. "The Adaptation of the Professional Soldier to New Training Methods." In *The Perceived Role of the Military*, edited by M. R. Van Gils, pp. 71–78. Rotterdam: Rotterdam University Press, 1971.

Frappat, [Capitaine de frégate]. "Plaidoyer pour l'initiative." *Revue maritime* 270 (1969).

Hennet, Léon. *Les Compagnies de cadets-gentilshommes et les écoles militaires.* Paris, 1889.

Herry, Joseph-L. *La Fonction militaire: évolution statutaire.* Paris: Berger-Levrault, 1976.

Hommes et Stratégies. "Chefs de corps et styles de commandement." Mimeographed. Neuilly, 1973.

————. "Commandants d'unités élémentaires et styles de commandement." Mimeographed. Paris, 1975.

Laulan, Robert. "Pourquoi et comment on entrait à l'Ecole royale militaire de Paris." *Revue d'Histoire moderne et contemporaine* 4 (1957): 141–50.

Lhoste, Michel. "L'Institution militaire, une organisation en crise." Ph.D. dissertation, Université Descartes, 1973.

Mandeville, Lucien. "Syndicalism in the French Military System." *Armed Forces and Society* 2 (1976): 529–52.

Mourot, Jean-Paul. *Evolution de la condition militaire: deux années d'effort, 1973–1975*. Paris: Jean Lopez, 1975.

"Propos sur le nouveau règlement de discipline générale." *Revue de Défense nationale* 22 (1966): 1956–62.

Tanant, G. *La Discipline dans les armées françaises*. Paris: Lavauzelle, 1938.

Vial, Robert. "De la discipline." *Revue de Défense nationale* 13 (1957): 1853–64.

The Military and Military Sociology

Aron, Raymond. *Le Grand Débat: initiation à la stratégie atomique*. Paris: Calmann-Levy, 1963.

Benkema, Herman. "The Social and Political Aspects of Conscription: Europe's Experience." In *War as a Social Institution*, edited by J. D. Clarkson and T. C. Cochran, pp. 113–29. New York: Columbia University Press, 1941.

Corvisier, André. *Armées et sociétés en Europe de 1494 à 1789*. Paris: Presses Universitaires de France, 1976.

Coulton, George C. *The Case of Compulsory Military Service*. London, 1917.

Curry, G. David. "A Comparative Analysis of Military Institutions in Developed Nations." Ph.D. dissertation, University of Chicago, 1976.

Feld, Maury D. *The Structure of Violence: Armed Forces as Social Systems*. Beverly Hills, Ca.: Sage Publications, 1977.

Guerlac, Henri. "Science and War in the Old Regime." Ph.D. dissertation, Harvard University, 1941.

Harries-Jenkins, Gwyn, and Van Doorn, Jacques, eds. *The Military and the Problem of Legitimacy*. Beverly Hills, Ca.: Sage Publications, 1976.

Howard, Michael. "The Acceptability of Military Force." *Adelphi Papers* 102 (1973): 2–13.

Huntington, Samuel P. *The Soldier and the State: The Theory and Practice of Civil-Military Relations*. New York: Random House, 1957.

Janowitz, Morris. "The Armed Forces and Society in Western Europe." *European Journal of Sociology* 6 (1965): 225–37.

———. "The Decline of the Mass Army." *Military Review* 50 (1972): 10–16.

———. "The Emergent Military." In *Public Opinion and the Military Establishment*, edited by Charles C. Moskos, pp. 255–70. Beverly Hills, Ca.: Sage Publications, 1971.

———. *Military Conflict: Essays in the Institutional Analysis of War and Peace*. Beverly Hills, Ca.: Sage Publications, 1975.

———. *The Professional Soldier: A Social and Political Portrait*. Glencoe: The Free Press, 1960.

Janowitz, Morris, and Little, Roger. *Sociology and the Military Establishment*. New York: Russell Sage Foundation, 1965.

Kourvetaris, George, and Dobratz, Betty. *Social Origins and Political Orientations of the Officier Corps in a World Perspective*. Denver: University of Denver Press, 1973.

Liebknecht, Karl. *Militarismus und Antimilitarismus*. Translated into English as *Militarism and Antimilitarism*. New York: H. Fertig, 1969.

Martin, Lawrence. "The Utility of Military Force." *Adelphi Papers* 102 (1973): 14–21.

Moskos, Charles C., Jr. "The All-Volunteer Military: Calling, Profession or Occupation?" *Parameters* 7 (1977): 2–9.

———. "The Emergent Military: Civil, Traditional or Plural." In *National Security and American Society*, edited by Frank Traeger and Philip Kronenberg, pp. 536–50. Lawrence: University of Kansas Press, 1973.

Speier, Hans. *Social Order and the Risks of War: Papers in Political Sociology*. New York: George W. Stewart, 1952.

Vagts, Alfred. *A History of Militarism*. New York: Meridian Books, 1959.

Van Doorn, Jacques. *The Soldier and Social Change: Comparative Studies in the History and Sociology of the Military*. Beverly Hills, Ca.: Sage Publications, 1975.

———, ed. *Armed Forces and Society: Sociological Essays*. The Hague: Mouton, 1968.

INDEX